OECD Investment Policy Reviews: Egypt 2020

OECD
BETTER POLICIES FOR BETTER LIVES

Please cite this publication as:
OECD (2020), *OECD Investment Policy Reviews: Egypt 2020*, OECD Investment Policy Reviews, OECD Publishing, Paris, *https://doi.org/10.1787/9f9c589a-en*.

ISBN 978-92-64-12288-8 (print)
ISBN 978-92-64-99939-8 (pdf)

OECD Investment Policy Reviews
ISSN 1990-0929 (print)
ISSN 1990-0910 (online)

Photo credits: Cover © Givaga/iStock/Getty Images Plus.

Corrigenda to publications may be found on line at: *www.oecd.org/about/publishing/corrigenda.htm*.

Foreword

This second *OECD Investment Policy Review of Egypt* uses the OECD *Policy Framework for Investment* to present an assessment of the investment climate in Egypt and to discuss the challenges and opportunities the Egyptian government faces in its reform efforts. It examines a broader range of policy areas in more depth than the first review. Chapters cover foreign investment trends and development benefits, the entry and operations of foreign investors, the legal framework for investment, investment promotion and facilitation, zone-based policies, tax policy and incentives, policies to promote and enable responsible business conduct, and infrastructure connectivity.

The Review was prepared in close collaboration with the General Authority for Investment and Free Zones (GAFI) and, until December 2019, with the Ministry of Investment and International Cooperation (MIIC). A draft version of the Review was presented and discussed before the OECD Investment Committee in Paris in October 2019.

The Review has been drafted under the supervision of Ana Novik, Head of the Investment Division, by a team led by Stephen Thomsen and comprising Fares Al Hussami, Alexandre de Crombrugghe, Sarah Marion Dayan, Hélène François, Alin Horj, Coralie Martin, Fernando Mistura, and Baxter Roberts from the Investment Division. The tax policy chapter was drafted by Steven Clark, Independent Consultant, under the supervision of the OECD Centre for Tax Policy and Administration. Secretariat inputs were received from Tihana Bule, Hans Christiansen, Korin Kane, and Joachim Pohl. The Review was undertaken in the framework of the *Project Enhancing the Investment Climate in Egypt,* and funded by the Middle East and North Africa Transition Fund of the G7 Deauville Partnership.

Table of contents

FIGURES

TABLES

Executive summary

Egypt is implementing ambitious reforms to stabilise its economy, attract investors, and spur durable economic growth. These efforts are having a positive effect. Since 2013, GDP growth has doubled, reaching 5.5% in 2019, the highest level in almost a decade. Foreign investment inflows have been steadily increasing since 2011, and despite more modest inflows over the past two years, in 2018 Egypt was the largest recipient of FDI in Africa and the second highest in the MENA region. Both the budget and current account deficit have narrowed in the past couple of years, and unemployment is decreasing. These positive gains will be tested in the near- to medium-term. Initial projections on the economic effects of the coronavirus pandemic portend declines in FDI in all economies for the coming year at least, along with disruptions to global value chains. A global recession appears likely. The steps the Egyptian government has taken to address its economic challenges, in recent years and in response to the pandemic, may help it weather some of the negative impacts of the current crisis. The new outlook makes continuing to advance Egypt's reform agenda all the more imperative.

Macroeconomic reforms adopted under an IMF-supported agenda that began in 2016 demonstrate the government's commitment to implementing meaningful, and at times difficult, measures. This includes the Central Bank's decision to allow the exchange rate to freely float, increasing competiveness of the long-overvalued Egyptian pound. The government has also implemented structural reforms to improve the business and investment climate and is moving forward with important regulatory reforms. The successive amendments of the Investment Law in 2015 and 2017 have sent strong signals that promoting and facilitating private investment is a government priority and essential to Egypt's economic growth. The legislation introduces a new incentives regime to encourage investment in the less developed regions of the country and new one-stop-shops to support business processes. This, and a modernised corpus of business legislation, mark a milestone in the country's efforts to provide a safer and more consistent regulatory environment for investors.

These recent reforms are important first steps. But advancing more inclusive and sustainable economic growth in Egypt will require strengthening these measures and implementing further near- and long-term reforms to improve the investment and business climate. These measures will be crucial to respond to the economic and social challenges caused by the coronavirus pandemic. Investment to emerging and developing economies is likely to be particularly affected, as disruptions to trade may prompt firms to reconsider their global supply chains. This could create opportunities. But depressed flows of capital and people risk exacerbating existing challenges. Among the greatest challenges Egypt's leaders face is to support job creation on pace with the country's growing population. Expanding the number – and crucially, the quality – of jobs will be central to economic growth, as well as to reduce inequality and support political stability. Inflation continues to be a burden on the cost of living, and unemployment, particularly among youth, women and the educated, remains high. Reforms could go further to support investment into activities with higher productivity potential, encourage SME growth and promote non-energy exports.

Despite liberalisation measures undertaken in the past decades, structural transformation of the economy has been limited in Egypt, impeding a sustained increase in labour productivity. Unnecessary restraints to competition caused by the presence of the state in the economy, excessive regulatory protection of incumbent firms, and complex administrative procedures are impediments to private sector development. Further reforms are required to provide clear and transparent regulatory and institutional frameworks.

Investment promotion activities in Egypt are sometimes hampered by a lack of common vision and of co-ordination across key public agencies and ministries. Indeed, co-ordination between government agencies in Egypt is a major challenge, aggravated by the country's complex institutional framework. GAFI's investment facilitation and regulating mandates are well developed but the agency could benefit from a clearer investment promotion strategy to better structure and monitor its activities, and to attract FDI in priority sectors.

Inconsistent and discretionary application of policies and regulations, particularly at the local level, also create confusion for investors. Authorities in Egypt have wide discretion to determine investment incentives, including land and tax subsidies, and beneficiaries. Minimising such discretion would reduce uncertainty for investors and limit the scope for corruption. The 2017 Investment Law includes many positive changes, including limiting the scope of corporate income tax holidays to free zone companies only. But levelling the playing field for investors in Egypt will also necessitate an examination of the benefits state-owned enterprises and well-connected firms receive.

Zone-based policies play an important role in the government's strategy to attract investment that promotes wider economic development. Zones can help compensate for a difficult business climate by offering special treatment to investors, streamlined business procedures, or better infrastructure than outside zones. Nevertheless, they risk becoming a substitute for addressing wider structural challenges, and investors might exploit incentives without embedding in the local economy, limiting potential spill-over benefits. Egypt has significantly improved the quality of its trade and transport infrastructure both in and outside zones in recent years. However, the government could strengthen its planning capacity and coordination for infrastructure projects, which require greater levels of investment.

The Egyptian government has taken steps to promote responsible business conduct (RBC), and Egypt has been an adherent to the OECD RBC instruments since 2007. However, civil society, including labour unions, should be empowered to perform their complementary role in monitoring the enforcement of newly enacted laws and the respect of enterprises for those laws. Civil society can also help ensure that human rights are protected, workers' rights are respected and that the environment is not degraded.

Based on the *Policy Framework for Investment*, this second *OECD Investment Policy Review of Egypt* was conducted together with GAFI and the former Ministry of Investment and International Cooperation (MIIC), in consultation with an inter-ministerial task force created for the *Review* under the leadership of MIIC. Assessing a broader range of policy areas in more depth than the first review, it takes stock of policy reforms, identifies several potential areas for reform, and provides policy recommendations for the government to consider. The Egyptian government has an opportunity to further strengthen its reform efforts in order to build a more sustainable and transparent investment environment, and in turn advance more inclusive growth.

Assessment and recommendations

Introduction

Egypt is implementing ambitious reforms to stabilise its economy, attract investors, and spur durable economic growth. These efforts are having a positive effect. Since 2013, GDP growth has doubled, reaching 5.5% in 2019, its highest level in almost a decade, according to the Central bank of Egypt (CBE). Foreign investment inflows have been steadily increasing since 2011, and despite more modest inflows over the past two years, in 2018 Egypt was the largest recipient of FDI in Africa and the second highest in the MENA region. Both the budget and current account deficit have narrowed, and unemployment is decreasing, from 13% to 7.5% by the second quarter of 2019. These positive gains will be tested in the near- to medium-term. Initial projections on the economic effects of the coronavirus pandemic portend declines in FDI in all economies for the coming year at least, along with disruptions to global value chains. A global recession appears likely. The steps the Egyptian government has taken to address its economic challenges, in recent years and in response to the pandemic, may help it weather some of the negative impacts of the current crisis. The new outlook makes continuing to advance Egypt's reform agenda all the more imperative.

The Egyptian government has taken substantial measures in the past few years to address its macroeconomic challenges. These form part of an ambitious agenda supported by a USD 12 billion Extended Fund Facility, agreed with the IMF in 2016. This agenda demonstrates the government's commitment to implementing meaningful, and at times difficult, reforms. Notably, the Egyptian Central Bank allowed the exchange rate to freely float to increase competiveness of the long-overvalued Egyptian pound and stop the depletion of foreign exchange reserves. To address its budget deficit, the government has reduced spending on energy subsidies, introduced a value-added tax (VAT), and curbed its public wage bill. Other fiscal-prudential plans include improving the tax administration and management of state-owned enterprises (IMF, 2018[1]).

The government has also implemented structural reforms to improve the business and investment climate and is moving forward with other reforms. The new Investment Law, adopted in 2017, is an important signal that promoting and facilitating private investment is a government priority and key to Egypt's economic growth. The legislation introduces an incentives regime to encourage local development in the poorer regions of the country and new one-stop-shops to support business processes. A revised bankruptcy act and companies law, passed in 2018, are positive developments towards fostering entrepreneurship and the growth of small and medium-sized enterprises (SMEs). The government has also established a Micro, Small and Medium Enterprise Development Agency (MSMEDA) to promote MSME growth and coordinate with all relevant stakeholders to this end. It also made progress in improving transparency and accountability of State-owned enterprises while advancing reforms to strengthen the independence of the Egyptian

Competition Authority and standardise public procurement. The government has also taken steps to improve access to land for investors.

The government has ambitious aims, outlined in its Vision 2030, to nearly triple GDP growth to 12%, reduce unemployment to 5%, and advance within the top 30 countries in terms of doing business. Despite positive reforms, clear challenges remain to these aims. Egypt only briefly reached GDP growth rates of above 9%, between 1976-1982, largely due to petroleum exports and an increase in foreign aid and capital following the country's shift towards an open market economy (Ikram, 2018[2]). Recent rebounds in investment and exports remain far below peaks reached in 2008, and both will be negatively affected by the coronavirus pandemic. Investment to emerging and developing economies is likely to be particularly affected, as disruptions to trade may prompt firms to reconsider their global supply chains. The Egyptian government has taken a series of measures in an effort to limit the human and economic impact of the pandemic. These include a fiscal stimulus package that will give grants to irregular workers and support to firms that continue to pay employees. Current tax holidays schemes have been extended and industrial sectors are eligible for gas and electricity subsidies. Firms in free zones may temporarily export to the local market at higher rates. The government is also working to further streamline procedures for investors through digitalised one-stop-shops. The rapid implementation of these measures may help the Egyptian economy to weather some of the negative effects of the current crisis. But in the long-term, advancing more durable economic growth will require higher and more sustained levels of investment and savings, as well as substantial improvements in productivity growth and export performance.

The government will also have to contend with ongoing socio-economic challenges, which are likely to be further exacerbated by the coronavirus pandemic and its economic aftermath. Positively, inflation, which spiked at more than 30% after the currency devaluation in 2017, has decreased substantially, reaching 5% in March 2020. The overall unemployment rate prior to the coronavirus pandemic had also been improving, dropping from 13% in 2013 to 10% in 2019, but remained at 20% for women and those with advanced degrees. Youth unemployment is 30%.[1] The current health crisis is putting further strain on the workforce. The government recognises that creating more and higher quality jobs is imperative for both economic growth and stability. Reforms could go further to support investment into activities with higher productivity potential, encourage SME growth and promote non-energy exports. Additional short-term and deeper structural reforms would help improve the investment climate and, in turn, advance more sustainable private sector growth.

The Egyptian government has an opportunity to further strengthen its reform efforts, in order to build a more sustainable and transparent investment environment. Based on an updated version of the *Policy Framework for Investment* (Box 1), this second *OECD Investment Policy Review of Egypt* identifies several potential areas for reform and provides policy recommendations for the government to consider. Implementing these reforms would help the government advance inclusive growth and reduce political and economic uncertainty. After an overview of trends in foreign investment and their socio-economic benefits (Chapter 1), the *Review* examines the country's wider regulatory framework on investors' entry and expansion (Chapter 2), legal framework for investment (Chapter 3), investment promotion and facilitation (Chapter 4), zone-based policies (Chapter 5), tax policy and investment incentives (Chapter 6), policies to promote responsible business conduct (Chapter 7) and infrastructure connectivity (Chapter 8).

Box 1. The Policy Framework for Investment

The Policy Framework for Investment (PFI) helps governments to mobilise private investment in support of sustainable development, thus contributing to the prosperity of countries and their citizens and to the fight against poverty. It offers a list of key questions to be examined by any government seeking to create a favourable investment climate. The PFI was first developed in 2006 by representatives of 60 OECD and non-OECD governments in association with business, labour, civil society and other international organisations and endorsed by OECD ministers. Designed by governments to support international investment policy dialogue, co-operation, and reform, it has been extensively used by over 25 countries as well as regional bodies to assess and reform the investment climate. The PFI was updated in 2015 to take this experience and changes in the global economic landscape into account.

The PFI is a flexible instrument that allows countries to evaluate their progress and to identify priorities for action in 12 policy areas: investment policy; investment promotion and facilitation; trade; competition; tax; corporate governance; promoting responsible business conduct; human resource development; infrastructure; financing investment; public governance; and investment in support of green growth. Three principles apply throughout the PFI: policy coherence, transparency in policy formulation and implementation, and regular evaluation of the impact of existing and proposed policies.

The value added of the PFI is in bringing together the different policy strands and stressing the overarching issue of governance. The aim is not to break new ground in individual policy areas but to tie them together to ensure policy coherence. It does not provide ready-made reform agendas but rather helps to improve the effectiveness of any reforms that are ultimately undertaken. By encouraging a structured process for formulating and implementing policies at all levels of government, the PFI can be used in various ways and for various purposes by different constituencies, including for self-evaluation and reform design by governments and for peer reviews in regional or multilateral discussions.

The PFI looks at the investment climate from a broad perspective. It is not just about increasing investment but about maximising the economic and social returns. Quality matters as much as the quantity as far as investment in concerned. It also recognises that a good investment climate should be good for all firms – foreign and domestic, large and small. The objective of a good investment climate is also to improve the flexibility of the economy to respond to new opportunities as they arise – allowing productive firms to expand and uncompetitive ones (including state-owned enterprises) to close. The government needs to be nimble: responsive to the needs of firms and other stakeholders through systematic public consultation and able to change course quickly when a given policy fails to meet its objectives. It should also create a champion for reform within the government itself. Most importantly, it needs to ensure that the investment climate supports sustainable and inclusive development.

The PFI was created in response to this complexity, fostering a flexible, whole-of-government approach which recognises that investment climate improvements require not just policy reform but also changes in the way governments go about their business.

For more information on the Policy Framework for Investment, see: www.oecd.org/investment/pfi.htm

Historical context

Economic reforms have improved macroeconomic conditions and opened the country to investment

Egypt's first episode of liberalisation began with a major reorientation of its economy in the 1970s under a policy of *Infitah* (open-door policy). The liberalisation reforms sought to attract foreign investment and move toward private sector-driven growth. The new posture contributed to rapid, but volatile GDP growth, with rates peaking at above 14% in 1976 (Figure 1). Positively, the level of labour productivity doubled between 1970 and the late 1980s. External factors aided this growth, including higher oil prices and the resumption of oil exports from the Sinai following a peace deal with Israel, along with higher worker remittances and a growth in tourism (Cammett et al., 2013[3]).

Figure 1. GDP growth (%) in Egypt 1995-2018

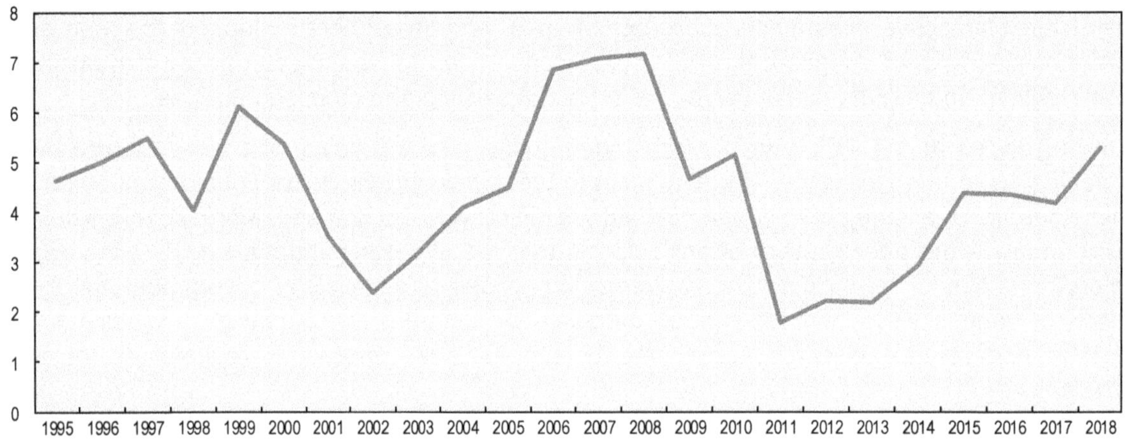

Source: World Bank Development Indicators Data

Infitah did not, however, radically change the structure of the economy or advance broad-based private-sector development, in contrast with other emerging countries that undertook similar liberalisation reforms over the same period. State-owned firms remained paramount in both strategic and non-strategic sectors. State spending on subsidies increased to 10% of GDP, following popular opposition to planned cuts. Non-oil exports remained weak, while imports and external debt grew. By the late 1980s, macroeconomic imbalances were once again acute.

The Egyptian government gradually adopted deeper reforms to stabilise and liberalise its economy over the next two decades. With the aid of a structural adjustment agreement with the IMF in 1991, Egypt's macroeconomic position improved. The government halved state expenditures to 30% of GDP by the early 2000s, and fully or partially privatised around 400 state-owned enterprises (SOEs) in a range of sectors, including banking. Spending on consumer subsidies decreased from 5.2% to 1.6% of GDP (Ikram, 2018[2]). Liberalisation of the financial sector and improvements to the business environment, coupled with record rates of global growth in the 2000s, helped draw a surge in foreign investment. FDI stock grew from 8% of GDP before the reforms to 35% in 2008, and FDI inflows nearly doubled between 2005 and 2008 (Figure 2). GDP growth remained uneven though averaged more than 7% between 2006 and 2008 (Figure 1). This period of growth was brief, however, and only benefited a small segment of the population. The 2007/2008 global financial crisis, followed by social unrest and political instability in 2011, precipitated a new slowdown.

The negative effects of political upheavals on economic growth and investment are well documented (Rodrik, 1989). Between 2011 and 2014, Egypt had six elections and five different governments. Uncertainty over the leadership's stability and posture prompted capital flight, and GDP growth during this period shrunk to an average of 2.4%. The average Egyptian firm experienced a 6.4% annual reduction in revenues and 1% drop in employment between 2009 and 2012 (EBRD, 2016[4]). Across the MENA region, political instability had a negative spill-over effect on investment, with some investors suspending their operations, downscaling their commitments, or withdrawing investments altogether. When President Abdel Fattah el-Sisi was elected in 2014, exports and foreign reserves were at their lowest levels in a decade, tourism revenue had dissipated, and poverty and unemployment were at ten-year highs (Ikram, 2018[2]).

In light of these challenges, the government quickly passed reforms to stabilise the economy and project a message of economic stability. Macroeconomic conditions are now improving, and FDI appears to be on an upward, albeit moderate, trend.

Figure 2. FDI inflows in Egypt and selected MENA countries

In USD million

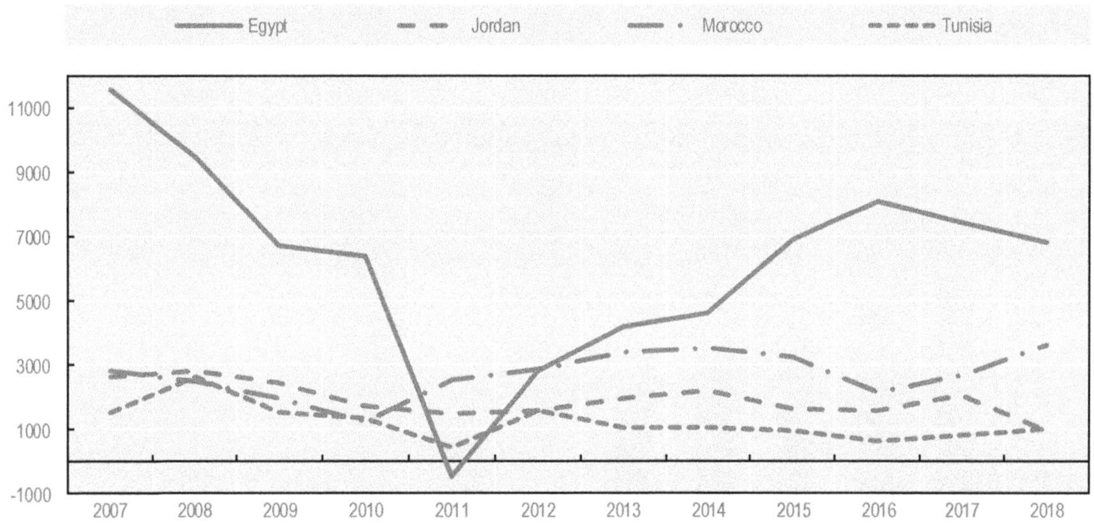

Source: OECD based on the IMF Balance of Payments database.

Further structural reforms would increase investment and labour productivity

Several interlinked economic challenges persist. While the state has gradually reduced its levels of public investment and employment since the *Infitah* period, the private sector did not fill, and has not filled, this gap. Private investment as a proportion of total fixed capital formation has remained at around 10% of GDP since the late 1990s (Figure 3). Formal private sector employment has also stagnated since the late 1990s at around only 13% of total employment (Assaad and Krafft, 2013[5]) (World Bank, 2014[6]).[2] Periods of growth in foreign investment have also not been sustained, and stock levels have remained lower than in other emerging economies, even at their peaks. Since 2012, the prospects for inward FDI have improved. At the end of 2018, FDI stock in Egypt was equal to 47% of GDP, above the MENA region (43%) and the OECD (40%) and below ASEAN (89%).[3]

Figure 3. Gross fixed capital formation: Public vs. private investment

% GDP

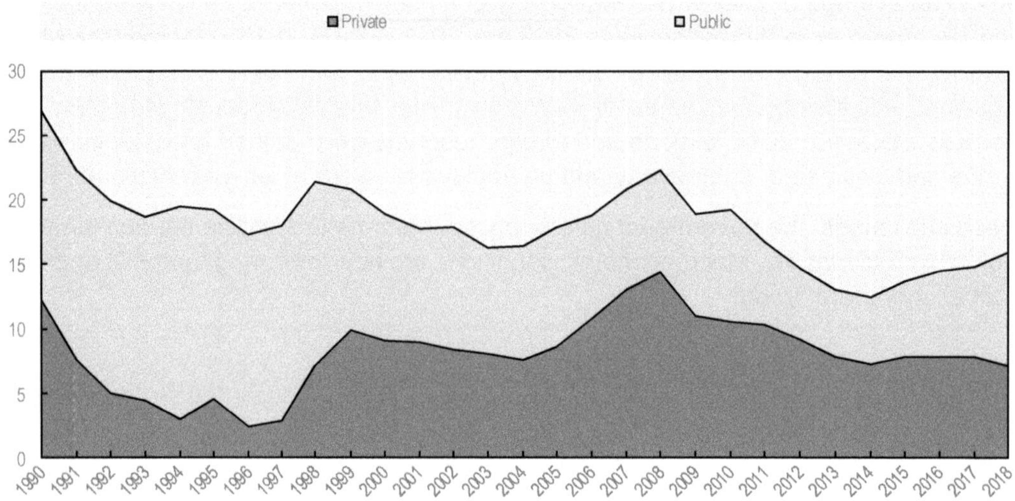

Source: OECD based on the World Bank Development Indicators Data.

Figure 4. Average contribution to GDP by main economic sector (%)

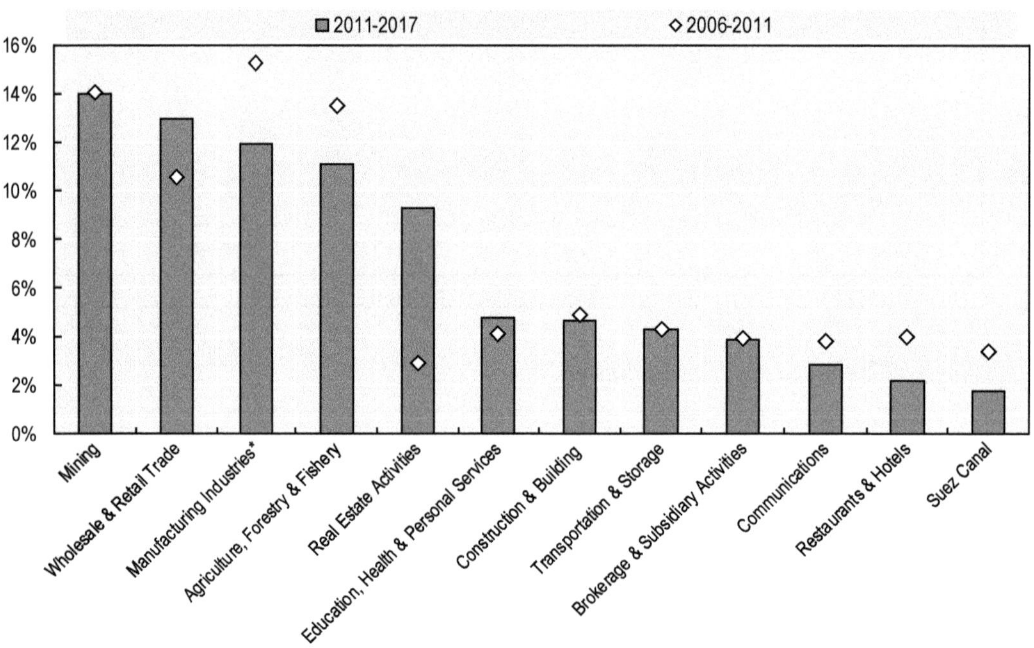

Note: *Manufacturing industries excludes oil refining (which accounts for 4% GDP). Average percent between 2006-2011 and 2011-2017 shown. Percentages calculated based on GDP at factor cost by economic activity. Data for 2006-2011 given at 2006/2007 prices, data for 2011-2017 at 2011/2012 prices. Only sectors with a high contribution to GDP depicted.
Source: OECD based on the Central Bank of Egypt.

Some of the main sectors contributing to economic growth are those with relatively low labour intensity, and therefore limited job-creating potential, such as natural resources and real estate. Between 2011 and 2017, oil and gas was the largest sector in terms of contribution to GDP (nearly 13%); followed closely by wholesale, retail, manufacturing and agriculture (Figure 4). Manufacturing was the leading sector in 2018, however. More than half of all FDI inflows go to the oil sector, and natural resources and agriculture account for more than 50% of Egypt's net exports (oil and gas alone account for more than 30%). While Egypt has diversified its production in the last couple of decades to include more manufacturing and services, the country remains specialised in low-value added activities within global value chains. Energy subsidies have also encouraged investment in energy-intensive rather than labour-intensive industries (Youssef et al., 2019). Egypt's reform program that started in 2016, gradually removed the energy subsidies to eliminate distortions and create right price signals. This should contribute to attracting investments in sectors with a competitive advantage.

Among the greatest challenges Egypt's leaders face is to support job creation on pace with the country's growing population. Expanding the number – and crucially, the quality – of jobs will be central to economic growth, as well as to reduce inequality and support political stability. The government is committed to making private investment, both domestic and foreign, the engine of growth and development, but further investment climate reforms are needed to achieve this ambitious goal, as described throughout this Review.

Improving the investment climate in Egypt: Main findings

Advancing more inclusive and sustainable economic growth in Egypt – and supporting the growth of higher-productive sectors with greater job-creating potential – will require further near- and long-term reforms to improve the investment and business climate. The government's recent macroeconomic, legislative and regulatory reforms are important first steps. The 2017 Investment Law demonstrates the high priority that the government places on promoting and facilitating private investment. FDI developments are positive signs of renewed investor confidence. Several areas of the investment climate could, however, be improved, and recent and planned reforms could be strengthened to enhance their impact.

The *Policy Framework for Investment* considers ways to improve the investment climate for both domestic and foreign enterprises. It looks not only at the policy framework necessary to stimulate investment but also at broader efficiency considerations and at the impact of investment on sustainability and inclusiveness.

Underpinning a positive investment policy framework is good governance. This includes transparency of government decision-making, inter-government co-ordination, and engagement with stakeholders. Investment climate reforms require an understanding of how different areas interact and hence the need for a whole-of-government approach. Co-ordination between government agencies in Egypt is a major challenge, given the country's complex institutional framework. Roles and responsibilities of investment-relevant ministries and implementing agencies are not always clear, and the division of labour can at times appear relatively artificial, although there have been some recent improvements in coordination, notably through the Investor Service Centres. Recent measures, such as the direct affiliation of GAFI to the Egyptian Council of Ministers, are expected to enhance effective cooperation with line government bodies.

Inconsistent application of policies and regulations and discords in administrative practices, particularly at the local level, also create confusion for investors. Authorities in Egypt also have wide discretion to determine investment incentives, including land and tax subsidies, and beneficiaries. When rules are applied on a case-by-case basis in a non-uniform and non-transparent manner across taxpayers, unfair competition results. It also creates opportunities for corruption. Levelling the playing field for investors in Egypt will also necessitate an examination of the benefits state-owned enterprises and well-connected firms receive, including inter alia preferential access to government contracts and exemption from certain laws and taxes.

Zone-based policies play an important role in the government's strategy to attract investment that promotes wider economic development. Zones can help compensate for a difficult business climate by offering special treatment to investors, such as tax or administrative incentives, streamlined business procedures, or better infrastructure than outside zones. Nevertheless, they risk becoming a substitute for addressing wider structural challenges, and investors might exploit incentives without embedding in the local economy, limiting potential spill-over benefits.

More broadly, a clear and transparent regulatory framework, developed through wide public consultations, can help to improve implementation of reforms. Civil society, including labour unions, should be empowered to perform their complementary role in monitoring the enforcement of newly enacted laws and the respect of enterprises for those laws. Civil society can also help ensure that human rights are protected, workers' rights are respected and that the environment is not degraded.

The section that follows reviews the assessments from each of the policy chapters, including the special focus on zone-based policies. The numerous policy options mix concrete measures that can be implemented relatively quickly and more aspirational recommendations, which will require more fundamental changes in the way the government goes about its business. Some measures can only be implemented over a long time horizon, while the government is already considering others. The aim is to provide a list of policy options in each area of the PFI for the Egyptian government to consider as it reforms it investment climate.

Regulations on investor entry and operations

A coherent investment policy is embedded in a regulatory framework that facilitates market entry, promotes fair competition and encourages international trade, including in services. Despite liberalisation reforms undertaken in the past decades, structural transformation of the economy has been limited in Egypt, impeding a sustained increase in labour productivity. The wider business climate continues to face several regulatory hurdles that limit private sector firms' entry and growth. Unnecessary restraints to competition caused by the presence of the state in the economy and by disproportionate regulatory protection of incumbent firms, and complex regulatory procedures are impediments to private sector development.

The creation of a more competition-friendly environment would allow for a better allocation of resources towards higher-productivity firms. It would enable new entrants and incumbents to bring in ideas and innovate and would encourage less productive firms to restructure or exit the market. The current reform project to strengthen the independence of the Egyptian Competition Authority (ECA) and increase its transparency and capacity is a positive development.

The government of Egypt has recently implemented further reforms to pursue investment liberalisation. The investment law does not discriminate between foreign and domestic investors. Restrictions on the entry and operation of foreign-controlled firms are nonetheless present in sector-specific legislations. These restrictions, while not particularly extensive, place an additional toll on the development of a thriving business sector. Not only might they discourage foreign investment inflows in the first place, they may also hold back potential economy-wide productivity gains associated with FDI.

Like most countries, Egypt has largely liberalised manufacturing industries to foreign investors, but a few backbone services activities are still partly off-limits. The implications go beyond forgone investments. By hindering contestability and competition in these sectors, restrictions potentially contribute to raising services input costs, such as logistics, for other economic sectors. Access to world-class services inputs through FDI has been shown to be crucial for moving manufacturing up the value chain and boosting growth and jobs in the services sector (OECD, 2015, 2018). In catching-up countries, lower productivity firms can achieve large productivity gains if they benefit from the expertise of foreign investors, if regulations do not impede these gains.

Egypt has fewer restrictions on foreign investment than other emerging economies, but higher regulatory barriers affecting the flows of goods and services. This has had a negative effect on the economy at large. Trade barriers have hurt export growth. Customs and administrative controls on imports (along with the long-overvalued pound) mean that it has long been more profitable to sell on the domestic market than to export. Import tariffs have meanwhile hampered Egypt's integration into global value chains (GVC) (Ikram, 2018[2]).

Policy recommendations

- Continue undertaking pro-competition reforms to further level the playing field between new entrants and incumbents, particularly SOEs, to allow for a better allocation of resources towards higher-productivity firms. Reforms could include reassessing regulatory protection of, and antitrust exemptions to, incumbent firms against their policy objectives and, when relevant, remove them.
- Egypt could benefit from adopting more transparent and less discretionary regulations on private firms' market entry, notably in network sectors. Such policies would reduce the impact of undesirable practices, such as corruption and cronyism, as well as potential *de facto* restrictions on private investors' access to certain competitive markets, particularly those where SOEs are operating.
- Consider reassessing existing restrictions to foreign investment, notably in services sectors, against their public policy objectives and, where relevant, streamline or remove them. Where such policies are deemed necessary, ensure that they are not greater than needed to address identified risks and concerns.

Investment policy

The government of Egypt is putting strong emphasis on adopting more modern investment legislation and regulations for investment. The new Investment Law, promptly followed by a modernised Companies Law, marked an important milestone in the country's efforts to provide a safer and more consistent regulatory environment for foreign and domestic investments. Yet, further reform endeavours are required to endow Egypt with clear and transparent regulatory and institutional frameworks governing business and investment activities. Overall, a more uniform and harmonised implementation of these regulations across the country would greatly enhance the enabling environment for investment.

One of the main avowed purposes of the new Investment Law was to create a more robust infrastructure for preventing and managing investment disputes. Despite the creation of new dispute settlement bodies, the current institutional setting for the resolution of investor-state disputes remains complex, and might therefore not serve its purpose in the most efficient way.

Egypt has a vast network of international investment treaties. Bearing in mind the existing scope for treaty shopping, Egypt should consider reviewing and considering possibilities for renegotiation, clarification and exit of investment treaties. Treaties with vague provisions concluded in the past may lead to undesirable interpretations in ISDS disputes.

GAFI, the Ministry of Justice and the Ministry of Foreign Affairs should continue to develop ISDS dispute prevention and case management tools. Egypt may also wish to consider efforts to raise awareness about Egypt's investment treaties and the significance of Egypt's international obligations under these investment treaties for the day-to-day functions of different government agencies and officials that regularly interact with foreign investors.

The complex landscape of public land ownership, and myriad approvals required to allocate land to investors, means that a substantial gap remains between land demand and supply in Egypt. The centralisation of investor requests for land under GAFI is an important improvement that appears to have enabled faster distribution of state-owned land to firms. But the government could consider taking further steps to centralise the allocation of land to investors, such as empowering one agency to allocate all publicly owned land, regardless of its sectoral use. More immediately, coordination between the many different government landowners should be significantly strengthened. GAFI's success in directing investors to the appropriate government landowner will depend on close intra-agency cooperation.

Short of a complete inventory and mapping of public land ownership, coordination challenges between agencies allocating public land are likely to persist. A complete registry would assist both GAFI in facilitating investment and firms in their location decisions. The Investment Map is a good step in this direction. Agencies could make public more comprehensive maps of land within their control, rather than only a selection of land available in zones, as is shown on the Investment Map.

The Egyptian government has taken substantial measures to improve standards of corporate governance for state-owned enterprises. Yet, the current dual regulatory system, under which only a subset of firms adhere to good corporate governance practices, falls short of levelling the playing field between SOEs and their private sector competitors. The government could do more to apply standards to all state-owned enterprises and take steps to minimise the market distortions of publicly-owned firms.

Policy recommendations

- For clarity and predictability purposes, and to avoid legal loopholes, adopt implementing regulations more promptly after the enactment of new legislation.
- Apply administrative procedures more consistently across all governorates and relevant public authorities. Strong, regular and transparent institutional cooperation mechanisms, including between central authorities and special economic zones, are needed on a more regular basis to provide for a more efficient administration of investment activities.
- Consider concrete reform options to streamline the current institutional infrastructure for investment dispute settlement. Clarify the respective mandate of each dispute settlement and prevention body, and avoid creating new bodies with similar mandates.
- Take steps to update Egypt's network on international investment treaties to bring them in line with government intent, Egypt's current priorities and more recent practices in investment treaty policy. Consider options to harmonise the content of overlapping bilateral and regional treaties.
- Centralise the allocation of land to investors, and improve day-to-day inter-agency coordination and exchange of information. The ongoing modernisation of the land cadastre is also encouraged.
- Further apply standards of Corporate Governance to State-Owned-Enterprises.

Investment promotion and facilitation policies

Investment promotion and facilitation policies can support the competitiveness of a country by branding it as a profitable investment destination, attracting quality investors and making it easy for businesses to establish or expand their operations. The General Authority for Investment and Free Zones (GAFI) is Egypt's investment promotion agency in charge of investment policy, promotion and facilitation. The government of Egypt, mostly through GAFI, has placed high priority on promoting and facilitating private investment, as demonstrated by the recent creation of flagship tools, such as the Investment Map and the Investors Services Centres. While the former is an innovative tool providing an array of information on existing investment opportunities by sectors and locations, the latter are fully-fledged one-stop shops aiming to facilitate the establishment of new businesses by providing required approvals, certifications and licences under the same roof.

Investment promotion activities in Egypt are sometimes hampered by a lack of common vision and of co-ordination across key public agencies and ministries. GAFI's recent affiliation to the Egyptian Council of

Ministers can nevertheless enhance effective co-operation with other government bodies involved in investment promotion and facilitation. GAFI's investment facilitation and regulating mandates are well developed but the agency could benefit from a clearer investment promotion strategy to better structure and monitor its activities, and to attract increased levels of FDI in priority sectors.

GAFI has the reputation of being a responsive and problem-solving organisation in the business community. Public-private consultations and aftercare services have recently improved but efforts need to be reinforced to make public-private dialogue more systematic and comprehensive. Involving all parts of government and representatives of different segments of the private sector is key to ensure an environment of trust and find ways to solve investors' challenges. Private sector representatives also report that administrative procedures and requirements tend to be burdensome after establishment – and fulfilling these requirements can be an impediment to their expansions and, at times, an incentive to divest. Improving these procedures, and the implementation of regulations, necessitates better co-ordination across government agencies.

Policy recommendations

- Prepare and disseminate a high-level investment policy statement to present the investment landscape in Egypt and its vision for FDI and supplement it with a well-articulated investment promotion strategy providing targets, tools and indicators to guide GAFI's activities and ensure that FDI attraction is well-aligned with national development objectives.
- Building on these strategic efforts, improve institutional co-ordination mechanisms on investment promotion and facilitation and clarify the roles and responsibilities of relevant ministries and implementing agencies;
- Build on the notable efforts to brand the country and guide potential investors to existing opportunities through the Investment Map to gradually conduct more systematic investor outreach and targeting activities to attract quality investments that can support sustainable and inclusive development.
- Continue and strengthen the monitoring and evaluation of the functioning and the performance of the Investors Services Centres to ensure, on the one hand, that investors are satisfied and, on the other hand, that the centres provide value for money;
- Pursue efforts to systematically revise existing administrative procedures and requirements to start and operate a business with a view to eliminating those which are deemed redundant or unnecessary; and
- Building on the recent efforts to systematise public-private sector consultations, establish a whole-of-government public-private dialogue platform to instigate an environment of trust between the government and the business community. Use it systematically to consult with the private sector, to seek business representatives' views on the main challenges to address, and to discuss government priorities and reforms.

Zone-based policies

Egypt has a longstanding history of relying on zone-based policies for development aims. Zones have become central growth locomotives of the Egyptian economy and, as in other emerging economies, they are home to large manufacturing activities. They have succeeded in attracting foreign investment, boosting participation in global value chains and creating jobs. By one estimate, they are home to at least one-tenth of the FDI stock, generate more than half of non-oil exports and employ nearly 2% of the national workforce.

Currently, seven types of zones co-exist in Egypt: public or private free zones, investment zones, technological zones, special economic zones, qualified economic zones, and industrial zones. Most are governed by specific laws, overseen by different ministries, operate under distinct regulatory and institutional frameworks, provide different types of incentives to investors, and often have overlapping goals.

Egypt Vision 2030 calls for "achieving coherence and integration among industrial and free zones, and domestic, regional, and global value chains". The complex and overlapping landscape of zones in Egypt has generated co-ordination challenges between government institutions over zones management. According to the Egyptian government, the regulatory framework for land management is clearly organising and defining the competency of the governmental ministries or authorities responsible for public land administration in zones. The patchwork of policies and regulations governing zones also makes it difficult to assess the benefits and costs of each zone type for investment and wider economic development. Further clarity on each zone's development aims, governance structure and legal and regulatory framework would help policymakers in better aligning zones' strategic objectives with Egypt's long-term development goals. This clarity is more than ever needed in a context where different institutions are rapidly increasing the number of their respective zones.

Zones have a mixed record in generating value-added, fostering innovation, and supporting diversification and sustainable development countrywide. In some zone types with generous fiscal incentives, they may be impeding fair competition between firms inside and outside of zones, at the risk of creating economic enclaves. They also impose a cost on government revenues, as the incentives granted to firms reduce the fiscal base. While foreign-owned businesses take advantage of such tax incentives, they often limit the deployment of local production sites in order to maintain some degree of locational mobility. Ties between zones and the local economy may be even narrower in the lower value-added segments of sectors such as textiles and clothing. Linkages between multinationals in Egyptian zones and local suppliers do sometimes exist, but policymakers could support their extension to further rely on higher-skilled labour or on R&D agreements.

Policy recommendations

- Better align the development objectives of zones in Egypt with national and local strategies as well as investment and trade goals, as stated in Egypt Vision 2030. The policy dialogue around the objectives should involve several ministries, the investment and export promotion agencies, the Industrial Development Agency, the SME agency, the SEZs authorities, governorates, and civil society.
- Assess the longer-term benefits and costs of creating new zones, notably free zones, or expanding existing ones, for sustainable development and economic welfare. For existing zones, balance the objective of expanding their activities with a transparent and sequenced plan to level the playing field between the special and the inland investment regimes, particularly with regard to corporate income tax incentives.
- Promote private investment in higher value-added segments of the manufacturing sector to unlock zones' export competitiveness potential. This includes promoting investment in capital-intensive, upstream stages of the manufacturing supply chains to modernise production capabilities. The government could support investments aimed at replacing ageing technology in SOEs, from which downstream firms in zones source their inputs.
- Better use zones as a tool to bridge investment and regional development policies. Cost-based incentives should be favoured over compulsory linkage requirements to strengthen linkages between MNEs in zones and suppliers located in the inland regime. Authorities at the national and zone level could better co-ordinate their efforts to promote the different tools incentivising linkages.

- Clarify zones' institutional and regulatory framework to ensure a level playing field between public and private investors. More systematically involve the private sector, local governorates and other relevant stakeholders in the decision-making process of zone authorities.
- Ensure that investors in zones comply with health, safety, labour and environmental norms and that these are in line with national and international standards. Monitor the impact of more flexible labour regulations, particularly in SEZs as they enjoy more flexible labour and social rules. Zone authorities should put in place independent mechanisms to monitor labour and environmental rights.

Investment incentives

The Egyptian government has made substantial improvements in its tax policy in recent years. The rationale behind the wide investment incentives offered by 2017 Investment Law is to boost domestic and foreign investments to spur economic growth, achieve inclusive development especially in lagging regions, generate employment, support SMEs development, increase exports and contribute to the formalization of the informal sector.

The 2017 Investment Law includes many positive changes, including limiting the scope of corporate income tax holidays to free zone companies only. Similarly, the 2015 amendment of the Law on Economic Zones of Special Nature no longer includes reduced corporate and income taxes for projects inside special economic zones. The government also has an extensive array of measures to protect the domestic tax base from cross-border tax minimisation techniques used by multinational enterprises (MNEs).

At the same time, the tax regime in Egypt remains highly complex, reflecting the multifaceted institutional framework surrounding overlapping zone-based strategies. A major concern is that officials have excessive discretion in deciding amounts of tax subsidy and beneficiaries, determined on a case-by-case basis. This hands-on approach runs counter to best practice that limits discretion by providing detailed legislation and regulations. Minimising discretion also improves outcomes by reducing uncertainty for investors, limiting scope for corruption of tax officials and revenue loss, and encouraging investment.

The new Investment Law No. 72 of 2017 has clarified the provision of special cost- and profit-based incentives. Article 11 provides a 50% discount off the investment costs for sector (A) and 30% for sector (B). Sector (A) covers investments in geographic locations most urgently in need of development according to the Investment Map and based on the data and statistics issued by the Central Agency for Public Mobilisation and Statistics. Sector (B) covers remaining areas in the country, in accordance with the distribution of the investment activities and for a number of identified projects. In addition, Article addresses taxes and duties of projects operating in public and private free zones. The government expects the new law to improve the institutional framework and tax regime in Egypt, which in return would facilitate investors' confidence and reduce uncertainty in the tax system.

Egypt's generous tax incentives to projects in free zones, including a corporate income tax holiday, also raises several concerns. Profit-based tax incentives, such as corporate tax holidays, are generally less efficient than cost-based tax incentives. Tax holidays to projects in free zone come with an export share requirement. The stated objectives are to enhance exports and increase foreign currency reserves. Although free zones in Egypt certainly stimulated exports, the extent to which their performance has met the objectives set by the government is an open question. Productivity growth may be hindered where tax relief encourages free zone firms to supply the domestic market where they enjoy a competitive advantage, rather than export markets where greater efficiency of business operations may be required to be competitive and profitable. Such concerns may arise even if free zone projects are subject to custom duties when they access the local market. Indirect tax relief in free zones also offers opportunities to evade taxes.

Policy recommendations

- To ensure consistency with overall tax policy and to strengthen accountability, the government is encouraged to consolidate tax incentive legislation and tax legislation and assign to the Ministry of Finance as primary responsibility to introduce tax incentive legislation.
- The tasks of monitoring compliance with tax incentives should be assigned to the Egyptian Tax Authority and strict penalty regimes should be exercised.
- The current project to switch to a fully electronic data management platform in the tax system is strongly supported.
- Redesign targeting criteria and clarify terms to minimise discretion in determining eligibility, and reduce discretion of officials in providing tax incentive relief.
- No longer provide free zone projects with a corporate income tax holiday (profit-based incentives), in line with the IMF recommendations to Egypt, and grandfather existing projects. Instead, extend investment tax allowances (cost-based tax incentives) of the Investment law to free zones projects.
- Apply strict penalty regimes for non-compliance with tax incentive laws and regulations.

Responsible business conduct

Promoting and enabling responsible business conduct (RBC) is of central interest to policymakers wishing to attract quality investment and ensure that business activity in their countries contributes to broader value creation and sustainable development. At global level, expectations and demands on RBC are rising, as reflected by a proliferation of high-level statements, national legislations, economic instruments and industry initiatives on RBC. Any company that wishes to integrate in the global economy and participate in trade and investment must be aware of the fact that their buyers, clients, and partners may have various obligations when it comes to RBC.

The notion that businesses should contribute to society is part of Egyptian business culture and rooted in Egyptian traditions. A number of programmes and initiatives that aim to address societal challenges from a business perspective exist in Egypt. These programmes have predominantly been based on philanthropy or social investments, but, in line with global trends, understanding of RBC in Egypt is evolving to align with the understanding that impacts on society and the environment are also a matter of core business operations.

The Egyptian government has taken steps to support various initiatives and promote RBC. Egypt is an adherent to the OECD RBC instruments since 2007 and the establishment of a National Contact Point (NCP) on RBC is an important milestone in this endeavour. Although the functioning of Egypt's NCP has not been consistent over the years, new developments, including the appointment of a contact person in 2019 demonstrate renewed efforts to promote RBC in Egypt. Continued co-operation with the OECD including participation in the Working Party on RBC offers an opportunity to renew various commitments on RBC, engage in dialogue with peers, and benefit from international good practices on RBC.

The Egyptian government has every interest in using the recent momentum on RBC in the country to promote a wide dissemination and implementation of internationally recognised RBC standards. This is especially true as a way to ensure that businesses conduct due diligence to identify, prevent, avoid and mitigate environmental and social risks which can have a significant impact on key economic sectors. For example, in the garment industry which is a strategic industry in Egypt, RBC can be instrumental in building a reputation for quality and sustainability that is increasingly essential. In infrastructure projects, risk-based due diligence can contribute to minimising potential environmental and social impacts.

Implementing RBC standards requires broad engagement with businesses but also with all stakeholders, including relevant government ministries and agencies, NGOs and trade unions. The government can take strategic actions to create an enabling environment for all relevant stakeholders to contribute to the design and implementation of RBC standards. A particular opportunity exists to promote collaborative initiatives.

Policy recommendations

- *Engage with other NCPs in order to build the capacities of the Egyptian NCP.* The NCP is an instrumental tool in the government policy toolbox that has so far been under-utilised. A well-functioning NCP can be instrumental for engagement with business and other stakeholders due to its unique non-judicial mandate and it can support the sound design and implementation of RBC-related policies.
- *Undertake a voluntary NCP peer review by 2023.* In line with calls from the international community and commitments made in June 2017 at the OECD Ministerial Council Meeting, Egypt is encouraged to undergo a voluntary peer review of its NCP. Peer reviews provide an important means to assess the practical aspects of NCP functioning and have been used by various government to assess opportunities for further improvements.
- *Develop a National Action Plan on RBC, in line with international best practice and in wide consultation with stakeholders.* A NAP process would be an opportunity to build multi-stakeholder support in key areas for Egypt's development trajectory and in complex areas where action by one stakeholder would not be enough. A consultative and inclusive NAP process is an opportunity to strengthen knowledge about the linkages of various policy areas that address business practices in the country and help build the capacity of Egyptian industry to participate in global supply chains.
- *Facilitate meaningful stakeholder engagement in the design and implementation of RBC policies and processes.* Particular attention should be paid to ensuring meaningful engagement in the early stages of policy development. In the planning and implementation of state-led projects, such as infrastructure projects, it is particularly important to meaningfully engage affected stakeholders.
- *Support, enable and promote RBC due diligence among businesses.* Egypt should explicitly support multi-stakeholder initiatives and promote broad dissemination and implementation of the OECD due diligence instruments. In particular, facilitating dialogue between various stakeholders in the garment sector and supporting application of the *OECD Due Diligence Guidance for Responsible Supply Chains in the Garment and Footwear Sector* in Egyptian factories would help improve industrial relations and enhance competitiveness of the garment sector.
- *Require the integration of RBC due diligence standards at all stages of infrastructure project life cycle, including in tendering and contracting processes.* Potential contractors and suppliers should be explicitly asked to follow international standards on RBC such as the OECD *Guidelines* and UN *Guiding Principles* and to demonstrate that they do so.

Infrastructure connectivity

Egypt has significantly improved the quality of its trade and transport infrastructure in recent years. However, the economy still faces important infrastructure challenges, coupled with considerable investment needs. According to the Ministry of Investment and International Cooperation, Egypt has directed around USD 61.4 billion to the infrastructure sector in the past five years to connect governorates, enhance accessibility and mobility of goods. The current levels of investment in infrastructure have raised questions whether Egypt may be able to sustain the current stock of infrastructure given its natural depreciation and aging, let alone expand it to meet growing demand. Bridging the financing gap requires a more cross-cutting approach to mobilise investment.

Infrastructure connectivity challenges in Egypt include a lack of multi-modal transport, an over-reliance on roads, a rail sector in need of further reform, and a fragmented port system. This leads to high transport costs and poor logistics performance compared to other countries in the region. Logistics costs in Egypt account for around 20% of GDP compared with a global average of 10-12% (IFC, 2013; World Bank, 2015). Overall, such bottlenecks constrain economic growth by around two percentage points per year, hindering the distribution of resources and contributing to a disproportionate concentration of economic activity in metropolitan areas (EBRD, 2017).

The need to improve connectivity is acknowledged in Egypt's "Vision 2030" and its transport and infrastructure plans, which aim to increase the capacity of the transport sector and boost its share in international and regional transport volumes. The Ministry of Transportation is also taking action to overcome such challenges, with the ongoing preparation of a plan to establish a network of logistical areas and villages. However, the government could strengthen its planning capacity and coordination for infrastructure projects. Currently, numerous infrastructure priorities are outlined in different strategies. The government intends to strengthen its fiscal planning by introducing the medium-term expenditure framework, which will set multi-year expenditure ceilings by major spending categories, including infrastructure (IMF, 2018).

Policy recommendations

- Clarify the regulatory frameworks for infrastructure investments to provide potential investors with clear, predictable and consistent policies. Currently, the public private partnerships (PPP) Law coexists with other channels of procuring infrastructure projects such as the public utilities legislation and a number of sector-specific or project-specific laws. The government should build a clearer and more transparent regulatory framework governing infrastructure activities.
- Provide more opportunities for private participation in infrastructure, including through PPPs. Despite Egypt's robust PPP regulatory framework, private sector participation in the infrastructure and energy sectors has been limited.
- Engage with stakeholders in local communities to ensure support for PPP projects. Currently, there is low public support for PPP projects, partly due to a lack of adequate community consultation to guide project selection and secure public support for projects. In order to gain more public support for infrastructure projects, the government needs to involve more systematically all the relevant stakeholders from the earliest stages of infrastructure planning to ensure support and that their needs – as well as social, economic, environmental and governance risks – are correctly assessed, addressed and adequately reflected in the contractual structures.
- Strengthen the capacity and co-ordination across the government for planning and assessing infrastructure priorities to ensure that infrastructure strategies are well integrated with other types of planning such as industrial development strategies and land use plans. For example, infrastructure plans in special economic zones such as the SCZone should be well connected with the hinterland. Achieving this also requires better co-ordination between different branches of government.

- Improve coordination of port and multimodal transport planning to facilitate more river-based transport. Currently, ports contribute less than 1% of inland transport, which is mainly due to the poor integration of river transport to the country's transport networks.
- Strengthen the legal framework for public procurement to increase tender participation and supplier diversity. Currently, the national public procurement legal framework is not considered to be clear, comprehensive, or conducive to a competitive procurement environment. While the 2016 Law on Public Procurement introduces procedures to enhance transparency and reduce discretion in public procurement, the consistent application and enforcement of the law by the involved procurement entities is weak.
- Ensure that infrastructure projects are grounded in efficiency rather than fiscal motivations. Currently, there is no legal requirement in Egypt for public entities to consider the costs of the whole life cycle of an infrastructure project or seek value for money. Building capacity among government entities to assess value for money over the lifecycle of an infrastructure asset is crucial to make sure that investments benefits Egyptian users and society at large.

References

Assaad, R. and C. Krafft (2013), "The Structure and Evolution of Employment in Egypt: 1998-2012", *Working Paper*, No. 805, The Economic Research Forum, Giza, http://www.erf.org.eg (accessed on 1 February 2019). [5]

Cammett, M. et al. (2013), *A Political Economy of the Middle East*, Routledge, https://www.routledge.com/A-Political-Economy-of-the-Middle-East-4th-Edition/Cammett-Diwan-Richards-Waterbury/p/book/9780813349381 (accessed on 13 December 2018). [3]

EBRD, E. (2016), *What's Holding Back the Private Sector in MENA? Lessons from the Enterprise Survey*, World Bank, Washington DC, http://www.ebrd.com (accessed on 29 January 2019). [4]

Ikram, K. (2018), *The Political Economy of Reforms in Egypt: Issues and Policymaking since 1952*, The American University in Cairo Press, Cairo. [2]

IMF (2018), "Arab Republic of Egypt : Third Review Under the Extended Arrangement Under the Extended Fund Facility, and Requests for a Waiver of Nonobservance of a Performance Criterion and for Modification of a Performance Criterion-Press Release; Staff Report; and Statement by the Executive Director for the Arab Republic of Egypt", *Country Report*, No. 18/213, IMF, Washington, DC, https://www.imf.org/en/Publications/CR/Issues/2018/07/12/Arab-Republic-of-Egypt-Third-Review-Under-the-Extended-Arrangement-Under-the-Extended-Fund-46061 (accessed on 8 January 2019). [1]

World Bank (2014), *More Jobs, Better Jobs: A Priority for Egypt*, World Bank, Washington, DC, http://siteresources.worldbank.org/INTMENA/Resources/EgyptJobsReportFinalcolor.pdf (accessed on 1 February 2019). [6]

Notes

[1] Based on ILO modelled estimates, data for female unemployment from 2019, data for youth and educated unemployment from 2017 (last year available).

[2] Based on panel data from the Egypt Labour Market Panel Survey between 1998 and 2012; formal employment is defined as employment that provides either a written work contract or social insurance (World Bank, 2014). According to ILO data, employment in the formal sector in Egypt has decreased since 2012, while share of informal employment has increased from 41% of total employment in 2012 to 53% in 2017.

[3] OECD calculations based on the IMF Balance of Payments and International Investment position database, the IMF World Economic Outlook database and OECD Foreign Direct Investment statistics database.

Chapter 1. Foreign investment trends and development benefits

This chapter reviews trends in foreign investment in Egypt and their development benefits using various national and international data sources. It looks at the performance of foreign investment relative to neighbouring and emerging economies as well as foreign investment distribution across economic activities and Egyptian governorates. The chapter also examines foreign investment development outcomes, including on productivity, labour market outcomes, export, and supply chain linkages with the local economy.

Egypt has a huge potential to leverage its strategic location, considerable market size and young workforce to attract untapped investment. Despite periods of increases over the last three decades, Egypt has not maintained stable investment and savings growth rates, both key engines of economic development. The contribution of investment to GDP has even declined since 1980 despite the progressive opening of the Egyptian economy to the private sector, initiated in the 1970s and referred to as *infitah* (open door policy). The investment-to-GDP ratio in 2017 was 15% in Egypt compared to 25-35% in Morocco, Turkey or Viet Nam.

Regulatory and institutional constraints, among other barriers, were the main causes of the sluggish improvement. The Egyptian state's shrinking contribution to investment since the late 1980s was also one of the factors behind the plunge in aggregate investment, as this decline was not compensated by an equivalent increase in private investment in the 1990s. The share of public investment fluctuated between 40% and 45% of total investment. In contrast, in the OECD area, public investment represents 15% of total investment.

Attracting foreign direct investment (FDI) is central to the development strategy of Egypt, particularly in light of lacklustre domestic saving and investment performance. Inward FDI surged in several waves over the last three decades, pushed, inter alia, by economic reforms. Macroeconomic stabilisation, the country accession to the WTO in 1995 and further liberalisation of cross-border investment in the early 2000s paved the way for a sustained wave of FDI increase between 2000 and 2007, amplified by record rates in global growth. Despite these periods of increases, Egypt's long-term FDI performance was nonetheless less impressive than of other emerging countries in Southeast Asia.

Encouraging prospects surround FDI performance in Egypt since 2012, despite the recent episodes of global and regional instability. The global financial crisis hit cross-border investment to Egypt harder and longer than to neighbouring countries. The external shock brought to light structural challenges in the economy impeding the deployment of foreign investment. These challenges included the overdependence on the public sector, limited product market competition and weak export diversification. The post-2011 instability in the region had a negative effect with some investors suspending their operations, downscaling their commitments or withdrawing their investments altogether. There is a surge in foreign investors' interest in Egypt in the last years, driven by macroeconomic stabilisation and market reforms, although fiscal constraints hit domestic demand.

FDI is present in few economic activities and concentrated in specific geographical areas. Foreign investment goes into natural resources, real estate, construction, and light manufacturing. Most of these sectors have limited innovation-creating potential due to their relatively low complexity. Meanwhile, greenfield FDI is taking place in promising sectors such as in chemicals and in renewable energies. FDI is also highly concentrated. The top five governorates accounted for 90% of FDI, while the bottom 22 governorates share the remaining 10%. This unequal distribution of FDI within Egypt is also found in other emerging countries.

The impact of FDI on sustainable development in Egypt is broadly positive, but could be significantly improved, notably in areas related to labour productivity. Foreign MNEs in the country are found to outperform local firms with respect to innovation, gender equality and energy efficiency. In contrast, they are not more productive nor pay higher than their domestic peers, in contrast with what is observed in other emerging countries. There is also ample room for foreign investment to further support Egypt's participation in higher value-added segments of global value chains (GVCs), notably by strengthening supply chain linkages through the importing of intermediate products.

Investment trends in Egypt since the post-*infitah* era

Despite remarkable periods of increases over the past three decades, Egypt has not maintained stable investment and savings growth rates, both key engines of economic development. The contribution of investment to GDP has gradually declined since 1980 despite the progressive openness of the Egyptian economy to the private sector, initiated in the 1970s and referred to as *infitah (*open-door policy*)* (Figure 1.1). The variations in investment trends have paralleled those in gross savings rate, except in the 1980s where their co-movement was disconnected. Investment and savings rates reached an all-time low of 13-15% of GDP in 2017, after a peak of roughly 30% in 1988 and 2008. Other countries with similar levels of per capita income registered stronger performance. In Morocco, Turkey or Viet Nam, investment and savings rates have fluctuated less than in Egypt over the last three decades, oscillating between 25% and 35% of GDP in 2017, depending on the country, which is twice as high as in Egypt.

Figure 1.1. Investment and savings trends in Egypt and other emerging economies

In percent of GDP

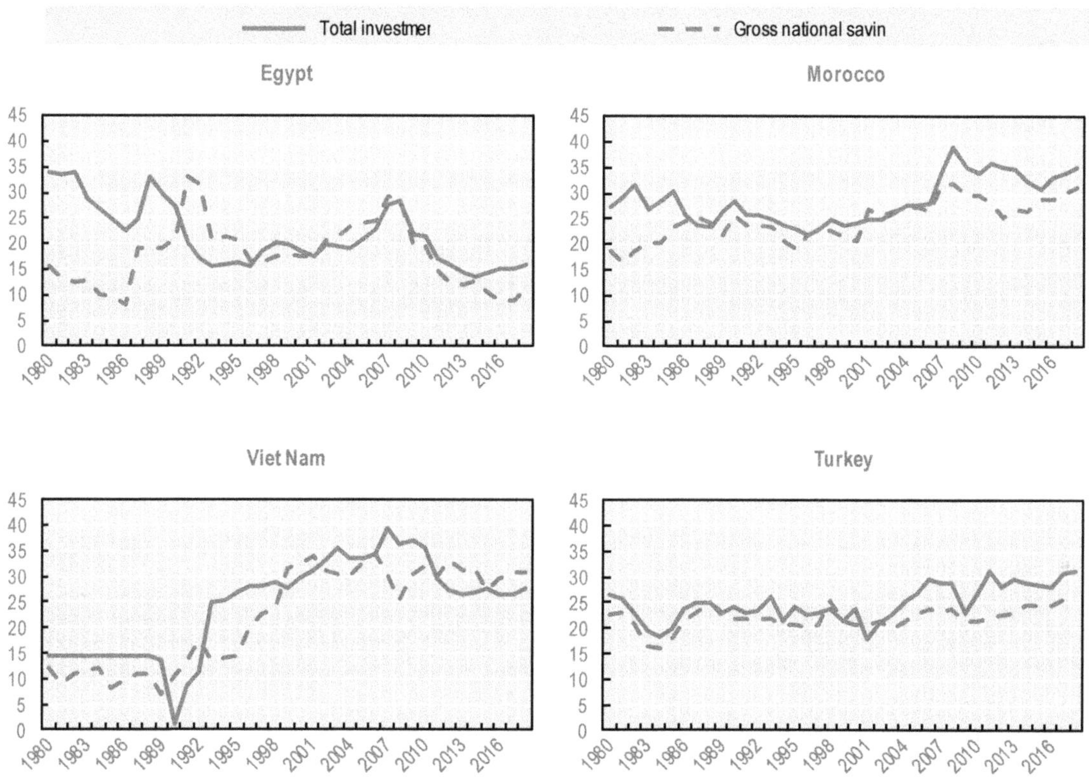

Source: OECD based on the IMF World Economic Outlook.

Multiple and evolving factors have been behind the decline in investment and savings rates in Egypt over the last three decades. Egypt's poor macroeconomic environment in the 1980s, among other challenges the economy was facing, was not conducive to private sector development. The country signed in 1991 an IMF-led stabilisation programme to correct important macroeconomic imbalances, in the form of a large government budget deficit. The government's stabilisation fiscal and monetary policy reforms successfully reduced budget deficits and increased credit available to the private sector, with little adverse consequences on output (Subramanian, 1997). The macroeconomic readjustments, coupled with other market-based reforms, helped contain the steep decline in investment and savings rates between 1988 and 1993 (Figure 1.1).

Regulatory and institutional constraints, among other barriers, were the main causes of the sluggish improvement in investment in the mid-1990s (Zaki, 2001). It is only in the late 1990s and mid-2000s that investment increased, a trend that was abruptly reversed by the 2007 global financial crisis. Investment and savings have witnessed a moderate improvement only since 2015, encouraged by a sequence of macroeconomic reforms and the decision to float the exchange rate in 2016. This decision contributed to the devaluation of the Egyptian pound, bringing the official rate closer to its black market counterpart, narrowing a gap that has deterred domestic and foreign investors in the past.

The Egyptian state's shrinking contribution to investment since the late 1980s was one of the factors behind the plunge in aggregate investment (Figure 1.2). This decline was not compensated by an equivalent increase in private investment in the 1990s. Despite their decline, public investments in non-infrastructure activities may have crowded out private investment in the country (Fawzy and El-Megharbel, 2004). The public sector continues to play a critical role in financing the Egyptian economy. Over the last ten years, the share of public investment fluctuated between 40% and 45% of total investment (i.e. public and private). In contrast, in the OECD area, public investment represents 15% of total investment and 3% of GDP.

Figure 1.2. Gross fixed capital formation: Public versus private investment

In percent of GDP

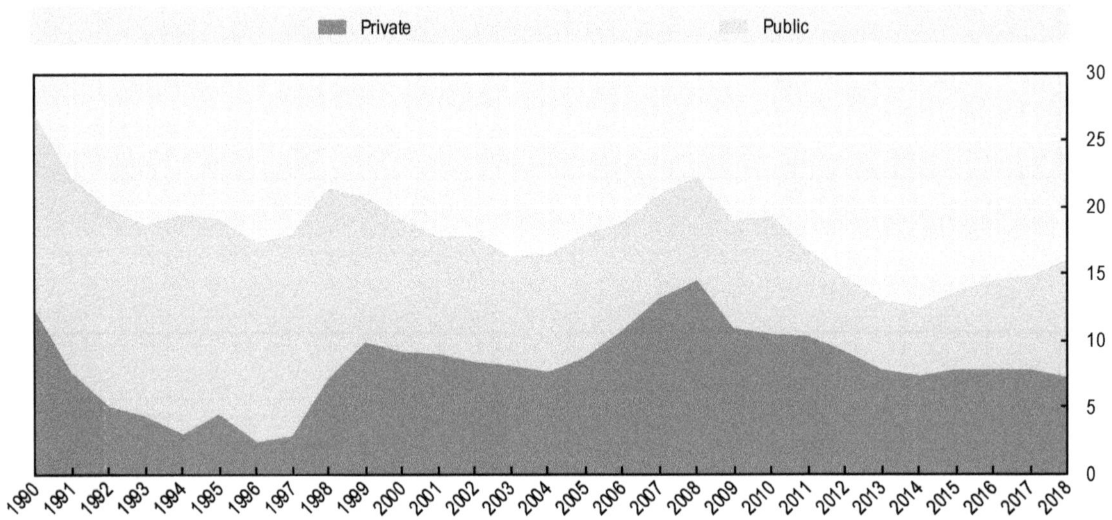

Source: OECD based on the World Bank Development Indicators.

Investment trends across economic sectors in Egypt indicate that private investors finance different types of activities compared to public actors (Figure 1.3). Private investment is predominant in manufacturing, real-estate projects, natural gas, communication, and tourism. In contrast, the public sector and state-owned enterprises (SOEs) invest typically in infrastructure and energy (i.e. electricity, transport and logistics, and water) as well as in health and education services. There are nonetheless activities in which both public and private actors invest. For instance, public investment in manufacturing represented 14% of total investment between 2011 and 2017. The distribution of investment between the public and private sector is altered by the fact that utilities sectors are totally or partly closed to private investors (see chapter 2). In OECD countries, education and transports receive most of public investments and more than half of it goes to regional and local areas.

Figure 1.3. Public and private investment by economic activities: Boom versus bust periods

Cumulated investment (in million LE)

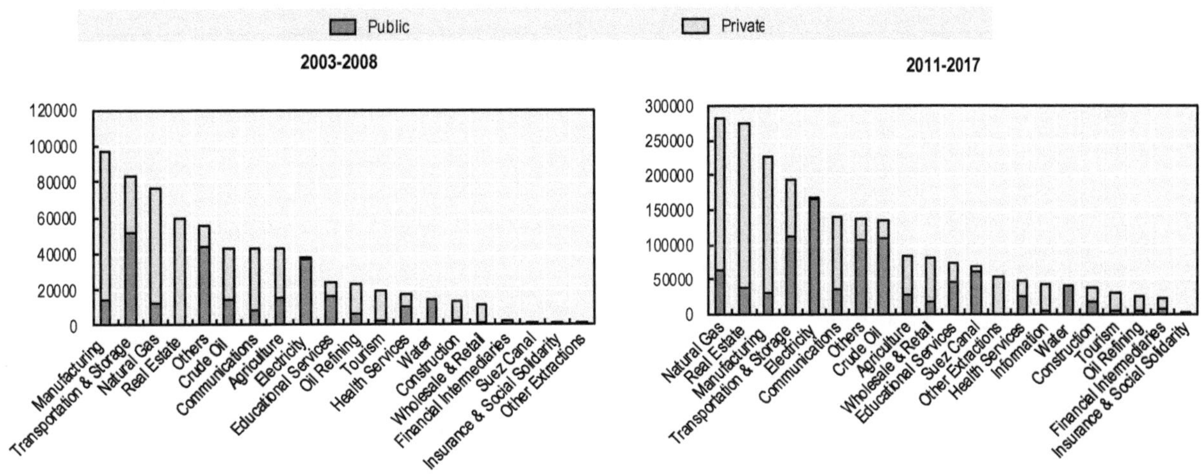

Note: Public investment includes investment by the government sector, economic authorities and SOEs. Data for the fiscal year 2016/2017 is preliminary.
Source: OECD calculations based on the Central Bank of Egypt statistics.

Long-term trends in foreign investment in Egypt

Attracting foreign investment is central to the development strategy of Egypt, particularly in light of lacklustre domestic saving and investment performance. Inward foreign direct investment (FDI) surged in several waves over the last three decades, pushed, among other reasons, by ambitious economic reforms that are discussed in the next chapters. The first wave of inward FDI increase was between 1985 and 1990. Macroeconomic stabilisation, the country accession to the WTO in 1995 and further liberalisation of cross-border investment in the early 2000s paved the way for a second and more sustained wave of FDI between 2000 and 2007, amplified by record rates in global growth. Over that period, the FDI stock to GDP ratio registered an impressive surge of 10 percentage points.

Egypt's long-term FDI performance has been remarkable in comparison with the wider MENA region but less with other emerging regions (Figure 1.4). Countries that underwent similar transformation of their economic systems, such as the economies in transition of Central and Eastern Europe or of Southeast Asia managed to cumulate higher FDI flows, relative to their respective economic size (UNCTAD, 2011). In the early 1990s FDI stock in Egypt represented around 25% of GDP, a ratio at that time higher than in the MENA and ASEAN regions as well as in the OECD area. Nonetheless, the growth of inward FDI into Egypt has not been sustained in a period when other developing countries, such as in the ASEAN group, attracted higher inflows. Overall FDI flows in Egypt witnessed strong periods of booms and busts.

Figure 1.4. FDI stock in Egypt compared to MENA and other economic groups

In percent of GDP

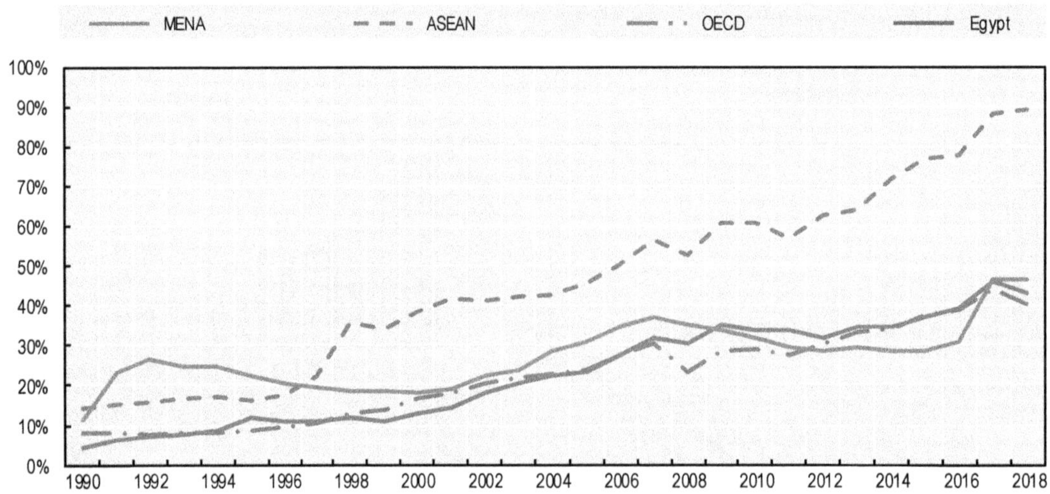

Note: MENA and ASEAN: Accumulation of BOP FDI flows were used when FDI stocks were not available for selected countries and/or historical years. Egypt: data for 1990-2003 correspond to accumulation of BOP FDI flows from 1977 onwards.
Source: OECD calculations based on the IMF Balance of Payments and International Investment position database, the IMF World Economic Outlook database and OECD Foreign Direct Investment statistics database.

The global financial crisis hit inward FDI to Egypt harder and longer than to other countries of the region (Figure 1.5). The external shock brought to light important structural challenges in the Egyptian economy impeding the deployment of foreign investment. These challenges, examined throughout this Review, included the overdependence on the public sector for economic activity, limited product market competition, inadequate infrastructure, and weak export diversification and structural transformation. FDI flows in Egypt recorded an all-time low in 2011 following the events witnessed by the region, including Egypt (Figure 1.5). These events have had negative spill-over effects on the attractiveness of the entire region with some investors suspending their operations, downscaling their commitments or withdrawing their investments altogether (OECD, 2014).

Figure 1.5. Inward FDI flows in Egypt in the aftermath of 2007 global financial crisis

In USD million

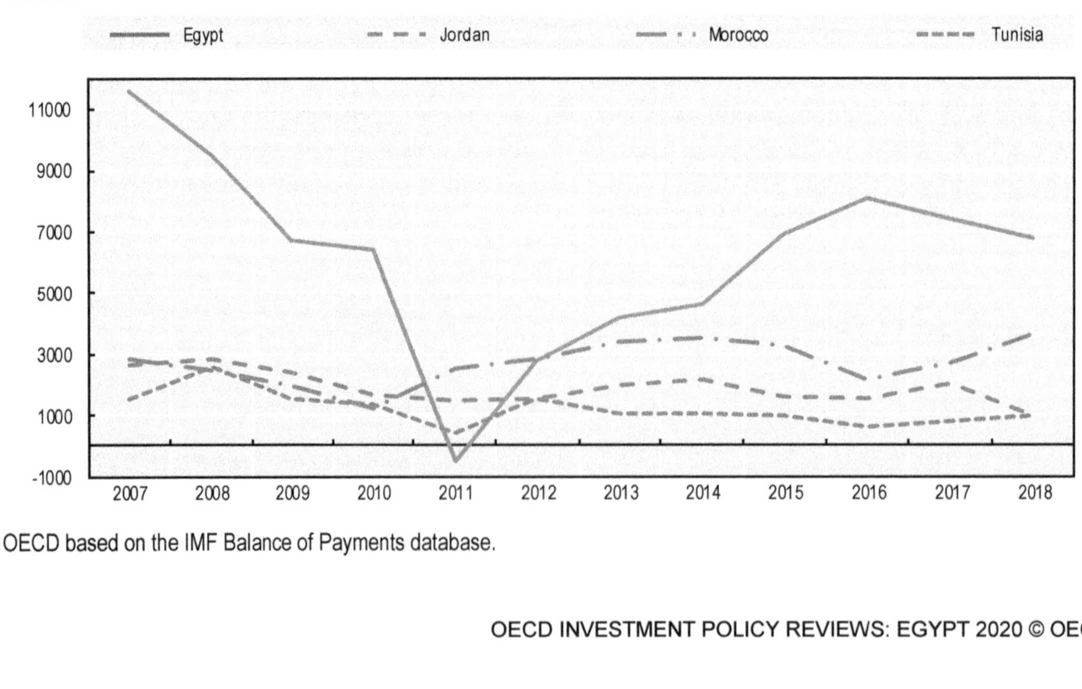

Source: OECD based on the IMF Balance of Payments database.

Egypt's FDI performance is improving

Between 2012 and 2016, FDI flows have been on an upward, albeit moderate, trend representing around 2% of GDP, still below the pre-2007 crisis levels of 8%. In 2016, Egypt was for the first time the largest recipient of FDI flows in the MENA region, ahead of Saudi Arabia, accounting for nearly 30% of total FDI flows received in the MENA region as a whole, compared to between 8% and 20% in 2005-14, excluding the negative FDI inflows recorded in 2011. Egypt also maintained in 2018 its position as the largest FDI recipient of foreign investment in Africa, although inflows decreased in comparison with 2016 and 2017 (UNCTAD, 2019 and Figure 1.5). End of 2018 the FDI stock in the country was equal to 47% of GDP, higher than in the MENA region (43%) and in the OECD (40%) and lower than in ASEAN (89%) (Figure 1.4).

Macroeconomic stabilisation and legislative reforms drove the important surge in foreign investors' interest in Egypt, even if budgetary measures also hit domestic demand. The recent surge in FDI may also reflect a challenge for domestic firms to finance themselves on the domestic market. Most of the recent foreign investments have been mergers and acquisitions or petroleum sector investments rather than new greenfield FDI projects (CBE, 2018 and 2019).

Foreign investment trends in Egypt by economic activity

In Egypt, as in most of the MENA region, FDI is concentrated in natural resources, real estate, construction, and light manufacturing (e.g. textiles). Most of these sectors have limited job-creating potential due to their relatively low labour-intensity. Since 2010, instability in the region has further skewed the sectoral composition of FDI towards the natural resources sector, which has been more immune to political shocks (OECD, 2014). FDI inflows in non-oil manufacturing and services sectors have stagnated, while these sectors have a higher propensity to create jobs and promote transfers of technology and managerial knowledge, making it more challenging for Egypt to participate in global value chains.

FDI flow statistics published by the CBE indicate that the oil sector represented the bulk of FDI received by Egypt over the last few years, followed by real estate and construction, which covers the purchase of land and homes by non-residents (Table 1.1). Manufacturing represented less than 10% of total inflows. Besides the real estate sector, services FDI was driven by financial activities. In contrast, communication and IT represented less than 4% of total inflows.

Table 1.1. FDI flows in Egypt by economic activity, as a share of total inflows

	2013/14	2014/15	2015/16	2016/17	2017/18	2018/19*
Oil	71.7	58.4	53.5	61.3	67.3	70.6
Manufacturing	2.0	2.3	3.4	5.8	10	7.1
Agriculture	0.2	0.0	0.0	0.2	0.1	0.6
Construction	2.2	6.0	1.5	0.9	4.5	2.3
Services	4	10.0	10.4	9.4	11.2	15.7
Real estate	1.4	6.2	3.6	3.1	2.7	8.8
Finance	1	2.0	3.8	1.6	1.9	1.9
Tourism	0.1	0.0	0.3	0.4	0.3	0.5
Communications	0.0	0.0	0.5	0.3	3.4	1.1
Other services	1.5	1.8	2.2	4.0	2.9	3.4
Unallocated	19.9	23.3	31.2	22.4	6.9	3.7

Note: *December-July 2018/19. 'Inflows' = increase in liabilities and differ from total net incurrence of liabilities published in Balance of Payments, which are defined as increases minus decreases in liabilities.
Source: Central Bank of Egypt, Annual reports of 2014/15; 2015/16; 2016/17; 2017/18 and Monthly Update of the External Position of the Egyptian Economy on July/December 2018/19.

FDI stock estimates by GAFI reveal a more diversified distribution across economic activities than with flows statistics of the last few years. Upstream oil and gas exploration and mining companies represented a quarter of the FDI stock in 2017. Foreign investment in this sector was nonetheless the lowest in terms of the number of FDI projects and of source countries.[1] The other leading FDI activities were finance and manufacturing and further behind construction, communication and information technology, tourism and agriculture. These estimations were based on a compilation system, designed by GAFI, to align Egypt with the definition of the IMF Balance of Payment Manual Sixth Edition (BPM6). Annex A provides a detailed assessment and recommendations on compiling FDI statistics in Egypt.

International data on announced greenfield FDI projects offer additional insights on cross-border investment by economic activity in Egypt. Real estate and natural resources alone represented 70% of greenfield FDI capital announced between 2006 and 2017 (Figure 1.6). The manufacture of chemicals and foodstuffs and renewable energy were the other most attractive sectors for FDI (16% of total greenfield FDI). Manufacturing activities such as automotive and textiles attracted much lower cross-border investment, even if FDI projects in textile were among the most numerous. This corroborates earlier evidence that foreign investment in textile and clothing was limited to the labour-intensive segments of the supply chain (Nugent and Abdel-Latif, 2010). Beyond real estate and tourism, services FDI was divided between financial and business services (largest in terms of project number), communication and logistics.

Figure 1.6. Greenfield FDI by economic activity, 2006-2017

Cumulative greenfield FDI capital between January 2006 and September 2017 in USD million

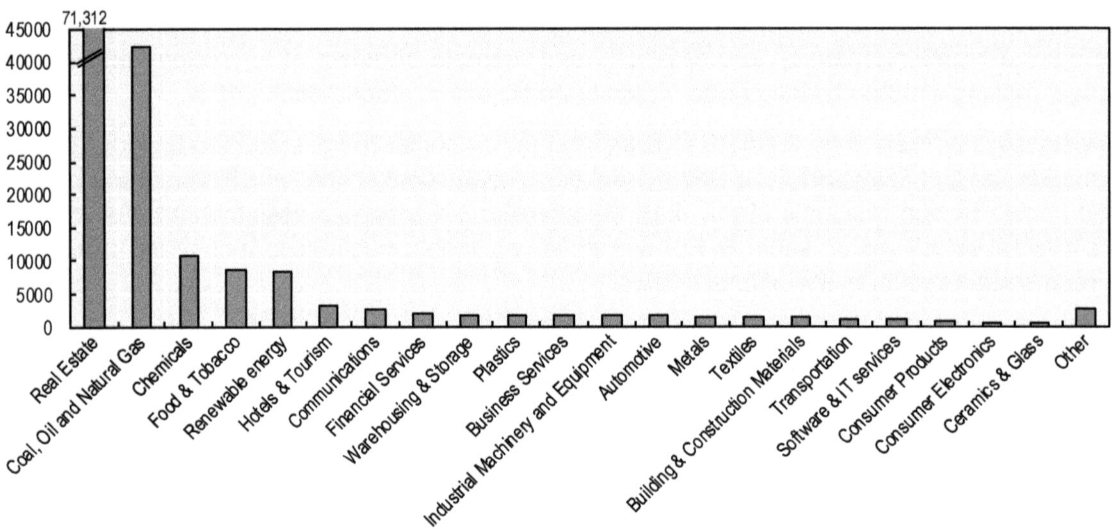

Source: OECD based on fDi Markets Database.

Trends in foreign investment in Egypt from a home country perspective

Another way of assessing FDI trends in Egypt is to examine which countries are the major investors in Egypt and what they report investing. Arab countries, EU member states, and the US are home to 90% of FDI flows in Egypt since 2004. Investors from these three regional blocks responded differently to a succession of global, regional, and domestic shocks that affected the Egyptian economy in the past decade. FDI from the countries of the European Union to Egypt proved resistant to the 2007 global financial crisis while investments from the US and, to a lower extent, Arab countries collapsed (Figure 1.7). End-2017 FDI flows from Arab States and the US to Egypt were still far below their pre-2007 crisis levels.

Figure 1.7. EU investment resisted more than other regions to global and domestic shocks

In USD million

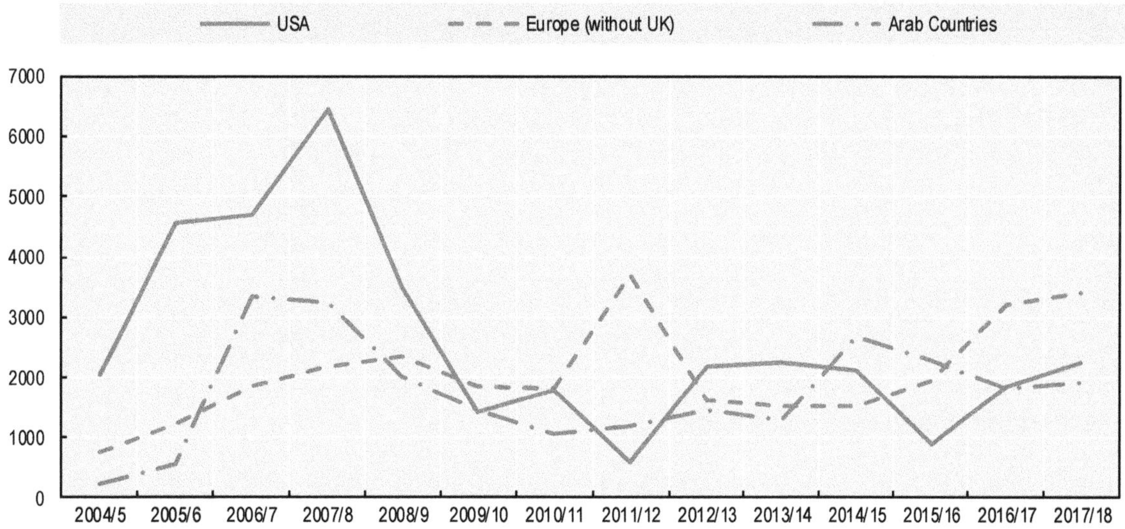

Note: Data for 2016/17 and 2017/18 is provisional.
Source: OECD based on Central Bank of Egypt statistics.

Estimates of bilateral FDI stocks, which were produced by GAFI from their developed compilation system, indicate that major investors in Egypt in 2017 were the United Kingdom, the Netherlands, the US, Italy, United Arab Emirates, Qatar, Saudi Arabia, Kuwait, Germany and Switzerland.[2] From the perspective of FDI flows, British and Dutch investment witnessed an exponential surge, most of it establishing projects in the capital-intensive hydrocarbons sector. Recently, some investments by the UK were undertaken in the higher education sector while Dutch companies invested in renewable energies. French FDI has remained rather immune to the instability triggered by the 2011 events. France has 160 subsidiaries, mostly large firms listed in the CAC 40 in a variety of sectors (agro food, transport, manufacturing, etc.). Most of the French-owned firms produce for the domestic or regional African market. Some companies have invested in R&D in sectors such as automotive equipment. Recently French investors have started to consider Egypt as a location for efficiency-seeking investments in connection with regional and global value chains. Outside of the top investors, Egypt has attracted rapidly growing investment from China over the last decade.

FDI statistics reported by home countries provide further indications on FDI trends in Egypt. Understanding patterns of cross-border investment is becoming increasingly difficult owing to the rise of special purpose entities and pass-through investments in third countries for fiscal reasons or to benefit from the protection of an investment treaty. Statistics by the CBE indicate that OECD member countries represented 77% of cumulated FDI inflows between 2004 and 2017. Table 1.2 shows the stock of FDI from OECD countries based on home country reporting. Companies from OECD countries invested USD 65 billion as of end 2016, equivalent to 66% of the total FDI stock in Egypt. The US, the Netherlands, and the UK report the three highest FDI positions among OECD countries. In contrast, the CBE flows statistics indicate that the Netherland is, by far, not among the top three investors in Egypt. Possible sources of discrepancy between OECD and CBE statistics are differences in valuation methodologies (OECD, 2020).

Table 1.2. FDI position of OECD member countries in Egypt

(2016 or nearest year available; USD million)

OECD Total	67507
United States	22202
Netherlands	20082
United Kingdom (2014)	9794
Italy	7445
Germany	1844
France	1655
Switzerland	978
Belgium	725
Spain	718
Greece	517
Other OECD	1547

Source: OECD International Direct Investment Database.

Recent estimates by GAFI of inward FDI positions compare immediate and ultimate investing countries.[3] Such evidence sheds further light on the top OECD investors in Egypt. The estimates suggest that the Netherlands, followed by Luxembourg and Belgium are, to varying degrees, pass-through countries for investments in Egypt. For instance, 80% of the investments immediately controlled by Dutch companies in Egypt have their ultimate controlling parents in Italy, the UK, the US, South Korea, and Mexico. According to GAFI, round tripping by Egyptian businesses, i.e. domestic firms that transit through a third country to invest in Egypt, is limited (0.13 USD billion).

Examining activities data of US MNEs affiliates in Egypt can yield further insights into the nature of their investment. By any measures, Egypt is one of the leading destination for US MNEs in the Middle East and Africa (Table 1.3). There is nonetheless space to attract additional US affiliates, which are significantly more active in other regional hubs such as South Africa and Turkey. Surprisingly, US MNEs in Morocco employ more people than in Egypt despite being less numerous, having lower sales, and providing lower compensation of employees. Statistics from the US Bureau of Economic Analysis indicate that the number of US affiliates in Egypt, their assets and their compensation of employees increased between 2009 and 2015. In contrast, US affiliates' sales and number of employees declined over the same period. The latter dropped from 40 000 to 31 000 employees.

Table 1.3. Activities of US MNEs in Egypt and selected emerging countries

(2015; USD million except employment)

	Affiliates #	Assets	Sales	Compensation of employees	Employment
Egypt	81	28 074	12 519	717	31 000
Jordan	11	1 691	1 047	85	2 500
Morocco	35	3 598	2 721	410	33 600
South Africa	267	56 248	46 904	4 641	169 500
Turkey	174	30 966	33 572	2 505	67 700
Viet Nam	67	15 308	7 882	696	71 300

Note: # only those affiliates with assets, sales or net income > USD 25 million.
Source: Bureau of Economic Analysis, US Department of Commerce.

Foreign investment distribution across Egyptian governorates

The distribution of cross-border investment is unequal across the 27 Egyptian governorates. Between 1992 and 2008, the neighbouring governorates of Cairo and Giza concentrated 60% of greenfield FDI. More recent data on announced greenfield FDI projects between 2006 and 2017 confirm the unequal distribution of FDI within Egypt. The top five governorates account for 90% of greenfield FDI, while the bottom 22 governorates share the remaining 10%. The governorates with low shares of FDI are mostly landlocked areas, with the exception of the greater Cairo area. Greenfield FDI in services, particularly in ICT and finance, are more concentrated in a small number of governorates, while manufacturing FDI projects are relatively more geographically dispersed (Hanafi, 2014).

Figure 1.8. The distribution of announced greenfield FDI capital across the 27 governorates

Cumulated greenfield FDI capital between January 2006 and September 2017

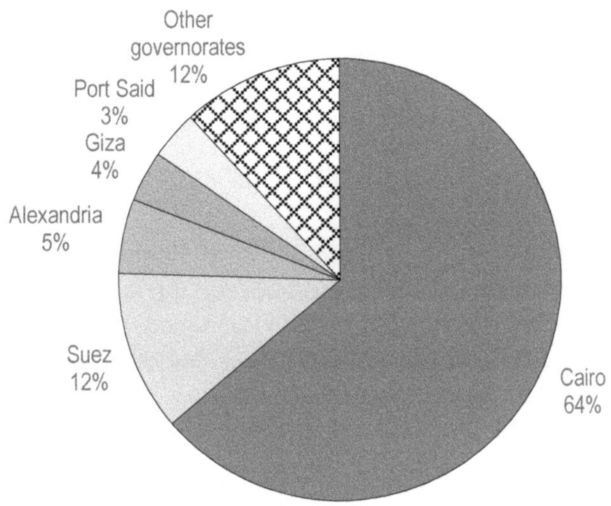

Source: OECD based on fDi Markets Database.

FDI trends within Egypt change when taking into account the size of the governorate. Relative to population levels, greenfield FDI is the highest in the governorates bordering the Suez Canal and Cairo and lowest in the more remote, less developed, governorates (Figure 1.8, 1.9). Variations in greenfield FDI per capita across governorates are massive, including within the top ten governorates such as Suez (USD 20 000), Cairo (USD 7 500) and Alexandria (USD 1 225). At the bottom end, greenfield FDI per capita in the governorates of Asyut, Fayoum, Louxor, Qena and 10 others is lower than USD 500.

Figure 1.9. Greenfield FDI per capita, by governorate

Cumulated greenfield FDI between January 2006 and September 2017 in USD; Population end 2015

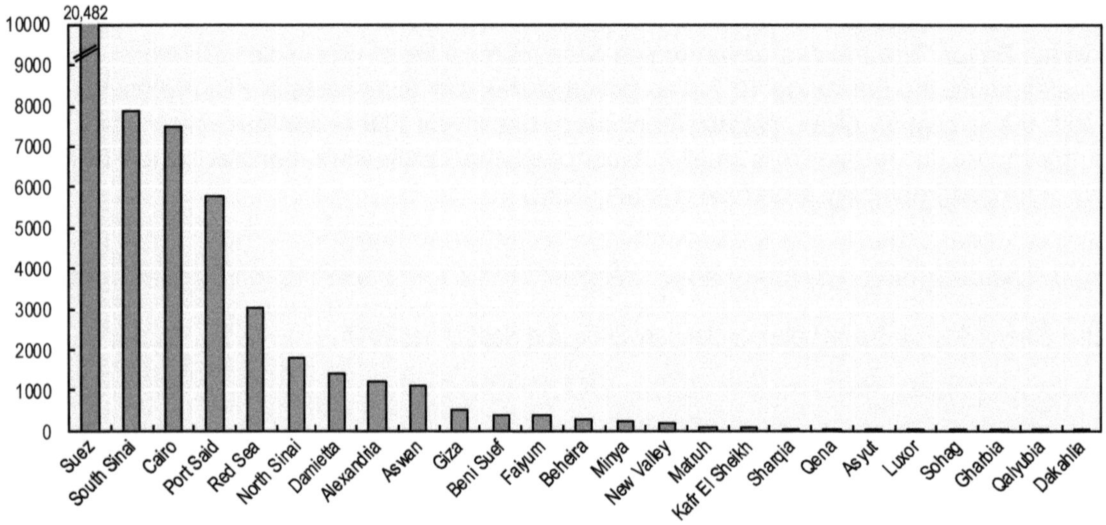

Source: OECD based on fDi Markets Database and the Central Agency for Public Mobilization and Statistics (CAPMAS).

The distribution of foreign multinationals is as unequal within Egypt as in other emerging countries. In Morocco, Tunisia, Turkey, or Indonesia the difference between the top and bottom regions, measured as the percentage of foreign-owned firms of total firms within the region, are higher than in Egypt. In Morocco, the four regions that contribute to 60% of the country's GDP, out of 16 regions, concentrate also 80% of total FDI stock (Ettoumi et al., 2015). More than 30% of Tunisia's FDI stock is concentrated in the capital and, overall, the coastal regions retain more than 80% of non-hydrocarbons FDI (OECD, 2017).

The unequal concentration of MNEs within Egypt, as for other countries, is largely the result of disparities in the level of economic activity across governorates. MNEs activity tends to be, to varying degrees, more concentrated spatially than domestic activity, in industrial or economic hubs, which may exacerbate within-country disparities. Recent evidence indicates that MNEs activity in Egypt is only slightly more concentrated than domestic economic activity, similar to other African countries, Chile or Mexico (Lejarraga and Ragoussis, 2019). Besides the level of economy activity, domestic private investment, well-functioning zones and labour abundance positively influence the distribution of FDI across Egypt's governorates. Sub-national policies such as the existence of One-Stop Shop offices in some specific regions are found not to affect the FDI distribution in the country (Hanafy, 2014).

Evidence from Cairo city, which extends over the governorates of Cairo, Giza and Qualyubia, sheds some light on the relationship between MNEs presence and local economic activity. At all levels, FDI numbers for Cairo indicate that its attractiveness for foreign investors is undisputed. Cairo may have overshadowed other cities or regions' ability to attract foreign investment, leading to population movements towards agglomeration centres. In response to this dilemma, and due to the growing congestion of Cairo city, Egypt has established industrial zones since the mid-seventies, which have increasingly attracted large, capital-intensive, FDI projects. The growing concentration of FDI in new industrial cities has been triggered by the availability of industrial land rather than attractiveness of these new locations (UN-Habitat and IHS-Erasmus University Rotterdam, 2018). This movement may nevertheless support a geographic dispersion of economic activities and improve the livelihood of the surrounding population.

The contribution of foreign investment to sustainable development in Egypt

FDI can benefit the host economy beyond its direct contribution to the capital stock. Under the right conditions, FDI in Egypt can raise productivity, boost exports and participation in global value chains (GVCs), and improve the standard of living of different segments of the population. It can contribute to job creation, human capital development, technological progress, knowledge diffusion, efficient reallocation of resources, and environmental greening. It can also serve as a conduit for domestic industries to access international markets and participate in global value chains. As such, FDI in Egypt can play an important role for progress towards the Sustainable Development Goals (SDGs).

Sustainable development benefits of FDI are not automatic. Different chapters of the Review examine how private sector reforms and selected policies in Egypt could enable FDI's potential to advance sustainable development. The following sub-sections use novel indicators the OECD developed to describe how foreign investment relates to aspects of sustainable development in host economies, including in Egypt (Box 1.1). The indicators monitor FDI outcomes on productivity and innovation, inclusiveness (i.e. employment and job quality, skills, and gender), and supply chain linkages in GVCs.

Box 1.1. The OECD FDI Qualities Indicators

FDI Qualities Indicators describe how FDI relates to sustainable development in host countries. They are structured around economic, social and environmental sustainability. An assessment of all 17 SDGs, and their corresponding targets, was undertaken to identify the spectrum of FDI Qualities – that is, areas where FDI contributes to achieving the SDGs. This assessment considers the extent to which FDI potential for advancing the SDGs is reflected in the OECD Policy Framework of Investment including related guidelines such as the OECD Guidelines on Multinational Enterprises and the OECD Policy Guidance for Investment in Clean Energy Infrastructure.

The FDI Qualities Indicators focus on five clusters: productivity and innovation, employment and job quality, skills, gender equality, and carbon footprint. For each of the five clusters, a number of different outcomes are identified and used to produce indicators that relate them to FDI or activity of foreign multinationals, allowing for comparisons both within and across clusters so as to identify potential sustainability trade-offs.

Taking into account the country-specific context, policymakers can use FDI Qualities Indicators to assess how FDI supports national policy objectives, where challenges lie, and in what areas policy action is needed. Indicators also allow cross-country comparisons and benchmarking against regional peers or income groups, which, taking into account the country context, can help to identify good practices and make evidence-based policy decisions.

An important value added of the FDI Qualities Indicators is that they reveal cross-country differences in how FDI relates to sustainable development. Existing studies touch upon some of the outcomes covered in this report, but generally only examine one dimension of sustainability, offering only a partial view of FDI's contribution to sustainable development, without revealing important cross-country and cross-cluster differences.

The impact of FDI on sustainable development can be direct and indirect, i.e. through spillover effects. Direct impacts relate to the activities of foreign multinationals and how they affect socio-economic and environmental outcomes. Indirect impacts refer to how foreign firms influence sustainable development through their interaction with domestic firms. FDI Qualities Indicators cannot fully disentangle both effects, but provide some direction as to what mechanisms are at play for a given sustainability outcome.

Source: OECD (2019a)

Foreign-owned firms outperform domestic ones in several development areas

Foreign manufacturers in Egypt are found to outperform local firms across several development areas, but not all (Figure 1.10 – panel A). The indicators show a stronger performance of foreign-owned firms in terms of process and product innovation, gender equality and energy efficiency. In contrast, the indicators reveal that foreign companies in Egypt do not have higher labour productivity levels nor pay higher wages than their domestic peers, as it is often the case in other countries (OECD, 2019a).

Figure 1.10. FDI relationship to sustainable development outcomes in Egypt

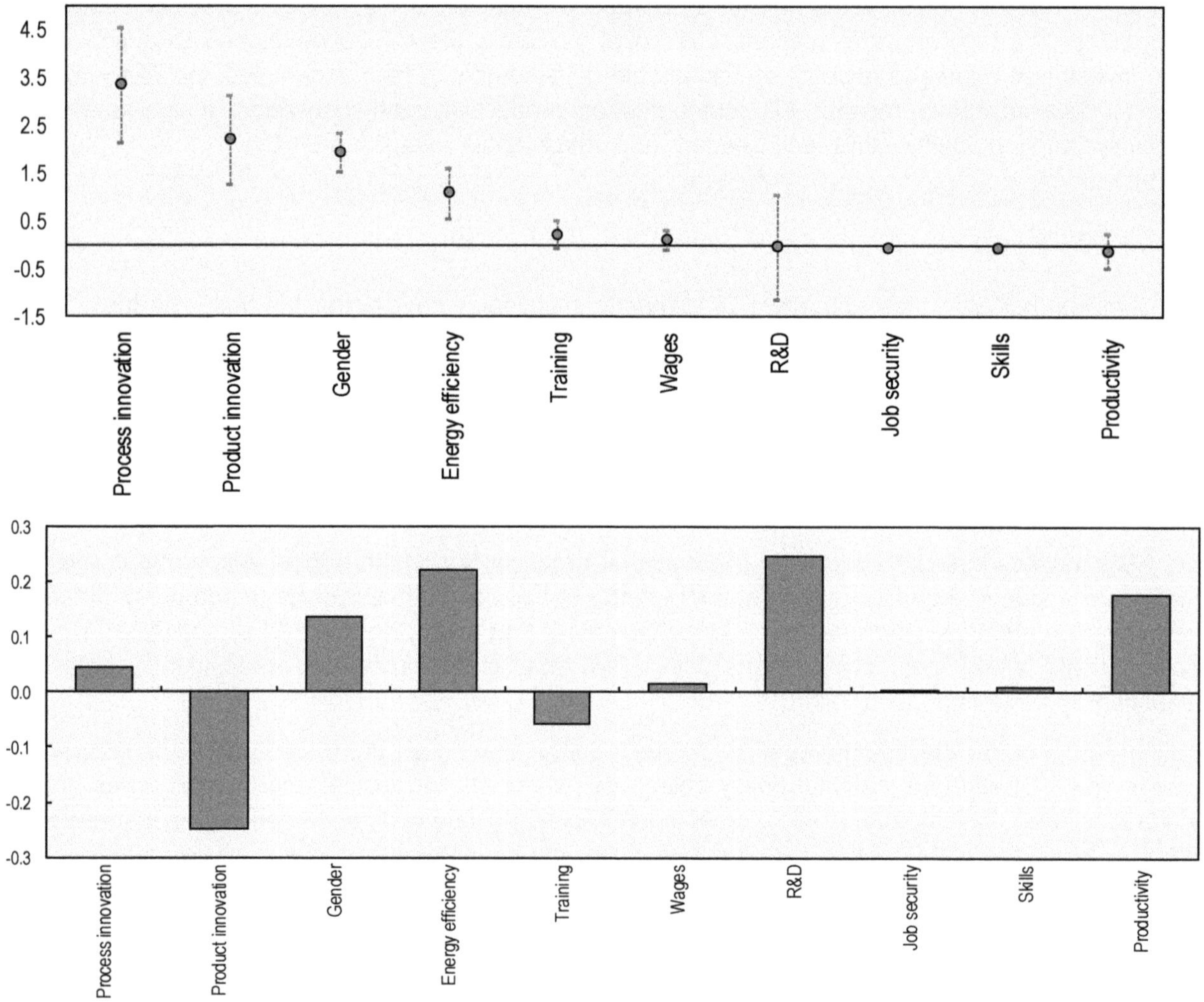

Note: Panel A includes confidence intervals for each indicator. The intervals report the extent of firm heterogeneity, i.e. the extent to which the data at the firm level vary around the mean. They also indicate whether the difference of average outcomes of foreign and domestic firms is statistically significant at the 95% level. If the confidence interval crosses the zero line, the difference of average outcomes of foreign and domestic firms is not statistically significant. For further details, see OECD (2019a).
Source: OECD based on the OECD FDI Qualities Indicators.

Affiliates of foreign firms may be less productive than domestically-owned firms when significant advantages, market protection and rents are given to domestic firms, often state-owned firms (OECD, 2019a). As described in chapter 2 of the Review, foreign firms established in Egypt may find it difficult to access a market dominated by protected state-owned firms, or their access is constrained due to regulatory and non-regulatory restrictions. It is important to note that there is a productivity premium of foreign firms in industries of the Egyptian economy where distortions are less important.

FDI in Egypt tends be concentrated into industries with better sustainability outcomes. FDI can lead to changes in the sectoral composition of the economic activity and may influence development positively or negatively if foreign firms directly or indirectly affect sectoral development outcomes. Figure 1.10 (B) shows whether FDI is concentrated in sectors with relatively higher or lower development outcomes. The results indicate that if MNE affiliates in Egypt are slightly less productive than domestic firms, they tend to be concentrated in more productive industries of the economy. In contrast, foreign investment tends to focus on economic activities where there is little product and process innovation.

A closer look at FDI and job creation shows that job created per dollar invested remain low compared to other countries, particularly for services investors (Figure 1.11). The majority of jobs remain heavily skewed toward low-skill and labour intensive activities. However, industries that require more technical skills, such as chemicals and electronic components, are beginning to attract more FDI, and account for growing shares of job creation.

Figure 1.11. Greenfield FDI and job creation in Egypt and other selected countries

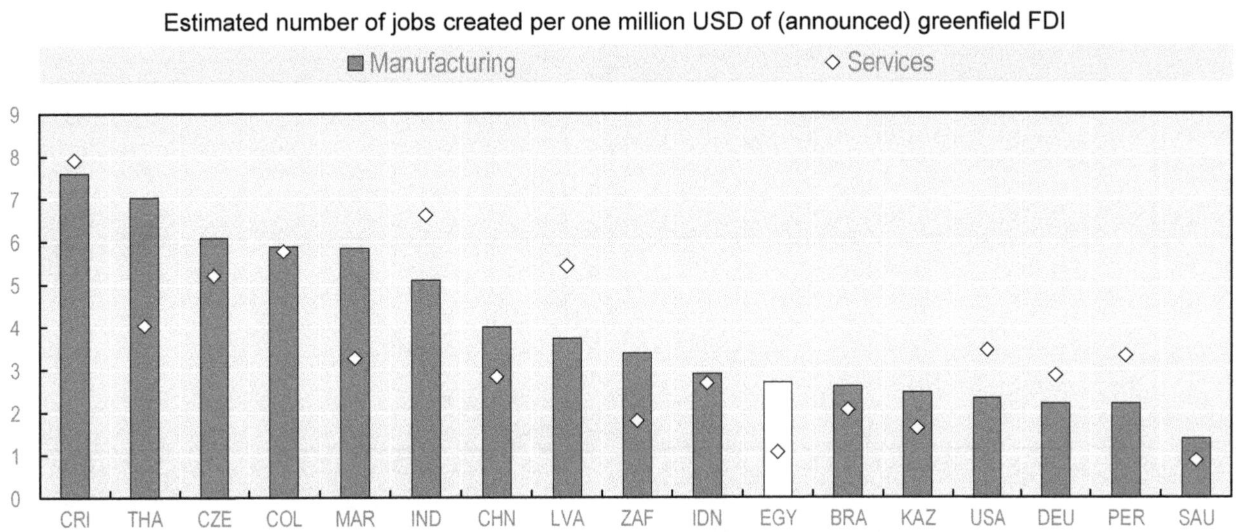

Source: OECD based on the OECD FDI Qualities Indicators and fDi Markets Database.

The role of foreign investment in boosting participation in global value chains

One objective of the Egypt 2030 vision is to maximise value added, increase local content in the manufacturing sector and decrease the trade deficit. Firms' participation in global value chains (GVCs) has been promoted as a key way to achieve higher export diversification and more sustainable and inclusive development. Along with trade, the "GVC revolution" has been driven to a large extent by MNEs through investment. FDI is not only a channel for exchanging capital across countries, it is also an important channel for exchanging goods, services, and knowledge and serves to link and organise production across countries.

Export of goods and services in Egypt have followed the same trend as FDI stock in the last three decades: a quasi-stagnant trend coupled with several boom and bust episodes (Figure 1.12). The export-to-GDP ratio deteriorated sharply following the 2007 global crisis and has been on a declining trajectory, even following the shallow recovery in the FDI stock in 2015. The history of the co-movement of FDI and export trends in Egypt is radically different from the one for other emerging countries. In Viet Nam, which opened up to the global economy in the 1980s, MNE affiliates played a key role in transforming the country into an export platform (OECD, 2019b). In the early 1990s, both countries had comparable FDI stock and export-to-GDP ratios. By 2016, FDI stock and export-to-GDP ratios in Viet Nam were respectively three times and 10 times higher than in Egypt.

Beyond the magnitude of exports and imports, the nature of traded products also matters for the development of the Egyptian economy and its integration in the global economy. The export basket of Egypt is relatively diversified but remains concentrated in lower value-added products. Trade in services, which constitutes a quarter of global trade, has become an increasingly important factor of global production as most goods require services for their fabrication. In Egypt trade in services represented only around 9% of GDP in 2016, compared to 15% in MENA (27% in Jordan, 23% in Morocco, 14% in Tunisia). Restrictions in services trade are still high in Egypt (Karam and Zaki, 2015).

Figure 1.12. Co-movement of FDI stock and exports in Egypt and Viet Nam

(% of GDP)

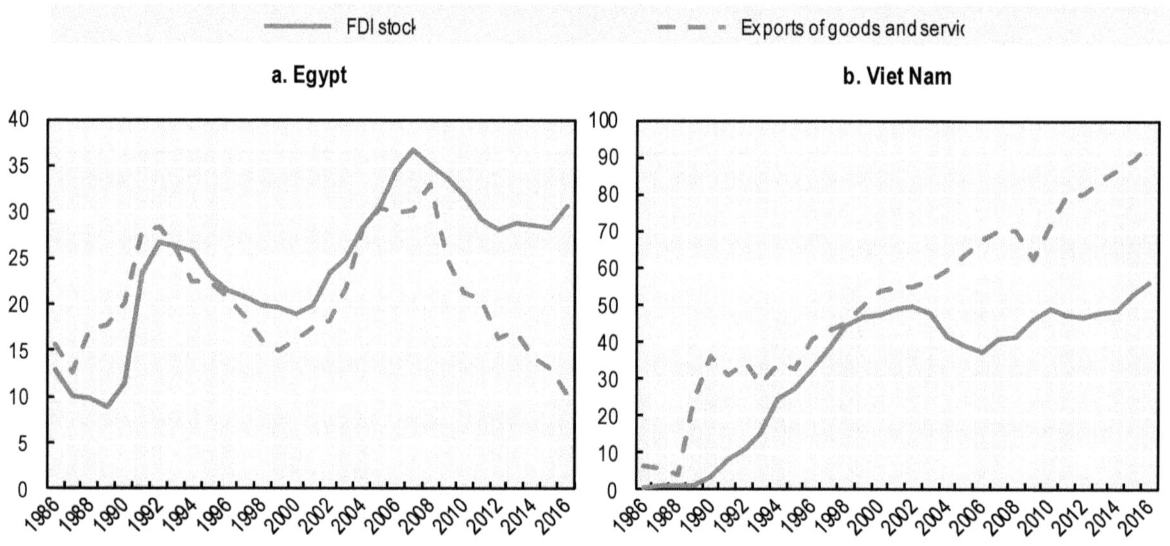

Source: OECD based on World Integrated Trade Solutions Database (WITS) and UNCTAD statistics.

Egypt has lower shares of participation in GVCs than other MED economies.[4] Larger countries such as Egypt may have lower backward participation, i.e. the value added used in a country's own exports, because of their higher local capacity for producing specific inputs, mostly in manufactured, fuel, and food supply chains. Lower participation in backward GVCs may also be driven by high import costs or restrictions. In contrast with Morocco or Tunisia, Egypt has more diversified trade and investment partners, beyond Europe. These partners have invested, *inter alia*, in the country's zones, on which the government relies to foster integration into GVCs and to promote local development.[5] Zones in Egypt are expected to reduce the lengthy and costly import-export procedures, which represent an important barrier for participation in GVCs.

There is ample room for foreign investment to further support Egypt's participation in GVCs. Egypt's low FDI stock-to-GDP is associated with an equivalently low participation in GVCs (Figure 1.13). In comparison, countries with higher ratios, such as Jordan, Tunisia or Viet Nam, are also participating more in GVCs. High regulatory and non-regulatory barriers on foreign investment and trade may impede the establishment of MNEs and their participation in GVCs. As discussed in other chapters of the Review, Egypt has moderate levels of regulatory restrictions on FDI in the manufacturing sector. Barriers on FDI and trade in services are however more important. This may impede the deployment of foreign investment in services sectors such as ICT, logistics, or transport, which are crucial for enhancing participation in GVCs.

The development impact of participation in GVCs has been limited, as Egypt has succeeded only to some extent to upgrade its position in supply chains. MNE investment motives and type of activity shape to some extent the development outcomes associated with participation in GVCs. The sectors that received the bulk of FDI in Egypt, e.g. real estate and petroleum activities, are also those with the least segmented supply chains (i.e. few intermediate inputs are needed to produce the final good). As a result, the country remains specialised in low value-added manufacturing activities within these chains leading to little overall developments in terms of types of jobs and income levels.

Figure 1.13. FDI in Egypt is associated with low participation in GVCs, 2009-2012

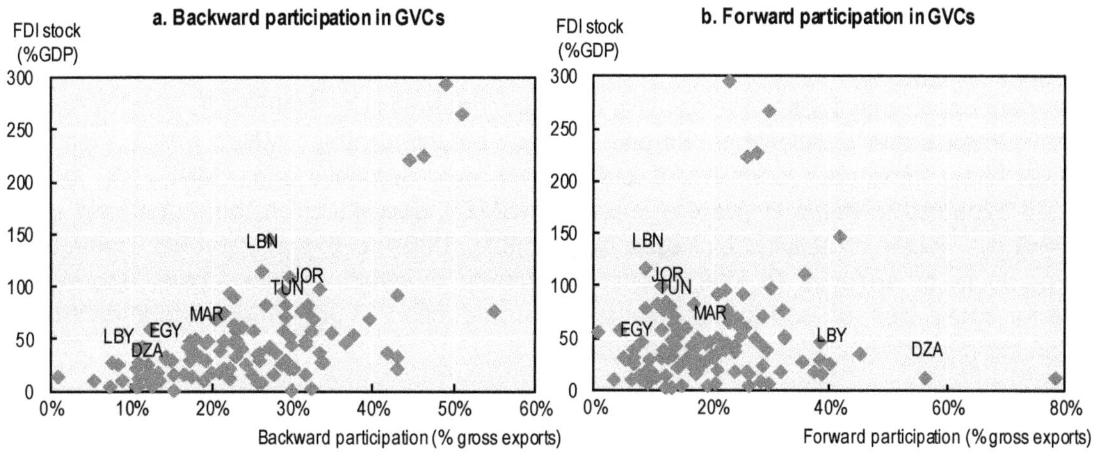

Source: OECD based on UNCTAD EORA GVC database, IMF BoP, and UNCTAD.

Attracting FDI inflows can stimulate GVC participation by upgrading the country's productive capabilities to manufacture products that are more complex. Recent evidence indicates that domestic firms more likely to supply foreign affiliates tend to introduce products that are more complex (Javorcik et al, 2018). In Egypt, additional FDI to the machinery and mechanical appliances, computers, chemicals industry and foodstuff industries would increase economic complexity (Box 1.2). As discussed in chapter 4, there is room for investment promotion activities, a relatively cost-effective activity, to be effective in channelling FDI to activities that would help Egypt move into sophisticated segments of the supply chain.

Box 1.2. Upgrading Egypt's productive capabilities: Where should FDI go?

Countries with comparable export levels can have different levels of complexity in their respective productive capabilities. This is the case when comparing Egypt to Viet Nam. In Viet Nam, half of Vietnamese exports are composed of electronic products. Despite increases in GDP per capita and in exports, Egypt's economic complexity index has been relatively stagnant since 1995. While Egypt has increased the diversity of its production, it has not moved into products that are more complex. It is still largely natural resource and agriculture based. Petroleum oils and gases account for over 30% of its net exports. When considering all natural resource-based or agricultural products, this share is above 50%.

Egypt's product space reveals the country should develop the machinery and chemicals and allied industry, and foodstuff since they would increase the country's product complexity index. It is well located in the product space and has, on average, shorter distances to more complex products. By moving into nearby, more complex, products using to a large extent productive knowledge that already exists within the country, Egypt can increase the complexity of its product space and improve its income level.

While products in the foodstuff and textile community are closer in distance in terms of productive knowledge and capabilities of the country, products in the machinery and chemicals and allied industry have a higher product complexity index. Therefore, developing them would have a larger impact on Egypt's average complexity. To meet this specific goal and to enhance production in other sectors, Egypt should focus on attracting sustainable FDI to existing industries with the aim of improving their productivity and ability to jump to nearby opportunities.

Source: Bustos S. & Yildirim M.A. (2017), Egypt's Manufacturing Sector: Seizing on an Advantageous Product Space Position, Policy Paper, May 2017, The Lebanese Center for Policy Studies.

The extent of MNE-SME supply chain linkages in Egypt

Leveraging FDI in Egypt to enhance supply chain linkages with small and medium enterprises (SMEs) can be an important opportunity for a more inclusive development trajectory. MNE-SME supply chain linkages involve the purchase and supply of goods and services between foreign MNEs affiliates and domestic SMEs. Given the performance premium of foreign firms over domestic ones, MNE-SME supply chain linkages are expected to result in positive impact on SMEs, depending on the extent and intensity of linkages and the sector of activity. Linkages may enable SMEs to export, develop managerial skills, upgrade products or services to international standards, innovate, reduce costs, improve working conditions for employees, or lead to more sustainable production.[6] Furthermore, the impact of linkages depends on the characteristics of SMEs themselves.

Manufacturing MNEs in Egypt source a large share of inputs locally

Foreign manufacturers established in Egypt source significantly more from local producers than from other countries in the MED region (Figure 1.14).[7] As in Indonesia or Viet Nam, MNE affiliates in Egypt source more than half of intermediate inputs from firms (both domestic and foreign) that produce locally. In Morocco and Jordan, this share is around 40% and in Tunisia less than 30%. These results mirror to some extent Egypt's low backward participation in GVC previously shown.

Variations between Egypt and other emerging countries may reflect differences in the sectoral structure of the economy, positioning within specific value chains and policy factors. For instance, significant local sourcing may be the result of a high local capacity for producing specific and competitive inputs. It may also indicate, however, higher trade barriers for imports of intermediate inputs. In the case of Egypt, the low sourcing of imported goods by foreign manufacturers may reflect local content requirements, as those in the Free Zones, or restrictions and lengthy procedures on imports. The differences in shares of local sourcing by foreign MNEs may thus not indicate better integration of the local firms in production networks of MNEs established in the MED region. Nevertheless, these shares do provide a reference point on whether some linkages exist in the first place.

In Egypt, as in the majority of MED economies, MNE affiliates in manufacturing are concentrated in the food and garment sectors. Accordingly, the shares presented in Figure 1.14 often represent an average of foreign firms' local sourcing practices in these sectors. In Egypt, foreign investors in manufacturing appear to have a diversified portfolio, from low-value added industries, such as food processing, to machinery production, a sector in which foreign manufacturers purchases of locally produced intermediates are relatively high (OECD, 2018).

Figure 1.14. Foreign MNEs in Egypt source more from local intermediates than MNEs in other countries

Foreign manufacturers' composition of intermediates sourcing, in % of total, 2013-2016

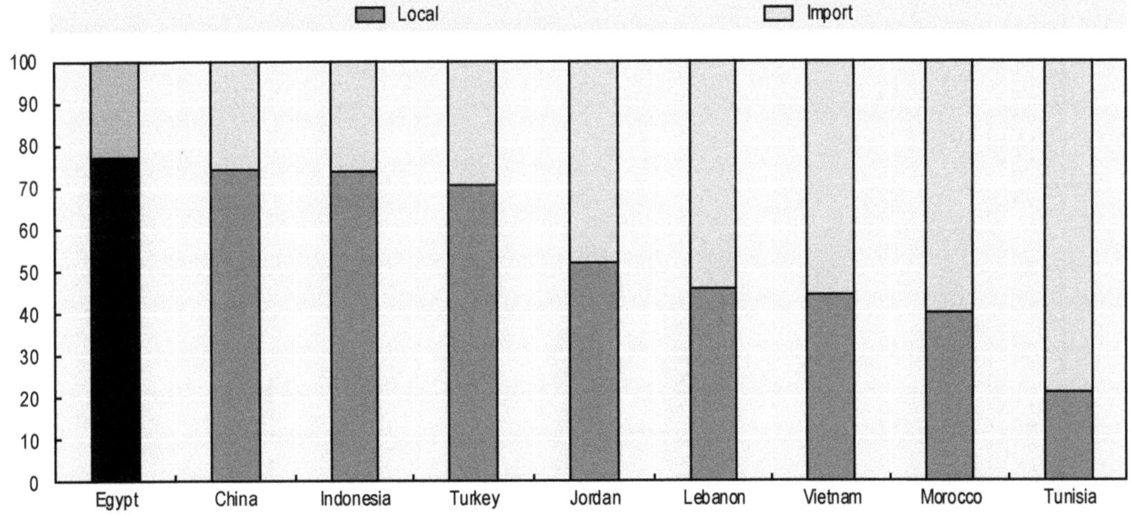

Note: The indicators in this figure include averages for manufacturing as a whole. It does not include services. *Source*: OECD estimates based on OECD-UNIDO (2019) and World Bank Enterprise Surveys.

MNE affiliates are a significant source of revenue for domestic suppliers

In terms of market size, MNE affiliates in Egypt represent a significant source of revenue for local suppliers. Nearly 20% of locally produced intermediate products are purchased by foreign-owned manufacturers in Egypt, although this share has declined slightly from 26% in 2013 to 17% in 2016. While important, the market created by MNE affiliates in Egypt contrasts with their high reliance on local intermediates relative to importing. Comparison with other emerging countries indicates that there is room for MNE affiliates to represent a bigger market for Egyptian suppliers. Foreign MNEs in Egypt represent a larger market for local suppliers than in Morocco or Turkey but much less than in Indonesia or Jordan (Figure 1.15, Panel A). MNE affiliates in Viet Nam do not represent a larger market for local intermediates producers than MNE affiliates in Egypt, despite their more important contribution to national economic activity.

Local suppliers of MNEs can be domestic large firms, domestic SMEs, or other foreign-owned firms.[8] SMEs in Egypt account for up to half of all inputs supplied to MNE affiliates, similar to Turkey and Tunisia. Large firms are also important suppliers. In Jordan and Indonesia, supplying relationships within foreign-owned firms are considerably higher than in Egypt (Figure 1.15, Panel B). Foreign MNEs often source from large first-tier international suppliers that are themselves MNEs for more capital-intensive and complex value chains/products (e.g. automotive) (OECD-UNIDO, 2019). From a policy perspective, different types of business linkages may have different effects on the local economy. For instance, investment that results in foreign-foreign linkages may be less effective in promoting greater inclusiveness than linkages between a foreign and a domestic firm.

Figure 1.15. Foreign MNEs are an important market for Egyptian SMEs

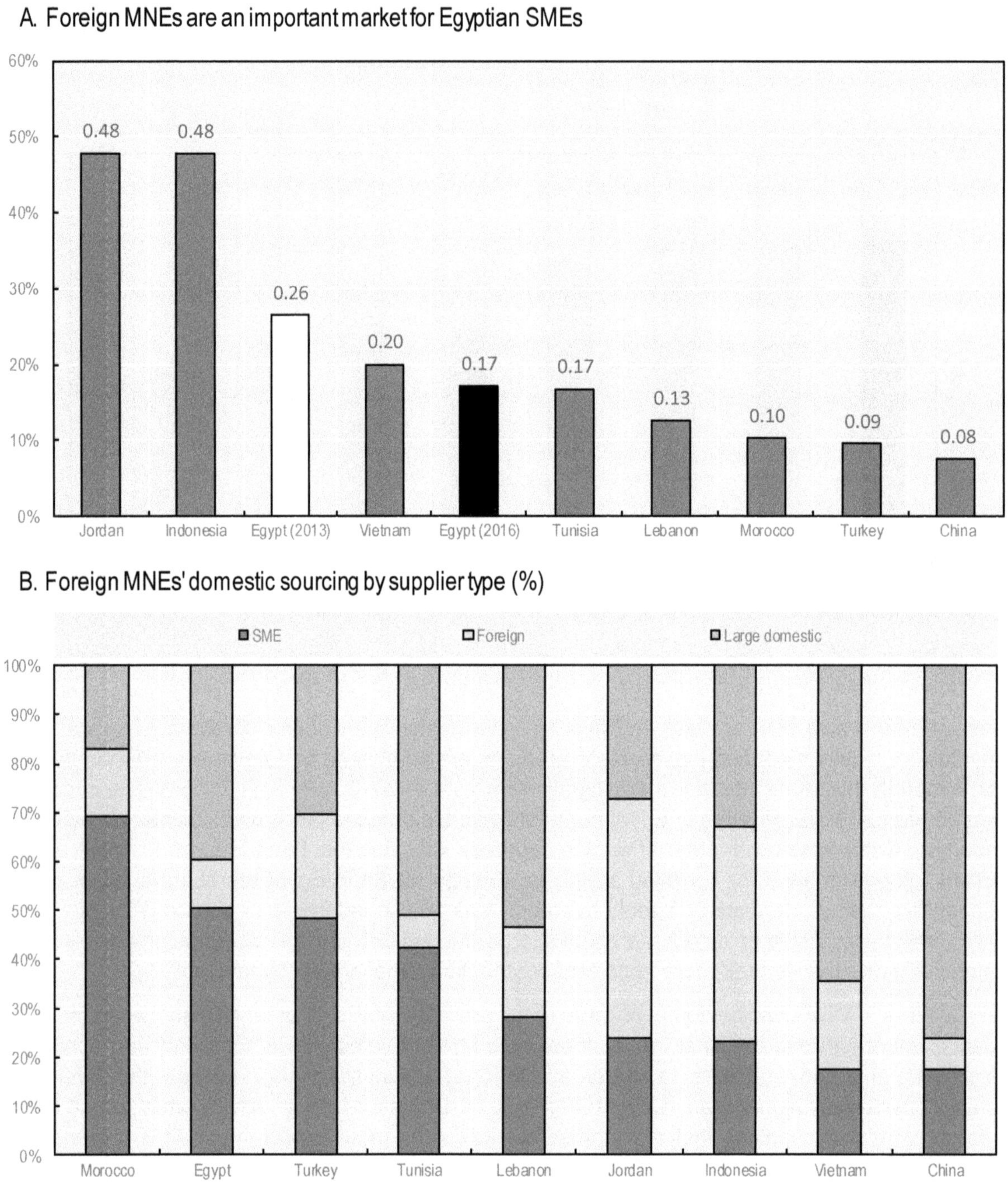

Note: The indicators in this figure include averages for manufacturing as a whole. It does not include services.
Source: OECD estimates based on OECD-UNIDO (2019) and on World Bank Enterprise Surveys.

References

AJG Simoes, CA Hidalgo (2011), The Economic Complexity Observatory: An Analytical Tool for Understanding the Dynamics of Economic Development, Workshops at the Twenty-Fifth AAAI Conference on Artificial Intelligence (2011).

Bustos S. & Yildirim M.A. (2017), Egypt's Manufacturing Sector: Seizing on an Advantageous Product Space Position, Policy Paper, May 2017, The Lebanese Centre for Policy Studies.

Central Bank of Egypt (CBE) (2019a), External Position of the Egyptian Economy

CBE (2019b), Annual Report 2017/2018

CBE (2018), Annual Report 2016/2017

CBE (2017), Annual Report 2015/2016

CBE (2016), Annual Report 2014/2015

Ettoumi Y, S.Toufik, S. Koubaa & IE. Hadad (2016), Regional attractiveness for Foreign Direct Investments in developing countries: empirical review, IOSR Journal of Business and Management, 2016;18 (10) :74-78.

Fawzy, Samiha & El-Megharbel, Nihal (2004), Public and Private Investment in Egypt: Crowding-Out or Crowding-In?, ECES Working Paper 96-A, the Egyptian Center for Economic Studies

Hanafy, S. (2014), Determinants of FDI location in Egypt: Empirical analysis using governorate panel data, No. 13-2015, Joint Discussion Paper Series in Economics.

Javorcik, B. S., Lo Turco, A., & Maggioni, D. (2017), New and Improved: Does FDI Boost Production Complexity in Host Countries? The Economic Journal.

Karam, F., & Zaki, C. (2015), Trade volume and economic growth in the MENA region: Goods or services? Economic Modelling, 45, 22-37.

Lejárraga, Iza; Ragoussis, Alexandros. (2018), Beyond Capital: Monitoring Development Outcomes of Multinational Enterprises, Policy Research working paper; no. WPS 8686. Washington, D.C.: World Bank Group. http://documents.worldbank.org/curated/en/342571545336579695/Beyond-Capital-Monitoring-Development-Outcomes-of-Multinational-Enterprises

Nugent, J. B., & Abdel-Latif, A. (2010), "A quiz on the net benefits of trade creation and trade diversion in the QIZs of Jordan and Egypt", In Economic Research Forum Working Papers (Vol. 514).

OECD (2020), *OECD Review of Foreign Direct Investment Statistics: Egypt.* www.oecd.org/investment/OECD-Review-of-Foreign-Direct-Investment-Statistics-Egypt.pdf

OECD (2019a), FDI Qualities Indicators: Measuring the sustainable development impacts of investment, Paris, https://www.oecd.org/investment/fdi-qualities-indicators.htm.

OECD (2019b), OECD Investment Policy Reviews: Viet Nam 2018, OECD Investment Policy Reviews, OECD Publishing, Paris, https://doi.org/10.1787/9789264282957-en.

OECD (2018), Making global value chains more inclusive in the MED region: The role of MNE-SME linkages, Background note prepared for the workshop "Business linkages in the MED region: Policies and tools", 17-18 April 2018, Beirut, Lebanon, http://www.oecd.org/mena/competitiveness/BN-Making-global-value-chains-more-inclusive-Beirut-042018.pdf.

OECD (2017), Making investment promotion work for sustainable development in the Southern Mediterranean: Focus on incentives and territorial development, Issues Note, October 2017, http://www.oecd.org/mena/competitiveness/REPORT-Regional-EU-OECD-IPA-Workshop-Paris-201710.pdf.

OECD (2014), “Protecting Investment in Arab Countries in Transition: Legal frameworks for investment in Egypt, Jordan, Morocco and Tunisia”, document prepared for the OECD Investment Committee, 4 November 2014, Paris, http://oecd.records.oecd.org/LES_RM/livelink.exe?func=ll&objId=7583945&objAction=properties&version=0&nexturl=http:%2F%2Foecd%2Erecords%2Eoecd%2Eorg%2FLES_RM%2Flivelink%2Eexe.

OECD-UNIDO (2019), Integrating Southeast Asian SMEs in Global Value Chains: Enabling Linkages with Foreign Investors, Paris, www.oecd.org/investment/Integrating-Southeast-Asian-SMEs-in-global-value-chains.pdf.

Subramanian, M. A. (1997), The Egyptian stabilization experience: An analytical retrospective, No. 97-105, International Monetary Fund.

UN-Habitat and IHS-Erasmus University Rotterdam (2018) “The State of African Cities 2018: The geography of African investment.” (Wall R.S., Maseland J., Rochell K. and Spaliviero M). United Nations Human Settlements Programme (UN-Habitat).

UNCTAD (2019), World Investment Report 2019, UNCTAD Publishing, Geneva.

UNCTAD (2011), Investment Policy Review Egypt, UNCTAD Publishing, Geneva.

Youssef, H., Alnashar, S. Bahaa Hamed; Erian, J., Elshawarby, A., Zaki, C. (2019), Egypt Economic Monitor : From Floating to Thriving – Taking Egypt's Exports to New Levels, Washington, D.C., World Bank Group.

Zaki, M. Y. (2001), IMF-supported stabilization programs and their critics: Evidence from the recent experience of Egypt, World development, 29(11), 1867-1883.

Annex 1.A. Measuring FDI and participation in GVCs

Compiling Foreign Direct Investment (FDI) statistics in Egypt

Internationally harmonised, timely, and reliable FDI statistics are essential for policymaking and to assess the trends and developments in FDI activity globally, regionally, and at the country level. FDI is one of the major types of investment included in the balance of payments (BOP) and international investment position (IIP) statistics. The International Monetary Fund (IMF), in its Balance of Payments and International Investment Position Manual, 6th edition (BPM6), and the OECD, in its Benchmark Definition of FDI, 4th edition (BMD4), present recommendations for compiling FDI statistics. The recommendations of the two agencies are aligned, but the OECD offers supplemental series that are particularly useful in analysing globalisation. The recommended measures of FDI statistics in these guidelines produce meaningful FDI statistics that are part of the larger System of National Accounts and, so, ensure that FDI statistics are compatible with other important economic statistics. Following the recommendations in the international guidelines is critical to producing relevant and coherent FDI statistics. The OECD also hosts the Working Group on International Investment Statistics (WGIIS), which serves as a forum for FDI statisticians from both OECD member countries and non-member countries to share best practices. The WGIIS also conducts research to improve the measurement of FDI.

The OECD conducted a review of FDI statistics of Egypt as part of the OECD project for Enhancing the Investment Climate in Egypt, through Equal Access and Simplified Environment for Investment and Fostered Investment Policy, Legal and Institutional Framework. The OECD prepared an assessment report on the FDI statistics of Egypt being compiled by the General Authority for Investment and Free Zones (GAFI). The review assessed their compatibility with the international guidelines (BPM6 and BMD4), assessed the data sources and estimation methods used, and examined both the feasibility and the usefulness of compiling additional series, such as by country of ultimate investor. The report uses the framework developed by the OECD for assessing the quality of macroeconomic statistics, which focuses on seven dimensions of quality: relevance, accuracy, credibility, timeliness, accessibility, interpretability, and coherence. The review was based on GAFI's replies to a questionnaire from the OECD on their compilation of FDI statistics, a presentation by three delegates from GAFI's FDI Intelligence Unit (FDIU) at the October 2016 WGIIS meeting of their FDI compilation system before the WGIIS delegates, and subsequent discussions with them about their system. A capacity-building workshop was organized in April 2018 in Cairo to present the OECD assessment report.

This annex provides a brief summary of the OECD assessment report on FDI statistics in Egypt. It starts with a description of the current system of compilation of FDI statistics in Egypt that are disseminated by the Central Bank of Egypt and its shortcomings. It, then, describes the new compilation system developed by GAFI and the improvements it could bring to the statistics. The annex concludes with a summary of OECD recommendations for further enhancing the quality of these statistics.

Current system for compilation of FDI statistics in Egypt

FDI statistics in Egypt are in a period of transition: the Central Bank of Egypt (CBE) and the Foreign Direct Investment Intelligence Unit (FDIU) of the GAFI signed a protocol that calls for cooperation in the compilation and dissemination of FDI statistics according to BPM6 and BMD4. While FDI statistics currently published by the CBE are based on BPM5, the new compilation system developed by the FDIU of GAFI is designed to produce FDI statistics in line with BMD4 and BPM6 standards.

Description

The CBE currently publishes FDI aggregate flows, positions and income as part of the BOP and IIP statistics in accordance with IMF BPM5 standards and following the IMF's Special Data Dissemination Standards' (SDDS) recommendations for timeliness. The BOP and IIP FDI statistics disseminated by the CBE use an International Transaction Reporting System (ITRS) as the primary data source for compiling FDI flows. The definition of FDI recommended in the international standards--non-residents' share of 10 percent or more of the capital in Egyptian enterprises--is used and is based on information from the Capital Market Authorities; direct investment in the petroleum sector is derived from the Ministry of Petroleum. For Inward investment, the GAFI provides data to the CBE on reinvested earnings that are used for capital expansions but not on all reinvested earnings realised by direct investment enterprises during the reporting period. Aggregate FDI statistics are presented according to the asset/liability principle as recommended in the latest international standards. In terms of valuation methods, FDI positions currently published as part of the IIP correspond to the accumulation of FDI flows.

The accessibility of FDI aggregates published as part of BOP and IIP is well ensured on the CBE website except for FDI income aggregates and the breakdown of FDI aggregates by instrument (i.e., equity capital, reinvestment of earnings, and intercompany debt). FDI inflows by partner country are also easily accessible from the CBE website in the Monthly Statistical Bulletin and from the time series database. However, detailed statistics by industry are only accessible in PDF format in the annual report and are less timely. The CBE publishes methodological information related to the compilation of BOP statistics under BPM5 while methodological information could not be located for the IIP nor for the inward FDI flows by partner country and by industry that are published by the CBE.

Issues

There are some important issues with the FDI statistics currently being disseminated by the CBE. First, and foremost, they do not follow the latest international standards—BPM6 and BMD4. In terms of coverage, FDI is composed of different components (equity capital, reinvestment of earnings and intercompany debt), and these components are not currently published by the CBE, which makes it difficult to determine whether certain components are included or not in the statistics. In addition, valuing direct investment positions by accumulating flows is not a method recommended in the international standards because this method fails to account for factors that can have a significant impact on FDI positions, including cumulative reinvested earnings, depreciation of fixed assets, and holding gains and losses at the direct investment enterprise. However, it is often the only option available when an ITRS is the data source. ITRS also raises other potential issues. For example, it is likely that the debtor/creditor principle might not be fully applied in the FDI statistics by partner country that are currently disseminated by the CBE because an ITRS tends to produce data based on the transactor principle.[9]

Further with regards to the detailed statistics by country and industry published by the CBE, these statistics are limited to inward FDI flows and do not cover FDI positions. As a result, Egypt does not participate in the IMF's Coordinated Direct Investment Survey (CDIS), which collects FDI position statistics by immediate partner country. Further, the asset/liability presentation is also used for inward FDI flows by partner country, which is not recommended. Rather, the directional presentation, which captures the direction and degree of influence of foreign investors, is recommended for the detailed statistics by partner country. Finally, detail by partner country are only available for the increases in liabilities, while decreases in liabilities are excluded. As regards inward FDI flows by industry that are currently disseminated by the CBE, they use an internal industry classification as opposed to the International Standard Industry Classification Rev 4 (ISIC4) recommended in BMD4.

Planned improvements with the new compilation system developed by GAFI

Description

GAFI developed a new compilation system for FDI position statistics based on financial statements of enterprises. GAFI had attempted in the past to collect information to compile inward FDI positions through an enterprise survey to support the Central Bank with the production of FDI positions as part of the IIP. However, the response rate was very low, and GAFI decided to abandon surveying enterprises and to look for an alternative. GAFI developed a compilation system based on financial statements that foreign-owned enterprises are required by Law to report to GAFI and other government authorities and where confidentiality of the information is also required by Law. GAFI's system is an ingenuous alternative to surveys, is very comprehensive, and should allow the compilation of inward FDI positions according to the latest international standards (BPM6 and BMD4). It will cover all the standard components (except for reinvestment of earnings from the petroleum sector). The new system will also improve various other aspects of coverage. For example, it uses the Framework for Direct Investment Relationships (FDIR) to identify all of the entities in a direct investment relationship, thus covering fellow enterprises.[10] In addition, the system seems to ensure good coverage of the various types of debt instruments in the position statistics and will be able to exclude debt between financial intermediaries as recommended in the international guidelines.[11] Finally, the system enables the maintenance of a complete and up-to-date register of information on Special Purpose Entities (SPEs), although information related to SPEs in Egypt is not yet separately available.[12]

With the signing of the protocol between the Ministry of Investment, CBE, and the Ministry of Petroleum in September 2016, the CBE will begin to disseminate the FDI position statistics compiled by the FDIU in Egypt's IIP once the transition to BPM6 has been completed. Under the protocol, the FDIU will be responsible for compiling and disseminating the detailed FDI position statistics by partner country and by industry. When the WGIIS Secretariat visited GAFI in April 2018, GAFI presented inward FDI positions by partner country and by industry for reference year-end 2016 and through June 30, 2017, indicating that the new system is able to produce timely estimates. Data and metadata information for inward FDI positions by partner country and by industry that GAFI will provide for the new system will be published when the first statistics from the new system are published.

In accordance with BMD4, the new system developed by GAFI for compiling inward FDI position statistics by partner country and by industry has been designed to compile the statistics on an extended directional basis as it includes entries for reverse investment transactions and transactions between fellow enterprises as well as information on the Ultimate Controlling Parent (UCP). The system also provides information for the part of Egypt's outward FDI position appearing in the financial statements of the companies covered. However, the latter field is not completely populated yet because the information is not readily available in the company financial statements.

In addition, in the compilation system developed by GAFI, the partner country allocation is currently based on the citizenship rather than the residency of the direct investor as is recommended in the international standards. GAFI has enabled the implementation of the residency principle in the compilation system, but it has not been used yet as there is need to populate the information on the residency of the investors. The FDIU has begun this process for some of the well-known Egyptian shareholders who are residents in other economy.

As regards the compilation of FDI flows by industry, the International Standard industry Classification Rev 4 (ISIC4) has been integrated in the compilation system developed by GAFI to produce inward statistics by industry in line with international recommendations. At the start of 2017, GAFI began to help the CBE with the allocation of FDI to activities. Prior to this help, the unallocated share was about 38%, but this fell to only 7% in FY 2017/18 with the assistance from the FDIU and further to 3% in the first quarter of FY2018/19. This highlights the potential benefits from cooperation between the CBE and the FDIU in the compilation of FDI statistics and that these benefits are not limited to improved position statistics but could also improve FDI transaction statistics as well.

The system is supported by an internal business registration database where all direct investment enterprises are registered. In addition to the information sourced from the financial statements of direct investment enterprises, the system will also use financial information on all the current Production Sharing Agreements (PSAs) on upstream exploration companies provided by the Ministry of Petroleum and information on real estate transactions from the CBE's ITRS. In addition, GAFI has completed a protocol with the Egyptian Financial Services Authority that will enable the coverage of the non-bank financial sector by providing information from their database of companies.

The response rate for the top 500 firms included in the sample is around 84% annually. In 2016, 2,529 companies'[13] financial statements were included in the sample, representing 8% of the firms, but 80% of the total capital of the population and 90% of the direct investment position. The mandatory nature of the data collection method (in Egypt, companies are required by Law to report their financial statements to the GAFI and other government authorities) helps to ensure high response rates. In addition, GAFI contacts companies directly when information from their balance sheets is missing or incomplete, which should also improve the response rate.

In terms of valuation methods, the compilation system developed by GAFI uses company financial statements, which is in line with the international recommendations; it will account for the factors missed by the accumulation of flows and, so, will produce better measures of FDI positions. The new system also allows for the compilation of FDI positions according to market values for listed equity positions and according to own funds at book value for unlisted equity positions. Using book values is not recommended because the books can encompass many different valuation methods, especially as the foreign direct investors may be following a variety of accounting methods. While the methods described in BMD4 for estimating unlisted equity can be difficult to implement, there is one method that is accepted as a measure of market value and is widely used by countries--the Own Funds at Book Value (OFBV).

GAFI is further improving its compilation system for both FDI flows and positions. Investment Law No. 72 of 2017 was amended to require firms to submit their financial data on a regular basis. Hence, the FDIU designed annual and quarterly reporting forms to compile FDI statistics in accordance with the recommendations in BPM6 and BMD4. The quarterly form will capture FDI flows while the annual form will be dedicated to capturing FDI positions. An online interface is being developed through which companies will be able to complete and submit these forms. The new approach will enable the FDIU to capture transactions that are not currently captured in the ITRS system, such as some in-kind investments and the part of retained earnings that are not used for capital expansion. Furthermore, data will be collected based on the residency of the investor rather than their citizenship. The FDI flows will be broken down into three components—equity capital, reinvestment of earnings, and intercompany debt—and positions will be broken down between equity and debt. In addition, sectoral and geographical breakdowns will be available.

Recommendations for further improving FDI statistics in Egypt

Currently, Egypt is disseminating FDI statistics under BPM5, and disseminates those statistics in line with timeliness recommendations of the IMF starting 1st of October 2019. The use of the new system developed by GAFI in the compilation of FDI statistics as part of the IIP would increase the quality of the statistics by closing gaps and following the latest international standards with no loss of timeliness. It would also enable Egypt to participate in the IMF's CDIS.. The use of the new system will also imply that significant efforts be dedicated to assist users understanding the possible significant revisions to the FDI series compared to what is currently published by the CBE. While the use of the new system developed by GAFI offers significant benefits in terms of higher quality FDI statistics, the need for cooperation between the different agencies, and particularly the FDIU and CBE, in compiling and disseminating FDI statistics poses threats to the quality of the statistics.

This leads to the first, overarching, recommendation: it is important that the agencies work together to ensure that the statistics compiled and disseminated by each agency are consistent with each other; this could mean, for example, producing a joint release and analysis of the FDI statistics. In addition, it is important that the statistics are perceived as objective by users.

The second key recommendation relates to improving alignment with the international standards. Items under this recommendation include: clarifying the treatment of SPEs within FDI statistics and exploring the feasibility of separately identifying FDI associated with SPEs in the statistics disseminated based on their identification within the source data; working to populate the information on residency so that the statistics can be compiled based on residency rather than citizenship; using the directional principle (or extended directional principle once information on the UCP is available) and the debtor/creditor principle for presenting the detailed statistics by immediate partner country and industry; and continuing to provide training in FDI concepts to staff as well as in related topics such as statistics, modelling, and the financial analysis of companies, to provide adequate IT resources, and to cooperate with the IMF's Middle East Technical Assistance Centre if possible.

The third recommendation is to improve the accessibility and usefulness of the FDI statistics to data users. Items under this recommendation include: providing more information on the overall response rate obtained from financial statements and on the comprehensiveness of the information collected to users so that they can evaluate the overall quality of the system; posting a methodology explaining the data sources, estimation methods, and any deviations from the international guidelines on the website; releasing an analysis with the release of the FDI statistics to help users better understand and interpret the statistics; ensure the accessibility of longer time series as well as detail by instruments for all series on the website; and consider creating a section on the website dedicated to the detailed annual FDI statistics by partner country and by industry.

The final recommendation is to explore further enhancements to the statistics. One of the most useful enhancements is the presentation of inward FDI position statistics by ultimate investing country, which should be feasible using the information from the new system, complemented by additional information for cases that may be more challenging than others. GAFI should also explore the possibility of publishing supplemental FDI series, such as on greenfield investment, as well as the possibility of publishing some economic variables, such as the turnover or capital expenditures, of FDI enterprises. However, Egypt should first focus on disseminating timely FDI positions and flows by immediate counterpart partner country that are in line with the international standards. Currently, only increases in liabilities are available by partner country while FDI positions are currently not disseminated by partner country.

Measuring participation in global value chains: Concepts and definitions

The flows of goods and services within global production chains are not always reflected in conventional measures of international trade. The international fragmentation of production has weakened the interpretability of trade data as intermediate goods and services cross borders several times on the way to their final destination. This is referred to as the double (or multiple) counting problem of international trade statistics.

Measuring Trade in Value-Added (TiVA) addresses this issue by considering the value added by each country in the production of goods and services that are consumed worldwide. This has led to the development of TiVA statistics providing new insights on GVCs, notably the OECD-WTO TiVA database.

For country coverage purpose, this chapter uses the UNCTAD EORA-GVCs database to measure Egypt and other MENA countries participation in GVCs. The database provides the following measures:

- Foreign value added (FVA) indicates what part of a country's gross exports consists of inputs that have been produced in other countries. It is the share of the country's exports that is not adding to its GDP.
- Domestic value added (DVA) is the part of exports created in-country, i.e. the part of exports that contributes to GDP. The sum of foreign and domestic value added equates to gross exports.
- GVC participation indicates the portion of a country's exports that is part of a multi-stage trade process, by adding to the foreign value added used in a country's own exports, referred to as *backward participation*, and the value added supplied to other countries' exports, referred to as *forward participation*. Forward participation captures the extent to which a given country's exports are used by firms in partner countries as inputs into their own exports.

The UNCTAD EORA-GVCs database draws upon information from a variety of primary data sources, principally on national Input-Output Tables. To deal with missing data, interpolation and estimation techniques are used. The database should be therefore used with some caution when interpreting results for data-poor countries.

Mechanisms of SME participation in GVCs via investment

Indicators in chapter 1 measure the extent and the type of linkages between MNE affiliates and the local economy. The indicators focus exclusively on the manufacturing sector and quantify the extent to which an MNE affiliate in a country purchases locally-produced intermediate inputs and how much it generate a market for intermediate goods produced by local businesses.

A backward linkage exists when SMEs purchase goods or services from foreign MNEs established domestically. A forward linkage exists when SMEs supply goods or services to foreign MNEs established domestically. Thus, basic SME integration in GVCs from the lens of investment can be considered as a complementary concept to a broader framework, focusing on SME participation in GVCs via trade. This investment channel could become a trade channel if inputs sold to foreign MNEs established domestically and these MNEs further process these inputs and then export.

SMEs can upgrade in GVCs through specific partnerships with foreign MNEs. From the lens of investment linkages, SME upgrading in GVCs is expected when stronger relationships, beyond just arm's length trade, with foreign MNEs are established (Figure below, bottom box). On the one hand, this may involve specific contractual arrangements with MNEs, such as supply/manufacturing agreements, licencing, R&D agreements, technology transfers, skills development, and quality support. On the other hand, supply chain linkages may be upgraded when SMEs receive inward FDI (partial or full acquisitions from foreign MNEs). Upgrading may involve getting better at producing goods, moving to different tasks within the value chain, or changing the activity altogether. It may also involve the development of improved managerial skills, compliance with international standards, innovation and improved working conditions and more sustainable production.

Annex Figure 1.A.1. Mechanisms of SME participation in GVCs via investment

How can SMEs participate in GVCs?

	Backward linkages	Forward linkages
Trade linkages (direct & indirect)	Import inputs	Export outputs
Domestic linkages with foreign investors	Source inputs from foreign MNEs	Supply outputs to foreign MNEs

How can SMEs upgrade to higher value added activities?	Strengthen GVC integration through: • **Partnering** with foreign MNEs established domestically • receiving **inward FDI**

Source: OECD based on OECD-UNIDO (2019)

Notes

[1] Ministry of Investment and International Co-operation (2017), Inward Direct Investment Position in Egypt, June 2017, Bulletin 1, Egypt.

[2] Ministry of Investment and International Co-operation (2017), Inward Direct Investment Position in Egypt, June 2017, Bulletin 1, Egypt.

[3] Ministry of Investment and International Co-operation (2017), Inward Direct Investment Position in Egypt, June 2017, Bulletin 1, Egypt. The analysis compared immediate and ultimate investing countries for a sample of top 10 investing companies of top 20 home economies.

[4] See annex A. for definitions.

[5] Chapter 5 provides an overview of foreign investment trends in Egypt's zones.

[6] Benefits of supply chain linkages for SMEs may differ if MNEs exert control and influence on SMEs (e.g. by engaging in specific contractual arrangements and support programmes, or by directly investing in SMEs), as compared to sourcing from SMEs through pure arm's length trade.

[7] See annex B. for more details on the mechanisms of SME participation in GVCs via investment

[8] SMEs are defined here as firms with less than 100 employees.

[9] The international guidelines recommend the debtor/creditor principle because it attributes the claims and liabilities to the country of the direct investor or direct investment enterprise involved in the transaction while the transactor principle records them with the party to the transaction, which may differ.

[10] Fellow enterprises are entities that are not in a direct investment relationship themselves but that do have a direct investor in common. Any transactions between fellow enterprises are deemed to be relevant

to direct investment because they result from the influence or control exerted by the common direct investor. The FDIR fully captures all direct investment relationships, including fellow enterprises.

[11] The latest international standards recommend excluding all debt between financial intermediaries, such as banks, from direct investment because this debt is more strongly linked to the role of parents and affiliates as financial intermediaries than to their direct investment relationship.

[12] Special Purpose Entities are entities whose role is to facilitate the internal financing of the MNE but that have little or no physical presence in an economy. BMD4 recommends that they be included in FDI statistics but that they be separately identified so that they can be excluded. By excluding such entities from their FDI statistics, countries have a much better measure of the FDI into their country that is having a real impact on their economy.

[13] The number of financial statements are for companies in the Investment Companies & Commercial Banks component excluding the Upstream Exploration and Real Estate components.

Chapter 2. **Regulatory overview of investors' entry and operations**

This chapter provides an overview of the regulations on investors' entry and operation in Egypt. It argues that, despite remarkable liberalisation reforms, structural transformation in Egypt has occurred at a slow pace. The creation of a more competition-friendly environment would allow for a better allocation of resources towards higher-productivity firms and would enable new entrants and incumbents to bring in new ideas and innovate. The chapter then examines the restrictions on cross-border investment and finds that restrictions on the entry and operation of foreign-controlled firms, while not particularly extensive in Egypt, place an additional toll on the development of a thriving business sector. Not only might they discourage foreign investment inflows in the first place, they may also hold back potential economy-wide productivity gains associated with FDI.

Summary and policy recommendations

A coherent investment policy is embedded in a regulatory framework that facilitates market entry, promotes fair competition and encourages international trade, including in services. The government of Egypt undertook impressive liberalisation in the past decades, but, despite these reforms, structural transformation of the economy has been limited, impeding a sustained increase in labour productivity. The wider business climate continues to face several regulatory hurdles that limit private sector firms' entry and growth. Beyond complex (albeit improving) regulatory procedures, a pervasive state presence in the economy and regulatory protection of incumbent firms are more common in Egypt than in OECD and many emerging countries.

The creation of a more competition-friendly environment in Egypt would foster market dynamics and allow for a better allocation of resources towards higher-productivity firms. It would enable new entrants and incumbents to bring in new ideas and innovate and would encourage less productive firms to restructure or exit the market. The current reform project to strengthen the independence of the Egyptian Competition Authority (ECA) and increase its transparency and capacity is a positive development.

The government has recently implemented further reforms to pursue investment liberalisation. The 2017 Investment Law does not discriminate between foreign and domestic investors. Restrictions on the entry and operation of foreign-controlled firms are nonetheless present in sector-specific legislation. These restrictions, while not particularly extensive, place an additional toll on the development of a thriving business sector, not only by potentially discouraging foreign investment inflows in the first place, but also by holding back potential economy-wide productivity gains associated with FDI. Like most countries, Egypt has largely opened manufacturing industries to foreign investors, but a few backbone services are still partly off-limits to foreign investors.

The implications may go beyond forgone investments. By hindering contestability and competition in these sectors, restrictions may possibly contribute to raising services input costs, such as logistics, finance or real estate, for other economic sectors or thwart potential quality improvements. Access to world-class services inputs, including through FDI in these sectors, has been shown to be crucial for moving manufacturing up the value chain and boosting growth and jobs in the services sector (OECD, 2019, De Backer et al., 2013). In catching-up countries, lower productivity firms can achieve large productivity gains if they benefit from the expertise of foreign investors, if regulations do not impede the necessary restructuring (Kalemli-Ozcan et al., 2014).

Policy recommendations

- Egypt could consider pursuing pro-competition reforms to further level the playing field between new entrants and incumbents firms, particularly SOEs, to allow for a better allocation of resources towards higher-productivity firms. Reforms include reassessing antitrust exemptions to incumbent firms, notably in commercial sectors and competitive markets against their policy objectives and, when relevant, removing them.
- Egypt could benefit from adopting more transparent and less discretionary regulations on firms' market entry, particularly in network sectors. Such policies would reduce the impact of undesirable practices, such as corruption and cronyism, on foreign and domestic investment prospects.
- Egypt could consider reassessing existing restrictions to foreign investment, notably in services sectors, against their public policy objectives and, where relevant, streamline or remove them. Where such policies are deemed necessary, ensure that they are not more restrictive than needed to address identified risks and concerns.

Structural transformation has been slow, despite liberalisation

The history of the Egyptian economy encompasses different eras where the public and private sectors came to play each more or less central roles in the economy. Opening up to private sector investments began in the 1970s, a reform period referred to as *Infitah* (i.e. *openness* in Arabic). The radical shift in government policy contributed to strong, albeit volatile, economic performance: labour productivity doubled between the early 1970 and late 1980s (Figure 2.1). Since then, Egypt has been facing severe structural challenges impeding a sustained increase in labour productivity. The public sector continues to dominate the economy and productivity gains in the past profited only a small, often politically connected, set of businesses (Diwan et al., 2015). The global financial crisis in 2008 and the post-2011 regional events aggravated these structural challenges. The level of labour productivity only recovered its pre-crisis peak of 2006 a decade later.

Figure 2.1. Evolution of labour productivity in Egypt since the *Infitah* era

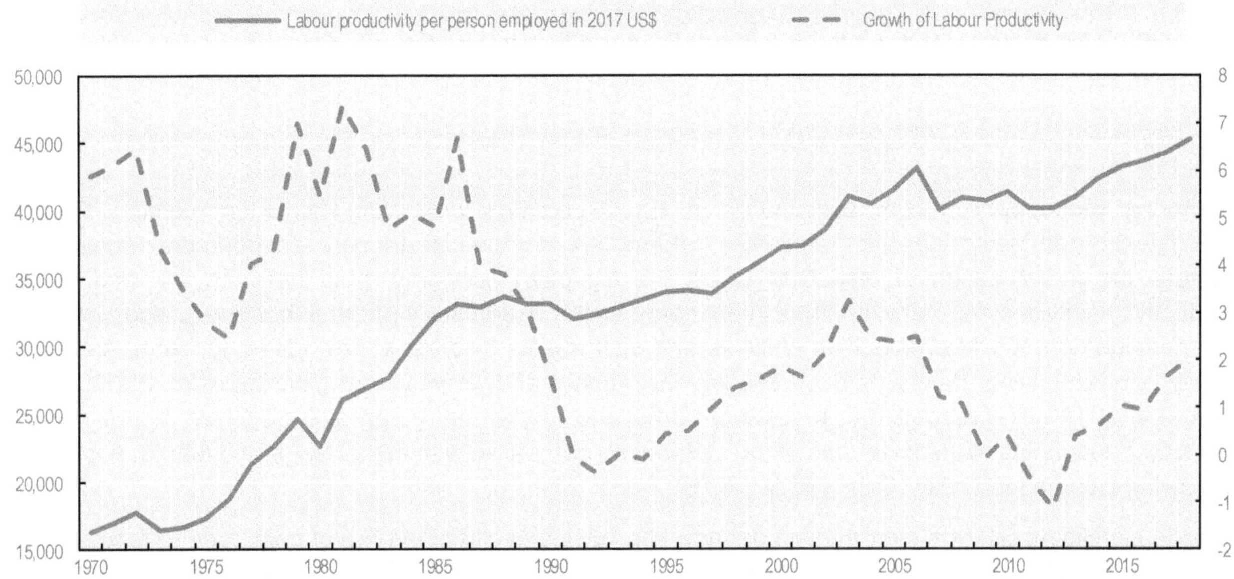

Note: The growth of labour productivity represents a five-years moving average.
Source: OECD calculations based on data from The Conference Board Total Economy database.

The productivity portrait depicted for Egypt becomes bleaker when examining total factor productivity (TFP) growth; corresponding to the residual of GDP growth that cannot be explained by pure production factor accumulation (labour and capital) and can thus be interpreted as firms' improvement in how these factors are combined to produce output. TFP growth in Egypt was, on average, negative throughout 1990-2016 (Figure 2.2, Panel A). The negative TFP trend suggests that structural transformation of the Egyptian economy has been occurring at a very slow pace. This is partly driven by the only slight adjustment over the last decades in the respective contributions of capital and labour to GDP growth. Other emerging countries that undertook similar market-based liberalisation reforms, such as Viet Nam in the 1980s (i.e. *Doi Moi*), were more successful in combining capital and labour to increase TFP, although the effects of reforms were only perceived after years (OECD, 2018).

Figure 2.2. GDP growth decomposition in Egypt and Viet Nam

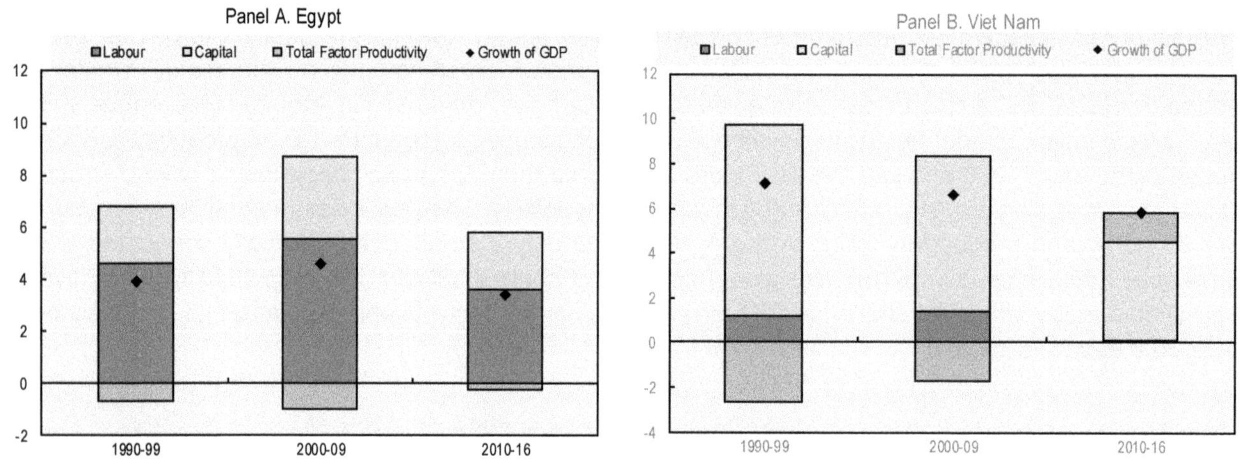

Note: For methodological details, see: https://www.conference-board.org/data/economydatabase/
Source: OECD calculations based on data from The Conference Board Total Economy database.

Pro-competition regulatory reforms encourage investors' entry and growth

Bolstering productivity growth sustainably in Egypt requires promoting fairer competition through countrywide and sector-specific regulatory reforms. A competition-friendly environment would help address the misallocation of resources within the Egyptian economy, both between low and higher productivity activities and between firms in the same sector. Regulatory reforms that encourage firm entry and development would enable new entrants and incumbents to bring in new ideas, innovate and raise productivity and living standards by increasing investment and employment (Alesina et al. 2005; Égert, 2016 and 2018). The reduction in regulatory barriers to market entry can also generate higher income gains for households at the lower end of the distribution compared with the average household, potentially narrowing income inequality (Causa et al., 2015).

Despite significant reforms over the last decade, the business climate in Egypt continues to face several regulatory hurdles that limit private sector firms' entry and growth. The *OECD Indicators of Product Market Regulation* (PMR) benchmark countrywide regulations for more than 60 countries.[1] According to Youssef et al. (2019), preliminary information for Egypt, collected in 2016 and based on the 2013 methodology[2], show that unnecessary restraints to competition caused by the presence of the state in the economy and by excessive regulatory protection of incumbent firms, and complex regulatory procedures are strong impediments to private sector development.[3] These regulatory impediments are considerably more important in Egypt than in OECD and other emerging countries, reducing potential cross-border investment (Fournier, 2015).

In Egypt, as in several other developing countries, state-owned enterprises (SOEs) dominate some markets and high levels of state control persist through regulations that protect current market structures (Ianchovichina and Mottaghi, 2013). State control over the economy in Egypt is characterised by the wide scope of public ownership in a variety of markets. Egyptian SOEs are concentrated in utilities sectors such as electricity, gas, transport and telecoms, as well as in the textile or extracting industries.[4] According to Youssef et al. (2019), the Egyptian government holds higher stakes in its companies than does the average emerging economy.

The governance of SOEs in Egypt could be further improved. Beyond the scope and extent of public ownership, Egyptian SOEs are insulated largely from market discipline and the regulatory privileges they receive are relatively more important than observed elsewhere. Such insulation from market rules may be more severe in the case of SOEs in the utilities and network sectors as they have their own separate laws while a large proportion of commercial SOEs fall under the Law of Public Sector Company and are subject to the Companies Law (World Bank, 2014a).[5] The governance framework of Egyptian SOEs can reduce their effectiveness and limit their incentives to upgrade their production and innovate. SOEs' capacity to supply goods and services at competitive prices can have an adverse impact on private sector establishments, particularly SMEs, as it affects production costs over the entire supply chain (Chapter 3 provides further evidence on SOEs in Egypt).

The complexity of regulatory procedures in Egypt to obtain licences and permits and the existence of regulations protecting incumbents are other important barriers to investors' entry and growth.[6] The 2017 Investment Law and the enlargement of one-stop-shop services through the establishment of the Investment Services Centres (ISC) should help simplifying regulatory procedures (Chapter 4 provides further information on ISCs). There are no indications of recent or upcoming reforms aiming at narrowing the protection of incumbent firms, and more particularly reducing the numerous antitrust exemptions for public enterprises. Publicly controlled firms in Egypt are subject to an exclusion or exemption, either complete or partial, from the application of the general competition law. While this might justified for some sectors, such exemptions are a problem when SOEs activities are commercial in nature and in competitive markets. They distort the competitive neutrality between state-owned and private businesses.

More transparent and less discretionary regulations on firms' market entry in Egypt would reduce the impact of undesirable practices, such as corruption and cronyism, on investment prospects. Evidence for Egypt, Lebanon, Tunisia or Indonesia has shown that crony behaviour by firms with special regulatory advantages lowers aggregate productivity, employment and innovation (Diwan and JI Haidar, 2016; Francis et al., 2018; Rijkers et al., 2014; Kochanova et al. 2018, World Bank, 2014b). Crony firms use and maintain their entrenched privileges thanks to preferential treatment or antitrust exemptions in network sectors. Their ties to the state, for instance through the presence of government individuals on the board of the companies, make them more likely to benefit from trade protection, energy subsidies, access to scarce land, or regulatory enforcement (Diwan et al., 2015). They can also hinder the entry of competitors by initiating *de facto* restrictions on the delivery of investment licences for domestic or foreign firms (World Bank, 2013; Chekir and Diwan, 2014). In Tunisia, connected firms were more likely to evade customs tariffs although this was reduced after 2011 (Rijkers, et al. 2014).

OECD indicators suggest that barriers to investment in Egypt are less an impediment to private sector development than are trade barriers, state control of businesses and regulatory protection of incumbents. Thanks to the successive waves of investment liberalisation reforms in previous decades, the entry and operations of foreign investors in Egypt are subject to less restrictive regulations than in other developing economies (see next section for a full analysis). Regulatory barriers affecting the flows of goods and services are relatively more important in Egypt than in other emerging countries, particularly those related to trade facilitation (e.g. the recognition of foreign regulations and the use of international standards). The requirements and procedures to obtain customs licences often represent an important challenge for companies, even more as several public entities are responsible for delivering those documents.

Pro-competition policy changes in Egypt may help unlock the expected impact of earlier liberalisation reforms on cross-border investment. The stringent laws regulating the access of new firms to markets and the expansion of their activities negatively affects the entry and retention of foreign investors despite moderate restrictions on cross-border investment. Even if moderate, FDI restrictions may still exacerbate the negative effect of market entry restrictions in network sectors on investment (Égert, 2016). In that context, investment liberalisation may not bear fruit, as some activities remain insulated from fair competition because of incumbents' privileges. The current reform project aiming to strengthen the independence of the Egyptian Competition Authority and increase its transparency and capacity is a positive development.

Restrictions on inward cross-border investment are not extensive…

Egypt is an adherent to the OECD *Declaration on International Investment and Multinational Enterprises*. As such, it voluntarily commits to accord national treatment – *i.e.* to treat foreign-owned or -controlled enterprises operating on its territory no less favourably than domestic enterprises in like situations – to foreign investors in its territory, subject to a list of exceptions. Under the *Declaration*, Egypt is also encouraged not to backtrack with regard to existing measures contained in the list of exceptions to national treatment (OECD, 2017a).[7]

In common with most adherents to the *Declaration*, Egypt maintains only a handful of statutory restrictions on FDI. The relative openness of its investment regime is attested by its position under the OECD *FDI Regulatory Restrictiveness Index* (Box 2.1). The extent of statutory discrimination against foreign investors in Egypt is higher than typically observed in the average OECD economy but remains below the average level of non-OECD economies included in the indicator (Figure 2.3) and is also only slightly higher than the average for non-OECD adherent economies.

Box 2.1. The OECD FDI Regulatory Restrictiveness Index

The OECD FDI Regulatory Restrictiveness Index seeks to gauge the restrictiveness of a country's FDI rules. The FDI Index is currently available for all OECD countries and over 30 non-OECD countries, including all G20 members and non-OECD countries adhering to the OECD Declaration on International Investment and Multinational Enterprises. It is used on a stand-alone basis to assess the restrictiveness of FDI policies in reviews of candidates for OECD accession and in OECD Investment Policy Reviews, including reviews of new adherent countries to the OECD Declaration.

The FDI Index does not provide a full measure of a country's investment climate since it does not score the actual implementation of formal restrictions and does not take into account other aspects of the investment regulatory framework which may also impinge on the FDI climate. Nonetheless, FDI rules are a critical determinant of a country's attractiveness to foreign investors and the Index, used in combination with other indicators measuring various aspects of the FDI climate, contributes to assessing countries' international investment policies and to explaining the varied performance across countries in attracting FDI.

The FDI Index covers 22 sectors, including agriculture, mining, electricity, manufacturing and main services (transport, construction, distribution, communications, real estate, financial and professional services). Restrictions are evaluated on a 0 (open) to 1 (closed) scale. The overall restrictiveness index is a simple average of individual sectoral scores. For a detailed description of the scoring methodology, please refer to the technical working paper by Kalinova et al. (2010). For each sector, the scoring is based on the following elements:

- the level of foreign equity ownership permitted,
- the screening/approval procedures applied to inward foreign direct investment;
- restrictions on key foreign personnel; and
- other restrictions, e.g on land ownership, corporate organisation (branching).

The measures taken into account by the Index are limited to statutory restrictions on FDI typically reflected in official OECD instruments on investment or identified in OECD Investment Policy Reviews and yearly monitoring reports. The FDI Index does not assess actual enforcement and implementation procedures. The discriminatory nature of measures, i.e. when they apply to foreign investors only, is the central criterion for scoring a measure. State ownership and state monopolies, to the extent they are not discriminatory towards foreigners, are not scored. Preferential treatment for special-economic zones and export-oriented investors is also not factored into the FDI Index score, nor is the more favourable treatment of one group of investors as a result of preferential treatment under international agreements.

Existing restrictions are mostly concentrated in a few services sectors: in construction, and maritime transport, foreign investment is only allowed in the form of joint ventures where foreign equity does not exceed 49%. Likewise, foreign investment in air transport is allowed up to 49% in companies involved in regular international and domestic flights (for both passenger and cargo services). Foreign investment is also limited in the case of commercial agency and import-trading businesses to only 49% of the equity or to natural persons who have had Egyptian nationality for at least 10 years.[8] Foreign participation in professional services, such as legal, accounting, architectural and engineering services is also subject to limitations.[9]

Foreign investors are also restricted from acquiring land and real estate in the Sinai Peninsula, which can only be owned by natural persons holding Egyptian nationality and by legal persons whose capital is totally owned by Egyptians. Even under a lease agreement, an equity limit of 49% applies for foreign investors in the Sinai region.

Figure 2.3. OECD FDI Regulatory Restrictiveness Index, 2018

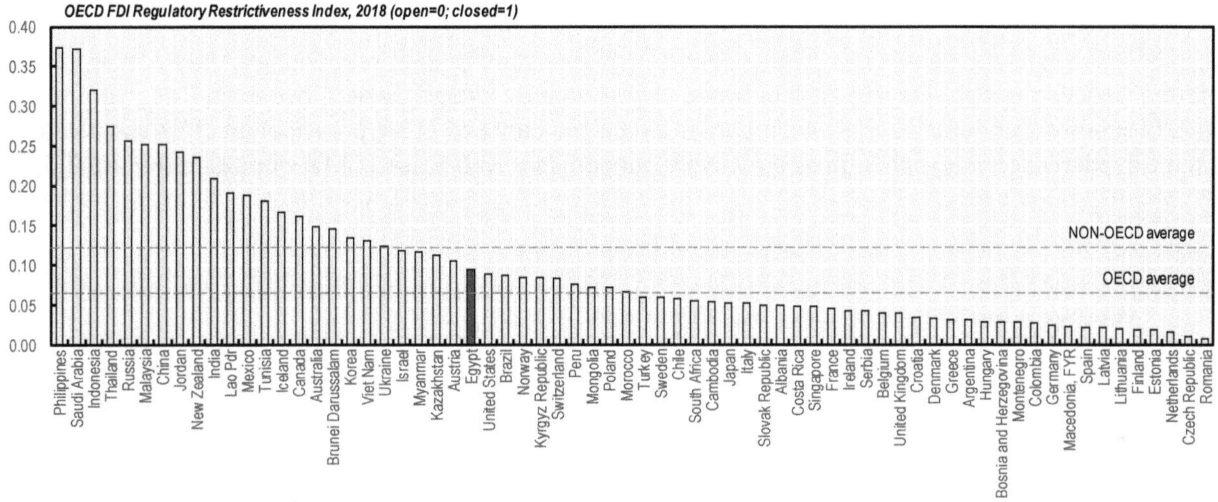

Note: The OECD *FDI Regulatory Restrictiveness Index* covers only statutory measures discriminating against foreign investors (e.g. foreign equity limits, screening & approval procedures, restriction on key foreign personnel, and other operational measures). Other important aspects of an investment climate (e.g. the implementation of regulations and state monopolies, preferential treatment for export-oriented investors and SEZ regimes among other) are not considered. Data reflect regulatory restrictions as of end-December. Please refer to Kalinova et al. (2010) for further information on the methodology.
Source: OECD FDI Regulatory Restrictiveness Index, www.oecd.org/investment/fdiindex.htm.

In other regions, foreign investment in land and real estate is forbidden except for business purposes or personal use. Non-Egyptian persons, including a locally incorporated company where Egyptian nationals do not own the majority of its capital, are allowed to own real estate needed for activities licensed by the government. They can also own up to two residential real estate units for family accommodation purposes, in an area not in excess of 4 000m^2 and not located in an historical site. They may not sell acquired properties for a minimum period of five years from the date of purchase, except if the property is located in certain touristic and new development areas specified in the legislation. Exemptions from such regulations are possible subject to the approval of the Prime Minister or the Cabinet of Ministers for properties located in touristic and new development areas (see section on land in Chapter 3).[10]

...but remaining restrictions may still curb foreign investments and hold back potential economy-wide productivity gains

Despite being relatively open to foreign investment, the effects of remaining restrictions in Egypt can still be sizeable. To some extent, it is tautological to say that when foreign investment is prohibited, an economy will receive no investment, but the evidence suggests that even partial restrictions can significantly curtail inward investment into both advanced and emerging economies (Nicoletti et al., 2003; Kalemi-Özcan et al., 2014; Fournier, 2015; Mistura and Roulet, 2019).

Recent OECD research (Mistura and Roulet, 2019) shows that the introduction of reforms leading to a 10% reduction in the level of FDI restrictiveness, as measured by the OECD *FDI Regulatory Restrictiveness Index*, could increase bilateral FDI inward stocks by around 2.1% on average across all countries. An illustrative simulation exercise, drawing on the baseline model, suggests that if Egypt were to reduce FDI restrictions to the level of Czech Republic, for instance, which is among the 5% most open economies in the sample, Egypt's bilateral inward FDI stocks could be expected to increase, all else equal, by up to 37% (Figure 2.4). The simulation is illustrative and, therefore, should be interpreted with caution.[11] Nonetheless, the exercise provides a sense of the importance of restrictions as barriers to investment.

Egypt's own experience seems to confirm that foreign investors tend to respond favourably to regulatory reforms enabling a level playing field between domestic and foreign-owned investors. The more recent wave of liberalisation reforms was accompanied by a significant rise in the participation of foreign investors in the Egyptian economy, although reforms were concomitant with a rise in FDI worldwide (Figure 2.5).

Figure 2.4. Simulated effects of FDI liberalisation in Egypt

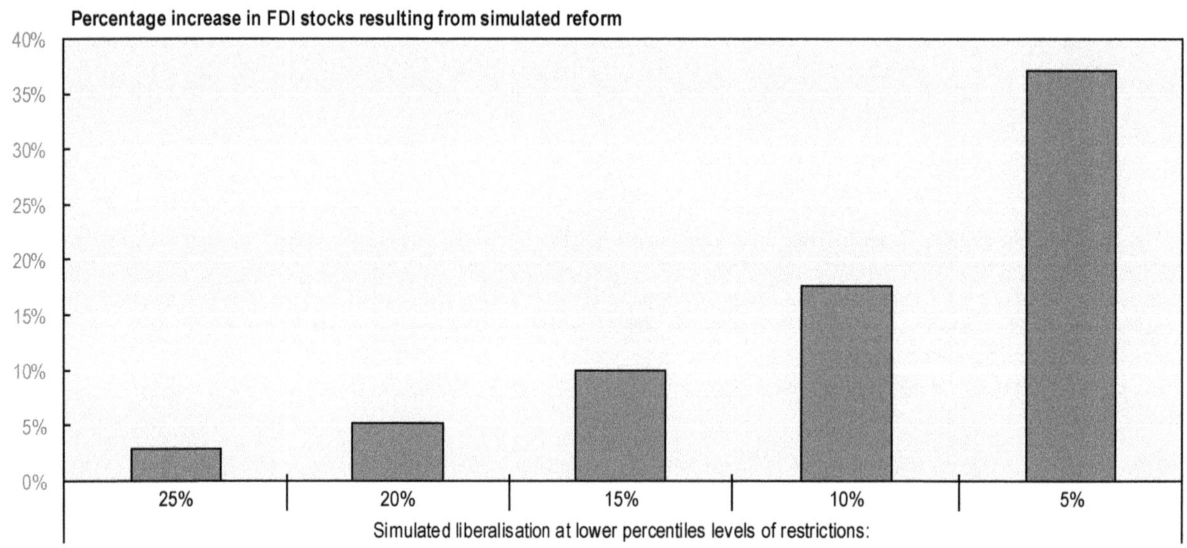

Note: The simulations are based on the partial elasticity of FDI to regulatory restrictions estimated in an augmented gravity model of bilateral inward FDI positions using a poisson pseudo-maximum likelihood estimator. Typical gravity variables and a series of other policy and non-policy factors are included (distance, contiguity, the existence of a common language, colonial ties, market size, economic growth, real exchange rates, similarity in size and factor resource endowments, trade openness, natural resource endowments, institutional maturity, FDI restrictions, participation in free trade areas, corporate tax and country and time-specific effects. The regressions cover bilateral FDI relationships between 60 countries over the 1997-2012 period.
Source: author's calculations based on Mistura and Roulet (2019).

Figure 2.5. Wave of liberalisation reforms and FDI stocks in Egypt

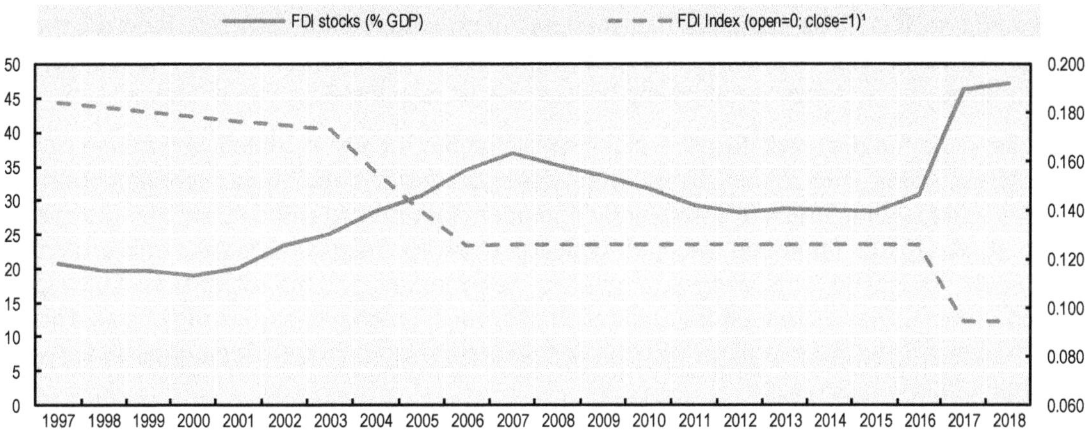

Note: [1]Index scores linearly interpolated over missing periods.
Source: author's calculations based on the OECD FDI Regulatory Restrictiveness Index and IMF World Economic Outlook and International Financial Statistics databases.

Figure 2.6. Remaining FDI restrictions place a larger toll on downstream manufacturing industries in Egypt

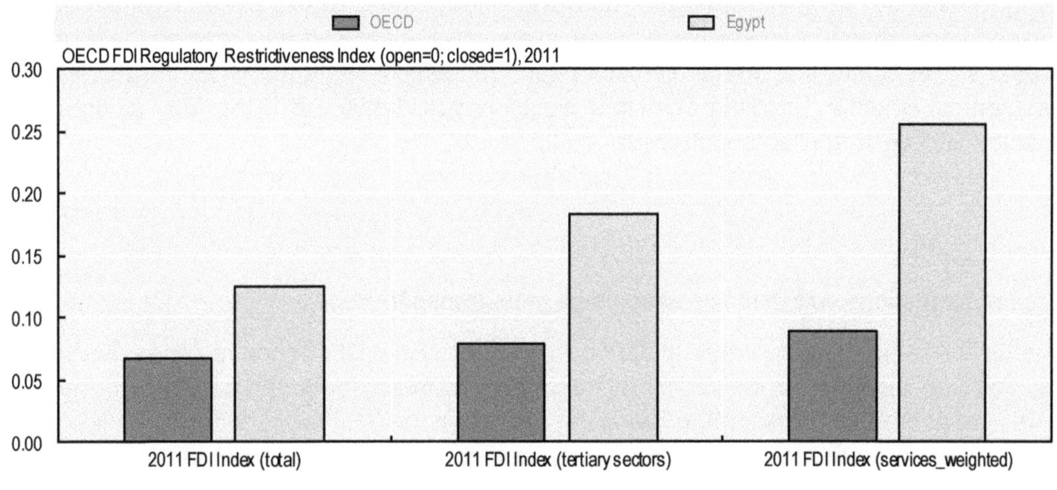

Note: The services weighted measure of FDI restrictiveness refers to the weighted average of the scores for nine services sectors covered by the Index (construction, transport, telecommunications, electricity, wholesale and retail distribution, financial and business services), where the weights are given by their respective shares in the total input costs of manufacturing sector. Data are from 2011. It is constructed as: $rest_{s,c} = \sum_j^J (w_{s,c,j} * Index_{j,c})$, where *rest* is the weighted FDI restrictiveness index faced by manufacturing sector *s* in country *c*; *w* is the share of service sector *j* in total inputs of manufacturing sector *s* in country *c*; and *Index* is the score of the OECD *FDI Regulatory Restrictiveness Index* of service sector j in country c.
Source: author's calculations based on the OECD *FDI Regulatory Restrictiveness Index*, the OECD Input-Output Tables and EORA World Input-Output Tables.

In addition, remaining restrictions may be more constraining for the development of the Egyptian economy than they might initially appear. Figure 2.6 compares Egypt's scores under the OECD *FDI Regulatory Restrictiveness Index* with the OECD average for the entire economy, tertiary sectors and as a weighted measure of services inputs to manufacturing sectors. Because of data limitations regarding inter-sector relationships across countries, the assessment is based on data from 2011, which is the latest available in a more consistent manner. As can be seen, the level of FDI statutory restrictiveness in Egypt then was already above the OECD average at the economy-level and was even higher across tertiary sectors too. This difference was even stronger when comparing the level of restrictiveness weighted by services inputs to manufacturing sectors. This suggests that manufacturing industries in Egypt tend to rely much more intensively on inputs from restricted services sectors than is the case across OECD economies, indicating that restrictions may have greater productivity-hindering effects in the Egyptian economy.

Worldwide, services have proved to be a significant channel for value added generation, including in manufacturing industries. The value created by services as intermediate inputs represents over a third of the total value added in manufacturing in over 60 countries spread across the Americas, Europe and Asia (De Backer et al., 2013). Improved services typically allow for relatively greater efficiency and lower transaction costs, facilitating firms' access to potential new markets and the expansion of their portfolio of products and services. The increased fragmentation of production chains across regions and globally has contributed to exacerbate the role played by network industries and complementary business services in supporting manufacturing operations.

A number of empirical studies have demonstrated the negative relationship between manufacturing productivity levels and barriers to competition and foreign participation in services sectors.[12] Market access reforms enable greater competitive pressures in services sectors and, consequently, higher productivity. In turn, this allows downstream manufacturers to benefit from higher quality services inputs or lower services input costs.

Egypt's strategy to channel investments into the Suez Canal Economic Zone (SCZone) may help to soften some of the potential constraints arising from restrictions on foreign investors, but it is not fully clear at this stage if they do so (Box 2.2). According to the government, there are no statutory differences between domestic and foreign investors inside the SCZone. In any case, such a strategy carries the cost of favouring some investors over others (i.e. foreign investors over domestic investors), which in itself should warrant an assessment of whether Egyptian investors would not be better off if the less stringent regulatory environment of SCZones applied countrywide.

Box 2.2. Transparency of FDI restrictions in the Suez Canal Economic Zone

The scope of restrictions on FDI in zones could be more transparent.

Investments inside the SCZone are regulated by the Law on Special Economic Zones. According to the SCZone website, there is no difference in treatments between national and foreign investors, i.e. companies are entitled to 100% foreign ownership, although the SEZ law is silent in this respect. In fact, according to the law, companies inside the zones remain subject to the provisions of other laws (e.g. sector-specific laws) unless if provided otherwise or inconsistently with provisions under the SEZ law. It remains, therefore, unclear if foreign investors operating from inside the Zones would be exempted, for instance, from nation-wide regulatory restrictions in the construction and maritime transport sectors, where foreign equity cannot exceed 49% of the capital. In the case such restrictions do apply in the SCZone, efforts should be made to assess whether they may discourage the development of the priority sectors targeted by the SCZone, i.e. manufacturing, transport and logistics and maritime-related services.

It is also important to examine the extent of state control on market access in the SCZone. If badly designed, regulations that protect current market structures, such as the preponderance of SOEs, may lead to de facto restrictions on foreign investment. On the legal front, Egypt made some improvements aiming at reducing anti - competitiveness practices. When they still exist in practice, such practices can hamper new foreign investors' entry.

Other countries have sometimes exempted SEZ investors from the application of national legislation or clarified in which sectors restrictions apply to FDI in SEZs. For instance, in several Asian countries, equity restrictions do not apply if the foreign investor located in the SEZ exports all or most of its output. In Indonesia, a negative list indicates all exceptions to national treatment, i.e. restrictions or other discriminatory measures that apply to foreign investors in general or in specific sectors or economic activities. One of the provisions of the negative list clearly stipulates that foreign investors in SEZs are entitled to 100% ownership. In China, a foreign investment negative list was issued in 2015 exclusively for the three pilot Free Trade Zones (Fujian, Guangdong and Tianjin). The negative list includes all the limitations and restrictions on foreign investment, including those stipulated in other laws, making it more intelligible for foreign investors. The Chinese FTZ example may be particularly relevant for Egypt, as they share the objective of using the zones as a laboratory for reforms that, if successful, could be replicated nationally.

Besides equity limitations, countries may sometimes regulate the entry and behaviour of foreign investors, including in SEZs, through screening and approval mechanisms. Although the number of countries resorting to screening for this purpose has substantially declined over time, such measures have not yet been completely eliminated. The SEZ law, while not explicitly making any distinction between foreign and domestic investors, stipulates, in art. 13, line 2b, that the Zone Authority shall define the requirements for delivering a licence. Projects may not be established in SEZs unless a prior written approval from the board of the SEZ Authority is obtained. More clarity on the criteria applied in such situations is warranted in implementing regulations, as well as regarding the possibility for investors to have recourse against authority decisions.

References

Alesina, A., Ardagna, S., Nicoletti, G., & Schiantarelli, F. (2005), Regulation and investment, *Journal of the European Economic Association*, 3(4), 791-825.

Chekir, H., & Diwan, I. (2014), Crony capitalism in Egypt, *Journal of Globalization and Development*, 5(2), 177-211.

De Backer, K. and S. Miroudot (2013), “Mapping Global Value Chains”, OECD Trade Policy Papers, No. 159, OECD Publishing, Paris. http://dx.doi.org/10.1787/5k3v1trgnbr4-en.

Diwan, I., & Haidar, J. I. (2016), Do political connections reduce job creation? Evidence from Lebanon, In *Economic Research Forum Working Paper* (No. 1054).

Diwan, I., Keefer, P., & Schiffbauer, M. (2015), Pyramid capitalism: political connections, regulation, and firm productivity in Egypt, World Bank.

Égert, B. (2016), Regulation, institutions, and productivity: new macroeconomic evidence from OECD countries, *American Economic Review*, 106(5), 109-13.

Égert, B. (2018), Regulation, institutions and aggregate investment: new evidence from OECD countries, *Open Economies Review*, 29(2), 415-449.

Fournier, J. (2015), “The Heterogeneity of Product Market Regulations”, *OECD Economics Department Working Papers*, No. 1182, OECD Publishing. http://dx.doi.org/10.1787/5js7xhxwrnwd-en

Francis, D., Hussain, S., & Schiffbauer, M. (2018), Do politically connected firms innovate, contributing to long-term economic growth? Policy Research Working Paper 8502, Washington D.C.

Kalemli-Ozcan, S., Korsun, V., Sorensen, B. E. and Villegas-Sanchez, C. (2014), “Who Owns Europe’s Firms? Globalization and Foreign Investment in Europe”.

Koske, I. et al. (2015), “The 2013 update of the OECD's database on product market regulation: Policy insights for OECD and non-OECD countries”, *OECD Economics Department Working Papers*, No. 1200, OECD Publishing, Paris. http://dx.doi.org/10.1787/5js3f5d3n2vl-en

Mistura, F. and C. Roulet (2019), "The determinants of Foreign Direct Investment: Do statutory restrictions matter?", OECD Working Papers on International Investment, No. 2019/01, OECD Publishing, Paris, https://doi.org/10.1787/641507ce-en.

Nicoletti, Golub, S., et al. (2003), "The Influence of Policies on Trade and Foreign Direct Investment", *OECD Economic Studies*, vol. 2003/1, https://doi.org/10.1787/eco_studies-v2003-art2-en.

OECD (2019), *OECD Investment Policy Reviews: Southeast Asia*, www.oecd.org/investment/oecd-investment-policy-review-southeast-asia.htm.

OECD (2018), *OECD Investment Policy Reviews: Viet Nam 2018,* OECD Investment Policy Reviews, OECD Publishing, Paris, https://doi.org/10.1787/9789264282957-en.

OECD (2017a), "National Treatment for Foreign-Controlled Enterprises: Including Adhering Country Exceptions to National Treatment", Paris, https://www.oecd.org/daf/inv/investment-policy/national-treatment-instrument-english.pdf.

OECD (2017b), The Size and Sectoral Distribution of State-Owned Enterprises, OECD Publishing, Paris. http://dx.doi.org/10.1787/9789264280663-en.

OECD (2015), *Policy Framework for Investment, 2015 Edition*, OECD Publishing, Paris, https://doi.org/10.1787/9789264208667-en.

Rijkers, B., Freund, C., & Nucifora, A. (2014), All in the family: State capture in Tunisia, The World Bank.

World Bank (2013), Investing in turbulent times, World Bank: Washington D.C., October.

World Bank (2014a), Corporate Governance of State-Owned Enterprises: A toolkit, The World Bank Group, Washington D.C.

World Bank (2014b), Jobs or Privilege: Unleashing the Employment Potential of the Middle East and North Africa, World Bank: Washington D.C.

Youssef, H., Alnashar, S. Bahaa Hamed; Erian, J., Elshawarby, A., Zaki, C. (2019), Egypt Economic Monitor: From Floating to Thriving – Taking Egypt's Exports to New Levels, Washington, D.C., World Bank Group.

Notes

[1] See www.oecd.org/economy/reform/indicators-of-product-market-regulation/ for further information on the OECD Indicators of Product Market Regulation.

[2] In 2018, the methodology used to collect the information and calculate the OECD PMR indicators was considerably modified.

[3] See Youssef et al. (2019) for a preliminary overview of the PMR Indicators in the Egypt's Economic Monitor of the World Bank.

[4] Based on statistics from 40 OECD and non-OECD countries, together, the electricity and gas, transportation, telecoms and other utilities sectors account for 51% of all SOEs by value and 70% by employment (OECD, 2017). Chapter 3 provides some data on SOEs prevalence in Egypt.

[5] Law of Public Sector Company's No. 203 of 1991 and Companies Law no. 159 of 1981.

[6] See Chapter 4 for a review of the procedures to obtain investment licences in Egypt.

[7] A list of these measures is provided during the adherence process and any new measure affecting foreign investment if formally required to be notified to the OECD Investment Committee.

[8] Registration in the Register of Commercial Agents and Intermediaries or in the Register of Importers is a condition for engagement in these activities. Until the entry into force of Law No. 7 of the year 2017 concerning the Importers Registry, only Egyptian nationals and fully owned and managed Egyptian companies were admitted into the Register of Importers. Since then, the registration of a legal entity, where the majority of its capital is held by Egyptians or naturalized Egyptians after the lapse of 10 years as of the date of their acquiring the Egyptian nationality, has also been permitted.

[9] The provision of professional services is largely restricted to Egyptian nationals. Incorporation is not permitted in most professional services, largely precluding the participation of foreigners as capital investors in such businesses. In legal services, a foreign firm may set up a representative office to advise clients on foreign and international law, but it cannot provide legal advice on the law of represent clients in Egyptian courts or advice. Only Egyptian nationals are allowed to appear before a court.

[10] Non-Egyptians may acquire vacant real estate in Egypt conditioned upon building within a period of five years from the date their ownership becomes effective (the date on which the realty is recorded at the competent Notary Public Office). Please refer to the following legislation for more information: Law 230 of 1996 Regulating the Ownership of Built Real Estate and Vacant Land by Non-Egyptians, and the Prime Ministerial Decree No. 548/2005.

[11] The effects of such a simulation depend logically on how restrictive is Egypt in relation to the simulated policy level. It also depends on many other conditions, such as the specification of the estimated model, the configuration of policies, and many exogenous elements. For instance, it neglects the needed efforts to implement any of the simulated policies.

[12] See OECD (2016) for empirical evidence and a review of the literature.

Chapter 3. Legal framework for investment

This chapter provides an overview of Egypt's legal framework for the protection of investment. It takes stock of the investment policies in force and examines the level of regulatory protection granted to both domestic and foreign investors since the enactment of the 2017 Investment Law, which constitutes a milestone in Egypt's recent efforts to reposition itself as an attractive and safe investment destination. The chapter looks into the rules for property protection, access to land and investor-state dispute settlement, and reviews its international investment treaty practice. It also explores Egypt's efforts to establish a corporate governance framework for state-owned enterprises, which play a major role in the country's economic landscape.

Summary and policy recommendations

The government of Egypt is putting strong emphasis on adopting more modern investment legislation and regulations for investment. The new Investment Law, promptly followed by a modernised Companies Law, marked an important milestone in efforts to provide a safer and more consistent regulatory environment for foreign and domestic investments. Yet, further reform endeavours are required to endow Egypt with clear and transparent regulatory and institutional frameworks governing business and investment activities. For clarity and predictability purposes, and to avoid legal loopholes, implementing regulations should also follow more promptly the enactment of new legislation. Likewise, a more uniform and harmonised implementation of these regulations across the country would greatly enhance the enabling environment for investment.

Policy recommendations

- The application of administrative procedures should be more consistent across all governorates and relevant public authorities. Strong, regular and transparent institutional cooperation mechanisms, including between central authorities and special economic zones, need to be put in place on a more regular basis to provide for a more efficient administration of investment activities.
- One of the main avowed purposes of the new Investment Law was to create a more robust infrastructure for preventing and managing investment disputes. Despite the creation of new dispute settlement bodies, the current institutional setting for the resolution of investor-state disputes appears overly complex and might therefore not serve its purpose in the most efficient way.
- Egypt has a vast network of international investment treaties. Bearing in mind the existing scope for treaty shopping, Egypt should consider reviewing and considering possibilities for renegotiation, clarification and exit of investment treaties. Treaties with vague provisions concluded in the past may lead to undesirable interpretations in ISDS disputes. Egypt should consider taking steps to update these treaties to bring them in line with government intent, Egypt's current priorities and more recent practices in investment treaty policy.
- GAFI, the Ministry of Justice and the Ministry of Foreign Affairs should continue to develop Investor-state Dispute Settlement (ISDS) dispute prevention and case management tools. Egypt may also wish to consider efforts to raise awareness about Egypt's investment treaties and the significance of Egypt's international obligations under these investment treaties for the day-to-day functions of different government agencies and officials that regularly interact with foreign investors.
- The complex landscape of public land ownership, and myriad approvals required to allocate land to investors, means that a substantial gap remains between land demand and supply in Egypt. The centralisation of investor requests for land under GAFI is an important improvement that appears to have enabled faster distribution of state-owned land to firms. But the government could consider taking further steps to centralise the allocation of land to investors, such as empowering one agency to allocate all publicly owned land, regardless of its sectoral use. More immediately, coordination between the many different government landowners should be significantly strengthened. GAFI's success in directing investors to the appropriate government landowner will depend on close intra-agency cooperation.
- Short of a complete inventory and mapping of public land ownership, coordination challenges between agencies allocating public land are likely to persist. A complete registry would assist both GAFI in facilitating investment and firms in their location decisions. The Investment Map is

a good step in this direction. Agencies could make public more comprehensive maps of land within their control, rather than only a selection of land available in zones, as is shown on the Investment Map.

- The government has taken substantial measures to improve standards of corporate governance for state-owned enterprises. Yet, the current dual regulatory system, under which only a subset of firms adhere to good corporate governance practices, falls short of levelling the playing field between SOEs and their private sector competitors. The government could do more to apply standards to all state-owned enterprises and take steps to minimise the market distortions of publicly-owned firms.

The domestic legal framework for investment protection

The Investment Law is central to business regulation

The degree of openness encountered by investors when establishing in Egypt, and the conditions they face in their on-going operations, is only one part of a broader investment environment. The protection of property, contractual rights and other legal guarantees provided to investors both in domestic legislation and in international agreements, combined with effective enforcement mechanisms and guarantees of access to efficient dispute settlement mechanisms are key building blocks of an enabling investment climate. When procedures for establishing investments and enforcing contracts are perceived as cumbersome and lack predictability, or when disputes cannot be resolved in a timely and cost-effective manner, investors may restrict their activities or refrain from engaging in the country. Providing strong, clear and predictable guarantees of legal protection for investors and offering reliable dispute resolution mechanisms are fundamental to reinforce investors' confidence. Enforcing regulatory reforms to set the conditions for a healthy and sound investment climate is a key priority in Egypt, where the business climate has considerably suffered from the economic and political turmoil in recent years.

Egypt has a long-standing tradition of economic liberalism and openness to foreign direct investment, which, coupled with a strong legalistic culture, has given rise to a succession of laws regulating investment.

The national programme of economic liberalisation, or *Infitah,* was introduced with the 1971 Law on Arab Capital Investment and Free Zones, the first ever legislation dedicated to investment in Egypt. The law provided legal guarantees and incentives and marked the establishment of the Investment and Free Zones Authority, which preceded GAFI. It also opened up to foreign investments from non-Arab countries. Partly hindered in its application by a number of inconsistencies in its provisions, it was abrogated in 1973 and replaced by the 1974 Law on Arab and Foreign Capital Investment and Free Zones, which provided a more comprehensive and coherent legal framework for investment.

The 1974 law broadened the scope of sectors opened to private investments and provided more incentives and guarantees to investors, hence signalling the government's willingness to take a pro-investment stance. Yet, the implementation of the law faced a number of challenges, mainly due to the vagueness of the provisions determining the scope of sectors open to private investment, including foreign investment, as well as of the provisions on applicable exchange rates and on incentives. In recognition of these weaknesses and of the subsequent lack of legal certainty for investors, the government adopted yet another new investment law, enacted in 1977. The amendment clarified the list of sectors open to foreign investment, introduced several dispute settlement options, including arbitration, and repealed procedural obligations for investment projects required by the then Company and Labour laws. Further amendments were introduced with the adoption of the Law No. 230 of 1989, which was subsequently repealed by a new Law on Investment Guarantees and Incentives, issued in 1997.

The 1997 legislation widened the scope of activities open to private investment and further relaxed the incorporation requirements for investing companies. It also reinforced the protection of investments against expropriation, with an explicit protection against "creeping expropriations" that may occur through administrative measures.

Recent regulatory amendments are improving the legal environment

The pace of reforms has accelerated over the past few years towards a modernised regulatory and institutional environment for investment. The aftermath of the 2011 events and of the subsequent political turmoil, during which numerous arbitration cases were brought against the state of Egypt, prompted the authorities to take steps to reposition Egypt as a safe investment destination. To respond to the pressing need to send a positive signal to both prospective and already established investors, the government introduced in 2015 substantial amendments to the 1997 Investment Law. The purpose of the in-depth revision of the law was to attract new investments to Egypt through more generous incentives and stronger guarantees, along with a streamlining of administrative obstacles and procedures.

The amendment brought substantial improvements to the core provisions of the investment legislation. It clarified and strengthened the role of GAFI as a one-stop-shop for investors operating in most sectors and streamlined the system for allocation of state land, pricing and zoning to clarify the institutional infrastructure governing the allocation of land outside of special economic zones. It also reaffirmed the core legal protections granted to investors and brought about a major change in the treatment of foreign investors by relaxing the available options to access dispute resolution mechanisms. In response to Egypt's increasing exposure to investor-state arbitration, a new dedicated chapter established three out-of-court committees to favour the amicable settlement of disputes between private investors and public institutions.

This first step on the path toward a more enabling regulatory and institutional environment for investment nevertheless gave rise to some criticisms from the business community. The initial delays in adopting the implementing regulations, without which the legislative provisions remained too vague to be effectively enforced, hindered the expected impact of the amendment. Pending the adoption of the implementing decrees, the level of guarantees provided by law remained uncertain and led the business community to adopt a "wait-and-see" position that did not enable the economy to get off the ground as quickly as expected.

Following the lukewarm reception of the 2015 amendment, and in a renewed attempt to signal the pro-investment stance of the government, MIIC and GAFI introduced a new investment law, issued by Law No. 72 of 2017, which formally replaced the Investment Law No. 8/1997 and its subsequent amendments. It was promptly followed by the adoption of the corresponding Executive Regulations in October 2017. With this latest reform, the government marked a major milestone and reaffirmed the strong political will to improve further the business environment and the competitiveness of the country. The substantive content of the new law was hence enriched, while retaining most of the main changes introduced by the 2015 amendment.

The formal adoption of a new law and the repeal of the previous legislation marked an important symbolic step that initiated a wider reform process to spur investment. It also improved the clarity of the overall investment regime by consolidating within a single piece of legislation the investment rules that were scattered under various laws and regulations.

The new law focuses on addressing the obstacles to investment and overcoming major procedural and substantive problems faced by investors. The amendment also introduced both a set of additional incentives and an explicit principle of social responsibility of investors.

One of the main goals of the amendment was to set the foundations for a clearer and more streamlined framework for investments, by prohibiting the application of ad hoc fees and financial and procedural requirements to specific projects unless such requirements are based on the opinion of GAFI's Board of Directors and of the Supreme Council of Investment. In the same vein, it is by virtue of the law that GAFI was given the mandate prepare an investment map in coordination and cooperation with all concerned state authorities and to be updated every three years. The law also gave authority to the Supreme Investment Council, headed by the President of the Republic, to develop a legislative and administrative reform plan for the investment environment and to approve policies and investment plan setting priorities for targeted investment projects.

Meanwhile, the 2017 amendment also introduced a set of additional advantages and incentives. It grants non-Egyptian investors residence in Egypt (Art. 3.4), and its executive regulations provide for additional guarantees for foreign employees. As further described in Chapter 4, in the same effort to shed light on available opportunities and advantages available to investors, the law provides for the development of an investment map that defines the investment type, regime, geographic areas, and sectors, in addition to the real-estate properties owned by the State or other public legal persons which are prepared for investment, and the arrangements and manner of disposal of such real-estate properties pursuant to the type of the investment regime (Art. 17).

Another prominent aspect of the amendment, as further developed in Chapter 7, is the emphasis given to the principle of investors' social responsibility. The new law authorises the investor to allocate a percentage of his annual profits to be used for establishing a social development system outside his investment project, through participating in one or more of the following areas: environmental protection, provision of health, social or cultural care services and programmes, supporting technical education or funding research, studies and awareness campaigns aimed at developing and improving production, as well as training and scientific research. The amount spent by the investor in one of these assignments is deductible in the application of the provisions of the Income Tax Law (91/2005).

In the same impetus for reform, the government adopted several key laws governing business activities. The Collateral Registry Law (115/2015) eased the use of movable assets as collateral by businesses and established an electronic collateral registry. In 2018, the revision of the Companies Law (159/1981) substantially enhanced the investment environment by broadening the scope of available corporate structures and providing the possibility of establishing sole person companies in Egypt. The Law on Streamlining Industrial Establishments Licensing (15/2017) was a long-awaited improvement to the existing licensing system, and the Law on Restructuring, Preventive Reconciliation and Bankruptcy in Egypt (the Bankruptcy Law, 11/2018), introduced, for the first time in Egypt, a non-jurisdictional restructuring mechanism for bankrupt businesses. The Law also gave authority to judicial courts to enforce restructuring plans for businesses and created a court-supervised mediation system.

This comprehensive set of reforms, together with the new Investment Law as amended by Law No. 141 of 2019, which streamlines and reinforces the administration of investment projects, forms a more coherent and enabling legislative corpus to reinforce investors' trust in the stability and certainty in the Egyptian regulatory and institutional ecosystem.

The business and the international community have praised this wave of legislative reforms, but have also called for further efforts to improve Egypt's image as an investment destination. Despite a now comprehensive set of well-drafted laws, the legal environment still suffers from a perceived lack of predictability.

The implementation of the provisions of the law and of the new mandate of GAFI is sometimes challenged by administrative practices, notably at governorate level. At central level, further coordination across ministries and public agencies, both in the policy-making process and in the operationalisation of reforms would also allow the existing investment regime to achieve its potential. GAFI's recent affiliation to the Egyptian Council of Ministers, by virtue of the Prime Minister Decree 38/2020, is expected to substantially enhance effective cooperation with all the government bodies in order to facilitate investment services.

Investors are protected by strong de jure guarantees of property rights

Egypt's domestic legal framework grants de jure property rights protections to investors that are consistent with high, modern standards of protection. The protection of investors' rights is recognised at constitutional and legislative levels, and, notwithstanding the application of bilateral investment treaty provisions, the same degree of legal protection and available incentives is granted to foreign and domestic investors.

The Investment Law provides the full spectrum of investment guarantees and protection standards that are required to provide a safe de jure regime for investors. It contains a provision granting fair and equitable treatment to both foreign and Egyptian investors, and a guarantee that the invested capital cannot be subject to any coercive or discriminatory measures.

The 2017 Investment Law provides protections against nationalisation and expropriation (Article 4). It also guarantees against sequestration and seizures, as well as the confiscation and freezing of property, except under court order. The state can only expropriate property for "public utility", with fair compensation and in a prompt manner. The law stipulates this value "shall equal the fair economic value of the expropriated property on the day preceding the expropriation decision date" (Article 4). Meanwhile, Article 6 of the Law 10 of 1990 on expropriation of real estate for public interest, amended in 2018, provides that the compensation is estimated at the rates prevalent at the time of the expropriation decision plus 20% of the estimated price. Seizure of capital is only allowed by virtue of a court judgment, except for tax and social insurance contributions. Likewise, licences granted and state-owned land or property allocated to an investment project cannot be withdrawn without prior notice given by GAFI.

"Public utility" is not defined in the Investment Law or in the Law on expropriation of real estate for public interest. Reports suggest that in practice, different government agencies have adopted different criteria for expropriation (of primarily informal settlements) in the public interest (Wang, 2017[15]). The large amount of informal housing, coupled with low registration, increases the likelihood of cases of expropriation of informal settlements. This is particularly the case in cities, where more than half of residents live in informal housing. Anecdotal evidence suggests that residents in these cases are compensated, but it is not clear who determines their remuneration and how this is calculated (El Rashidi, 2018[22]).

As for ISDS cases, most of the expropriation cases pending before ICSID arbitral tribunals relate to political instability between 2011 and 2014 and were caused by the cancellation of sales of state-owned assets.

The Investment Law also details procedures for the state to recover land in the case of a breach of contract. If an investor commits a material breach of the terms of the contract, and does not rectify this after receiving written notice, GAFI may withdraw real-estate properties allocated for the project. The state can also recover property if: the investor does not receive the property within 90 days; it does not start the project within 90 days (if there are no obstructions and without reasonable excuse); it violates conditions of payment; or it changes the purpose for which the property was allocated (Article 67). In all cases, GAFI must inform the investor of the violations, allow the investor to comment, and give "an adequate grace period to rectify the causes of the breach" (Article 5).

A comprehensive yet complex framework for protecting intellectual property rights

The legal regime for protecting intellectual property (IP) rights comprises several pieces of legislation, including the 2002 Intellectual Property Rights Law, which unified former IP laws to bring Egypt's legal IP regime in line with its obligations under the WTO Trade-Related Aspects of Intellectual Property Rights (TRIPS) Agreement. The adoption of Law (15/2004) on E-signature and the Establishment of the Information Technology Industry Development Authority (ITIDA) completed the new legal arsenal for a more up-to-date system of IP protection.

ITIDA is a public authority affiliated to Ministry of Communications and Information Technology, which aims to "develop Egypt's competitive advantages as a one-stop shop for foreign direct investors seeking to enhance their global offering and providing the Egyptian IT industry with the right tools to increase IT/ITES exports." ITIDA has the authority to deposit, record, and register the original software and databases submitted by entities or individuals, who publish, print, and produce thereof in order to protect copyrights and other rights.

More recently, the 2014 Constitution reinforced IP rights (art. 69), providing that "the state shall protect all types of intellectual property in all fields". It established a "specialised body" to uphold the rights of Egyptians and their legal protection, as regulated by law.

Egypt is party to the main international conventions on IP rights, such as the Berne Convention on Copyright, the Paris Convention on Industrial Property and the Madrid Agreement. The government developed an IP Rights Action Plan to bring its IP system in line with the WTO's Trade-Related aspects of Intellectual Property Rights (TRIPS) commitments. There is a strong awareness, at the highest level of the government, of the immediate benefits of having a robust IP policy (Box 3.1).

Box 3.1. The benefits of IP rights in developing countries: The shifting debate

Traditionally, a limited number of developed countries in which a high proportion of the world's R&D was concentrated were the main "demandeurs" of strong IP rights internationally. Four recent developments are helping to broaden acceptance of the benefits of intellectual property rights.

More firms in more developing countries are now producing innovative products and thus have a direct stake in the protection of intellectual property rights. In Brazil and the Philippines short-duration patents have helped domestic firms to adapt foreign technology to local conditions, while in Ghana, Kuwait, and Morocco local software firms are expanding into the international market. India's vibrant music and film industry is in part the result of copyright protection, while in Sri Lanka laws protecting designs from pirates have allowed manufacturers of quality ceramics to increase exports.

A growing number of developing countries are seeking to attract FDI, including in industries where proprietary technologies are important. Foreign firms are reluctant to transfer their most advanced technology, or to invest in production facilities, until they are confident their rights will be protected.

There is growing recognition that consumers in even the poorest countries can suffer from the sale of counterfeit goods, as examples ranging from falsely branded pesticides in Kenya to the sale of poisoned meat in China attest. Consumers usually suffer the most when laws protecting trademarks and brand names are not vigorously enforced.

There is a trend toward addressing intellectual property issues one by one, helping to identify areas of agreement and find common ground on points of difference.

Source: (OECD, 2015a).

Strong legislative and political efforts have been made in the past 20 years to meet the standards required under Egypt's international commitments, but the domestic IP regime still lags behind and the enforcement of IP legislation continues to be perceived by the private sector as inefficient. IP rights are enforced in Egypt through a wide array of administrative and judicial institutions. Despite the creation, by virtue of the 2014 Constitution, of the high-level IP body, the institutions remain poorly equipped to enforce the protection of IP rights. Further political impetus and greater financial resources are needed to streamline the administration of IP rights and to meet the international standards that Egypt has committed to implement. The body created by the Constitution could hence play a greater coordination role to orchestrate the various responsibilities and powers scattered across public bodies and ministries.

Within the judiciary, the economic courts are specialised in disputes related to intellectual property, and judges are regularly trained on IP law enforcement. Parties have the obligation to seek amicable settlement first, by filing their case with the Economic Courts Preparation Panel. Meanwhile, arbitration remains available as a way to settle an IP dispute, in the event the concerned parties have mutually agreed to recourse to alternative dispute resolution mechanisms. Yet, the management and settlement of IP cases by Economic Courts is reported to remain too lengthy.

Access to dispute settlement and prevention

The national justice system has a fundamental role to play in reinforcing competitiveness and robust economic growth in Egypt. Its efficient functioning is key for setting the conditions for a healthy and competitive business climate. The judiciary is endowed with specialised economic and commercial courts, respectively in charge of economic and commercial disputes relating to the state economic activity, and of commercial disputes which do not involve public authorities.

In parallel to its courts system, Egypt has increasingly made available alternative dispute resolution mechanisms for resolving commercial and investment disputes. When investors perceive a lack of independence and efficiency of the court system, they tend to favour alternative dispute resolution means to settle their business disputes This is especially true in Egypt, where the reputation as a stable jurisdiction has been by the political turmoil of the past years. Along with international investment arbitration, which is provided through international investment treaty provisions (see section below), commercial arbitration has thus become the most common way of resolving business disputes before private arbitration centres, such as the Cairo Regional Centre for International Commercial Arbitration.

Despite the major role played by private institutions in steering and managing business cases, the government has remained very proactive in institutionalising mediation mechanisms to avoid having claims escalate into international arbitration proceedings, both among private parties and against public authorities. The 2015 amendment established three different committees: the Grievances Committee, the Ministerial Committee for Resolving Investment Disputes, and the Ministerial Committee for the Settlement of Investment Contracts Disputes (Box 3.2). Each committee has a different membership and is regulated by a set of specific regulatory provisions.

The 2017 Investment Law brought further clarification and emphasis on the importance of investors' access to alternative dispute resolution mechanisms. The overall purpose of the new institutional infrastructure is to endow the government with more robust dispute avoidance, prevention and management mechanisms, and the inter-ministerial committees were established as part of a broader effort to optimise the defence of the state in the event of international investment disputes, which represent a growing challenge for the government of Egypt. GAFI is particularly aware of the importance of preventing disputes at an early stage and is recognised by the business community for its very active role in mediating at an early stage emerging disputes. GAFI has made strong efforts to establish a formal dispute prevention and early alerts mechanism to forestall potentially very costly international arbitration proceedings that may stem from investor-state disputes.

The respective roles, functioning and affiliation of each body mentioned above could however be further clarified, and it is not always clear whether the authorities themselves have a clear view on the allocation of responsibilities and of the lines of accountability. For example, it is not clear, under the new 2017 law, whether the MCRID is affiliated to the Cabinet or GAFI, while the previous legislation expressly provided that the MCRID be established under the auspices of the Cabinet. Likewise, the legal community has expressed concerns over the lack of clarity regarding the right to submit an investment contract dispute to the MCSICD. The regulatory provisions are not explicit as to whether such recourse is exclusively afforded to the investor or to the disputing governmental bodies as well. In the event of failure of settlement negotiations, there is no clear provision stating that the investor can then submit the dispute to the MCRID prior to resorting to arbitration or litigation.

Box 3.2. Egypt's new institutional framework for the prevention of investment disputes

The 2017 Investment Law created new mechanisms dedicated to dispute resolution, giving investors more options when facing a dispute, without prejudice to the inalienable right of the investor to recourse to the judiciary. Dedicated inter-ministerial bodies were created, as follows:

1. Grievance Committee (Article 83 of the Investment Law):

The Grievance Committee's role is to look into the grievances against administrative resolutions passed by GAFI or other administrative bodies having competence to grant approvals, permits and licences. This committee is chaired by a justice of an authority from among the judiciary. The committee must decide on the grievance within 30 days. In addition, the committee's resolution is final and binding on all bodies, without prejudice to the investor's right to appeal against the committee's resolution before the Judiciary.

2. Ministerial Committee for Investment Disputes Resolution (MCIDR) (Article 85 of the Law):

MCIDR is competent to look into the claims or disputes arising between investors and the state, or any body, authority or company affiliated to the state and relating to a wide range of administrative issues including licensing and land allocation. The Investment Law states that MCIDR resolutions are, upon the approval by the Council of Ministers, enforceable and binding on the appropriate administrative bodies and have the same effect as the writ of execution.

3. Ministerial Committee for Investment Contracts Disputes Settlement (MCICDS) (Article 88 of the Law):

Chaired by the prime minister, the MCICDS is competent to settle any disputes arising out of the investment contracts to which the state, or any body, authority, or company affiliated to the state is a party. It investigates and handles any disagreements arising among the parties to investment contracts. In order to do so and with the consent of such contracting parties, MCICDS may reach any required settlement to redress imbalances in such contracts and to extend the time limits, terms or grace periods stated in the contracts. The Law states that the settlement is, upon the approval by the Council of Ministers, enforceable and binding on all the bodies, and has the same effect as the writ of execution.

4. GAFI Dispute Settlement Centre (Article 90 of the Law):

Along with the ministerial dispute committees, the Investment Law establishes a Mediation Centre, under the auspices of GAFI, to settle investment disputes which might arise among investors. The Mediation Centre is governed by a board of directors, composed of five members appointed by Prime Ministerial Decree. Since its creation, the centre has dealt with more than 200 claims, out of which about 60% were amicably settled. GAFI Dispute Settlement Centre is also competent to deal with investors' grievances filed against any state entity.

Source: Zulficar and Partners (2018), GAFI

Concerns were also raised about potential overlaps between MCRID and the Grievances Committee. For example, an investor could, by virtue of Art. 83 of the Investment Law, submit to the Grievances Committee a dispute that arises as a result of GAFI's violation of provisions of the Law. Alternatively, the same investor could also, by virtue of Art. 85 of the same legislation, submit the same dispute arising out of GAFI's violation of provisions of the new Investment Law to the MCRID. It is essential to quickly address such overlaps and to clarify whether it is an intentional choice to give investors the right to choose between the two recourse options. If so, it is then important, for legal predictability purposes, to clarify if the investor has to opt for one recourse, or whether he can proceed with the two recourses simultaneously or subsequently, and which decision should prevail.

The strong momentum for favouring dispute prevention mechanisms offers a welcome alternative to both the judicial courts, which are less specialised in business matters and suffer from lengthy delays in settling pending cases, and private arbitration centres, which are too costly for small investors. Yet, the newly established institutional infrastructure poses many unanswered questions and has yet to prove itself as an efficient mechanism to prevent disputes and reassure investors about the ability of public authorities to act neutrally when preventing and settling business disputes.

Land access and tenure rights

Land access and security are an investment constraint in many countries. In Egypt, the complexity of the land administration system and shortage of land appropriate for investment present challenges for new investors. The ability to acquire and secure rights to land and property are important prerequisites for prospective investors. Investors need to be confident that their land rights are properly recognised and that they are protected against forced evictions without compensation. Land registers can enhance tenure security. When comprehensive and properly maintained and publicised, registers can limit the time to acquire land tenure rights, reduce corruption, and facilitate tax collection. In order to provide land tenure rights, the land administration should be accessible, reliable and transparent (OECD, 2015[1]).

The Egyptian government has in the past decade significantly improved procedures to access and register land for industrial purposes. Reforms since 2015 have helped enable the state to allocate around 1.8 times more land to investors than it distributed over the previous eight years (IMF, 2017[2]). Management of investor requests for land is now centralised under one agency, GAFI, and a new digital Investment Map helps improve transparency of public land ownership. The Investment Map includes information on projects of all sizes, indicating how close the projects are to key facilities (transport links, schools and hospitals) and provides a platform where investors and government officials can connect. Furthermore, the map indicates the location of ongoing development projects enabling investors to plan ahead for investment projects. Despite land allocation being decentralised, a central land allocation system has been put in place, which allows for the reservation of land electronically through the system (Investment Map Portal1). In addition, a cabinet decree issued in October 2019 states that allocation of industrial land can only be done through the online Investment Map Portal. The Investment Map is considered a very important step towards unifying the processes for land allocation even if the ownership is decentralised (see chapters 4 and 5).

As a result of these various efforts, the number of firms reporting access to land as a major or severe constraint has nearly halved since 2007 to 15% (WB Enterprise Survey, 2016). Very few firms list land access as the biggest obstacle to the business environment in Egypt. But according to government officials, access to land is one of the top hurdles for new investors. Unaddressed, issues related to land availability and tenure affect the stability and developmental impact of FDI.

Land-related challenges in Egypt stem from a number of factors. These include the country's geography and overly complex legal and institutional frameworks (dozens of laws govern land ownership and registration), which has made land registration difficult (World Bank, 2015[3]). But many of the issues related to land tenure in Egypt involve the management and distribution of public land. The government controls up to 95% of Egyptian territory, much of it desert. Ownership is fragmented: 11 ministries, at least 13 different government agencies and 27 governorates hold territory along a mix of sectoral and geographic lines (World Bank, 2006[4]). Despite progress towards streamlining information on ownership to investors, land administration remains highly complex. The quality of land administration is among the lowest in the region (9 out of 30 compared to 14.2 for MENA), according to the World Bank's 2019 Doing Business

Report (World Bank, 2019[5]).[2] This makes it difficult for investors to determine ownership and purchase land at market value and hinders the government's ability to distribute land efficiently.

There have been a number of improvements with regards to dealing with land registration and access. The 2017 Investment Law clarifies the land acquisition procedures. As with investors competing to acquire real property required to set up investment projects, investors who meet the technical and financial conditions required for investment shall be selected according to a point system and based on preference principles including the value of the bid offered by the investor or other technical or financial specifications. If this proves difficult, then the highest bid is accepted. According to article 54 in the executive regulation, governmental entities shall provide a decision within a week. In addition, GAFI works in coordination with other governmental entities to further facilitate investors' access to lands.

Main policy recommendations

Improve coordination among government landholders and strengthen centralisation of land requests

The complex landscape of public land ownership, and myriad approvals required to allocate land to investors, means that there remains a substantial gap between land demand and supply in Egypt. The centralisation of investor requests for land under GAFI is an important improvement that appears to have enabled faster distribution of state-owned land to firms. But the government could consider taking even further steps to centralise the allocation of land to investors, such as empowering one agency to allocate all publicly-owned land, regardless of its sectoral use. More immediately, coordination between the many different government landowners should be significantly strengthened. GAFI's success in directing investors to the appropriate government landowner will depend on close inter-agency cooperation. There are reports that agencies have been slow to share their available land plots with GAFI, despite their legal obligation to do so.

Increase transparency of public land ownership

Short of a complete inventory and mapping of public land ownership, coordination challenges between agencies allocating public land are likely to persist. A complete registry would assist both GAFI in facilitating investment and firms in their location decisions. The Investment Map is a good step in this direction. Agencies could make public more comprehensive maps of land within their control, rather than only a selection of land available in zones, as is shown on the Investment Map.

Adopt more transparent processes for pricing and allocation of public land

There is no overarching authority on land allocation, pricing and development which has allowed different government agencies to pursue their own ad hoc policies. The Investment Law specifies some requirements for the valuation process, but all landholders could be more transparent about how they determine land use, select investors, and determine land pricing. This would help reduce the potential for speculation and corruption in public land sales. The government could consider naming an independent auditor to evaluate pricing set by different agencies.

Improve tenure security by streamlining registration procedures

The government should continue its efforts to ease the number of procedures and cost to register property. This includes addressing challenges of registering informal residents. Notably, reforms could ease requirements of complete records of past ownership. The Egyptian Survey Authority should be strengthened to fulfil its mission to develop and maintain an up-to-date land registry.

Box 3.3. Legal framework for land tenure in Egypt

No one overarching law on public land management or use exists. Laws related to land tenure set out different procedures for registration, requirements for land use, and terms for ownership/lease depending on the location and owner of the land, making for a complex legislative framework.

Property law in Egypt falls under the Civil Code (adopted in 1949) and a series of subsequent laws on land rights, foreign ownership and management of public land. The legal framework allows for private ownership, public ownership, cooperative/collective ownership, lease, waqf land (reserved for religious or charitable purposes), and some forms of encroachment (FAO, 2009[6]). The Civil Code grants ownership after 15 years of unchallenged possession or use of land, but this does not apply to state-owned land. All unregistered land is technically public land. There are restrictions on the sale/lease of public land (discussed below), notably for any land deemed of military or strategic importance, including the Sinai.

Foreigners are restricted from owning certain types of land. These are set out in three laws: No. 15 of 1963, No. 143 of 1981, and No. 230 of 1996. Law 15 (1963) stipulates that foreigners (natural or legal) are prohibited from owning agricultural lands, as well as areas "susceptible of cultivation, fallow lands and desert lands" (United Arab Republic, 1963[7]). Law 143 (1981), also known as the Desert Land Law, places limits on the ownership of desert land, which the Law defines broadly as all territory two kilometres outside city borders (GAFI, 2017[8]). Partnerships and joint stock companies can own desert land up to 42 km2 (10 000 feddans) and 210 km2 (50 000 feddans) respectively, if Egyptian nationals own at least 51% of the capital. A 1998 amendment (Law 55) allows the government to treat Arab nationals as Egyptians for ownership purposes.

Law 230 (1996) sets out further conditions for foreign ownership. With some specific exceptions, non-Egyptians are limited to two real estate properties for accommodation, the area of which cannot exceed 4 000 square metres and must not be a historical site. It is not clear what classifies as a historical site. The Cabinet of Ministers set specific requirements for ownership in tourist areas. Foreign owners are prohibited from selling land for five years from the property registration date, and holders of vacant land must build within five years (GAFI, 2017[8]).

Complex public land administration delays allocation of land to investors

Companies and government officials cite timely access to land as a key barrier to new investment in Egypt. The greatest challenge, according to GAFI, is that the lack of available land suitable to investors' needs, including with appropriate infrastructure and access to markets and workers. This is partly a geographical challenge: cities are overcrowded and the vast majority of Egyptian territory is desert, often not well connected to hubs and under-developed. But the gap between land supply and demand is largely due to Egypt's complex and fractured system of public land administration which has caused uncertainty over ownership and delays in allocating land to investors.

Around 90-95% of Egyptian territory is state owned. More than 40 laws and executive orders stipulate which government entities control what land, whether the land can be disposed of, and who has a say in determining land use (Sims, 2015[9]) (World Bank, 2006[4]). A minority of public land is reserved for security or other state purposes. The remaining territory either has a governing authority, which in many cases can allocate land to investors, or does not yet have a designated use and no specific controlling entity.

Control of designated public land is complex: 11 ministries, at least 13 government entities and 27 governorates hold land along a mix of sectoral and geographic lines. Figure 3.1 depicts the main agencies involved in state land management. By law (143 of 1981 and 7 of 1991), Governorates manage public land located inside historical urban limits (known as the zimam), and in most cases, within 2km of this boundary. Less than 5% Egyptian territory falls within the zimam; the rest is by law "desert land". Outside the zimam, control of designated desert public land is divided among ministries and agencies based on sector and land-use.

Figure 3.1. Institutional framework of state land management

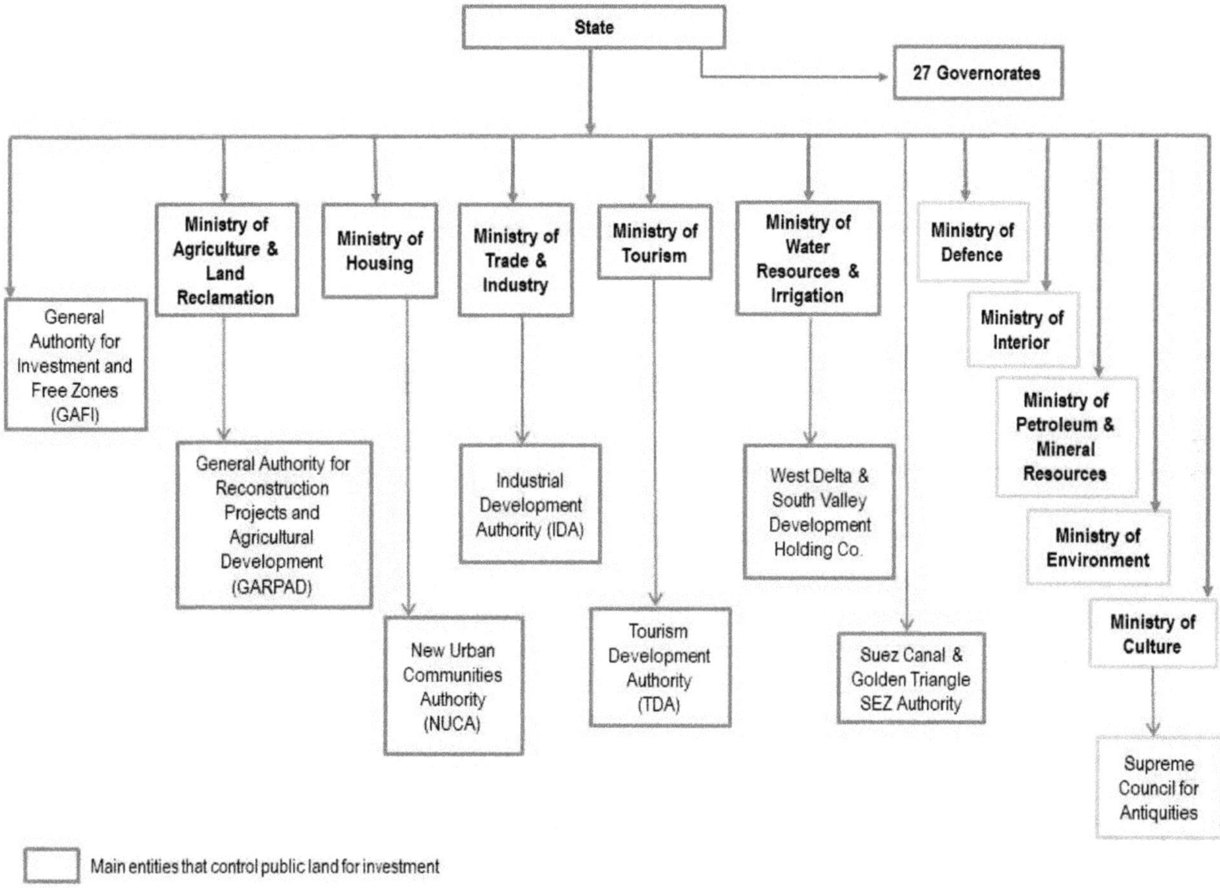

Note: Only entities with a major stake in land management presented. Entities in blue are the main holders of public land distributed to investors.
Source: Reproduced and adapted from (World Bank, 2006[4]).

A mix of laws and de facto practice grants certain agencies priority in claiming/requesting control over undesignated desert land and determining its use. Law 143 of 1981 (Desert Land Law) gives the Ministry of Defence first right to claim any territory for military or strategic purposes. The Ministry of Agriculture and Land Reclamation has second rights to name undesignated territory for agricultural development, in coordination with the Ministry of Defence. The Ministry of Housing, Utilities and Urban Development can identify land for new urban areas, subordinate to the claims of the defence and agriculture ministries, while the Tourism Development Authority can demarcate territory for tourism projects (Law 7 of 1991).

In practice, however, other ministries and agencies delimit lands based on their historical value, extractive potential, conservation needs, and potential for industrial use (Sims, 2015[9]) (World Bank, 2006[4]). The hierarchy of these claims is not codified in law, leading to competition between agencies. The National Centre for Planning of State Land Use has the mandate to coordinate between agencies and set coherent plans for land use, but in practice, there is no overarching authority on land allocation and development. In most cases, agencies only gain control over a specific plot of land through an executive decree (of which there are hundreds), and the decision-making process of determining land use is often opaque.

Four government agencies, two SEZ authorities and two holding companies manage most of the desert public land designated for development. Together, they control around 10% of Egypt's total territory. Table 1 shows the estimated amount of land managed by each entity, though the dearth of publicly available reports on state land ownership means that many of these figures are out of date. The data nonetheless suggest that the vast majority of designated state desert land is earmarked for agriculture, followed by industrial projects and new town development. Other agencies, including GAFI, manage a smaller amount of land through their oversight of free and investment zones. Once allocated state land, investors are prohibited from changing the original designated land use (2017 Investment Law).

Table 3.1. Main agencies controlling public land for development

Entity	Authority/Ministry	Estimated land controlled, in km2 (year)
General Authority for Reconstruction Projects and Agricultural Development (GARPAD)	Ministry of Agriculture and Land Reclamation	71 400 (2010)
Suez Canal & Golden Triangle SEZ Authorities	Prime Minister	9 761 (2018)*
Industrial Development Authority (IDA)	Ministry of Trade and Industry	7 938 (2018)*
New Urban Communities Authority (NUCA)	Ministry of Housing	3 574 (2010)
West Delta & South Valley Development Holding Company	Ministry of Water Resources and Irrigation	2 730 (2006)
Tourism Development Authority (TDA)	Ministry of Tourism	575 (2006)

* Estimates for 2018 reflect data GAFI made available that year.
Source: GAFI, (Sims, 2015[9]), (World Bank, 2006[4]).

Although there have been efforts to increase transparency of land available to investors (discussed below), there is no cadastre or complete map of which government entities control what territory. There is only one modern map with a rough estimate of agencies' control, published by the government in 2001, and at the limiting scale of 1:1 000 000. Despite the adoption of decrees detailing land boundaries, some governorates lack knowledge about new settings of lands, and there are reports that agencies have conflicting understandings of the land they manage (Sims, 2015[9]). Notably, some governorates ignore the out-of-date zimam boundary, exerting de facto control over surrounding desert land. Governorates have the legal right to manage public land 2km outside the zimam, but only if no sectoral agency has claimed the area for their use. This means that in many cases neither investors nor the government has a clear picture of which entity owns what plot of land, particularly in areas bordering urban centres.

The entity controlling designated desert land in most cases has the authority to allocate parcels to investors. But this often requires approvals from other government bodies, such as the MoD or local branches of other ministries, a process that can take months (World Bank, 2006[4]). As a result, large portions of designated public land remain unavailable to investors. The government is well aware of these challenges, and as the next section outlines, is taking some measures to centralise land allocation.

Reforms seek to ease land access for investors, primarily in zones

The government has made significant improvements in the past decade, and notably in the past two years, in easing the process of acquiring land for investors. Management of investor requests for land is now centralised under GAFI. The 2017 Investment Law gave the agency and its Investor Service Centres (ISCs) the mandate to direct investors interested in a specific area to the appropriate controlling authority. A new digital Investment Map lists parcels of land available for investment by location and sector, detailing the governing authority of each free plot and their contact information. (The Law stipulates that all agencies must provide GAFI with detailed maps of land in their jurisdiction open to investors). The Investment Map centralises procedures for obtaining lands across the country, which is expected to greatly improve the access to land. It also streamlines the process of identifying available land parcels, which previously required a lengthy coordination with different agencies and governorates. The government has other plans to improve distribution to investors, including allowing governorates to update the Investment Map directly.

Due in part to these reforms, in 2016 and 2017 the government allocated 16.9 million m^2 of industrial land, nearly 1.8 times the amount distributed over the previous eight years (IMF, 2017[2]).Fewer firms now report problems with land access: around 15% of firms considered access to land as a major or severe constraint to their operations in 2016, compared to nearly 27% in 2007 (World Bank, 2009[10]). The most recent data show no substantial difference in opinion between foreign and domestic firms (World Bank, 2016[11]).

While GAFI and the ISCs serve as the link between investors and landowners, GAFI does not allocate land used for industrial purposes: this remains the purview of the Industrial Development Authority (IDA). In ensuring transparency of IDA's land distribution processes and simplifying the institutional framework of public land management, the government is considering establishing a committee to review processes and set standards for industrial land allocation (Government of Egypt, 2018[12]). The government has made a similar proposal to the IMF.

The Investment Map is a positive step towards transparency of public land ownership, but it primarily shows plots of land available in economic, industrial or other types of zones, reflecting the government's strategy of zone development. Zones have also not solved issues with land access. Surveys suggest that availability of land is actually a greater obstacle for firms located in industrial zones than those outside (22% of firms in IZs reported land access as a major or severe challenge to their operations, compared to 11% of firms outside zones) (World Bank, 2016[11]). This could be due to differences in firm size; most firms in industrial zones are larger and require more land. There is also limited space in zones in areas highly sought out by investors. Incentives to investors, including cheap or free land in zones, has raised competition over land parcels (and the responsibility of zone authorities to allocate land to businesses efficiently). According to GAFI, there is not enough available land for new investments or for the expansion of existing businesses in public free zones, a point which was confirmed in discussions with firms located in the coveted public free zones of Alexandria.

Improvements to land registration but tenure security not widespread

As with land access, the government has made clear progress in easing property registration processes for investors. Compared to a decade ago, the registration process now takes less than half the time and, at 1.1% of the property value, is roughly 1/6th of the cost (Wang, 2017[13]) (OECD, 2007[14]) (World Bank, 2019[5]). Around 95% of agricultural land is now registered, but property registration remains time-consuming and can be arduous in practice. It requires nine procedures (two more than a decade ago), and takes an average of 76 days, more than double the average amount of time in the MENA region. This is despite many previous reform efforts, including in 2006 to establish a one-stop-shop for property registration, which aimed to reduce the time to one week (OECD, 2007[14]). Egypt ranks 130 of 190 economies in terms of ease of registering property in the World Bank's Doing Business index, lower than most other countries in the region (with the exception of Algeria, Libya and Syria) (World Bank, 2019[5]). Box 3.4 lists the current procedures required to register property for firms under the inland (standard) investment regime in Cairo.

The vast majority of land and private property in Egypt is not registered. The last cadastral survey dates to 1940, and there is no cadastral map with full details on government land ownership (Sims, 2010[15]). The Egyptian Survey Authority, the body responsible for conducting cadastral mapping, lacks technical capacity and has few digital records (Chemonics International, 2005[16]). Only around 10% of urban land is registered (compared to 90% of agricultural land) (Wang, 2017[13]). The disparity is due to a fragmented legal framework for property registration. In agricultural areas, the government has worked to transfer land registered under a deed system (set up in the 1946 Deed Law, No. 114) to a title registration system, notably through a push in 2006 to automate title registration. Urban areas still use the deed system, largely due to a gap in the 1964 Title Law (No. 142), which does not permit the registration of apartment units (Wang, 2017[13]) (World Bank, 2006[4]).

Box 3.4. Property registration procedures in Egypt

Firms under the inland regime, operating in Cairo:

Registering purchased property in most cases involves nine steps. However, these steps are relevant only if the property the buyer is purchasing is already registered and has no title disputes. Only around 10-15% of all private property is registered (Sims, 2015[9]).

Parties procure an official property tax statement from the local Property Tax Authority Office, which proves the property is registered at the Authority, has had a tax assessment, and has no mortgages. This costs EGP 2.25.

Parties get certificate from District Land Registry with details on the property ownership and encumbrances. This costs EGP 30.

Buyer submits a request to register the property with Real Estate Registry, for a maximum fee of EGP 2 000 (for property larger than 300 m2).

Egyptian Surveying Authority (ESA) conducts site inspection and a produces a report, a process that can take a month.*

Both the Measurement Department and the Real Estate Registry must approve the ESA's report, which may take 21 days. The Registry then accepts the registration request (step 2) and gives the parties a stamped contract form.

Lawyers representing the parties send the completed contract to the Lawyers Syndicate, which verifies the lawyers' syndicate identification and registration. In 2018 this cost 1% of the property value (up to EGP 25 000), a 0.5% increase from 2017.

Parties submit the contract to the Real Estate Registry for review and approval, which can take 10 days.

Parties stand before Notary Public, which oversees signing of contract and authenticates it.

Buyer gives notarised contract to Real Estate Registry for review, if approved the Registry gives a registration number, confirming the property registration. This may take 10 days.

Note: *The step has no cost if amount not specified.
Source: (World Bank, 2019[5]); 2017 Investment Law, (Egypt.gov website)

Issues with tracing ownership have been a key impediment to registering land. Unlike title registrations, which prove legal ownership of a plot of land, a deed system is a public record of a transaction between two parties. The deed registration process in Egypt is time consuming, costly and reportedly fraught with forgeries and petty corruption, as land ownership and transactions records (required for registration) are incomplete (USAID, 2010[17]) (Sims, 2010[15]). In urban areas, the low percentage of registered land under the deed system is also due to the prevalence of informal settlements; estimates suggest that more than half of Cairo's residents live in informal housing (Sims, 2015[9]). Many property transactions rely on informal procedures and contracts (Sims, 2010[15]).

The low registration rate negatively affects tenure security, as unregistered land is technically state property. Reliable land titling and property registrars help landholders to seek legal redress in case of violation of property rights. For businesses, better land rights and registries facilitate investment decisions. Transparent, complete and secure land registration is also associated with greater access to credit, as land titles offer a form of collateral. As the majority of property in Egypt is not registered, it is often difficult to prove ownership, complicating and significantly lengthening the process of taking out a mortgage (EBRD, 2012[18]). (The 2001 Real Estate Finance Law sets out details of issuing mortgages). In 2015, the government passed a Movable Securities Law (No.115) allowing the use of other types of assets as collateral, including equipment, crops, current and future receivables and intellectual property rights, which helps facilitate loans to SMEs for example.

Reforms to land registration

The 2017 Investment Law eases some procedures required for property registration. Companies under the law are exempt from taxes and fees involved with land registration (Article 10). New Investor Service Centres (ISCs) have the mandate to receive investor applications and issue approvals, permits and licences (Article 21). For investors, the process of land registration is simplified in industrial zones and other zone types. Investors receive their property licences from zone authorities and/or GAFI. In public free zones and special economic zones, land is licensed to investors under a usufruct system (Article 37). Real-estate property in other zones may be purchased, leased, leased-to-own, or licensed for usufruct (Article 58). The law stipulates that for some sales and lease-to-own transactions, property titles are transferred to the investor after the investor pays in full and begins production, or in some cases, completes the project (Article 62).

The government is also taking steps to improve the land registration procedures. There are reports in the Egyptian press that parliament is considering a new real estate registration law, which will reduce the cost and steps involved in property registration. These efforts are a step towards improving tenure security. But to be successful, the government should evaluate lessons from the many previous efforts to broaden participation in land registers, including schemes to sell titles to informal residents (Sims, 2016[19]). Notably, reforms should address the continued high cost of registration and ease requirements of complete records of past ownership. The Egyptian Survey Authority, responsible for cadastral mapping, should be strengthened to be able to carry out its mission of developing a comprehensive and up-to-date land registry.

Gaps in transparency of state role in land market

The Egyptian state, as the largest landholder in the country, dominates the land market. Its role as both owner and price setter has led to public controversies over corruption and nepotism in land sales (Sims, 2015[9]). A lack of transparency on how land is valued and how buyers are selected has contributed to an uneven playing field for investors and lost revenue for the government, as well as land speculation. One fifth of firms see the price of land as a substantial barrier to investment (World Bank, 2016[11]). Details in the investment law on procedures for valuing land is a step towards standardising the evaluation process. The government could, however, further increase transparency of its land pricing, and in particular, weigh the benefits of selling or renting land to investors at reduced cost.

The Investment Law states that one of five different entities estimates the sale, rent or usufruct price for land based the purpose of the allocated land.[3] These are: the General Authority for Government Services, Supreme Committee for Pricing of State-Owned Lands at the Ministry of Agriculture, New Urban Communities Authority, Tourism Development Authority, and the Industrial Development Authority (Article 64). The entity should include "experienced representatives as members in the estimation committees" and finalise estimations within 30 days of requests. The executive regulations of the Law detail that the estimation will involve examining the prices of adjacent property, costs of preparing the property (with infrastructure and utilities), the investment activities, and other relevant technical elements (Article 52). This evaluation is in most cases valid for one year.

A risk is that government agencies involved in evaluating land value are not neutral. The law states that the authority with jurisdiction over the land pays a fee to the entity that estimates the price (Article 64 of the Law and 53 of the Executive Regulations). But several of the entities in charge of estimating prices also control land: IDA, the New Urban Communities Authority and the Tourism Development Authority are among the largest holders of land earmarked for development in Egypt (Table 1). IDA has the authority to allocate land to investors. The Llw does not seem to prevent these authorities from setting their own land prices.

There is further potential for conflicts of interest. The law permits authorities overseeing land to have a stake in investment projects under their jurisdiction, via either in-kind shares or a partnership (Article 58). This requires approval from the Cabinet of Ministers. One of the five aforementioned government agencies estimates share prices. Once again, it appears that in some cases an agency can benefit from setting its own land sale/rent/usufruct prices and share prices. Elsewhere the Law states that in the case of publicly owned land, either GAFI or the administrative authority will "indicate" the price of the land (Article 59). It is not clear if this means that the authority overseeing the land has a final say in the value estimation.

In practice, public land is often dispersed at below-market rates as an investment incentive. The Investment law also permits the free disposal of state-owned property (primarily in zones) to investors, if the investment is for "the sole purposes of development", and with approval through decree from the Cabinet of Ministers (Article 60). In this case, the investor must provide a cash guarantee of up to 5% of the value of the investment costs – one of the key incentives of the law. Firm-level evidence reveals that "access to land at a reduced or no cost" is the most important reason behind manufacturing firms' choice to locate in an industrial zone (World Bank, 2016[11]). This incentive is not without distortive risks; cheaper land has created a shortage of land in zones, as discussed earlier.

The pricing of public land also tends not to be transparent. Several highly publicised court cases have involved the sale of land at what was perceived to be below-market value. There have been instances of purchasers of public land re-selling at up to 100 times the original price (Sims, 2015[9]). The government has put in place regulations to discourage land speculation, and the High Price Appeals Committee should act as a regulatory body. But the lack of transparency on land pricing, and on the selection of buyers, means that the potential for speculation and corruption in public land sales persists.

The government has recognised that selling industrial land at nominal, pre-determined prices is "not optimal for the future allocation of land, as it forgoes revenue for the state and creates opportunities for rent seeking" (from the government's Memorandum of Economic and Financial Policies) (IMF, 2018[20]). In 2018, it proposed to create a working group, under the prime minister, tasked with reforming how industrial land is priced and allocated. The reforms will include reducing restrictions on land use and "market-based land allocation mechanisms that ensure open, transparent and competitive bidding process" (IMF, 2018[20]). The government also intends to digitalise the industrial land tender process, allowing investors to bid and submit documents online. These reforms, if implemented, will be a positive step, but the effect will be limited if the reforms are only applied to industrial land and not to land held by other sectoral agencies.

Investment treaties

Investment treaties (also referred to as international investment agreements or IIAs) are another component of Egypt's investment policy framework. Investment treaties entered into between two or more states typically protect certain investments made by nationals of a contracting state in the territory of another contracting state. Investment treaties include both bilateral investment treaties (BITs) and investment chapters in trade agreements. This section addresses treaty-based protection for covered investors. Increasingly, investment treaties also address market access for foreign investment (addressed separately below).

Protections afforded under investment treaties generally arise in addition to and independently from domestic law protections. Treaty-based protections generally only cover investors defined as foreign. Treaties also define types of investments and investors that are covered, frequently in broad terms.

The majority of Egypt's investment treaties grant covered investors two different types of rights:

Substantive rights to standards of treatment for covered investments (such as protections against expropriation or discrimination, or against unfair treatment); and

Procedural rights to enforce government obligations in the treaty, often through investor-state dispute settlement (ISDS) mechanisms. These generally permit covered investors to bring claims against the host state for breach of the treaty before arbitral tribunals.

One of the main reasons motivating certain countries to conclude investment treaties has been to seek to attract foreign investment, and yet the assumption that investment treaties would encourage foreign investment has been difficult to establish as a factual matter despite a multitude of studies.[4]

Most of Egypt's investment treaties contain features common to so-called first generation treaties. Concluded in the 1980s and 1990s, these include vague substantive provisions that have been broadly interpreted in ISDS cases and provide little procedural guidance for ISDS. Recent treaties concluded by other states have rejected this approach in favour of more precise definitions of the scope of government obligations and increased regulation of ISDS. These changes often reflect government efforts to improve the balance between covered investor protection and the right to regulate.[5]

Many governments have been substantially revising their investment treaty policy in recent years.

The European Union's (EU) rejection of investor-state arbitration has transformed EU policy – and it continues to evolve under increasing public and academic questioning, and growing constraints imposed by EU law.

Long-standing supporters of investment treaties like the United States have recently expressed fundamental doubts about treaty-based investor protection and have exited or sharply narrowed the substantive provisions and scope of ISDS, notably in the United States-Mexico-Canada Agreement (USMCA) signed in November 2018 with Canada and Mexico.

Chinese investment treaty policy is still in flux, with pressures to strengthen covered investor protection in the context of growing outward investment accompanied by concerns about the reputation of Chinese business abroad and the possible exposure to claims which have remained minor to date.

The Comprehensive and Progressive Agreement for Trans-Pacific Partnership (CPTPP) reflects the expansion of an updated North America Free Trade Agreement (NAFTA)-inspired investment treaty model to a broader range of 11 economies including relations between advanced economies, notwithstanding US rejection of the treaty.

States in Southeast Asia have taken steps towards an ASEAN-driven landscape for regional investment policy, with a strong focus on intra-region liberalisation and protection through both domestic laws and international treaties including the ASEAN Comprehensive Investment Agreement and a host of ASEAN-led investment agreements with third states such Hong Kong (China) (2017), India (2014) and China (2009).

Major G20 capital importers like India, Indonesia and South Africa have all rejected and exited first generation investment treaties with some exiting the system more broadly. Brazil has developed a new model for investment treaties focused on investment facilitation and using state-to-state dispute settlement without ISDS.

Multilateral reform of ISDS is now underway. Following inter-governmental debate, the UNCITRAL Commission entrusted its Working Group III in July 2017 with a broad mandate to work on possible reforms for ISDS. The sixty government members of UNCITRAL as well as many government observers – including Egypt – have found by consensus that reforms should be developed to address concerns raised with eleven different issues relating to ISDS.

GAFI announced in March 2016 that it was undertaking a new investment treaty reform programme based on two main objectives: updating Egypt's model BIT and reviewing and amending Egypt's existing investment treaties.[6] GAFI has confirmed that the process of updating Egypt's model BIT seeks to respond to domestic and international developments regarding investment policy, enhance the role of FDI in achieving sustainable development and establish a new balance between the rights and obligations of investors and the state These reform efforts will undoubtedly be informed by Egypt's considerable first-hand experience with ISDS cases: it is the fifth most frequent respondent state for known ISDS claims worldwide with at least 34 ISDS claims filed against Egypt.

This section outlines the current status of Egypt's investment treaties and the historical development of Egypt's policy towards investment treaties before identifying considerations that may assist Egypt in achieving its desired balance in investment treaty policy in the future.

Overview of Egypt's investment treaties

Egypt has a broad range of investment treaties. GAFI indicates that as of September 2019 Egypt has concluded 111 BITs, 72 of which are currently in force.[7] Egypt has BITs in force with all of the G7 states except the EU and all but three of the member states of the EU (Estonia, Ireland and Lithuania) as well as several other major capital-exporting states in the G20 group including Argentina, Australia, China, Korea, the Russian Federation and Turkey.

Egypt has a large number of signed investment treaties that are not in force. According to publicly-available information, Egypt had signed at least 101 BITs and, together with multilateral treaties, has concluded treaty relationships with at least 122 countries as of May 2019.[8] The reasons for non-ratification are not clear. GAFI indicates that non-ratification may be linked to assessments of Egypt's economic interests in respect of these treaties. In any case, many of these treaties are older treaties containing vague provisions now seen as outdated due to broad and varying interpretations in ISDS cases – few if any states are today ratifying treaties dating from this era. The analysis here generally addresses investment treaties in force except where otherwise indicated.

Egypt's investment treaties are primarily composed of a majority of first generation BITs. The majority of Egypt's BITs (77) were signed between 1990 and 2005.

In addition to concluding BITs, Egypt has several trade agreements in force that do not contain investment protections, including with Turkey in 2005 and the EFTA states (Iceland, Liechtenstein, Norway and Switzerland) in 2007. Egypt has signed Trade and Investment Framework Agreements (TIFA) with the United States (1998) and the European Union (2001). In June 2013 the EU and Egypt began talks about a Deep and Comprehensive Free Trade Agreement, which is planned to include an investment chapter, but negotiations are currently on hold.[9] Egypt has also signed the SADC-EAC-COMESA Tripartite Free Trade Agreement and the African Continental Free Trade Agreement in 2015 and 2018 respectively; negotiations regarding investment issues are yet to start under either of these two frameworks.

At the regional level, Egypt has signed plurilateral agreements with investment protections, most importantly the Unified Agreement for the Investment of Arab Capital in the Arab States (1980) (the Arab Investment Agreement) and the Agreement for Promotion, Protection and Guarantee of Investments among Member States of the Organisation of Islamic Cooperation (1981) (the OIC Agreement).[10] The remaining plurilateral agreements contain general investment promotion commitments or investment protection obligations without binding enforcement mechanisms.

The OIC Agreement and the Arab Investment Agreement provide for ISDS. Investor claimants have invoked the OIC Agreement in at least seven ISDS disputes since 2011[11] (none of which involve Egypt) despite uncertainties in the agreement's appointing authority mechanism.[12] OIC governments are currently discussing proposals to replace investor-state arbitration under that treaty.[13]

At a global level, Egypt has signed and ratified three important multilateral treaties related to enforcement of arbitral awards, including in ISDS cases under investment treaties – the New York Convention,[14] the Washington Convention[15] and the Riyadh Agreement.[16]

It is difficult to be precise about the status of Egypt's investment protection treaties due to insufficient and inconsistent publicly-available information. Comprehensive information on the existence of Egypt's investment treaties, along with any protocols, amendments, earlier versions of renegotiated treaties and in-force status, is not available. Egypt has made some of its investment treaties available on the official website of the Ministry of Foreign Affairs (MFA)[17] in multiple languages (e.g. Egypt's BITs with Uzbekistan and Viet Nam), but many of Egypt's treaties are not available on this website.[18] Some are accessible as part of the United Nations Treaty Collection and other foreign government or third-party websites.[19] Some of Egypt's investment treaties have been made available by the MFA in an Arabic-language version only, even though they are available elsewhere online in other languages.[20] Several Egyptian BITs that are not in force are available for download on the MFA website with no indication about their current status.[21] This includes the Egypt-Indonesia BIT which is understood to have been terminated recently by a unilateral notification from Indonesia.

From publicly-available information, Egypt appears to have treaty protection in force for almost all of its inward and outward FDI stock.[22] A detailed summary of FDI flows into and out of Egypt is provided in Chapter 1, but for current purposes it is notable that Egypt is the only country in the world to have 100% treaty coverage for its total inward FDI stock. Four BITs cover over 85% of Egypt's inward stock[23] while eight other investment treaties cover the remaining inward stock (Figure 3.2).[24]

Egypt's investment treaties cover almost 90% of its outward FDI stock, with five BITs responsible for the vast majority of this coverage.[25] Likely reflecting the use of corporate structuring, Egypt's recent BIT with Mauritius (2014) added treaty coverage to 20% of Egypt's outward FDI stock. Many investment treaties that Egypt has concluded cover none of Egypt's FDI stock or only negligible portions of it. This is a common phenomenon in many countries' treaty samples around the world.

Figure 3.2. Approximate evolution of Egypt's inward and outward FDI stock coverage from investment treaties in force

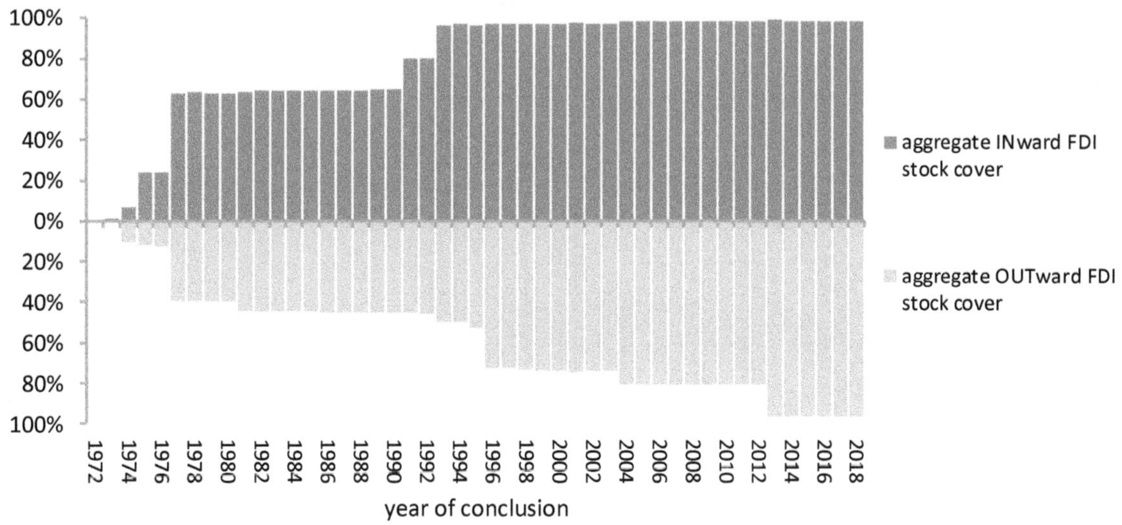

Source: OECD calculations based on OECD treaty database; FDI data was taken from OECD FDI database and IMF Direct Investment Positions and reflects FDI stock as of 2016 rather than historical values.

Egypt's evolving policies towards investment treaties

Based on available information, it appears that Egypt has investment treaties in force with a diverse set of economies: large and small, advanced and developing. In terms of geographical distribution, the majority of Egypt's BITs in force today are with partners in Europe and Asia/Oceania. Almost one third of the total BITs that Egypt has signed are with African states but very few of these treaties appear to be in force.

Aside from the early regional treaties within the League of Arab States and the Organisation for Islamic Cooperation, Egypt's first investment treaties in the 1970s and 1980s were concluded predominantly with capital-exporting countries like the United States, Japan and several European countries.

From 1990 until 2005, Egypt concluded treaties with countries from all corners of the globe, including with capital-importing partners that had smaller economies compared to Egypt at the time[26] (see Figure 3.3 below for a timeline of Egypt's concluded treaties). This development accompanied the Egyptian government's economic reform and structural adjustment programme introduced in 1991 with IMF and World Bank support.

Figure 3.3. Evolution of Egypt's investment treaty relations

Signed relationships shown with the dashed line; in-force relationships shown with the solid blue line.

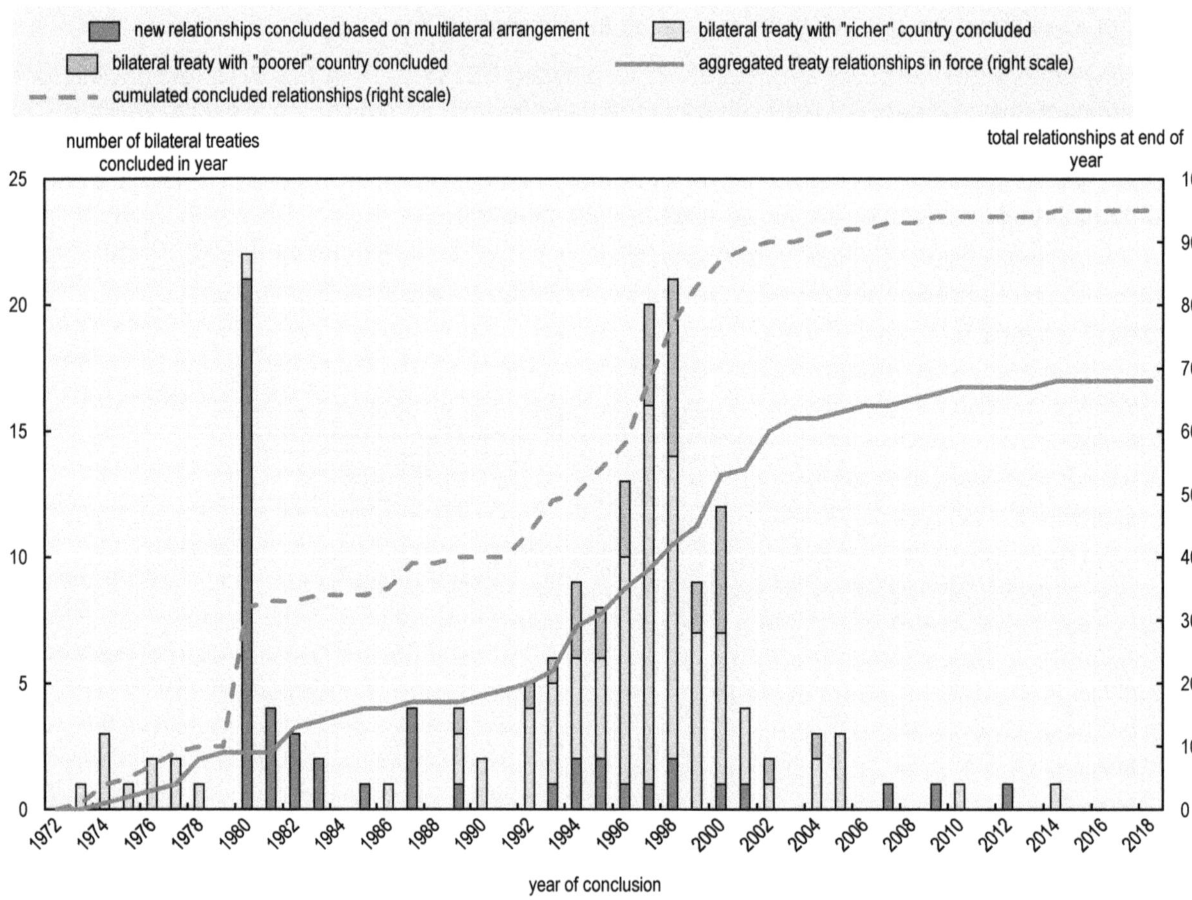

Source: OECD calculations based on OECD treaty database; World Bank data on GDP.

In 2002, GAFI was empowered under Presidential Decree No. 79/2002 to establish a one-stop shop for foreign investors in Egypt. GAFI conducted an internal review of Egypt's BITs in the early 2000s, which identified a lack of consistency in the content of Egyptian BITs and the absence of links between BIT content and Egypt's economic priorities.[27] This review process led to a reform programme for Egypt's investment treaties launched in 2005 and a model BIT adopted in 2007 with assistance from UNCTAD.[28] The main objectives of these reform efforts included achieving consistency within Egypt's BIT programme and restoring a sustainable balance between seeking to attract FDI and Egypt's right to regulate.[29] In 2006, Presidential Decree No. 266/2006 was issued to grant the Ministry of Investment the mandate for negotiating and concluding IIAs with other countries under this new approach.

Egypt has concluded five new investment treaties since 2005.[30] The slowing and recent reversal in the number of existing investment treaty relationships in force is a broad phenomenon reflecting the policies of many governments. As for other governments, this may reflect Egypt's experiences as a respondent in ISDS claims.[31] In Egypt's case, it may also reflect Egypt's development priorities in recent years following a period of political and social unrest that began in 2011. At the same time, as noted, Egypt already has broad treaty coverage for both inward and outward FDI stock leaving little need for any potential additional coverage.

Alongside its treaty-making activities in recent years, another notable development occurred in July 2007, when Egypt became the 40th country, as well as the first Arab and African nation, to adhere to the OECD's *Declaration on International Investment and Multinational Enterprises* (the OECD *Declaration*). The OECD *Declaration* is a policy commitment made by OECD countries and selected other states to improve the investment climate, encourage the positive contribution multinational enterprises can make to economic and social progress and minimise and resolve difficulties which may arise from their operations (see further discussion in Egypt's approach to responsible business conduct in Chapter 7).

Following a brief description of Egypt's experience with ISDS cases, the balance of this chapter seeks to offer insights and recommendations that may assist Egypt in this reform process.

Treaty use: ISDS claims under Egypt's investment treaties

Egypt and Egyptian nationals have a long history of practical experience with investment treaties as a basis for legal claims by investors. As of May 2019, 38 claims were known to have formally been brought against Egypt while four publicly-known claims have been brought by Egyptian investors under Egyptian investment treaties.

Egypt as a respondent in ISDS cases

Egypt is the fifth most frequent respondent state for known ISDS claims worldwide.[32] Based on publicly available information, investors have filed at least 38 ISDS claims against Egypt: 33 under the auspices of the ICSID Convention[33] and five with *ad hoc* arbitral tribunals constituted under the UNCITRAL Arbitration Rules.[34] Egypt has also been a respondent in four cases brought before the Arab Investment Court, an institution created under Article 28 of the Arab Investment Agreement (1980).

The first known ISDS cases brought by foreign investors against Egypt in the 1980s were not filed pursuant to investment treaties but rather an ICSID arbitration clause in Egypt's former investment law.[35] The first ICSID arbitration brought against Egypt under an investment treaty was filed in July 1998.[36] At least six of the treaty-based claims against Egypt since then have been filed by American investors under the United States-Egypt BIT (1986) while the rest have been filed by investors of various nationalities (predominantly from European countries) under at least 18 different BITs. Thirteen of the 35 treaty-based claims were filed from 2011 to 2013. While the level of public information regarding the most recent cases filed against Egypt is not uniform, it appears that several of them arise from events that occurred during a period of political and social unrest beginning in 2011.

Egypt's ISDS disputes have primarily concerned tourism, infrastructure, natural resources, textiles and manufacturing projects. Several of the recent ISDS cases filed against Egypt are linked to the introduction of new labour legislation, court rulings affecting commercial transactions, and alleged government interference in natural resources projects. Fourteen of the 38 investor claims known to have been filed against Egypt were pending as of May 2019.

Five of the 24 concluded investor claims are known to have resulted in awards of monetary compensation in favour of the investor. Seven were dismissed on jurisdictional or merits grounds. Sixteen claims are known to be have been settled and discontinued by the parties. Settlement terms are unknown in 14 of the 16 cases, but may involve substantial payments – two of the settlements involved multi-million dollar payments to investors[37] while two others came after the investors secured substantial awards of damages from arbitral tribunals.[38]

Nine cases involved applications under the ICSID Convention to annul the arbitral tribunal's award (four made by Egypt and five made by investors). Two of these annulment applications were dismissed, one was upheld in part and led to a partial annulment of the tribunal's award, and the remaining cases were settled or discontinued before an annulment decision was rendered.

Damages awards in some cases have been very large. Public reports indicate that Egypt faces a USD 2 billion liability for damages in one recent case.[39] Egypt also has further possible exposure to several large damages claims being pursued by investors in its pending cases.[40]

Egyptian investors as claimants in ISDS cases

Although it is difficult to be precise given the confidentiality of certain ISDS proceedings, at least five Egyptian investors are known to have brought ISDS claims against some of Egypt's treaty partners (Algeria, Canada, Kuwait and Lebanon).[41] As of June 2019, three claims were still pending. Notably, one Egyptian investor, acting as the single beneficial owner for a group of companies, is reported to have caused the filing of two overlapping ISDS claims against Algeria in relation to a telecommunications investment, using different corporate entities and treaties.[42]

Reconsidering Egypt's investment treaty policy

Egypt's investment treaties, especially the BITs, show many features associated with first-generation investment treaties concluded in great numbers in the 1990s and early 2000s, notably a lack of clarity of the meaning of key provisions, absence of rules that most would consider to be essential and ubiquitous in a domestic law context, and extensive protections for covered investors. This scenario entails exposure, especially given that many Egyptian treaties have vague standards of protection and very little regulation of ISDS. In order to better address the balance between investor protection and the government's right to regulate, Egypt could pursue several different courses of action separately or in tandem.

This section examines three key aspects of treaty policy reform: (a) the scope of two important substantive protections, namely the fair and equitable treatment (FET) and most-favoured nation (MFN) treatment standards; (b) ISDS mechanisms; and (c) other aspects of investment treaty reform.

a. Two central substantive aspects of investment treaties

Fair and equitable treatment clauses

The fair and equitable treatment (FET) standard is almost always at the centre of investment treaty policy debates and claims by investors under investment treaties. References to fair and equitable treatment were an almost universal feature in investment treaties for many years. Most FET clauses were agreed before the rise of ISDS claims related to this treatment standard. Starting around 2004, broad theories for the interpretation of autonomous FET clauses by arbitral tribunals quickly emerged as the number of ISDS cases increased. FET is now invoked in a great number of ISDS cases – including the vast majority of known ISDS cases brought against Egypt. Arbitral tribunals have often made damages awards to covered investors based on breaches of this treatment standard.[43]

Many older FET provisions do not provide guidance about what treatment will be considered fair and equitable. FET appears in 94% of Egypt's investment treaties that are in force.[44] These FET provisions generally provide little or no guidance on interpretation of this standard.[45]

Many arbitral tribunals deciding ISDS cases involving FET claims since 2004 have established lengthy shopping lists of alleged elements of unqualified FET.[46] Among other things, some arbitral tribunals have considered unqualified FET clauses to require the host state to act in a consistent and transparent manner, free from arbitrariness and discrimination, and in good faith without transgressing the legitimate expectations of the investor. Some interpretations of FET, in particular those involving legitimate expectations, place significant restraints on the right to regulate including through non-discriminatory regulation.[47] In addition, arbitral tribunals have taken different approaches leading to considerable uncertainty for investors and states alike.

Governments have reacted to these developments in various ways, including by adopting more restrictive approaches to FET in recent treaties (Box 3.5).

Box 3.5. Recent approaches to the FET provision

Recent investment treaties indicate that states are becoming more active in the ways in which they specify or address absolute FET-type obligations. Uncertainties about FET and its scope have also led some governments to exclude it from their treaties. Some important recent approaches are outlined below.

The MST-FET approach – express limitation of FET to the minimum standard of treatment under customary international law (MST)

This approach has been used in a growing number of recent treaties, especially in treaties involving states from the Americas and Asia (Gaukrodger, 2017). It has recently been excluded by its initial sponsors, the NAFTA governments, in favour of a much more limited set of protections in the USMCA (see below). In addition to using MST-FET, the Comprehensive and Progressive Trans-Pacific Partnership Agreement (2018) (CPTPP), contains a carve-out to address legitimate expectations, and requires the claimant to establish any asserted rule of MST-FET by demonstrating widespread state practice and *opinio juris*, which is difficult to do. (Art. 9.6 (3)-(5), fns 15 and 17, Annex 9A). This approach has since been replicated by other states (see, e.g. Australia-Indonesia CEPA (2019), Art. 14.7). Only three of Egypt's investment treaties[1] and the COMESA Agreement[2] expressly link FET to the customary international law standard for the treatment of aliens.

The defined-list approach – closed lists for the elements of FET

Recent treaties negotiated by the European Union, China, France and Slovakia contain a defined list of elements of the FET obligation. This approach adopts a positive list system to limit the elements of FET standard, including elements such as a denial of justice, fundamental breach of due process, targeted discrimination on manifestly wrongful grounds, and/or abusive treatment of investors. The ASEAN-China Investment Agreement (2009) FET provision is narrower and is limited expressly to a prohibition on denials of justice. Legitimate expectations are not generally included as an element of FET in any treaty; however, certain treaties of this type allow for possible consideration of them in narrowly defined circumstances. This approach can result in a broader concept of FET than MST-FET, especially if state practice and *opinio juris* are required to establish rules under MST-FET. In addition, the parties to CETA adopted a joint government interpretation to clarify that the treaty does not create greater rights for foreign investors than those available to domestic investors.[3]

The recent India-Belarus BIT (2018) is an example of a treaty that in effect combines the above two approaches. Reference is made to MST and a closed list of elements is provided. The words fair and equitable are not used.

Exclusion of FET

Some recent NAFTA cases have adopted relatively broad interpretations of MST-FET despite repeated NAFTA government submissions to the contrary. The recently-concluded USMCA updating NAFTA generally excludes FET-type provisions entirely from the scope of ISDS (except for a narrow class of cases involving certain government contracts). ISDS under the USMCA generally applies only to claims of direct expropriation and post-establishment discrimination (and only to Mexico-United States relations).

All of these approaches are more specific than the broad, unqualified language of most Egyptian investment treaties that only refer to fair and equitable treatment.

1. Canada-Egypt BIT (1996); https://treaty-accord.gc.ca/text-texte.aspx?id=101524&lang=eng&_ga=2.144461749.1820137988.1553769576-626902904.1553510907, Belgium/Luxembourg-Egypt BIT (1999): https://treaties.un.org/doc/Publication/UNTS/Volume 2218/v2218.pdf; Mauritius-Egypt BIT (2014), https://arbitration.org/sites/default/files/bit/egypt_mauritius_english.pdf.

2. COMESA Agreement (2007), Article 14: "Member States shall accord fair and equitable treatment to COMESA investors and their investments, in accordance with customary international law. Fair and equitable treatment includes the obligation not to deny justice in criminal, civil, or administrative adjudicatory proceedings in accordance with the principle of due process embodied in the principal legal systems of the world. ... Paragraph 1 of this Article prescribes the customary international law minimum standard of treatment of aliens as the minimum standard of treatment to be afforded to covered investments and does not require treatment in addition to or beyond what is required by that standard."

3. Joint Interpretative Instrument on the Comprehensive Economic and Trade Agreement (CETA) between Canada & the European Union and its Member States, *Official Journal of the European Union*, 14 January 2017, pp. 3-8, https://eur-lex.europa.eu/legal-content/EN/TXT/PDF/?uri=CELEX:22017X0114(01)&from=EN.

The prevalence of unqualified FET obligations in Egypt's treaty practice contrasts with the practice of many other states, including most of Egypt's partners in Africa and the MENA region. These vague provisions create uncertainty as to the scope of Egypt's FET obligations and exposure to expansive interpretations by arbitral tribunals in ISDS cases. Clarification of government intent could improve predictability for the government, investors and arbitrators alike, limit treaty impact on the right to regulate, and reduce Egypt's exposure to damages claims.

One way to achieve further clarity would be to consider developing joint interpretative declarations or protocols to existing investment treaties with treaty counterparties as well as other states and stakeholders.[48] Egypt may also wish to consider incorporating recent investment treaty drafting practices with respect to FET in its new draft model BIT.

Most-Favoured Nation treatment

Egypt's investment treaties systematically grant most-favoured nation (MFN) treatment which requires Egypt to treat covered investments at least as favourably as it treats comparable investments by investors from third states. As with its FET provisions, the MFN obligations in Egypt's investment treaties are primarily broadly-worded with little guidance on how they are to be interpreted or applied.

MFN clauses in investment treaties can have a range of unintended consequences. These provisions can but do not necessarily allow for claimants in ISDS cases to engage in "treaty shopping" – a phrase used to describe the routing of an investment through an often complex company structure in order to gain access to treaty protections where they were not previously available, as well as the process of seeking to gain access to more favourable investment treaty protection (see further detail on treaty shopping below). Some arbitral tribunals have allowed investors to use MFN provisions to "import" substantive or procedural provisions from other investment treaties that they consider more favourable than the provision in the treaty under which their case is filed.[49] There is also considerable uncertainty regarding the interpretation of textual aspects of MFN clauses such as the meaning of "treatment" and "like circumstances" which appear in many MFN clauses.

Recently, an increasing number of governments concerned about the use of MFN clauses in ISDS cases have clarified their intent. Some have clarified that the treatment referred to in MFN provisions refers essentially to treatment of third country investors under domestic law, not to investment treaty provisions.[50] It is understood that the MFN provision in Egypt's new model BIT may include this clarification. As mentioned above, Egypt is currently conducting consultations with public and private stakeholders regarding its proposed new model BIT, including on the content of the MFN clause. Other treaties – like the Mauritius-Egypt BIT (2014) – clarify that MFN treatment does not extend to the ISDS provisions in other investment treaties, thereby avoiding the risk of arbitral tribunals interpreting an unqualified MFN clause in this way. India reacted strongly to an interpretation of an MFN clause in an ISDS case and has removed MFN entirely from its new model investment treaty.[51]

Governments have also increasingly clarified their intent with regard to what constitute comparable investments for purposes of MFN provisions. Many investment treaties require that the MFN treatment be accorded in "like circumstances" in order for the MFN clause to be applicable but do not provide further guidance, although this is changing. For example, the recent USMCA further clarifies that the "like circumstances" inquiry includes consideration of whether the relevant treatment distinguishes between investors or investments on the basis of legitimate public welfare objectives.[52]

Arbitral interpretations in ISDS cases allowing reflective loss and broadly interpreting MFN pose important obstacles to the effectiveness of investment treaty reform. There are a number of reform options that Egypt may wish to consider in this respect (see subsection (c) below regarding treaty shopping).

b. Investor-state dispute settlement (ISDS) mechanisms

ISDS mechanisms are included in the majority of Egypt's investment treaties, allowing covered foreign investors to bring claims against Egypt in investor-state arbitration, in addition or as an alternative to domestic remedies.[53] Investor-state arbitration involves arbitration tribunals selected on a case-by-case basis to adjudicate disputes in an approach derived from international commercial arbitration.

Like many other first generation treaty samples, almost all of Egypt's treaties regulate ISDS very lightly leaving substantial decisional power to arbitrators, or to claimants and their counsel. For example, (i) only two of Egypt's treaties[54] contain time limits for covered investor claims – a feature that is standard in domestic law systems and that has become more commonplace in IIAs concluded since 2005; (ii) only 14 of Egypt's investment treaties contain express references to the governing law in ISDS cases and those treaties use a range of different formulations; (iii) many of Egypt's treaties give claimants and their counsel substantial power over key procedural issues, including the identity of the appointing authority, through the investor's unilateral choice among several arbitration institutions;[55] (iv) none expressly provide for non-disputing government party interventions on issues of interpretation in ISDS cases; (v) none address transparency in ISDS; and (vi) only one of Egypt's investment treaties addresses the remedies that may be awarded by an arbitral tribunal.[56]

Egypt may wish to consider assessing its policy approach to ISDS mechanisms in general and, in particular, whether the low level of regulation of ISDS mechanisms in its existing treaties appropriately reflects its policy objectives. Recent treaty practice indicates that some states are beginning to circumscribe the limits of ISDS mechanisms in great detail[57] while others propose to reject ISDS mechanisms altogether in favour of alternative approaches. The European Commission, for example, proposes to set up a permanent court and an appellate tribunal to resolve investor-state disputes. This approach has been included in three IIAs negotiated by the EU as of May 2019.[58] Recent IIAs concluded by Brazil dispense with binding forms of ISDS altogether in favour of state-to-state disputes and designating domestic entities ("National Focal Points") to act as an ombudsperson by evaluating investor grievances and proposing solutions to a Joint Committee comprised of government representatives from both states (see, for example, Brazil-Chile FTA (2018) and Brazil-Ethiopia BIT (2018)). South Africa has terminated its BITs with European countries and now permits, under domestic legislation, foreign investors to bring direct claims against the government in domestic courts.

As mentioned above, multilateral reform efforts are underway, with a large number of governments participating in the UNCITRAL Commission's Working Group III having agreed by consensus that reforms to ISDS mechanisms are desirable to address a wide range of government and civil society concerns with the current system of investment arbitration.[59]

c. Other considerations for investment treaty reform

Clearer specification of investment protection provisions would help to reflect government intent more effectively

Investment protection standards in older investment treaties around the world have often been unqualified and relatively vague. The absence of detailed guidance gives ISDS tribunals broad discretion to interpret these provisions and thereby to determine the scope of protection. Many provisions in Egypt's investment treaties – beyond those discussed in some greater detail here – lack specific language to indicate government intent as to their scope and meaning. More specific language in investment protection provisions would lead to increased predictability that would benefit investors, governments and arbitrators in ISDS cases.

Specifications should reflect policy choices informed by Egypt's priorities. Policy-makers need to consider the costs and benefits of these choices and their potential impact on foreign and domestic investors, together with Egypt's legitimate regulatory interests and potential exposure to investment claims. Egypt should continue its efforts to update its treaties and its dialogue with treaty partners regarding amending existing treaties, issuing joint interpretative declarations to clarify government intent, or terminating treaties that no longer reflect current government policies.[60]

Combatting "treaty shopping"

Egypt may wish to consider strengthening its investment treaties with features to combat the rise of claims brought by investors who engage in treaty shopping. As mentioned above, this phrase is used to describe, among other things, the routing of an investment through an often complex company structure in order to gain access to treaty protections or to more favourable ones. It is also used to refer to the use of MFN clauses to "import" provisions from other treaties.

Investor claimants may seek to use treaty shopping to circumvent recent reformed investment treaties by bringing claims through companies incorporated in states that still have protections under first generation treaties, thereby undermining reform efforts in individual treaties. While some features to combat this behaviour appear scattered throughout Egypt's investment treaties, they are far from universal.

Ways to limit treaty shopping include:

- Seeking to engage in investment treaty reform across the full network of treaties;
- Barring ISDS claims by investors for reflective loss (Box 3.6);
- Specifying in the definition of covered investors that the ultimate owner who controls an investment, either directly or indirectly, must be a national of the home state treaty party,[61] or requiring investors

to have substantial business activities, the location of their effective management or some other substantial connection to the home state;

- Regulating the criteria for admission of a foreign investments (e.g. compliance with host state law or a registration requirement) and extending treaty protections only to established investments (although this may be considered to conflict unacceptably with liberalisation objectives);
- Denial of benefits clauses which allow host states to deny the benefits of the treaty, including access to ISDS mechanisms, to investors who are unable to meet specific criteria, such as corporate seat, ultimate ownership, or substantial business presence requirements; and
- Clarifying that MFN treatment does not permit an investor to import substantive or procedural rights from third-party Egyptian investment treaties, thereby preventing the investor from cherry-picking a preferred set of provisions from other treaties.

Box 3.6. The unique ISDS approach to reflective loss

Shareholders incur reflective loss if a company in which they hold shares suffers a loss that results, in turn, in the shareholders suffering a commensurate loss, typically a loss in value of the shares. Creditors of an injured company also typically suffer reflective loss. Reflective loss is generally contrasted with direct injury to shareholder rights, such as interference with shareholder voting rights. Claims for direct injury to shareholders are generally uncontroversial; such losses occur infrequently.

Corporate law systems generally bar claims for reflective loss. Where a company is injured, the claim belongs to the directly-injured company. Only the company can recover the loss. Shareholder claims for loss derived from the company loss are generally barred. This universally-applied general rule has both procedural and substantive benefits. Procedurally, it achieves judicial economy by limiting claims, avoiding inconsistent outcomes, facilitating amicable settlement, and precluding double recovery by the company and shareholders for the same loss. It is seen as fair in particular to defendants who are not subjected to multiple claims for the same alleged injury.

In ISDS, in contrast to normal corporate law principles, arbitrators have generally allowed shareholders to claim against governments for reflective loss. This has given rise to the many of the policy issues such as multiple claims from the same injury, leading to millions of dollars in additional legal costs for the same dispute. Egypt has recently experienced some of the high costs arising from the reflective loss interpretation in the cases arising from the East Mediterranean Gas S.A.E gas pipeline project, which involve multiple company and shareholder claims arising from the same dispute and risks of double recovery.

Extensive analysis and discussion of shareholder claims for reflective loss at the OECD have demonstrated that the availability of reflective loss claims in ISDS raises a broad range of policy issues for governments including those identified above. Reflective loss claims are a causal factor in many of the concerns being addressed in multilateral ISDS reform work being conducted by the UNCITRAL Commission's Working Group III. To date, no convincing policy arguments have been identified to explain the unique ISDS approach allowing for the general acceptance of reflective loss claims. Given that it provides claimants with exceptional benefits and greatly expands the number of actual and potential ISDS cases, however, only government-led reform is likely to address the issues.

Consistency of plurilateral and bilateral investment agreements

Egypt may wish to explore the possibility of harmonising regional investment treaty policies through existing regional frameworks. As mentioned above, Egypt – like many other countries in the MENA region – has a considerable number of overlapping treaty relationships between its BITs and multilateral agreements that duplicate treaty protections with individual countries. Moreover, many of the provisions in the OIC, COMESA and Arab Investment Agreements reflect an outdated treaty design that may undermine Egypt's efforts to review and reform its BITs if they were to remain in place in their current form: covered investors could conceivably circumvent Egypt's BITs in the future by choosing to bring an ISDS claim under a more favourably-worded multilateral treaty.

If one or more of the regional groupings of states to which Egypt participates wishes to create a fully integrated investment area, significant differences in investment protections in bi- and multilateral agreements do not contribute to this goal. Egypt may wish to bear these concerns in mind when preparing its new model BIT and engaging in discussions regarding reform efforts in these multilateral fora. There may be scope, for example, to develop a modern balanced approach in plurilateral investment agreements while exiting overlapping BIT relationships to reduce fragmentation in the regional investment treaty regime. The intra-ASEAN Comprehensive Investment Agreement (2009), the Comprehensive and Progressive Agreement for Trans-Pacific Partnership (2018) and the proposed Regional Comprehensive Economic Partnership (RCEP) are prominent recent examples that Egypt may wish to consider in terms of coordinated efforts to harmonise regional investment policy.

Ensuring policy space while attracting better quality investment

Egypt may wish to consider ways in which it can guarantee a higher degree of legitimate regulatory freedom and attract sustainable, quality FDI through its new model BIT and discussions with treaty partners regarding possible amendments to existing BITs. These concerns would appear to align with Egypt's Sustainable Development Strategy (Egypt's Vision 2030) and the clear focus on sustainable development as part of the new Investment Law.[62]

Aside from addressing FET provisions, as discussed above, one way to achieve greater regulatory space would be to provide expressly for it. A growing number of recent treaties clarify that non-discriminatory measures adopted by the state parties in relation to designated objectives (e.g. environmental, labour, health, social welfare or consumer protection objectives) will not breach their obligations under the treaty with respect to the treatment of covered investments.[63] The upshot of such provisions is that investors are barred from invoking certain measures as the basis for claims against host states under ISDS mechanisms.

Responsible business conduct

Egypt may also wish to consider addressing sustainable development and responsible business conduct considerations in its investment treaties. Three of Egypt's BITs, as well as the OIC, COMESA and Arab Investment Agreements, make express reference to these objectives.[64] Other recent treaties clarify the state parties' understanding that it is inappropriate to encourage investment by investors of the other contracting party by relaxing environmental or health measures,[65] exclude investments procured by corruption from the scope of protections under the treaty,[66] recognise that investments should contribute to the economic development of the host state,[67] and recognise the importance of requiring companies to respect corporate social responsibility norms.[68]

As many of these areas are addressed in Egypt's new Investment Law,[69] Egypt may wish to consider cross-referring to these domestic law obligations in its investment treaties or ensuring that protection under all of its investment treaties is restricted to investments made in accordance with Egyptian law. Several of Egypt's treaties stipulate expressly that only investments made in accordance with host state laws will be protected under the treaty. Such requirements serve as a filter mechanism that can potentially incentivise investors to be more mindful of their obligations under domestic law. The issue of whether such a requirement is implicit appears uncertain in ISDS in light of inconsistent decisions, and an express clause removes doubt in this regard.

Developing proactive approaches to prevention of ISDS claims and case management

Egypt may wish to review its strategy with respect to prevention and early settlement of investment-related disputes and its approach to case management of ISDS cases. Recent domestic legislative developments are encouraging in this respect. As outlined above (Box 3.2), the new Investment Law and its implementing regulations establish a number of non-binding dispute resolution options, including a Grievance Committee to investigate investor complaints, two different ministerial committees and a new arbitration and mediation centre to resolve investment disputes.

Egypt may wish to consider additional options to complement these encouraging steps towards promoting out-of-arbitration dispute settlement. Efforts to build awareness within government ministries, agencies and local or sub-national government entities regarding Egypt's obligations under investment treaties and the potential impact that government decisions may have regarding investor rights under investment treaties is likely to be worthwhile. A communication protocol regarding important decisions made below ministerial level that may adversely affect investment projects should also be implemented. One OECD member country has recently reported successful outcomes with ministerial committees to consider pre-arbitration notices of dispute filed by investors under investment treaties. Evaluating investor claims candidly before any form of binding arbitration is initiated can be an important step in preventing a protracted and costly legal process. In some cases, it may be prudent to engage internal or external legal counsel to provide an independent legal assessment of the strengths and weaknesses of the investor's claims to inform governmental decision-making and identify opportunities for early settlement or compromise.

Several states that have been frequent respondents in ISDS cases – including Argentina, Spain, the United States, Canada and Mexico – have capitalised on their own ISDS experiences to develop dedicated teams of government lawyers who now handle exclusively all ISDS cases brought against their government with no reliance on external counsel. Egypt may wish to explore ways to learn from these experiences with these states and other OECD members. While this option naturally involves considerable planning and resources to coordinate, it may be worth considering for the future if external legal fees pose budgetary concerns.

d. Treatment of domestic and foreign investors

It is clear from Egypt's new Investment Law that Egyptian policy makers are seeking to guarantee a sound investment climate for both domestic and foreign investors. Parts of Egypt's legal framework applicable to investment protection, including the new Investment Law, apply equally to both domestic and foreign investors.

Egyptian law also contains instruments that exclusively cover only some foreign investors, such as its investment treaties and the possibility left open in Article 3 of the new Investment Law for preferential treatment of foreigners subject to approval from the Cabinet of Ministers.

More favourable regulatory conditions for certain investors based on nationality can distort efficient investment decisions and lower overall investment.[70] Where corporate nationality is easily modified through corporate structuring, nationality-based preferences can be easily exploited by investors that would not ordinarily benefit from them. Treaties designed to protect foreign investment from a particular jurisdiction can easily be used by domestic investors or third-country investors advised by legal counsel experienced in ISDS disputes (Box 3.6). At the same time, some governments consider that they need to provide certain extra incentives and guarantees to seek to attract foreign investment because they believe FDI will increase productivity, jobs and innovation. The balance between these interests is a delicate one and may evolve over time.

Investment treaties as tools to liberalise investment policy

While liberalisation provisions are common features of international trade agreements, they have been much less common in investment treaties. However, investment treaties are being used increasingly to liberalise investment policy by facilitating the making or establishment of new investments, such as by removing regulatory restrictions on FDI. (Investment liberalisation generally is discussed in Chapter 2.)

While econometric studies have failed to establish a clear link between investment protection and FDI flows, some show that reducing barriers and restrictions to foreign investments (whether through investment treaties or otherwise) does lead to more FDI flows.[71] Evaluation of preferential regimes for protection of covered investors under investment treaties should include their potential dissuasive impact on incentives for investment liberalisation.

One important way that investment treaties may be able to foster liberalisation is by extending the national treatment (NT) and MFN treatment standards to investors seeking to make investments, i.e. the pre-establishment phase of an investment. Another way is through clauses prohibiting measures that block market access.[72]

Overall, provisions that seek to foster liberalisation are not a common feature of Egypt's investment treaties. Only a few of Egypt's treaties grant so-called pre-establishment NT and MFN treatment to investors. Egypt's BITs with Canada and the United States, for example, provide that the treaty parties shall permit the establishment of a new business enterprise or acquisition of an existing business enterprise on a basis no less favourable than that which is accorded to their own and third-state investors.[73] Provisions of this type are typically accompanied by certain exclusions (Box 3.7). Egypt may wish to consider more widespread inclusion of such liberalisation provisions into new or existing investment treaties.

Box 3.7. Negative and positive list-approaches to NT and MFN exceptions

When countries grant national and/or most-favoured nation treatment, whether pre- or post-establishment, they typically do so subject to reservations. There are two broadly different approaches.

A negative list-approach typically provides that MFN and NT are generally afforded, except for specific exceptions or provisions (negative lists). The Canada-Egypt BIT (1996), for example, provides that the governments may adopt and maintain measures not conforming with the MFN and NT provisions in certain sectors and with respect to matters specified in the Annex to the BIT (Articles III and IV).

A positive-list approach specifies that MFN and NT liberalisation provisions only apply to specific identified sectors (positive lists). Generally, the negative list-approach is seen as more conducive to investment liberalisation particularly over time with the development of new areas of economic activity that are not covered by negative lists.

e. Procedural considerations: exit and renegotiation

Given the current state of its investment treaties as discussed above, Egypt may wish to consider reviewing its existing agreements to ensure that they reflect government intent and sound practices emerging in recently-concluded treaties around the world. A growing number of states are prioritising efforts to exit first-generation investment treaties, as Egypt will no doubt be aware after the recent unilateral denunciations of Egyptian BITs by Indonesia and India. Review and renegotiation of investment treaties takes time, however, and the option to terminate a treaty is not necessarily available at any moment, as the relevant provisions on temporal validity in the treaty may place limits on exit options (see Box 3.8 on designs of temporal validity provisions in investment treaties).

Box 3.8. Designs of temporal validity provisions in investment treaties

Unlike most international treaties, which can be denounced at relatively short notice, investment treaties typically contain clauses that extend their temporal validity for significant periods of time. Three designs can be found, often cumulatively in the same agreement: First, most investment treaties set and initial validity period of often 10 years or more, counting from the treaty's entry into force; after that period, many treaties only allow states parties to denounce the treaty at the end of specific intervals of often 10 years or more; finally, treaty obligations almost universally continue to apply for a sunset period after the termination of the treaty, again for periods of typically 10 years or more. Many treaties thus bind the states parties for at least two decades, and in some extreme cases for up to 50 years.

Treaty designs that automatically extend the validity of the treaty for fixed terms are included in around 30% of the global treaty stock, but this design is used less frequently in recent time. This design tends to prolong the period for which states parties are bound without granting additional benefits in terms of predictability for investors: on the contrary, the oscillating residual treaty validity is hard to grasp and predict without detailed study, and drops to very short residual validity of no more than six months (see figure below).

Figure 3.4. Residual treaty validity

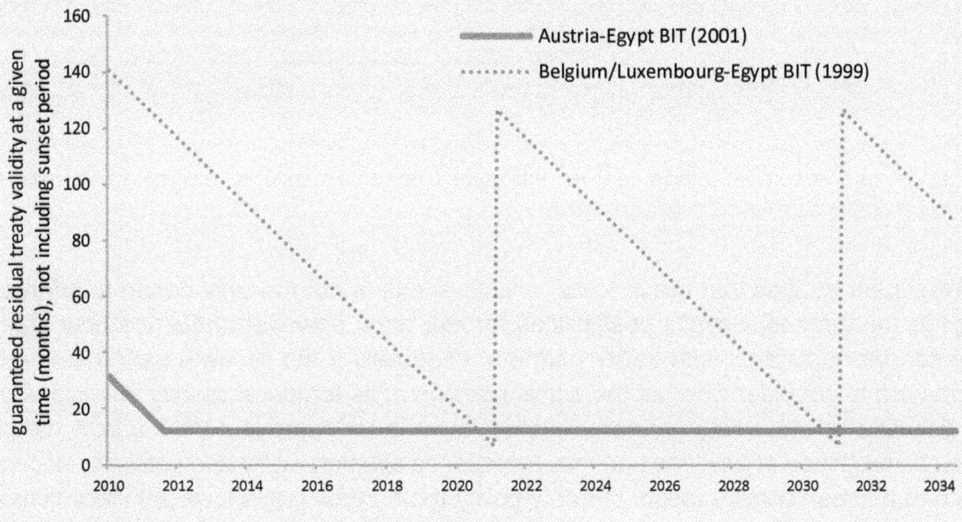

Source: Adapted from OECD work on temporal validity under IIAs (Pohl, 2013).

Many of Egypt's investment treaties that are currently in force contain temporal validity provisions that will operate to delay possibilities for unilateral exit from the treaty. All of Egypt's treaties contain an initial validity period of between 5 and 20 years. Roughly half of Egypt's BITs provide for an automatic renewal period after the period of initial validity and allow either state party to denounce the treaty within 6 or 12 months (depending on the treaty) of the expiry of the renewed period. Treaties that renew for fixed terms require more monitoring, as they limit the possibilities to update or unilaterally end the agreement. If no termination is effected in the defined notice period, the treaty is automatically renewed for the agreed period, thereby committing Egypt to these treaties for a further 15 or 20 years in some cases before the next opportunity to terminate the treaty will arise. Even if Egypt were to terminate successfully its treaties, almost all will continue to apply for a survival period of at least 10 years or more in the majority of cases, which leaves Egypt potentially exposed to investor claims under ISDS provisions far beyond the termination date.

Based on available treaty data for Egypt BITs (which remains incomplete for the reasons explained above), it appears that Egypt will be bound by at least one treaty until 2032 (Italy-Egypt BIT (1989)), and even if it were to unilaterally withdraw from all of its investment treaties at the earliest possible occasion, effects of its past treaty policy could bind Egypt until 2049 (Figure 3. 5).

Figure 3.5. Projection of the temporal validity of Egypt's investment treaties (light blue) compared to global sample (dark blue)

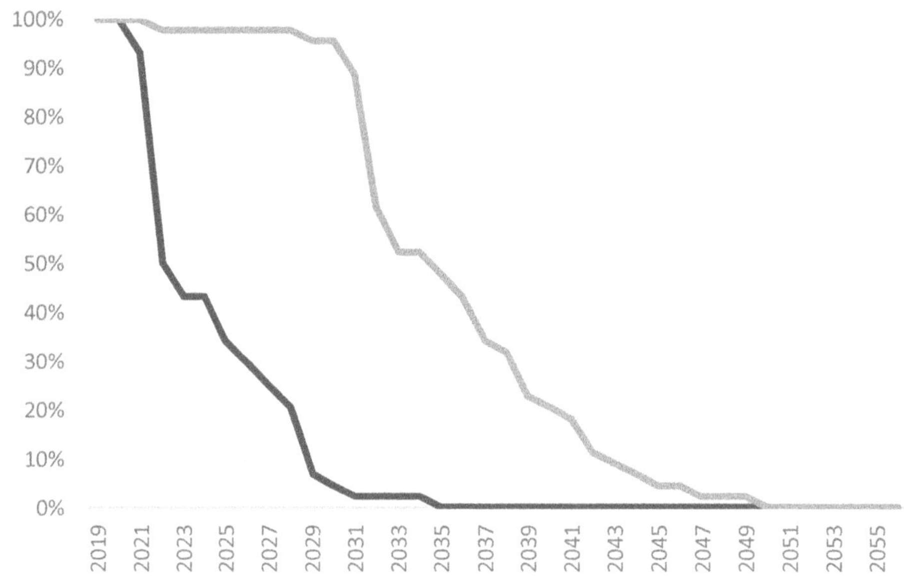

Source: OECD calculations based on OECD treaty database. Projections based on a hypothetical scenario of unilateral denunciation of all treaties in the available sample at the earliest possible occasion.

For those investment treaties that are in force, unilateral exit is not the only option to address perceived shortcomings in the treaties. Egypt's possibilities for exit may, however, influence how amendments or agreed exits can be negotiated with treaty partners, especially if the renewal period is imminent. Egypt may therefore wish to consider whether the current design of its temporal validity provisions can serve its interests in discussions with treaty partners. Another avenue for improvement is a joint interpretation to a treaty. These can be issued at any time and may represent a simpler, faster and politically-acceptable device through which to address some aspects of treaty policy if the treaty text allows sufficient scope to achieve the jointly-desired interpretation. Egypt may wish to consider examples of recent joint interpretations signed by other states or develop a model for joint interpretations for its BITs through consultations with interested stakeholders. It may also be prudent to consider revising existing provisions on temporal validity systematically in the context of amendments or renegotiations of existing treaties to remove lock-in provisions and reduce post-termination sunset periods. Egypt's new model BIT may be an appropriate place to reconsider the government's stance on temporal validity.

Recommendations

Review and consider possibilities for renegotiation, clarification and exit of investment treaties. Bearing in mind the existing scope for treaty shopping, Egypt should consider its treaty network as a whole during such an exercise. Treaties with vague, unqualified provisions concluded by Egypt in the past may attract undesirable interpretations in ISDS disputes. Egypt should consider taking steps to update these treaties to bring them in line with government intent, Egypt's current priorities and more recent practices in investment treaty policy as described above in this Chapter. In many instances, this can likely be achieved through amendments or joint interpretations agreed with treaty partners. Termination or replacement of older investment treaties by consent or unilateral action may represent an appropriate last resort in order to manage exposure and safeguard the government's right to regulate in the public interest.

Manage potential exposure under existing investment treaties proactively. GAFI, the Ministry of Justice and the Ministry of Foreign Affairs should continue to develop ISDS dispute prevention and case management tools. Egypt may also wish to consider efforts to raise awareness about Egypt's investment treaties and the significance of Egypt's international obligations under these investment treaties for the day-to-day functions of different government agencies and officials that regularly interact with foreign investors.

Improve access to public information on investment treaties and ISDS cases. Egypt should consider providing a comprehensive list and complete copies of all Egyptian investment-related agreements in Arabic and English on the website of the Ministry of Foreign Affairs. Accessible information regarding Egypt's investment agreements and Egypt's policy regarding investment treaties reflects two of the core objectives of Egypt's new Investment Law – transparency and equal opportunity among investors. Transparency could also be improved with respect to Egypt's ISDS cases. Egypt is not a signatory of the 2014 United Nations Convention on Transparency in Treaty-based Investor-State Arbitration (the Mauritius Convention) – a multilateral effort to address concerns regarding the lack of transparency in ISDS cases by establishing a set of procedural rules for making information publicly available on ISDS cases. It is also unknown whether Egypt has agreed to adopt the UNCITRAL Rules on Transparency in Treaty-based Investor-State Arbitration in ISDS cases since those rules took effect in April 2014.

Corporate governance of state-owned enterprises

State-owned enterprises[74] (SOEs) in Egypt, as in many countries, are prevalent in sectors such as utilities, infrastructure and finance, whose performance affects both broad segments of the population and the business sector. Good governance of state-owned companies is critical to ensure their positive contribution to economic efficiency and competitiveness. SOEs can address market failures, ensure quality public service delivery and contribute to the broader economy – when they operate efficiently, transparently and on a level playing field with private enterprises. When SOEs operate inefficiently and subject to weak governance, they can negatively affect wider economic growth, crowd out more productive private sector activity and strain public resources. Worse, poorly governed or regulated state-owned firms can be abused for political patronage or self-enrichment, reducing the confidence of the public and private investors (OECD, 2015[21]) (OECD, 2018[22]).

Good corporate governance – which involves the relationships between a company's management, board, shareholders and other stakeholders – can create market confidence and business integrity. For state-owned firms, good governance involves: (i) professionalising the state as an owner; (ii) making SOEs operate with similar efficiency, transparency and accountability as good practice private enterprises; and (iii) ensuring that competition between SOEs and private enterprises is conducted on a level playing field (OECD, 2015[21]). Box 3.9 presents the main policy recommendations of the OECD *Guidelines on Corporate Governance of State-Owned Enterprises*.

The Egyptian government has taken substantial measures to improve standards of corporate governance for state-owned enterprises. A Law on Public Sector Enterprises sets out rules of governance based on international best practices for a selection of firms, and since 2006, Egypt has had a voluntary but encouraged code of corporate governance for SOEs. The government also announced plans to improve transparency of SOE finances, aims and cost to the state budget. These efforts are important advancements, but the current dual regulatory system, under which only a subset of firms adhere to good corporate governance practices, falls short of levelling the playing field between SOEs and their private sector competitors. The government could do more to apply standards to all state-owned enterprises and take steps to minimise the market distortions of publicly-owned firms.

SOE landscape and challenges

The state is a significant economic actor in Egypt. While privatisation programmes in the 1990s and 2000s substantially reduced the economic role of the government, companies owned (in full or part) by the state remain dominant in network sectors (including utilities and transport) and prevalent in many others, including manufacturing, services, banking and real estate. According to the OECD's preliminary Product Market Regulation (PMR) information based on Youssef et a. (2019), the state owns majority shares of the largest firms in the electricity, gas, telecom and transport sectors. See Box 3.9 for a brief background on the SOE landscape in Egypt.

Box 3.9. Brief history of SOEs in Egypt

The role and weight of state-owned enterprises has been a central question in Egyptian economic policy since the founding of the modern Egyptian state. In the 1950s and 1960s Egypt pursued a radical transformation of the economy based on a socialist development model and protectionist trade policies of import substitution industrialisation. State-owned enterprises were seen as essential sources of industry growth, job creation and self-sufficiency. By 1961, the state controlled all banking, insurance, utilities, maritime and air transport, most large-scale industry, as well as many service sectors (Cammett et al., 2013[23]). Economic growth from the strategy was short-lived; inefficient public-sector enterprises soon became widely considered a burden on high budget deficits and public debt (Bromley and Bush, 1994[24]).

Egypt began liberalisation reforms under a policy of *infitah* (open-door policy) in the 1970s, but state-owned firms remained paramount in both strategic and non-strategic sectors. At the end of the decade output from SOEs contributed to 13% of GDP, and state firms accounted for 60% of value added in manufacturing, nearly double the average for developing countries (Cammett et al., 2013[23]). Privatisation efforts did not begin until 1991, promoted under the terms of structural adjustment agreements with the World Bank and IMF. According to some estimates, over the next two decades the government oversaw the full or partial privatisation of around 400 SOEs in a range of sectors, and cut SOE debt by nearly 75% (Raballand et al., 2015[25]). Compared to other countries in the MENA region, Egypt, Morocco and Tunisia were the only states to significantly reduce the size and number of state-owned enterprises (OECD, 2012[26]).

While lauded by international financial institutions, there was popular opposition to privatisations, which many believed led to layoffs and benefited politically connected businesses (OECD, 2013[27]). Sales of state-owned firms subsequently halted during the period of political instability between 2011 and 2014, and some sales were challenged in court (Adly, 2017[28]). The government is now planning partial divestments from a selection of enterprises (see Divestment plans appear well defined). Yet available information makes it clear that firms owned in full or part by the state remain an important facet of the business sector, including in manufacturing, energy, electricity, banking and construction.

By some accounts the commercial role of the state has expanded in recent years, with firms diversifying into new sectors and taking a greater role in large-scale infrastructure projects (Marshall, 2015[29]) (Abul-Magd, 2014[30]). SOE companies also became major food producers and public contractors and increasingly participated in joint public-private ventures in strategic sectors (Marshall and Stacher, 2012[31]).

The full extent of the state's role in the economy is unknown. Some reports suggest that public sector firms account for 30% of GDP, but it is not clear whether this figure includes joint public-private ventures or companies owned in full by the state (IMF, 2017[2]). According to Central Bank figures, "public companies" accounted for nearly 16% of all investment in the 2016-17 fiscal year, and "economic authorities" another 10%.[75] A subset of 121 state-owned companies generated revenues of EGP 91 billion in the same year, accounting for around 4.6% of GDP (Ministry of Public Enterprise, 2017[32]). State-owned banks control 40% of the domestic banking sector (US Department of Commerce, 2018[33]). There is however no complete list of the number and names and finances of SOEs in Egypt, nor of their finances.

Gaps in transparency are exacerbated by the dispersed nature of public ownership in Egypt. Ministries control portfolios of SOEs directly or through holding companies, which manage sub-groupings of firms by industry. There is no overarching policy or co-ordinating entity to ensure each ministry follows the same procedures on managing or disclosing information on SOEs. Some ministries do not report which companies they control. The Ministry of Public Enterprise Sector appears to oversee the largest number of firms (121), via eight holding companies. Many sectors considered strategic, including electricity, telecommunications and petroleum, are controlled by their corresponding line ministry (the ministries of electricity and energy, communications and information technology, and petroleum, respectively) (Raballand et al., 2015[25]). In some cases, presidential decrees have created holding companies with no apparent overseeing ministry, such as for Egypt's national airline holding company (OECD, 2014[34]).

This dispersed model of SOE ownership carries an inherent risk of conflict of interest; ministries are often simultaneously responsible for owning SOEs (and benefiting from their success) and regulating them. The establishment of holding companies can improve governance, by transferring shareholding functions away from the ministry (OECD, 2018[22]). In practice however, the independence of holding companies varies widely. Dispersed SOE ownership can also lead to discordant approaches to SOE oversight. As shown in Box 3.10, establishing central co-ordinating entities could help ensure harmony of policies across the different bodies overseeing state-owned firms (OECD, 2015[21]).

Many SOEs in Egypt receive fiscal and quasi-fiscal subsidies that burden the state budget and create market distortions. This includes inputs at below market prices, which can impose high opportunity costs on the government and economy. Inputs frequently come from other SOEs, whose reduced profit in turn affects government revenue (OECD, 2013[27]). Preferential inputs include free land and the ability to defer gas and electricity payments (Egypt Council of Ministers, 2018[35]). SOEs in Egypt often benefit from preferential access to government contracts and, at times, debt relief from state-owned banks.

Further, some state firms are exempt from certain laws. All public utilities, including state-owned electricity companies, are not subject to the Competition Law (private utilities can apply to the Competition Authority for total or partial exemption) (OECD, 2013[27]). Combined, these benefits to SOEs impede competition and create barriers to entry for private-sector firms. There is a risk that SOEs crowd out not only products and services but also access to credit. Some banks may hesitate to back private sector enterprises in sectors perceived to be in competition with state-owned firms.

Despite substantial fiscal and other support, many state-owned firms are not profitable. State holding companies in the food industries, electricity, storage and aeronautics sectors reported receiving grants or subsidies equal to double their combined profits in fiscal year 2015-16 (Ministry of Finance, 2016[36]). While the eight holding companies under the Ministry of Public Enterprise Sector earned revenues equal to 4.6% of GDP in fiscal year 2016-17, their profits accounted for only 0.4% of GDP. The same year, two holding companies (in pharmaceuticals and textiles) posted losses of more than EGP 0.5 and 2.7 billion (Figure 3.6). The debts of these holding companies reportedly exceed EGP 40 billion (El-Fiqi, 2018[37]).

Box 3.10. Main policy recommendations of the OECD Guidelines on Corporate Governance of State-Owned Enterprises

The state exercises the ownership of SOEs in the interest of the general public. It should carefully evaluate and disclose the objectives that justify state ownership and subject these to a recurrent review.

The state should act as an informed and active owner, ensuring that the governance of SOEs is carried out in a transparent and accountable manner, with a high degree of professionalism and effectiveness.

Consistent with the rationale for state ownership, the legal and regulatory framework for SOEs should ensure a level playing field and fair competition in the marketplace when SOEs undertake economic activities.

Where SOEs are listed or otherwise include non-state investors among their owners, the state and the enterprises should recognise the rights of all shareholders and ensure shareholders' equitable treatment and equal access to corporate information.

The state ownership policy should fully recognise SOEs' responsibilities towards stakeholders and request that SOEs report on their relations with stakeholders. It should make clear any expectations the state has in respect of responsible business conduct by SOEs.

State-owned enterprises should observe high standards of transparency and be subject to the same high quality accounting, disclosure, compliance and auditing standards as listed companies.

The boards of SOEs should have the necessary authority, competencies and objectivity to carry out their functions of strategic guidance and monitoring of management. They should act with integrity and be held accountable for their actions.

Source: OECD (2015), OECD Guidelines on Corporate Governance of State-Owned Enterprises, 2015 Edition, OECD Publishing, Paris, https://doi.org/10.1787/9789264244160-en.

Figure 3.6. Financial performance of holding companies under Ministry of Public Enterprise Sector in 2016-2017

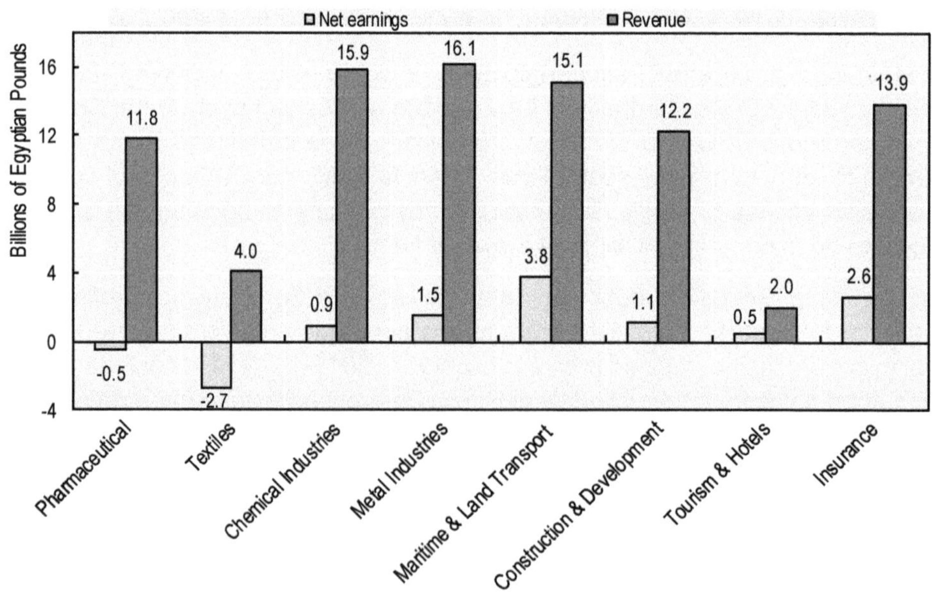

Note: Fiscal Year 2016-17.
Source: OECD calculations based on data from the Business Sector Information Centre (http://www.bsic.gov.eg/Mowazant_Rep.asp).

Successive Egyptian governments have recognised the inefficiency and distortive nature of many state-owned enterprises. But SOEs in Egypt, as elsewhere, often have development aims, notably boosting employment, that have proven difficult to reconcile with reforms. The state is one of the largest employers in Egypt. Aggregate figures of SOE employment vary; data from a 2014 labour force survey suggest that public-sector corporations employ 3.6% of the total workforce (ILO, 2014[38]). Company-level figures demonstrate that employment-generating goals often outweigh efficiency objectives, contributing to SOEs' large debt (OECD, 2013[27]). The government in the 1990s used a variety of measures to reduce worker opposition to SOE restructuring and privatisation, including consultations with labour unions, allowing employees to purchase company shares at a reduced cost, termination bonuses and incentives for early retirement. Though these approaches are commonly used in other countries, the results and impact on public opinion in Egypt were mixed (Kauffmann and Wegner, 2007[39]). Few firms assumed the responsibility for the rehabilitation of workers. Offering training for younger employees, redeployment or outplacement services, or short-term job protection, in consultation with employee representatives, can help reduce the negative social costs of reforming underperforming SOEs (Broughton and Manzoni, 2017[40]). Several OECD countries have sought to assist SOE employees through employment retention guarantees (OECD, 2018[41]).

Good corporate governance addresses some of the aforementioned challenges involved with state economic ventures. Clarifying the objectives and improving the performance of state-owned firms can help minimise market distortions and state budgetary pressures.

Advancements on corporate governance of some SOEs

The government has some laudable measures in place to foster standards of corporate governance for state-owned enterprises. Law 203 on Public Sector Enterprises, adopted in 1991, sets out rules of governance based on international best practices for a selection of state-owned firms. SOEs covered by the law must follow provisions of the general Companies Law (159/1981) governing private sector firms and should not receive special benefits or legal exemptions. The law also sets out procedures for the constitution of the general assembly and board, quorum requirements, rules for selection of board members, and requirements for reporting and external audits (OECD, 2012[26]) (Raballand et al., 2015[25]). These provisions are a positive step toward levelling the playing field between SOEs and their private sector competitors. The law also helps alleviate inherent conflicts of interest when a governmental body acts as both an owner and a manager, by transferring management responsibilities away from the overseeing ministry. The Ministry of Public Enterprise Sector oversees firms in a range of sectors and does not set sectoral regulations.

The law is not a comprehensive framework for SOE governance, however. It initially aimed to improve governance of 314 companies slotted for privatisation, transferring their ownership to holding companies under the supervision of what is now the Ministry of Public Enterprise Sector. More than half of the companies have been sold in full or part; the ministry now controls 121 firms (called "affiliate companies") under eight holding companies in manufacturing, transport and service sectors (Figure 3.6). The law therefore only to applies to these 121 companies and does not cover firms in strategic sectors, including security, banking, telecommunications and water.

Reports also suggest that some provisions of Law 203 are not adhered to in practice, notably related to reporting on finances (Hassouna, 2018[42]). Government influence also remains paramount (Raballand et al., 2015[25]). The law stipulates that the overseeing minister nominates board positions in holding companies, which in turn nominate boards for affiliate companies. These appointments are political decisions, which may undermine oversight of company performance. Experience shows that these practices often compromise the objectivity and independence of boards and curtail their ability to perform effectively, i.e. to oversee company strategy and management, absent political interference (OECD, 2012[26]).

Commendably, Egypt became the first country in the region to develop a Code of Corporate Governance of the Public Enterprise Sector in 2006. The code, based on the OECD SOE Guidelines (Box 3.10), is an important reform towards improving SOE governance and operations and complements law 203 and the general corporate governance code for the private sector (adopted in 2005). The code's recommendations include many best practices: ensuring the existence of an effective regulatory and legal framework for SOEs, guidelines for the state as an owner, equitable treatment of shareholders, relationships with stakeholders, transparency and disclosure, and responsibility of boards of directors (Egyptian Institute of Directors, 2006[43]). The Ministry of Public Enterprise Sector set up a committee in 2017 to review the corporate governance code for SOEs, to strengthen its standards and bring its provisions in line with the OECD's updated SOE Guidelines (OECD, 2018[22]).

The code is voluntary, and it appears that adherence varies substantially among Egyptian SOEs. Firms that sell minority stakes on national stock exchanges tend to have higher standards of corporate governance, due to transparency and disclosure requirements of the country's Capital Market Law, and efforts to appeal to foreign investors (Hassouna, 2018[42]). Other firms, notably Egypt Air Holding Company, do not fall under law 203 but were corporatised under special legislation (in this case via a 2002 presidential decree), which mandates it operate as if "it were privately owned without any interference from the government" (OECD, 2014[34]). Some firms follow some of the code's guidelines, such as on information disclosure, but many practices are apparently applied in an ad hoc rather than formal manner. In terms of monitoring, the Central Auditing Authority can audit any company in which the state controls more than 25% of shares. These reports are generally not public, and there are questions about their thoroughness (OECD, 2012[26]) (Hassouna, 2018[42]).

While law 203 and the corporate governance codes are important advances in improving governance of state-owned firms, they fall short of levelling the playing field between SOEs and their private sector competitors. The government could consider making elements of the codes mandatory for all SOEs. These standards should be sufficiently flexible to accommodate the variety of commercial and non-commercial objectives of SOEs. To that end, clarifying and disclosing SOE objectives could help shield them from political interference that can hinder their efficiency and make them more accountable to the public (OECD, 2018[22]). More broadly, governments can benefit from following the OECD SOE Guidelines, as well as the corporate governance guidelines for the private sector, outlined in the G20/OECD Principles of Corporate Governance. Aligning SOE and private sector practices helps ensure fair competition (OECD, 2015[44]).

Progress towards transparency

A good corporate governance framework includes high levels of transparency and disclosure. The government has taken steps to increase transparency of public sector firms. Notably, it plans to publish a "comprehensive report on state-owned enterprises", which will include a "full list of the companies owned by the government, broken down by industry, policy objectives… and type of ownership (e.g. majority or minority-owned)". The report will also include information on the government's ownership policy, the impact of public sector enterprises on government finances, and details on individual companies' finances (including subsidies), board members and management. The government will publish the report annually (IMF, 2018[20]). If enacted, this is a significant step towards improving transparency of public enterprises and making them more accountable in the eyes of the public and investors.

The government does make available financial information on a subset of SOEs. The Business Sector Information Centre, a body under the Ministry of Public Enterprise Sector, publishes the latest financial summary reports (including year-end profits, revenues, investments and exports) of the eight holding companies (and their affiliate companies) under the Ministry. The Ministry of Finance also has publicly accessible financial records on 19 holding companies (including the eight controlled by the Ministry of Public Enterprise Sector), and 23 firms, including in the oil and gas and electricity sectors. These are fairly detailed, including information on current financial position, grants or subsidies received, income statements, distribution of profits, and statements of cash flows. The Ministry of Finance website also discloses budgets and spending of 47 "economic authorities". The disclosures demonstrate that the government delivered on pledged reforms: in 2012, the Ministry of Finance announced it would improve reporting on financial accounts of some public sector companies (Raballand et al., 2015[25]).

There are currently, however, no publications showing aggregate financial data for SOEs. Individual holding companies and firms sometimes publish annual reports and information on boards of directors, though this seems to be done on an ad hoc basis. The government's plans to release aggregate reports on all enterprises in the state's ownership portfolio will require coordination across government. It is not clear if one state body has the mandate and resources to lead this effort. If realised, this mapping will be critical to enacting further improvements to corporate governance (OECD, 2018[22]).

Divestment plans appear well-defined

The Egyptian government announced in 2017 a five-year plan to re-start partial divestments of SOEs, after a period of few privatisations since 2011. It intends to float minority shares (between 15-30%) of at least 23 state-owned firms in a range of sectors including banking and financial services, oil and gas, petrochemicals, transport and logistics, and real estate. Table 3.2 presents the list of firms under consideration, ten of which are already listed on the Egyptian stock exchange (Ministry of Finance, 2018[45]). In line with international best practices, the government established an inter-ministerial committee in charge of developing a plan for partial sales, and consulted with independent banking and legal firms to identify viable companies and determine valuation (IMF, 2018[46]).

The government's stated objectives are to raise funds and increase liquidity in the country's capital market. But it has also said it hopes the sales will improve the governance, transparency and performance of SOEs (IMF, 2018[46]). There is some evidence that larger ownership by foreign investors in Egypt has had a positive impact on the performance of privatised firms. This seems to be due however to changes in the board of directors and management rather than the sale itself, emphasising the importance of good corporate governance for all firms (Omran, 2009[47]).

The state's communication to the public on the rational for divestment and process is also a positive step. Privatisations (full and partial) have in the past been met with strong public opposition, including labour strikes, due in part to perceptions that they will lead to layoffs (OECD, 2012[26]). Moreover, a lack of transparency in previous sales fuelled popular allegations that state assets were transferred at a fraction of their market value to parties affiliated with the government (OECD, 2013[27]). It is important that the government continue to inform the public on the progress of the divestment programme, including on how companies are valued.

The government postponed the divestment programme at the end of 2018 to the following year, citing negative stock market performance across emerging economies. Reports suggest it could alter the stated list of public offerings and will proceed with plans depending on market conditions.

References

Abul-Magd, Z. (2014), *Egypt's Adaptable Officers: Power, Business, and Discontent*, Analysis No. 265, https://www.ispionline.it/sites/default/files/pubblicazioni/analysis_265__2014.pdf (accessed on 14 December 2018).

Abdel Wahab, M. S. (2017) "Investment Arbitration: The Chronicles of Egypt: A Perilous Path to Pass", Chartered Institute of Arbitrators, *Arbitration*, Volume 83(1).

Adly, A. (2017), "Too Big to Fail: Egypt's Large Enterprises After the 2011 Uprising", *Carnegie Endowment for International Peace*, https://carnegie-mec.org/2017/03/02/too-big-to-fail-egypt-s-large-enterprises-after-2011-uprising-pub-68154 (accessed on 14 December 2018).

Ahram (2016), "Egypt approves delegating industrial land allocation to Industrial Development Authority", *Ahram Online*, http://english.ahram.org.eg/NewsContent/3/12/223618/Business/Economy/Egypt-approves-delegating-industrial-land-allocati.aspx.

Aisbett, E., Busse, M. and Nunnenkamp, P. (2018) "Bilateral investment treaties as deterrents of host country discretion: the impact of investor-state disputes on foreign direct investment in developing countries", *Review of World Economics*, Vol. 154, No. 1, pp. 119-155.

Alschner, W. and Skougarevskiy, D. (2016) "Rule-takers or rule-makers? A new look at African bilateral investment treaty practice", University of Bern World Trade Institute, Working Paper No. 7.

Assaad, R. and C. Krafft (2013), "The Structure and Evolution of Employment in Egypt: 1998-2012", *Working Paper*, No. 805, The Economic Research Forum, Giza, http://www.erf.org.eg (accessed on 1 February 2019).

Australian Government (2010), "Bilateral and Regional Trade Agreements", Productivity Commission Research Report, Australian Government, November 2010.

Berger, A., Busse, M., Nunnenkamp, P. and Roy, M. (2013) "Do Trade and Investment Agreements Lead to More FDI? Accounting for Key Provisions Inside the Black Box", *International Economics and Economic Policy*, Vol. 10, No. 2, pp. 247-275.

Bonnitcha, J. (2017) "Assessing the Impacts of Investment Treaties: Overview of the Evidence", International Institute of Sustainable Development (IISD) Report, September 2017.

Bonnitcha, J., Skovgaard, L. N. and Waibel, M. (2017) *The Political Economy of the Investment Treaty Regime*.

Bromley, S. and R. Bush (1994), "Adjustment in Egypt? The Political Economy of Reform", *Review of African Political Economy*, Vol. 21/60, pp. 201-213, https://about.jstor.org/terms (accessed on 13 December 2018).

Broughton, A. and C. Manzoni (2017), *Employment in privatised utilities: A higher risk of precariousness?*, European Parliament, Committee on Employment and Social Affairs, http://www.europarl.europa.eu/RegData/etudes/STUD/2017/602061/IPOL_STU(2017)602061_EN.pdf (accessed on 20 December 2018).

Bureau of Economic and Business Affairs (2018), *Egypt: 2018 Investment Climate Statements*, US Department of State, Washington, DC, https://www.state.gov/e/eb/rls/othr/ics/2018/nea/281657.htm (accessed on 11 October 2018).

Cammett, M. et al. (2013), *A Political Economy of the Middle East*, Routledge, https://www.routledge.com/A-Political-Economy-of-the-Middle-East-4th-Edition/Cammett-Diwan-Richards-Waterbury/p/book/9780813349381 (accessed on 13 December 2018).

Chemonics International (2005), *Cadastral Survey and Mapping Issues Report*, USAID, Washington, DC, https://pdf.usaid.gov/pdf_docs/PNADG846.pdf (accessed on 7 November 2018).

Diwan, I., P. Keefer and M. Schiffbauer (2015), "Pyramid Capitalism: Cronyism, Regulation, and Firm Productivity in Egypt", *Center for International Development Working Paper*, No. 291, Harvard University, Cambridge.

EBRD (2012), *Commercial Laws of Egypt: An Assessment by the EBRD*, EBRD, https://www.ebrd.com/downloads/sector/legal/egypt.pdf (accessed on 6 November 2018).

Egypt Council of Ministers (2018), *Important decisions to collect electricity and gas receivables in the public sector companies*, Presidency of the Council of Ministers News Release, http://www.cabinet.gov.eg/Arabic/MediaCenter/CabinetNews/Pages/des.aspx (accessed on 6 December 2018).

Egyptian Institute of Directors (2006), *The Code of Corporate Governance for the Public Enterprise Sector*, Ministry of Investment, Arab Republic of Egypt, https://ecgi.global/code/code-corporate-governance-state-owned-enterprises-egypt.

El-Kady, H. (2012) "Egypt's Bilateral Investment Treaties: A Straitjacket in a New Era of Foreign Investment Re-regulations?", *Transnational Dispute Management*, (2012:3).

El Rashidi, Y. (2018), "Why Do We Destroy What Makes Us?", *The New York Times*, https://www.nytimes.com/2018/11/05/opinion/cairo-heritage-development-maspero-.html (accessed on 14 November 2018).

El-Fiqi, M. (2018), "Egypt's public-sector revamp", *Ahram*, http://english.ahram.org.eg/News/310625.aspx (accessed on 30 November 2018).

European Bank for Reconstruction and Development, European Investment Bank and The World Bank (2016), *What's Holding Back the Private Sector in MENA? Lessons from the Enterprise Survey*, World Bank, Washington DC, http://www.ebrd.com (accessed on 29 January 2019).

FAO (2009), *Egypt: Country Profiles*, Food and Agricultural Organisation of the United States, Gender and Land Rights Database, http://www.fao.org/gender-landrights-database/country-profiles/countries-list/national-legal-framework/rights-entrenched-in-the-constitution/en/?country_iso3=EGY (accessed on 6 November 2018).

GAFI (2017), *Land and Real Estate Ownership Laws*, GAFI, http://www.gafi.gov.eg/English/StartaBusiness/Laws-and-Regulations/Documents/LandandRealEstateOwnershipLaws.pdf (accessed on 29 October 2018).

Gaukrodger, D. (2018) "Appointing Authorities and the Selection of Arbitrators in Investor-State Dispute Settlement: An Overview", OECD Consultation Paper, March.

Gaukrodger (2017a) "The balance between investor protection and the right to regulate in investment treaties", *OECD Working Papers on International Investment*, No. 2017/02, OECD Publishing, Paris, https://doi.org/10.1787/82786801-en.

Gaukrodger, D. (2017b) "Addressing the balance of interests in investment treaties: The limitation of fair and equitable treatment provisions to the minimum standard of treatment under customary international law", *OECD Working Papers on International Investment*, No. 2017/03, OECD Publishing, Paris, https://doi.org/10.1787/0a62034b-en.

Gaukrodger, D. (2016) "The legal framework applicable to joint interpretive agreements of investment treaties", *OECD Working Papers on International Investment*, No. 2016/01, OECD Publishing, Paris, https://doi.org/10.1787/5jm3xgt6f29w-en.

Gaukrodger, D. (2014a) "Investment Treaties and Shareholder Claims for Reflective Loss: Insights from Advanced Systems of Corporate Law", *OECD Working Papers on International Investment*, No. 2014/02, OECD Publishing, Paris, https://doi.org/10.1787/5jz0xvgngmr3-en.

Gaukrodger, D. (2014b), "Investment Treaties and Shareholder Claims: Analysis of Treaty Practice", *OECD Working Papers on International Investment*, 2014/03, OECD Publishing, Paris, https://doi.org/10.1787/5jxvk6shpvs4-en.

Gaukrodger, D. (2013) "Investment treaties as corporate law: Shareholder claims and issues of consistency. A preliminary framework for policy analysis", *OECD Working Papers on International Investment*, No. 2013/3, https://doi.org/10.1787/5k3w9t44mt0v-en.

Gaukrodger, D. and Gordon, K. (2012) "Investor-State Dispute Settlement: A Scoping Paper for the Investment Policy Community", *OECD Working Papers on International Investment 2012/03,* OECD Publishing, Paris, https://doi.org/10.1787/5k46b1r85j6f-en.

Gordon, K. and Pohl, J. (2015) "Investment Treaties over Time – Treaty Practice and Interpretation in a Changing World", OECD Working Papers on International Investment, 2015/02, OECD Publishing, Paris, https://doi.org/10.1787/5js7rhd8sq7h-en.

Government of Egypt (2018), "Press Release: Meeting of the Ministerial Economic Committee", *Cabinet, Government of Egypt*, http://www.cabinet.gov.eg/Arabic/MediaCenter/CabinetNews/Pages/Meeting-of-the-Ministerial-Economic-Committee.aspx (accessed on 2 November 2018).

Hassouna, M. (2018), *The Corporate Governance Experience Under the Egyptian State-Owned Assets Management Programme*, OECD, Lisbon, Portugal.

Ikram, K. (2018), *The Political Economy of Reforms in Egypt: Issues and Policymaking since 1952*, The American University in Cairo Press, Cairo.

ILO (2014), *ILO STAT Employment*, International Labour Organization, https://www.ilo.org/ilostat/faces/wcnav_defaultSelection;ILOSTATCOOKIE=g0OIADPeJNYmTdU-HHVqzl6yNh5k4Bxkohubn42z9gVIOI69g9R8!-951333532?_afrLoop=924201898642560&_afrWindowMode=0&_afrWindowId=null#!%40%40%3F_afrWindowId%3Dnull%26_afrLoop%3D924201898642560%2 (accessed on 7 December 2018).

IMF (2018), "Arab Republic of Egypt : 2017 Article IV Consultation, Second Review Under the Extended Arrangement Under the Extended Fund Facility, and Request for Modification of Performance Criteria-Press Release; Staff Report; and Statement by the Executive Director for the Arab Republic of Egypt", *Country Report*, No. 18/14, IMF, Washington, DC, https://www.imf.org/en/Publications/CR/Issues/2018/01/22/Arab-Republic-of-Egypt-2017-Article-IV-Consultation-Second-Review-Under-the-Extended-45568 (accessed on 30 November 2018).

IMF (2018), "Arab Republic of Egypt : Third Review Under the Extended Arrangement Under the Extended Fund Facility, and Requests for a Waiver of Nonobservance of a Performance Criterion and for Modification of a Performance Criterion-Press Release; Staff Report; and Statement by the Executive Director for the Arab Republic of Egypt", *Country Report*, No. 18/213, IMF, Washington, DC, https://www.imf.org/en/Publications/CR/Issues/2018/07/12/Arab-Republic-of-Egypt-Third-Review-Under-the-Extended-Arrangement-Under-the-Extended-Fund-46061 (accessed on 8 January 2019).

IMF (2018), "IMF Team Reaches Staff-Level Agreement on the Fourth Review for Egypt's Extended Fund Facility", *IMF Press Release No. 18/405*, https://www.imf.org/en/News/Articles/2018/10/31/pr18405-imf-team-reaches-staff-level-agreement-on-the-fourth-review-for-egypts-eff (accessed on 28 January 2019).

IMF (2017), "Arab Republic of Egypt: Selected Issues", *Country Report*, No. 18/15, IMF, Washington, DC, https://www.imf.org/en/Publications/CR/Issues/2018/01/22/Arab-Republic-of-Egypt-Selected-Issues-45569.

Kauffmann, C. and L. Wegner (2007), “Privatisation in the MEDA Region: Where do we Stand?”, *Development Centre Working Paper*, No. 261, OECD, Paris, http://www.oecd.org/dev/wp (accessed on 20 December 2018).

Marshall, S. (2015), *The Egyptian Armed Forces and the Remaking of an Economic Empire*, Carnegie Endowment for International Peace, Washington, DC, https://carnegieendowment.org/files/egyptian_armed_forces.pdf (accessed on 14 December 2018).

Marshall, S. and J. Stacher (2012), “Egypt’s Generals and Transnational Capital”, | *Middle East Research and Information Project*, Vol. 42/Spring, http://www.merip.org/mer/mer262/egypts-generals-transnational-capital (accessed on 13 December 2018).

Ministry of Finance (2018), “News Release: Implementation of an ambitious program of government proposals to provide financing for Egyptian companies”, *Ministry of Finance*, http://www.mof.gov.eg/Arabic/MOFNews/Press/Pages/news-a-18-3-18.aspx (accessed on 13 December 2018).

Ministry of Finance (2016), *Final account of the budgets of economic units*, Ministry of Finance, http://www.mof.gov.eg/Arabic/عناوين%20رئيسيه/Pages/hessab_khetamy.aspx (accessed on 6 December 2018).

Ministry of Finance (2016), *Questions about the Value-Added Law Guide*, Ministry of Finance, Cairo, http://www.mof.gov.eg/MOFGallerySource/Arabic/PDF/Questions_about_the_value-added_law_guide.pdf (accessed on 3 December 2018).

Ministry of Industry and Trade (2018), *Approval by the House of Representatives of the Law of the General Authority for Industrial Development*, Ministry of Industry and Trade, http://www.mti.gov.eg/Arabic/MediaCenter/News/Pages/%D9%85%D9%88%D8%A7%D9%81%D9%82%D8%A9-%D9%85%D8%AC%D9%84%D8%B3-%D8%A7%D9%84%D9%86%D9%88%D8%A7%D8%A8-%D8%B9%D9%84%D9%89-%D9%82%D8%A7%D9%86%D9%88%D9%86-%D8%A7%D9%84%D9%87%D9%8A%D8%A6%D8%A9-%D8%A7%D9%84%D8%B (accessed on 2 November 2018).

Ministry of Public Enterprise (2017), *Estimated budgets of holding companies*, Business Information Center, http://www.bsic.gov.eg/Mowazant_Rep.asp (accessed on 6 December 2018).

Moataz, H. (2012) “Opportunity Egypt”, GAFI Presentation on the Egyptian experience with BITs.

Moataz, H. (2015) “Toward balanced Arab regional investment regulations”, Columbia FDI Perspectives No. 163 (21 December 2015).

Mossallem, M. A. (2016) “Bilateral Investment Treaty Overview – Egypt”, *Investment Claims*, http://oxia.ouplaw.com/abstract/10.1093/law:iic/ov-eg.document.1/law-iic-ov-eg?prd=IC

OECD (2018), *Privatisation and the Broadening of Ownership of State-Owned Enterprises*, OECD, Paris, https://www.oecd.org/daf/ca/Privatisation-and-the-Broadening-of-Ownership-of-SOEs-Stocktaking-of-National-Practices.pdf (accessed on 5 February 2019).

OECD (2018b), “Background information on treaty shopping”, Agenda and Conference Material for the OECD’s 4th Annual Conference on Investment Treaties (12 March 2018), http://www.oecd.org/daf/inv/investment-policy/4th-Annual-Conference-on-Investment-Treaties-agenda.pdf.

OECD (2016), *Limiting Base Erosion Involving Interest Deductions and Other Financial Payments, Action 4 - 2016 Update: Inclusive Framework on BEPS*, OECD/G20 Base Erosion and Profit Shifting Project, OECD Publishing, Paris, https://dx.doi.org/10.1787/9789264268333-en.

OECD (2016b), "The impact of investment treaties on companies, shareholders and creditors", in *OECD Business and Finance Outlook 2016*, OECD Publishing, Paris, pp 223-253, https://dx.doi.org/10.1787/9789264257573-en.

OECD (2015), *Designing Effective Controlled Foreign Company Rules, Action 3 - 2015 Final Report*, OECD/G20 Base Erosion and Profit Shifting Project, OECD Publishing, Paris, https://dx.doi.org/10.1787/9789264241152-en.

OECD (2015), *G20/OECD Principles of Corporate Governance*, http://www.oecd.org/corporate/principles-corporate-governance

OECD (2015), *OECD Guidelines on Corporate Governance of State-Owned Enterprises, 2015 Edition*, OECD Publishing, Paris, https://dx.doi.org/10.1787/9789264244160-en.

OECD (2015), *Policy Framework for Investment, 2015 Edition*, OECD Publishing, Paris, https://dx.doi.org/10.1787/9789264208667-en.

OECD (2014), *Airline Competition Note by Egypt to the Competition Committee meeting 18-19 June 2014*, OECD, Paris, http://www.oecd.org/officialdocuments/publicdisplaydocumentpdf/?cote=DAF/COMP/WD(2014)32&docLanguage=En (accessed on 6 December 2018).

OECD (2014b) Business Climate Review of Egypt: Investment Policies and Public Private Partnerships

OECD (2014c), *Protecting Investment: Legal Frameworks for Infrastructure Investment in Egypt, Jordan, Morocco and Tunisia*, OECD Publishing, Paris, http://www.oecd.org/mena/investment (accessed on 7 January 2019).

OECD (2013), *State-Owned Enterprises in the Middle East and North Africa: Engines of Development and Competitiveness?*, OECD Publishing, Paris, https://doi.org/10.1787/9789264202979-en.

OECD (2012), *Towards new arrangements for state ownership in the Middle East and North Africa.*, OECD Publishing, Paris, https://doi.org/10.1787/9789264169111-en

OECD (2007), *OECD Investment Policy Reviews: Egypt 2007*, OECD Investment Policy Reviews, OECD Publishing, Paris, http://dx.doi.org/10.1787/9789264034624-en.

OECD (forthcoming), *State ownership in the Middle East and North Africa: Comparison with international practices and policy options for reform*, OECD Publishing, Paris.

Omran, M. (2009), "Post-privatisation corporate governance and firm performance: the Role of Private Ownership Concentration, Identity and Board Composition", *Working Paper*, No. 495, Economic Research Forum, http://erf.org.eg/wp-content/uploads/2014/08/495.pdf (accessed on 13 December 2018).

Pohl, J. (2018) "Societal benefits and costs of International Investment Agreements: A critical review of aspects and available empirical evidence", *OECD Working Papers on International Investment*, No. 2018/01, OECD Publishing, Paris, https://doi.org/10.1787/e5f85c3d-en.

Pohl, J. (2013) "Temporal Validity of International Investment Agreements: A Large Sample Survey of Treaty Provisions", *OECD Working Papers on International Investment*, No. 2013/04, OECD Publishing, Paris, https://doi.org/10.1787/5k3tsjsl5fvh-en

Pohl, J., K. Mashigo and Nohen, A. (2012) "Dispute Settlement Provisions in International Investment Agreements: A Large Sample Survey", *OECD Working Papers on International Investment*, No. 2012/02, OECD Publishing, Paris, https://doi.org/10.1787/5k8xb71nf628-en.

Raballand, G. et al. (2015), "Middle East and North Africa Governance Reforms of State-Owned Enterprises (SOEs) Lessons from four case studies (Egypt, Iraq, Morocco and Tunisia)", No. ACS15142, World Bank Group, Washington, DC, http://documents.worldbank.org/curated/en/829511468279359781/Middle-East-and-North-Africa-Governance-reforms-of-state-owned-enterprises-SOEs-lessons-from-four-case-studies-Egypt-Iraq-Morocco-and-Tunisia.

Said, E. G. (2016) Statement by Ms. Eman Gamal Said, Head of International Cooperation Department of GAFI, to the UNCTAD Expert Meeting on Taking Stock of IIA Reform, Geneva (16 March 2016).

Sims, D. (2016), *Securing Land Tenure in Egypt: Who Needs Registered Titles?*, Metropolitics.eu, https://www.metropolitiques.eu/Securing-Land-Tenure-in-Egypt-Who-Needs-Registered-Titles.html (accessed on 9 January 2019).

Sims, D. (2015), *Egypt's Desert Dreams, Development or Disaster?*, The American University in Cairo Press, Cairo, https://play.google.com/books/reader?id=j4gCCgAAQBAJ&hl=en&pg=GBS.PT3 (accessed on 2 November 2018).

Sims, D. (2010), *Understanding Cairo: the logic of a city out of control*, The American University in Cairo Press, Cairo.

Skovgaard Poulsen, L. N. and Aisbett, E. (2013) "When the claim hits: Bilateral investment treaties and bounded rational learning", *World Politics*, Vol. 65, No. 2, pages 273-313.

Thomson Reuters (2018), *Lending and taking security in Egypt*, Thomson Reuters, https://uk.practicallaw.thomsonreuters.com/6-633-8846?transitionType=Default&contextData=(sc.Default)&firstPage=true&comp=pluk&bhcp=1#co_anchor_a577911 (accessed on 14 November 2018).

Transparency International (2018), *The Officers' Republic*, Transparency International, London, http://ti-defence.org/wp-content/uploads/2018/03/The_Officers_Republic_TIDS_March18.pdf (accessed on 6 December 2018).

UNCTAD (2016) "Taking stock of IIA Reform", IIA Issues Note (2016:1).

UNCTAD (2012) Report on the Implementation of the Investment Policy Review – Egypt.

United Arab Republic (1963), "United Arab Republic: Law Prohibiting Foreign Ownership of Agricultural Lands", *International Legal Materials*, Vol. 2/3, https://www-jstor-org-s.acces-distant.sciences-po.fr/stable/20689630?pq-origsite=summon&seq=1#metadata_info_tab_contents (accessed on 29 October 2018).

US Department of Commerce (2018), *Egypt Country Commercial Guide*, Export.gov, International Trade Administration, https://www.export.gov/article?id=Egypt-Banking-Systems (accessed on 7 December 2018).

USAID (2010), *Property Rights and Resource Governance: Egypt*, USAID, Washington, DC, http://usaidlandtenure.net/egypt (accessed on 29 October 2018).

Walid, B. H. (2006) "The First Arab Investment Court Decision", *Journal of World Investment & Trade*, Vol. 7, No. 5, pages 699-721

Wall R.S., Maseland J., R. and Spaliviero M (eds.) (2018), *The State of African Cities 2018: The geography of African investment*, United Nations Human Settlements Programme (UN-Habitat), https://unhabitat.org/books/the-state-of-african-cities-2018-the-geography-of-african-investment/ (accessed on 7 November 2018).

Wang, C. (2017), *Egypt - Policy note on public land acquisition and institutional reforms: application of eminent domain principles*, World Bank, Washington, DC, http://documents.worldbank.org/curated/en/330071507119993972/Egypt-Policy-note-on-public-land-acquisition-and-institutional-reforms-application-of-eminent-domain-principles (accessed on 10 October 2018).

World Bank (2018), *Doing Business 2019: Economy Profile Egypt, Arab Rep.*, World Bank, Washington, DC, http://www.doingbusiness.org/content/dam/doingBusiness/country/e/egypt/EGY.pdf (accessed on 2 November 2018).

World Bank (2018), *World Bank Doing Business 2018: Egypt*, World Bank Group, Washington, DC, http://documents.worldbank.org/curated/en/338781509694287582/pdf/120885-WP-PUBLIC-DB18-EGY.pdf (accessed on 29 October 2018).

World Bank (2016), *Egypt, Arab Rep: Enterprise Survey (ES) 2016*, Ref. EGY_2016_ES_v01_M.

World Bank (2015), *World Development Indicators*, World Bank Data, https://data.worldbank.org/indicator/AG.LND.AGRI.ZS?locations=EG (accessed on 17 October 2018).

World Bank (2014), *Jobs or Privileges: Unleashing the Employment Potential of the Middle East and North Africa*, World Bank, Washington DC, http://documents.worldbank.org/curated/en/791831468059652277/pdf/888790MNA0Box382141B00PUBLIC0.pdf (accessed on 31 January 2019).

World Bank (2014), *More Jobs, Better Jobs: A Priority for Egypt*, World Bank, Washington, DC, http://siteresources.worldbank.org/INTMENA/Resources/EgyptJobsReportFinalcolor.pdf (accessed on 1 February 2019).

World Bank (2009), *From Privilege to Competition Unlocking Private-Led Growth in the Middle East and North Africa*, World Bank, Washington, DC, http://siteresources.worldbank.org/INTMENA/Resources/Privilege_complete_final.pdf (accessed on 17 October 2018).

World Bank (2006), *Egypt - Public land management strategy : Policy note*, World Bank, Washington, DC, http://documents.worldbank.org/curated/en/289771468037496435/Policy-note (accessed on 11 October 2018).

Youssef, H., Alnashar, S. Bahaa Hamed; Erian, J., Elshawarby, A., Zaki, C. (2019), Egypt Economic Monitor: From Floating to Thriving – Taking Egypt's Exports to New Levels, Washington, D.C., World Bank Group

Zulficar & Partners (2018), Dispute Prevention and Settlement Mechanisms in Egypt, Working Note, Cairo.

Notes

[1] Investment Map: (www.investinegypt.gov.eg).

[2] The index looks at five dimensions related to land administration: "reliability of infrastructure, transparency of information, geographic coverage, land dispute resolution, and equal access to property rights" (World Bank, 2019[5]).

[3] This does not apply to Public Free Zones, where the Board of Directors determines the value per square meter of land for usufruct, on an annual basis (Article 82 of Executive Regulation). SEZ authorities also set land plot prices for lease or usufruct.

[4] See Pohl, J. (2018); Aisbett, E. et al. (2018); Bonnitcha, J. (2017); Bonnitcha, J. et al. (2017).

[5] Gaukrodger (2017a); Gaukrodger (2017b.)

[6] Said, E. G. (2016).

[7] According to publicly-available information and the OECD's database of international investment agreements, Egypt has signed at least 104 treaties that contain investment protections, with at least 49 BITs and one multilateral treaty in force.

[8] For example, Egypt appears to have at least three or four different investment treaty relationships with several countries – including Comoros, Jordan, Morocco, Qatar, Saudi Arabia, Somalia, Sudan and the United Arab Emirates – but not every treaty relationship appears to be in force.

[9] The European Commission published a Trade Sustainability Impact Assessment in 2014 in support of negotiations of a DCFTA between the EU and Egypt.

[10] Egypt has signed a number of pluri-lateral agreements related to investment. Within the framework of the League of Arab States, Egypt has signed the Agreement on Arab Economic Unity (1957); Agreement on Investment and Free Movement of Arab Capital Among Arab Countries (1970); Convention establishing the Inter-Arab Investment Guarantee Corporation (1971); Unified Agreement for the Investment of Arab Capital in the Arab States (1980) (the Arab Investment Agreement); Agreement on the Encouragement and Protection of Investments and Transfer of Capitals among Arab Countries (2000); Agreement on the Settlement of Investment disputes in Arab Countries (2000); Agadir Agreement with Jordan, Morocco and Tunisia (2004, 2007); and Greater Arab Free Trade Area with all 18 MENA countries (1997, 2005). Within the framework of the Organisation of the Islamic Conference, Egypt has signed the Agreement for Promotion, Protection and Guarantee of Investments among Member States of the OIC (1981) (the OIC Agreement); and Articles of Agreement of the Islamic Corporation for the Insurance of Investment and Export Credit (1992). Within the framework of the Common Market for Eastern and Southern Africa, Egypt has signed the Treaty Establishing the Common Market for Eastern and Southern Africa (1993) (the COMESA Agreement); and Tripartite Free Trade Area agreement between COMESA, EAC and SADC (2015).

[11] *Hesham Talaat M. Al-Warraq v Republic of Indonesia* (ad hoc, UNCITRAL, final award rendered in December 2014); *Kontinental Conseil Ingénierie v. Gabonese Republic* (ad hoc, UNCITRAL, final award rendered in 2017); *D.S. Construction FZCO v Libya* (ad hoc, UNCITRAL, claim filed in October 2016); *Itisaluna Iraq LLC, Munir Sukhtian International Investment LLC, VTEL Holdings Ltd., VTEL Middle East and Africa Limited v Republic of Iraq* (ICSID Case No. ARB/17/10, claim filed in April 2017); *undisclosed investor v Oman* (ad hoc, UNCITRAL, claim filed in 2017); *beIN Corporation v Kingdom of Saudia Arabia* (UNCITRAL, ad hoc, claim filed in October 2018); *Trasta Energy Ltd v Libya* (ad hoc, UNCITRAL, claim filed in January 2019).

[12] Gaukrodger, D. (2018), fn. 5; Investment Arbitration Reporter (2017).

[13] OIC (2019), para 6(III); Investment Arbitration Reporter (2019).

[14] Egypt acceded to the Convention on the Recognition and Enforcement of Foreign Arbitral Awards (the New York Convention) on 9 March 1959 following Presidential Decree No. 171 of 1959 in February 1959.

[15] Egypt signed on 11 February 1972 the Convention on the Settlement of Investment Disputes between States and Nationals of Other States 1965 (the Washington Convention or ICSID Convention), which entered into force with respect to Egypt on 2 June 1972.

[16] Egypt signed the Riyadh Agreement for Arab Judicial Cooperation (the Riyadh Agreement) on 6 April 1983, which was ratified in 2014 following Presidential Decree No. 286 of 2014 and Ministerial Decree No. 43 of 2014.

[17] https://www.mfa.gov.eg/English/Ministry/TreatiesAndDocs/Pages/default.aspx.

[18] For other examples, such as Egypt's BIT with Armenia, several pages are missing from the English version of the treaty on the MFA's website.

[19] Egypt's BITs with Australia, Bahrain, Burundi, Czech Republic, Ethiopia , France, Greece, Hungary, Iceland, Italy, Japan, Kazakhstan, Latvia, Lebanon, Libya, Malawi, Malaysia, Mali, Mauritius, Oman, Portugal, Qatar, Russian Federation, Slovak Republic, Slovenia, Somalia, Sudan, Tunisia, Turkmenistan and the United Arab Emirates do not appear on the MFA's website.

[20] See, for example, Egypt's BITs with Argentina, Canada, Croatia, Denmark, Finland, Germany, South Korea, Kuwait, Mongolia, Morocco, Netherlands, Nigeria, Poland, Romania, Serbia, Singapore, Spain, Sri Lanka, Sweden, Switzerland, Syria, Thailand, Turkey, Ukraine, United Kingdom, United States and Yemen.

[21] See, for example, Egypt's BITs with Chile, Georgia, North Macedonia, South Africa and Zambia.

[22] The coverage is assessed based on FDI stock data (2016 or, where 2016 data was unavailable, data of preceding years, giving preference to more recent data, based on data released by OECD and IMF) and investment treaties in force in May 2019. For several reasons, reported FDI stock data is not a valid measure for assets that benefit from treaty protections (Pohl (2018)) and available data does not allow to determine ultimate ownership of assets. The proportions of FDI stock data may nonetheless serve as a rough approximation of stock held by the immediate investing country to illustrate features and outcomes of Egypt's past investment treaty policies.

[23] Italy-Egypt BIT (1989); Netherlands-Egypt BIT (1996); United Kingdom-Egypt BIT (1975); United States-Egypt BIT (1986).

[24] Belgium/Luxembourg-Egypt BIT (1999); Denmark-Egypt BIT (1999); France-Egypt BIT (1974); Germany-Egypt BIT (2005); Greece-Egypt BIT (1993); Spain-Egypt BIT (1992); Switzerland-Egypt (2010); OIC Agreement (1981)

[25] Canada-Egypt BIT (1996); China-Egypt BIT (1994); France-Egypt BIT (1974); Italy-Egypt BIT (1989); Mauritius-Egypt BIT (2014).

[26] The comparison of GDP per capita in PPP terms between Egypt and its respective treaty partner was determined for the year when the treaty was concluded; where this data were not available, data for the earliest year available for the country-pair were used. The values of per capita GDP PPP in current terms were taken from the World Bank's World Development Indicators as of mid-2018.

[27] Moataz, H. (2012); UNCTAD (2012).

[28] GAFI indicates that the 2007 model BIT is available for download on UNCTAD's Investment Policy Hub database.

[29] Moataz, H. (2012); UNCTAD (2012).

[30] GAFI indicates that these BITs were signed with Ethiopia (2006), Iceland (2008), Switzerland (2010), Burundi (2012) and Mauritius (2014). Egypt's BITs with Switzerland and Mauritius are available on the MFA website.

[31] Skovgaard Poulsen, L. N. et al. (2013).

[32] The discussion here refers only to known claims. Under many Egyptian investment treaties, claimants can often select arbitration rules under which claims must remain confidential. Governments also can prefer individual claims to remain confidential to avoid embarrassment. The number of actual ISDS claims against Egypt appears likely to be higher based on confidential pending cases. Egypt indicated in a prospectus for a public bond offering issued in February 2018 that "[t]here are 20 investment treaty arbitrations and international litigation proceedings against Egypt, of which nine are ICSID arbitrations." Governments have worked collectively at UNCITRAL Commission meetings to provide for greater transparency in light of the public interest and impact on public budgets at issue in ISDS. As of May 2019, Egypt is not a signatory of the 2014 United Nations Convention on Transparency in Treaty-based Investor-State Arbitration (the Mauritius Convention) – a multilateral effort to address concerns regarding the lack of transparency in ISDS cases by establishing a set of procedural rules for making information publicly available on ISDS cases.

[33] https://icsid.worldbank.org/en/Pages/cases/AdvancedSearch.aspx.

[34] *Yosef Maiman, Merhav (MNF), Merhav-Ampal Group, Merhav-Ampal Energy Holdings v. Arab Republic of Egypt*, PCA Case No. 2012/26 (Egypt-Poland BIT); *Mohamed Abdel Raouf Bahgat v. Arab Republic of Egypt*, PCA Case No. 2012-07 (Finland-Egypt BIT); *Nile Douma Holding v. Egypt* (Bahrain-Egypt BIT); *MetroJet (Kogalymavia) Limited v Egypt* (Egypt-Russia BIT); *Prens Turizm Kuyumculuk Tasimacilik ve Dis Ticaret Limited v Egypt* (Egypt-Turkey BIT). It has also been reported that Saudi investors initiated three arbitrations against Egypt under the OIC Agreement (1981) in 2014 relating to hotel and tourism investments but none of the three claims ultimately proceeded due to the OIC Secretariat's reluctance to make default arbitrator appointments after Egypt declined to nominate an arbitrator.

[35] *Southern Pacific Properties (Middle East) Limited v. Arab Republic of Egypt* (ICSID Case No. ARB/84/3); *Manufacturers Hanover Trust Company v. Arab Republic of Egypt and General Authority for Investment*

and Free Zones (ICSID Case No. ARB/89/1). The investors in these cases are understood to have invoked an ICSID clause in Law No. 43 of 1974 Concerning the Investment of Arab and Foreign Funds and the Free Zones, as amended by Law No. 32 of 1977. Law No. 43 repealed the prior investment regime established by Law No. 65 of 1971, which had been issued by President Sadat on 23 September 1971 and published in the Official Gazette on 30 September 1971.

[36] *Wena Hotels Limited v. Arab Republic of Egypt* (ICSID Case No. ARB/98/4).

[37] It has been reported by Bloomberg and Global Arbitration Reporter that a settlement deal in *Fund III Egypt, LLC, LP Egypt Holdings I, LLC and OMLP Egypt Holdings I, LLC v Arab Republic of Egypt* (ICSID Case No. ARB/16/37) involved a payment of approximately USD 20 million and that Egypt agreed to pay USD 54 million to the investor as part of a settlement deal in *Indorama International Finance Limited v Arab Republic of Egypt* (ICSID Case No. ARB/11/32).

[38] *Southern Pacific Properties (Middle East) Limited v Arab Republic of Egypt* (ICSID Case No. ARB/84/3), Award, 20 May 1992 (awarding the investor approximately USD 27.7 million plus interest); *Waguih Elie George Siag and Clorinda Vecchi v Arab Republic of Egypt* (ICSID Case No. ARB/05/15) Award, 1 June 2009 (awarding the investor approximately USD 74.6 million plus interest).

[39] *Unión Fenosa Gas, S.A. v. Arab Republic of Egypt* (ICSID Case No. ARB/14/4), Award, 31 April 2018. Egypt filed for annulment of the tribunal's award under Article 52 of the ICSID Convention in January 2019 and the annulment proceedings remain pending as of May 2019.

[40] See, for example, *Abd-El-Aziz Saleh Esmail Abdallah Al-Rashed, Awrad International Holding, International Holding Project Group and others v Arab Republic of Egypt* (ICSID Case No. ARB/18/31) (reported to involve damages claims by Kuwaiti investors of around USD 15 billion); *Yosef Maiman, Merhav (MNF), Merhav-Ampal Group, Merhav-Ampal Energy Holdings v Arab Republic of Egypt* (PCA Case No. 2012/26) and *Ampal-American Israel Corp., EGI-Fund (08-10) Investors LLC, EGI-Series Investments LLC, BSS-EMG Investors LLC and David Fischer v Arab Republic of Egypt* (ICSID Case No. ARB/12/11) (two related cases reported here and here to involve damages claims totalling over USD 1 billion).

[41] *Eastern Company S.A.E. v Lebanon* (CRCICA, award issued in June 2002); *Orascom Telecom Holding S.A.E v People's Democratic Republic of Algeria* (PCA Case No 2012-20, consent award issued on 12 March 2015); *Global Telecom Holding S.A.E. v Canada* (ICSID Case No ARB/16/16, claim registered on 6 June 2016); *Almasryia for Operating & Maintaining Touristic Construction Co. L.L.C. v State of Kuwait* (ICSID Case No ARB/18/2, claim registered on 14 February 2018); *Ayat Nizar Raja Sumrain and others v State of Kuwait* (ICSID Case No ARB/19/20, claim registered on 30 June 2019).

[42] *Orascom TMT Investments S.à.r.l. v People's Democratic Republic of Algeria* (ICSID Case No. ARB/12/35), Award, 31 May 2017.

[43] According to case analysis covering the period 1997 to mid-2018 and made publicly available by UNCTAD, out of 499 cases for which data on alleged breaches was available, investors worldwide have invoked the standard in 411 claims, or 82%, and tribunals have found a breach in 104 cases.

[44] Egypt's BITs with Albania, Georgia, Iran, Japan, Libya, Palestine, the United States and Uzbekistan do not provide for FET (but only the BITs with Albania, Japan and the United States are in force); nor do the regional OIC and Arab Investment Agreements. At least two of Egypt's BITs contain FET wording in the preamble only rather than in the main text of the treaty: see Azerbaijan-Egypt BIT (2002); Turkey-Egypt BIT (1996). This is a common trait of Turkey's investment treaty practice. Brazil, Turkey and Japan have

a lower rate of FET provisions in their concluded investment treaties but these countries' treaty samples are considerably younger than Egypt's, on average, which makes Egypt's regime unique in this respect.

45 There are a few exceptions. For example, one of Egypt's early investment treaties links FET to domestic law obligations: see Finland-Egypt BIT (1980), Article 2(1): "Each Contracting State shall, subject to its laws and regulations, at all times ensure fair and equitable treatment to the investments of nationals and companies of the other Contracting State." Another gives examples of prohibited conduct: see Article 3: "Chacune des parties contractantes s'engage à garantir un traitement juste et équitable sur son territoire et sa zone maritime pour les investissements des nationaux et sociétés de l'autre partie contractante, excluant la prise de toute mesure injustifiée ou discriminatoire qui pourrait entraver en droit ou en fait la gestion de ces investissements ou leur maintenance, ou leur utilisation, ou la jouissance ou leur liquidation." At least two of Egypt's BITs contain a unique "non-impediment" qualification to the FET obligation but this is unlikely to have particular significance in the interpretation of FET in practice: see Article 3 of the France-Egypt BIT (1974): "Each Contracting Party shall undertake to accord in its territory just and equitable treatment to the investments of nationals and companies of the other Party *and to ensure that the exercise of the right so granted is not impeded either de jure or de facto*." (Emphasis added.). See also Chile-Egypt BIT (1999), Article 4(1).

46 Gaukrodger, D. (2017b), pp. 14-15.

47 Gaukrodger, D. (2017b).

48 For a recent example, see the Joint Interpretative Declaration between Columbia and India (2018) regarding the Columbia-India BIT (2009). See also Gaukrodger, D. (2016); Gordon, K. and Pohl, J. (2015).

49 See, e.g., *Emilio Agustín Maffezini v. Kingdom of Spain* (ICSID Case No. ARB/97/7). For a recent discussion of the uncertainty surrounding the interpretation of MFN clauses in ISDS disputes, see Batifort, S. and Benton Heath, J. (2018) "The New Debate on the Interpretation of MFN Clauses in Investment Treaties: Putting the Brakes on Multilateralization", *American Journal of International Law*, Volume 111, Issue 4 (October 2017), pp. 873-913.

50 See, e.g., EU-Canada CETA (2016), Article 8.7(2): "For greater certainty, the [most-favoured-nation treatment] does not include procedures for the resolution of investment disputes between investors and states provided for in other international investment treaties and other trade agreements. Substantive obligations in other international investment treaties and other trade agreements do not in themselves constitute 'treatment,' and thus cannot give rise to a breach of this Article, absent measures adopted or maintained by a Party pursuant to those obligations." See also OECD (2018b), "Background information on treaty shopping", Agenda and Conference Material for the OECD's 4th Annual Conference on Investment Treaties (12 March 2018).

51 The arbitral tribunal in the *White Industries* case allowed the investor to import an "effective means" clause from a third-party treaty via the MFN clause in the India-Australia BIT with no analysis of how it considered the relevant MFN clause to operate: *White Industries Australia Limited v. Republic of India*, UNCITRAL, *ad hoc*, Final Award, 30 November 2011, paras 11.2.1-11.2.9.

52 United States-Mexico-Canada Agreement (2018), Article 14.5(4) ("For greater certainty, whether treatment is accorded in "like circumstances" under this Article depends on the totality of the circumstances, including whether the relevant treatment distinguishes between investors or investments on the basis of legitimate public welfare objectives.")

[53] Egypt's BITs with Qatar (1990), Tunisia (1989) and Uzbekistan (1992) do not contain ISDS provisions. Likewise, Egypt's early BITs with Germany (1994), the Netherlands (1976) and Switzerland (1974) did not contain ISDS provisions but these BITs have all been replaced with newer treaties that contain ISDS mechanisms.

[54] Canada-Egypt BIT (1996), Article XIII(3)(d); Switzerland-Egypt BIT (2010), Article 12(5).

[55] Gaukrodger, D. (2018).

[56] Canada-Egypt BIT (1996), Article XIII(9).

[57] See, for example, Australia-Indonesia CEPA (2019), EU-Canada CEPA (2016).

[58] See EU-Canada CETA (2016), EU-Viet Nam Investment Protection Agreement (2018); EU-Singapore Investment Protection Agreement (2018).

[59] See, generally, UNCITRAL Commission, Working Group III, "Investor-State Dispute Settlement Reform".

[60] For a recent example, see the Joint Interpretative Declaration between Columbia and India (2018) regarding the Columbia-India BIT (2009). See also Gaukrodger, D. (2016).

[61] See, e.g., Arab Investment Agreement (1980), Article 1(4) (defining an "Arab citizen" protected by the Agreement as "an individual or a body corporate having the nationality of a State Party, provided that no part of the capital of such body corporate belongs either directly or indirectly to non-Arab citizens. Joint Arab projects which are fully owned by Arab citizens shall be deemed to be included within this definition in instances where they do not have the nationality of another State").

[62] Article 2 of the new Investment Law provides: "Investment in the Arab Republic of Egypt aims at improving the national economic growth rates and the domestic production rates, as well as provision of employment opportunities, promotion of exports, and boosting of competitiveness which contribute to achieving the comprehensive and sustainable development. Investment is governed by the following principles: ... 2. Consideration of all aspects with social dimension, protection of the environment and the public health. ... These investment principles apply to the Investor and the State, each in their respective areas of responsibility."

[63] See, for example, Australia-Indonesia CEPA (2019), Article 14.16; United States-Mexico-Canada Agreement (2018), Article 14.17; Brazil-Chile FTA (2018), Article 8.17; Argentina-United Arab Emirates BIT (2018), Article 11.

[64] See Canada-Egypt BIT (1996) (in a general exceptions clause), Mauritius-Egypt BIT (2014) (in the preamble text and the security exceptions clause); Switzerland-Egypt BIT (2010) (in the preamble text); OIC Agreement (1981) (in the preamble and Article 3); COMESA Agreement (1994) (in the preamble and Articles 3, 72, 122, 123, 126, 129 and 154); Arab Investment Agreement (1980) (in the preamble).

[65] See, for example, Japan-Viet Nam BIT (2003), Article 21; Netherlands Model BIT (2018), Article 6(3); Argentina-United Arab Emirates BIT (2018), Article 12.

[66] See, e.g., Brazil-Chile FTA (2018), Article 8.16.

[67] See, e.g. China-Peru FTA (2009), which states in the preamble that the State Parties "RECOGNIZE that this Agreement should be implemented with a view toward raising the standard of living, creating new employment opportunities, reducing poverty and [...]".

[68] See, e.g. Australia-Indonesia CEPA (2019), Article 14.17; United States-Mexico-Canada Agreement (2018), Article 14.17; Brazil-Chile FTA (2018), Article 8.16.

[69] See, for example, Articles 3 and 15 regarding corruption and corporate social responsibility.

[70] See, for example, the findings of the Australian Productivity Commission: Australian Government (2010), "Bilateral and Regional Trade Agreements", Productivity Commission Research Report, Australian Government, November 2010.

[71] Berger et al., 2013.

[72] See, for example, EU-Canada CETA (2016), Article 8.4; EU-Vietnam FTA (2018), Article 8.4.

[73] Canada-Egypt BIT (1996), Article II(3); United States-Egypt BIT (1986), Article II(1), (2). Some other Egyptian treaties extend MFN and NT treatment to "activities associated with" investments, which arguably also covers pre-establishment activities: see, for example, China-Egypt BIT (1994), Article 3(2). Others clarify that MFN and NT treatment only applies after an investment is established in the territory of one of the treaty parties: see, for example, Turkey-Egypt BIT (1996), Article II(2).

[74] State-owned enterprises mentioned in the present report refer to enterprises engaged in commercial and non-commercial activities, and owned by a wide range of public authorities, including sectoral ministries and the military authorities.

[75] Economic authorities are public bodies that manage, regulate or provide services. They include some corporatised entities, such as the Egyptian General Petroleum Corporation, as well as railway and port authorities, and authorities in charge of free, investment and special economic zones. While some of these entities are involved in economic activity, they are for the most part government branches and are not included in this analysis.

Chapter 4. Investment promotion and facilitation

This chapter analyses the investment promotion and facilitation policies in place in Egypt, examines the institutional framework for investment promotion and facilitation, with a particular focus on the role and activities of GAFI, highlights key reforms and measures implemented by the government to attract foreign investment and improve the business environment and also identifies remaining challenges and proposes recommendations to address them.

Summary and policy recommendations

Investment promotion and facilitation policies can support a country's competitiveness of by branding it as a profitable investment destination, attracting quality investors and making it easy for businesses to establish or expand their operations. These measures can not only support the creation of an attractive economy but also help ensure that foreign investments generate positive spill-overs through the development of poorer areas, linkages with domestic companies and skills transfer. It is important that these efforts complement – and do not replace – measures to ensure a sound investment policy framework.

In Egypt, the new Investment Law from 2017 demonstrates the high priority that the government places on promoting and facilitating private investment. The law's most notable features are the creation of Investors Services Centres supporting the establishment of new businesses and the implementation of an investment incentives' regime aiming at promoting local development in poorer regions of the country. Investment promotion instruments have also been put in place, such as the Investment Map – an innovative and interactive software to present investment opportunities by sectors and locations.

The General Authority for Investment and Free Zones (GAFI) is a large investment promotion agency (IPA) in charge of investment policy, promotion and facilitation. It was under the authority of the Ministry of Investment and International Co-operation (MIIC) until December 2019, when it was brought under the authority of the Prime Minister. GAFI's investment facilitation and policymaking mandates are well-developed but could have a tendency to overshadow its investment attraction efforts. The country looks to promote increased levels of foreign direct investment (FDI) but lacks a clear, nationwide and well-articulated strategy to do so. In the business community, GAFI has the reputation for being a responsive and problem-solving organisation, but co-ordination among key public agencies and ministries can be improved.

Policy recommendations

- Prepare a high-level investment policy statement to present the investment landscape in Egypt and its vision for FDI, highlight key government orientations and business climate reforms, and showcase the country's commitment to private investment;
- Supplement it with a well-articulated investment promotion strategy providing targets, tools and indicators to guide GAFI's investment promotion and facilitation activities and ensure that FDI attraction is well-aligned with national development objectives;
- Building on these strategic efforts, improve institutional co-ordination mechanisms on investment promotion and facilitation and clarify the roles and responsibilities of relevant ministries and implementing agencies;
- Consider strengthening the separation between GAFI's policymaking responsibilities and its promotion and facilitation tasks or dividing the agency into two distinct entities– one in charge of negotiating treaties, regulating investment and reviewing applications, and the other responsible for investment promotion and facilitation.
- Build on the notable efforts to brand the country and guide potential investors to existing opportunities through the Investment Map to gradually conduct systematic investor outreach and targeting activities to attract quality investments that can support sustainable and inclusive development.
- Continue and strengthen the monitoring and evaluation of the functioning and the performance of the Investors Services Centres to ensure, on the one hand, that investors are satisfied and, on the other, that the centres provide value for money;

- Pursue efforts to systematically revise existing administrative procedures and requirements to start and operate a business with a view to eliminating those which are deemed redundant or unnecessary; and
- Building on the recently established monthly public-private sector meetings at the MIIC, establish a whole-of-government public-private dialogue platform to instigate an environment of trust between the government and the business community. Use it systematically to consult with the private sector, to seek business representatives' views on the main challenges to address, and to discuss government priorities and reforms.

The institutional framework for investment promotion and facilitation in Egypt

A network of public agencies with GAFI as the main national IPA

Recognising the importance of private investment for economic and social development, most countries in the world have established IPAs dedicated to promoting and facilitating investment, often with a particular emphasis on attracting multinational enterprises (MNEs) and capturing the benefits of FDI.

In the vast majority of countries, IPAs are major players in the implementation of four core functions:

- *image building* consists of fostering the positive image of the host country and branding it as a profitable investment destination;
- *investment generation* deals with direct marketing techniques targeting specific sectors, markets, projects, activities and investors, in line with national priorities;
- *investment facilitation, retention and aftercare* is about providing support to investors to facilitate their establishment phase as well as retaining existing ones and encouraging reinvestments by responding to their needs and challenges; and
- *policy advocacy* includes identifying bottlenecks in the investment climate and providing recommendations to government in order to address them.

While the first two functions relate to investment promotion (i.e. marketing a country or a region as an investment destination and attracting new investors), the latter two deal with investment facilitation (i.e. making it easy for investors to establish, operate and expand their existing investments) (Novik and de Crombrugghe, 2018). Investment promotion is meant to attract potential investors that have not yet selected an investment destination, whereas facilitation starts at the pre-establishment phase, when an investor shows interest in a location. As such, and as will be explained below, investment promotion and attraction is primarily the business of IPAs while facilitation is not limited to IPAs and involves a whole-of-government approach.

Large differences exist among IPAs in terms of institutional settings, governance policy, strategic priorities, and investment promotion tools and activities. The way governments around the world organise their institutional framework for investment promotion and facilitation responds to their policy objectives and the priority they give to investment. These choices can greatly influence their success in attracting investment in the most efficient and effective manner.

The investment promotion landscape in Egypt is dominated by GAFI, which is the leading public agency in charge of investment promotion, facilitation and regulation. GAFI is a large organisation with numerous mandates that go beyond the scope of investment promotion and facilitation. It is the operational arm of the government and its main action is based on five major pillars:

1. Attraction, reinvestment and expansion of foreign investment;
2. Stimulation of domestic investment;

3. Development of investment services;
4. Management of free zones and development of investment zones to accelerate the expansion of competitive strategic clusters; and
5. Institutional support to entrepreneurship development and stimulation of innovation development.

Although GAFI is the main national IPA in Egypt (see section below for a more detailed analysis), other parts of the government are, in one way or another, involved in investment promotion and facilitation activities. The Ministry of Trade and Industry – particularly the Industrial Development Authority (IDA), one of its main executive arms – is active in promoting FDI in Egypt's industrial sectors, notably through the development of industrial zones (see Chapter 5 on zone-based policies). With the authority over industrial land – and access to land being a major recognised investment climate challenge – the IDA has a key role to play in the country's investment attraction strategy.

As GAFI is responsible for free zones, investment zones and technology zones, a relatively artificial division of labour has been established between the two ministries to oversee the development of zones and the promotion and facilitation of investment into these zones. Some promotional activities are duplicated, which is not efficient in terms of government resources nor beneficial in providing a clear message to investors. GAFI and IDA are seeking to co-ordinate on investment projects, especially those inside industrial zones, but these two agencies would have an interest in co-operating more closely in order to rationalise resources and to conduct a more efficient investment promotion strategy. In this regard, GAFI's recent affiliation to the Egyptian Council of Ministers (Prime Minister Decree 38/2020) is expected to enhance effective co-operation with all the government bodies involved in investment promotion and facilitation.

The General Authority for the Suez Canal Economic Zone (SCZA) is another important actor involved in investment promotion and facilitation in a strategic location of the country. The SCZA has the mandate to manage and promote the SCZone, through state-of-the-art facilities and services as well as a variety of financial and non-financial incentives for investors willing to set up in the SCZone. It has executive powers of regulation and approval – including the full authority to oversee all areas of operation, staffing, budget and funding, partnerships with developers and business facilitation services. Relevant ministries are also part of the SCZA's board.

GAFI's organisational characteristics

In the context of the EU-OECD Programme on Promoting Investment in the Mediterranean, Egypt recently participated in a survey of IPAs conducted by the OECD (Box 4.1). The results serve as the basis of some of the comparative analysis conducted in this chapter, which benchmarks GAFI against its regional peers and against agencies from other regions.

Box 4.1. The OECD-IDB survey of investment promotion agencies

The OECD and the Inter-American Development Bank (IDB) have partnered to design a comprehensive survey of IPAs. The questionnaire provides detailed data that reflect the multiple recent policy developments as well as rich and comparable information on the work of national agencies in different countries.

In 2017-2018, the survey was shared with IPA representatives from 32 OECD and 19 Latin America and Caribbean (LAC) countries. In 2018, 10 national agencies from the Mediterranean (MED) region participated in the same survey, which was displayed in the form of an online questionnaire and divided into nine parts:

- Basic profile;

- Budget; Personnel;
- Offices (home and abroad);
- Activities;
- Prioritisation;
- Monitoring and evaluation;
- Institutional interactions; and
- IPA perceptions on FDI.

The results of the survey are gathered and presented in comprehensive IPA mapping reports, which provide a full and comparative picture of IPAs in selected regions. The reports are benchmarking agencies against each other as well as the average IPA in a region against other regions.

Objectives and mandates

IPAs can be either fully dedicated to investment promotion and facilitation – and exclusively focus on the four core functions mentioned above – or be part of a broader agency that includes additional mandates, such as the promotion of exports, innovation, regional development, outward investment and domestic investment, among others. In practice, most IPAs around the world have multiple mandates and conduct activities that go beyond inward foreign investment promotion. In OECD economies, the most frequent combination of mandates in IPAs are with export promotion (56% of agencies) and with innovation promotion (same percentage) (OECD, 2018a).

GAFI reported in its responses to the IPA survey to have 9 official mandates (out of 18 possible mandates):

1. Inward foreign investment promotion;
2. Outward investment promotion;
3. Domestic investment promotion;
4. Operation of one-stop shop;
5. Screening and prior approval of investment projects with foreign participation or investor registration;
6. Negotiation of international trade, investment and other agreements;
7. Management of special free zones and investment zones;
8. Granting fiscal incentives; and
9. Granting non-financial incentives.

Although large differences exist across agencies, including within the same regions, IPAs in OECD countries as well as in Latin America and the Caribbean (LAC) have generally fewer mandates, with an average of 5.7 and 6.3 different mandates respectively under the agency's responsibility (Figure 4.1). GAFI's total number of mandates is nonetheless overall in line with the average for the Mediterranean (MED) region of 8.6 mandates.

Figure 4.1. Number of mandates of GAFI and selected other national IPAs

(Out of a total of 18 possible mandates)

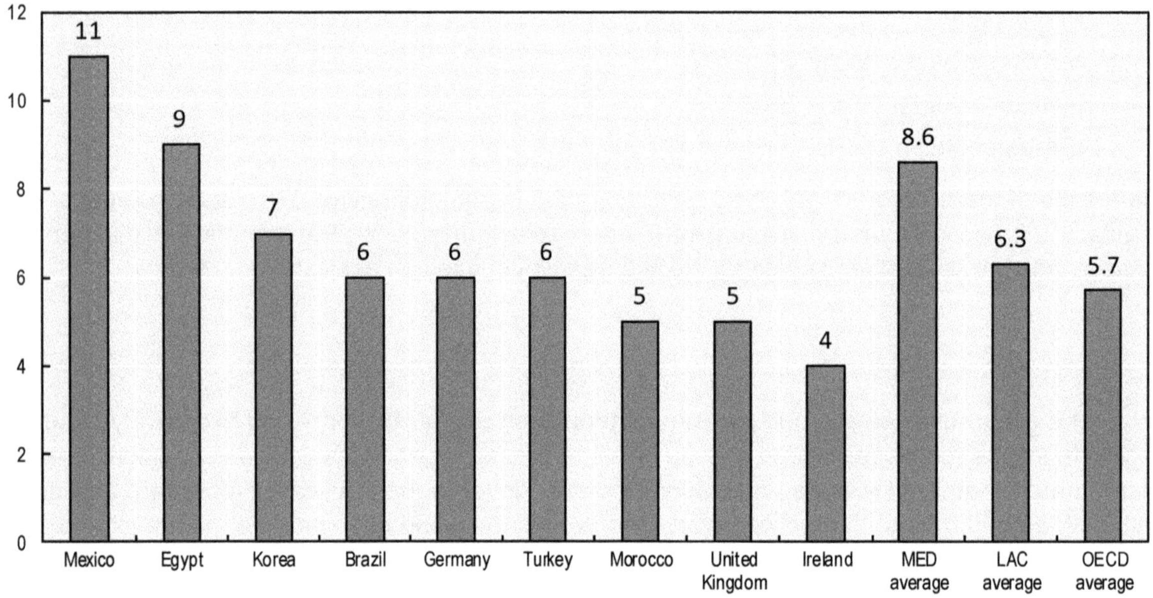

Source: Based on OECD (2018a), OECD (2019) and Volpe Martincus and Sztajerowska (2019).

GAFI's number of mandates reflects its wide scope of responsibilities and activities, which are strongly articulated around investment, both domestic and foreign, as no other policy area (such as export promotion, which is often combined with investment promotion) is included in GAFI's official mandates. This reflects the importance of investment in Egypt's overall development policy and demonstrates a coherent approach to making investment work for growth and prosperity – notably by including foreign investment promotion, domestic investment promotion and the operation of a one-stop shop under the same umbrella. While this is often the case in MED agencies, it is less frequent across IPAs in OECD countries (Figure 4.2).

Figure 4.2. GAFI's mandates and their frequency across MED and OECD agencies

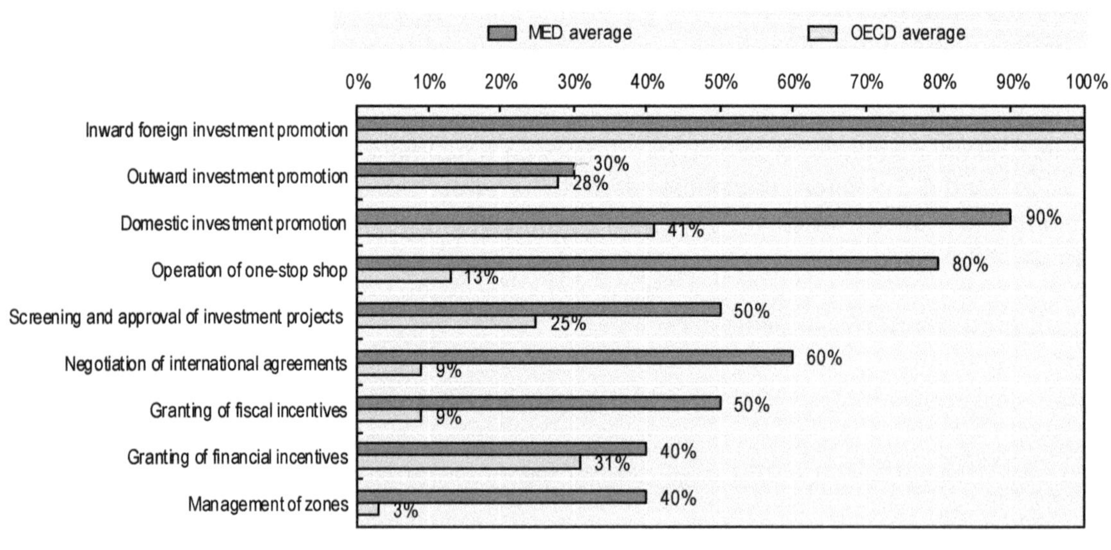

Source: Based on OECD (2018a) and OECD (2019).

It is not a common practice in IPAs to combine regulation and promotion of investment under the same roof, however, and there might be a risk of mixing the two. Some studies show that those IPAs focusing exclusively on investment promotion achieve significantly higher results in attracting investors than those which carry out both regulatory/administrative and promotional activities (World Bank, 2011). The reason behind this finding is that attracting FDI and ensuring that investors comply with legal requirements are two different functions with different objectives and that require different skillsets. Investors contacted by the IPA may wonder whether it is intended to solve their problems or to create new ones. The IPA is often expected to represent private investors' interests within government and it will be less credible to do so and to influence policymaking if it is the same agency that regulates them.

A long-term alternative would be to divide GAFI into two separate entities – one in charge of negotiating treaties, regulating investment and reviewing applications, and the other responsible for investment promotion and facilitation. If this option is considered, the policy part of GAFI would operate as a ministry and its promotion part could increasingly take more autonomy from it. The fact that GAFI has now been moved under the prime minister's responsibility is an opportunity to make this distinction clearer and operational. In most countries, especially in the OECD area, the ministry in charge of investment is responsible for policymaking and, if appropriate, other regulatory aspects such as reviewing investment proposals and monitoring companies' projects. Meanwhile, the IPA is more autonomous from the ministry, sometimes with private sector participation, seeking to find a balance between following the government's strategic orientations and representing the views of investors. This consideration directly relates to GAFI's legal status and governance policy, examined below.

Governance policy

The governance of an IPA relates to the way it is supervised, guided, controlled and managed. IPAs' governance policies are often dictated by their institutional contexts and broader political choices. It affects their legal status, reporting lines and managerial structure, including the role of their board in case they have one.

IPAs can usually be created as: *i)* part of a ministry; *ii)* an autonomous public agency; *iii)* a joint public-private body; or *iv)* a fully privately-owned organisation. GAFI belongs to the second category, as it is an autonomous public agency (reporting to the MIIC until the end of 2019 and now to the prime minister). Autonomous public agencies are the most common forms of IPA legal status according to the IPA surveys conducted by the OECD. All IPAs in the MED region and 60% of those in the OECD are autonomous public agencies (OECD, 2018a and 2019). Across OECD agencies, the second most frequent legal status – just below a third – are governmental IPAs (part of a ministry) and the remaining 9% are private or semi-private.

A key component of an IPA's governance policy is the existence and role of a board. When a board exists, it is meant to supervise or advise the work of the agency, or both, with an independent perspective. Boards vary greatly from one IPA to another; they can be of advisory nature or with a high degree of decision-making power. GAFI's board has changed quite frequently over the past years and has often been limited to a few members. In 2017, the board was reformed in line with the provisions of the Investment Law and has since then been composed of eight members, six of which are from the public sector (including two from GAFI's senior management), and two from the private sector.

Having private sector representatives on the board is a positive initiative, as it ensures that the views and interests of businesses are taken on board in GAFI's broad strategic directions. But it should not be taken for granted that the perspective of the private sector is fully or necessarily represented in all of GAFI's decisions, as it is difficult for a few individuals to represent the views of all companies, given their diversity in terms of economic sector, size, geographic location and specific contexts and challenges. As a matter of comparison, in OECD IPAs, boards are often larger (around ten people on average) and members include just below 40% of private sector representatives on average – the remaining being representatives of the public sector, research and academia, civil society or other areas. In MED agencies, public sector members tend to dominate but the private sector is often well represented – proportionally more than in Egypt (Figure 4.3). Other stakeholders, including from civil society or academia, could also be represented in GAFI's board – as in the case of some OECD and MED agencies – to help better address their concerns in the agency's activities. More importantly, having private sector representatives in the board should not substitute for wide and systematic private sector consultation platforms and mechanisms (see section 3 below on facilitating investments and reinvestments).

Similarly, in most other IPAs – both in MED and OECD countries – public sector members of the board come from other ministries and government agencies, not only to provide complementary skillsets to the strategic decision-making but also to allow for smoother inter-institutional co-ordination. GAFI could consider expanding its board to integrate new members from other ministries and agencies, which would help better align and co-ordinate its activities with other parts of government.

Figure 4.3. Board members in GAFI and selected other IPAs

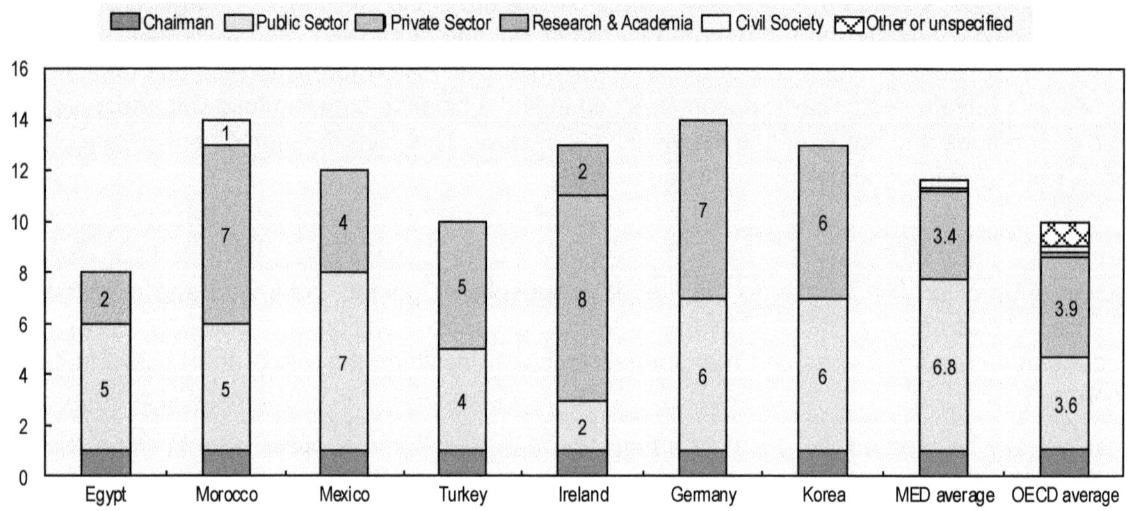

Source: Based on OECD (2018a) and OECD (2019).

Promoting and attracting investment: strategy and tools

To attract FDI in support of national economic objectives, a government first needs to design a clear and well-defined strategy to provide an overall direction, with specific targets and means to achieve the set targets. Depending on the government's objectives, three different types of investment strategies exist:

1) National policy statements on investment, which present and describe the investment landscape and the government's strategic orientations;
2) Investment promotion strategies that define the government's main targets, tools and performance indicators to attract inward foreign investment; and
3) Comprehensive investment strategies that outline in an action plan the government's objectives and reform plans to foster investment and the roles and responsibilities of all relevant government bodies.

Annex 1.A provides a comparative overview of these different strategies, which could help the government of Egypt in its future investment strategy making. It is recommended that the authorities prepare both an overarching policy statement on investment, to give broad orientations to its institutions and a clear vision to the international business community, and a more-focused investment promotion strategy to guide GAFI in its activities and ensure they are well-aligned with national development objectives.

Preparing a high-level investment policy statement

Governments often prepare an investment policy statement prior to the design of – or in parallel to – a more detailed and specific investment promotion strategy. As explained in Annex 1.A, investment policy statements are meant to present the institutional and regulatory landscape for investment in the country as well as the government's strategic orientations and measures to foster investment. Investment policy statements aim to demonstrate a political commitment in favour of private investment. They are relatively short and meant to be widely disseminated, including among the international business community.

Box 4.2. Ireland's 2014 FDI Policy Statement

The Policy Statement on Foreign Direct Investment in Ireland was published by the Irish Department of Jobs, Enterprise and Innovation in July 2014 under the authority of the former Minister. It was released halfway through the government's term (2011-16).

Its purpose is to take stock of the foreign investment policy implemented during the past three years (and sometimes beyond) and to highlight recent achievements and ongoing reforms. It also presents the government's strategic vision for 2014-20 by identifying areas for improvement, but without providing a detailed set of measures to be adopted. To justify these strategic choices, the statement brings to the fore some empirical research work on the impact of investment policies on the economy. An overview of this strategic vision is given through the minister's foreword, which indicates that this policy was designed through a whole-of-government approach to create quality jobs and improve the quality of life of the Irish.

The Policy Statement includes an introduction that describes global investment trends, Ireland's performance in attracting FDI and its contribution to the national economy. The overarching objectives of this FDI strategy are also presented and include the necessity to create employment and enhance national productivity. The strategy aims to contribute to the development of key industrial sectors through the creation of ecosystems and to enable access to global value chains for Irish-owned enterprises. Amongst its objectives, three strategic elements are identified in the strategy:

1. identifying promising sectors based on the Irish industry's strengths;
2. identifying strategic FDI source markets; and
3. facilitating different modes of investment, including greenfield investments, mergers and acquisitions and partnerships with research institutions.

The document identifies strategic policy enablers to reach these objectives: fostering Ireland's key differentiators (human resources, R&D and urban planning); developing sectoral ecosystems; preserving a competitive tax system and maintaining business cost levels; developing infrastructure; and guaranteeing the access to real-estate. For all dimensions, a stocktaking of reforms is made. Actions to be implemented are also identified for each area, although they remain rather general, as they do not provide precise details on the way these actions should be put into effect.

Finally, the Policy Statement briefly presents IDA Ireland, the Irish IPA. It describes its mandate and those from related national agencies such as Enterprise Ireland and the Science Foundation Ireland and recommends the development of a new strategy in line with this FDI Policy Statement.

Source: OECD based on https://dbei.gov.ie/en/Publications/Publication-files/Forf%C3%A1s/Policy-Statement-on-Foreign-Direct-Investment-in-Ireland1.pdf.

The example of Ireland is particularly enlightening, as the complementarity and usefulness of both its *Policy Statement on Foreign Direct Investment* and its investment promotion strategy (*Winning: Foreign Direct Investment 2015-2019*) are very clear. Ireland's policy statement takes stock of past reforms, paves the way for future actions and reflects the government's willingness to put FDI at the heart of economic development (Box 4.2). It also recommends the development of a new investment promotion strategy, which was subsequently designed and is more operational and specific, as it lays down the country's investment opportunities and targets as well as its value proposition – from both a national and sub-national perspective.

The Egyptian authorities should consider preparing and disseminating a national policy statement on investment, as this is the most overarching option and would allow the government to translate its vision into investment objectives and priorities while providing overall guidance to implementing institutions. In line with MIIC's report on "Investing in Development for the SDGs" (2018a), the national policy statement would be an opportunity to demonstrate the government's commitment to foster investment but also to showcase the economy's openness to FDI, as reiterated in the new investment law. Recent and upcoming reforms should also feature in the document, which would provide a positive signal to potential and existing investors and help raise Egypt's profile among the international business community.

Disseminating the national policy statement would also provide overarching guidance for the authorities to prepare more detailed roadmaps and strategic documents, including GAFI's investment promotion strategy, but also in-depth sectoral strategies and a national investment reform action plan that involves all parts of government.

...together with a well-articulated investment promotion strategy

An investment promotion strategy is a more focused and operational policy tool, usually designed by or for the national IPA. It should focus on inward foreign investment and define the major objectives, tools and activities to attract investment, including specific targets and performance indicators to evaluate success, priority sectors and countries for FDI attraction, and the role and responsibilities of the IPA and other agencies to support these objectives or targets.

Investment promotion strategies are prepared to ensure that promotion efforts are well-targeted and contribute to the government's broader national development objectives. They revolve around the question of what to promote (i.e. sectors, countries, projects, investors) and how to implement this promotion in practice. They should rely on a solid evaluation of the economy's strengths, weaknesses, opportunities and threats (SWOT), as there is a risk associated with focusing on specific sectors or picking winners if these decisions are made based on political agendas rather than on carefully crafted economic rationales.

Virtually all IPAs target some investments over others in performing their functions, even without a clear investment promotion strategy in place. According to the OECD survey of IPAs in the MED region, GAFI seems to have well-focused investment promotion activities, as the agency selects sectors, countries, projects and investors in its FDI attraction efforts. Across IPAs in the OECD, only 41% combine these four layers of priorities (OECD, 2018a). Across MED agencies, the majority prioritise countries (90%), sectors (90%) and projects (70%), but Egypt is the only one to also prioritise investors (OECD, 2019).

Prioritising sectors, countries, projects and investors should be conducted according to a set of well-defined criteria in line with national development objectives. The way Egypt selects its criteria for prioritising investment projects, for example, reflects its desire to maximise the potential impact of FDI on society, including with criteria such as the impact of investment projects on jobs, wages, exports, innovation and regional development (Table 4.1). GAFI is interestingly one of the few agencies not to consider the size of investment when prioritising investment projects.

Table 4.1. Criteria used for prioritisation of investment projects by GAFI and selected other IPAs

	Egypt	Morocco	Turkey	Mexico	Poland	UK	Ireland	Korea
Priority Sector	√	√	√	√	√	√	√	√
Priority Country of Origin			√			√		
Mode of Entry			√			√		√
Size of Investment		√	√	√	√	√	√	√
Investment Horizon / Duration	√			√	√	√	√	
Type of Investor				√		√		
Size of the Company			√			√		
Nationality of Investor						√	√	
Company's Engagement in FDI	√	√	√			√	√	
Impact on Job Creation	√	√	√	√	√	√	√	√
Impact on Wages	√			√			√	
Impact on Exports	√	√	√	√		√	√	√
Impact on Innovation	√	√	√	√		√	√	√
Impact on Regional Development	√	√	√	√		√	√	√
Impact on Tax Revenue								
Impact on Country's Image		√	√				√	
Impact on Local Firms' Capacities	√	√	√	√			√	
Impact on Competition			√	√				√
Sustainability	√	√	√	√		√		√

Source: Based on OECD (2018a and 2019).

Priority sectors for economic development are presented in Egypt 2030, but a more specific list of priority sectors and industries for investment – notably FDI – has not been clearly identified. GAFI and the IDA (under the Ministry of Industry and Trade) have each established their own lists of sectors, which seem to be based on a politically negotiated split. GAFI identified labour-intensive, export-oriented, and research and development (R&D)-oriented sectors for FDI promotion, which could potentially include any sector. The Investment Law targets the following industries: renewable energy; tourism; automotive; wood, packaging and chemicals; pharmaceuticals; food and agricultural products. Key industrial sectors identified by IDA include chemicals, engineering, textiles/ready-made garments, food, and building materials – which are not so different from those identified by the Investment Law.

According to GAFI's senior management, an investment promotion strategy is in place but not publicly available or shared internally with other ministries or public agencies. The strategy is said to be based on Egypt 2030 and aimed at guiding GAFI's overall activities, but it does not include detailed investment promotion targets and indicators. It is important that the investment promotion strategy and its main features are developed in co-ordination with other key ministries as investment priorities need to be aligned with other major policy strategies – including trade, innovation, industry and skills. Additionally, making GAFI's investment promotion strategy publicly available would not only support inter-governmental co-ordination, but would also help raise Egypt's positive image within the international business community and inform it about priority sectors and investment opportunities.

The investment promotion strategy should also be very clear and specific about the targets as well as the tools and performance indicators to reach the set targets. It should provide clear indications on how to implement it, i.e. how the staff should be organised internally, what are the main activities it should focus on, what are the key performance indicators to measure outputs and outcomes, and the collaboration mechanisms in place to work with other relevant public agencies and stakeholders (e.g. the private sector).

Implementing investment promotion tools and activities

GAFI is organised by geographic locations and specific investment promotion activities are conducted accordingly by the agency's different teams. Proactive investor targeting and lead generation activities remain relatively limited, as GAFI is focusing on branding the country as an attractive investment destination, providing information to interested investors, helping them establish (i.e. see below the Investors Services Centres) and supporting those that encounter problems. The agency also recently established a unit dedicated to domestic investment promotion.

The 2017 Investment Law provides little information on the four IPA core functions described above, particularly those relating to investment promotion and attraction. According to the OECD survey of IPAs, GAFI allocates its employees equally to image building, investment generation and investment facilitation and retention activities (30% of staff each). Figure 4.4 shows that this estimated share for image building, similarly to the MED average (28%), remains much higher than in the OECD and LAC regions (17% and 18% on average respectively).

Figure 4.4. Estimated use of staff across the four investment promotion functions in GAFI and in the average IPAs of selected regions

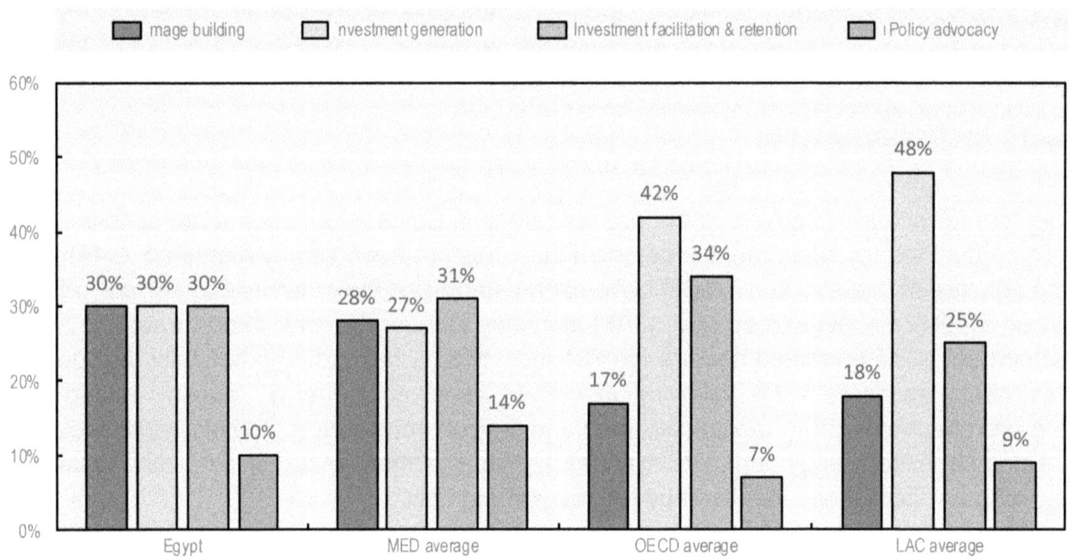

Source: Based on OECD (2018a), OECD (2019) and Volpe Martincus and Sztajerowska (2019).

Conversely, the estimated percentage of staff dedicated to investment generation is slightly higher than the MED average (27%), but significantly lower than the average for OECD and LAC countries (42% and 48% respectively). This reflects the fact that agencies from more advanced countries usually use fewer resources to work on branding or improving their country's image and dedicate most of their promotion efforts to more focused FDI attraction and generation activities. The investment facilitation and retention function is more homogeneous across regions. Its relatively high estimated share in Egypt reflects the importance of the Investors Services Centres in GAFI. Policy advocacy is another function that is relatively similar across Egypt and the three regions.

One of GAFI's new investment promotion flagship instruments is the Investment Map, launched in February 2018. This tool presents, on an interactive map of Egypt, different investment opportunities by sectors and geographic locations, including those in all the different zones, and provides information on existing utilities, the distance to ports and airports, and other logistical information (Box 4.3). It is a horizontal tool by nature and serves the purpose of different functions, notably image building, investment generation and investment facilitation. The Investment Map also reflects improved co-ordination efforts by the government, as investment opportunities from all sectors and in all types of zones are centralised in this tool. Having a single entry point for investors makes it both more efficient for the Egyptian authorities and more helpful for investors to make fully informed investment decisions.

The Investment Map can thus prove a very useful tool for prospective investors. It testifies to how to best use knowledge sharing and information dissemination as catalysts for investment. Focusing investment promotion efforts on specific, ready-made projects is common in other countries and regions, and can constitute a good selling point for some specific investors, but targeting should not be limited to this practice, as most businesses appreciate flexibility as to where and how their investments will be channelled.

Box 4.3. Egypt's Investment Map

To overcome potential information gaps on investment opportunities in Egypt, the MIIC introduced an Investment Map that provides a comprehensive view of the many investment opportunities across the country. In order to encourage new projects and business opportunities, the map allows any potential investor to search and discover opportunities by geographical location and economic sector as well as all major national projects including the mega projects. The map also outlines all the different zones and incentives, including industrial, investment, technology and free zones, in addition to development projects categorised by the relevant development partners. The map provides investors with case studies and information about other investors operating within the market.

The first phase of the investment map was finalised in 2017, including the design, structure and data collection for the map. The final format of the map provides the user with a 360-degree image of all investment opportunities. Upon choosing and selecting a potential opportunity, a short description of the project is provided, in addition to the main information and statistics about the governorates in which it is situated (such as land area, employment rate, etc.). The map also indicates the main utilities surrounding the projects, such as airports, ports, hospitals, universities, technical centres, governmental services and touristic locations. The map specifies the type of contract for the project (rent, holding, usufruct, etc.) and the relevant governmental entity to contact.

The second phase of the map is completed. It included the design and implementation of a management system that ensures the sustainability of the portal. The system provides access to governorates and relevant authorities to collaborate in order to update the data and provide additional investment opportunities.

Source: MIIC (2019).

Additionally, albeit very innovative and informative, the Investment Map remains a simple information portal. Egypt should complement these efforts with more direct marketing techniques to identify and approach potential investors that can support national economic priorities, as laid out in the national investment strategy (see above). Investment generation requires thorough sector-specific knowledge and a good understanding of MNEs' internationalisation strategies (OECD, 2011). The Egyptian commercial services, which are located in key overseas markets, support the country's investment generation activities. They are very active in attracting specific investors, including in all types of zones. Given that these services are also mandated to work on trade facilitation, they report to both the Ministry of Trade and Industry and the local ambassador. They have a working relationship with GAFI but no reporting line.

To enhance investor targeting efforts, GAFI's senior management would also be well advised to consider restructuring its staff according to economic sectors rather than geographic locations, as is the case in most IPAs based in OECD countries. GAFI's staff members have to be able to grasp companies' investment location decision processes and identify their requirements long before their investment decision is taken, to effectively respond to their needs and enquiries during their investigation phase and influence their decision making. Strong sector knowledge is a key success factor in such activities.

From a broader investment promotion perspective, the plethora of zones in Egypt play a crucial role in the country's investment promotion strategy. Many other countries across the world opt for zone-based policies to attract investors, create jobs and increase export earnings. Common features of zones include a geographically defined area and streamlined procedures – such as for customs, special regulations, tax holidays – which are often governed by a single administrative authority. In Egypt, free zones, investment zones and technology zones are under the responsibility of GAFI while industrial zones are under the authority of the Ministry of Industry and Trade. SEZs report directly to the office of the prime minister. Chapter 5 examines in detail the specificities, roles and performance of Egyptian zones.

Finally, the investment incentive scheme constitutes one of Egypt's major investment promotion tools. The 2017 Investment Law introduced a new incentives' classification with two categories, A and B, based on three criteria:

1. The geographical location (Suez Canal special economic zone, Golden Triangle special economic zone and other, less developed, regions as determined by a Ministerial Cabinet's decision)
2. The type of investment (labour-intensive; small and medium-sized enterprises; or export-oriented) and
3. The sector (renewable energy; tourism; automotive; wood, packaging and chemicals; pharmaceuticals; food and agricultural products).

Investments complying with criteria 1 fall under category A (50% discount of the investment costs for a maximum of seven years) and those with criteria 2 and 3 under category B (30% discount of the investment costs for the same amount of time). A detailed analysis of Egypt's investment incentives scheme can be found in Chapter 6 on Tax Incentives for Investment.

Investment facilitation services and activities

Investment facilitation starts when an investor shows interest in a location. It includes the way enquiries are handled by the relevant authorities, notably the IPA, and measures to reduce potential obstacles faced by investors once they have decided to invest. But investment facilitation does not stop there: encouraging the expansion of existing investors and helping them overcome the challenges they face in operating their business is at least as important as facilitating new investments. Aftercare measures can be influential in companies' decisions to stay in the country and reinvest, and policy advocacy is a powerful instrument to bolster reforms and enhance the business environment by leveraging the private sector's feedback.

Starting a business: the Investors Services Centres

One of Egypt's flagship investment climate reforms is the establishment of the Investors Services Centres (ISC), as promulgated by the 2017 Investment Law. The ISCs were set up to grant the approvals, certifications and licences that are necessary for establishing and operating a company. They are typical examples of what are commonly known as one-stop shops, which consist in placing officials from different government agencies and ministries under the same roof to centralise administrative procedures and requirements for incoming investors. One-stop shops have been established in various parts of the world, often under the IPA and are frequently geared towards foreign businesses.

ISCs in Egypt include full start-to-end services to investors, including services related to establishing companies and their branches, approving the minutes of their boards of directors and their general assemblies, issuing approvals and permits and allocating the necessary real estate for the establishment of projects (MIIC, 2018b). As of September 2019, 10 ISCs had been established and were operating in the country, and ISCs are expected to be established in all 27 governorates. Depending on their level of development and geographic location, each ISC has a different number of external agencies and ministries represented. In Alexandria, for example, 28 other ministries and public agencies were represented in their ISC as of mid-2018. Several ISCs have now reached 66 entities according to government sources. ISCs are also increasingly integrating digital tools for business registration, such as the electronic signature service that enables reducing the time needed for certain procedures. The law also gives the possibility to create private accreditation offices, licenced and registered by GAFI, that deliver all permits. As such, the government seeks to engage the private sector in the licensing process and to expand the possible channels for business registration.

Integrating fully-fledged ISCs under its responsibility makes GAFI a "facilitation-oriented" IPA, offering a wide range of government services to incoming investors. As such, the wide scope of its administrative support services makes GAFI very competitive vis-à-vis other IPAs in the MED region – and even more so vis-à-vis those from OECD and LAC regions (Figure 4.5). The same services that are offered by GAFI are only available in 86% of MED agencies, 67% of OECD agencies and 63% of LAC agencies on average.

Figure 4.5. IPA services aiming to assist investors with administrative procedures in Egypt and in selected regions

(% of IPAs performing the activities)

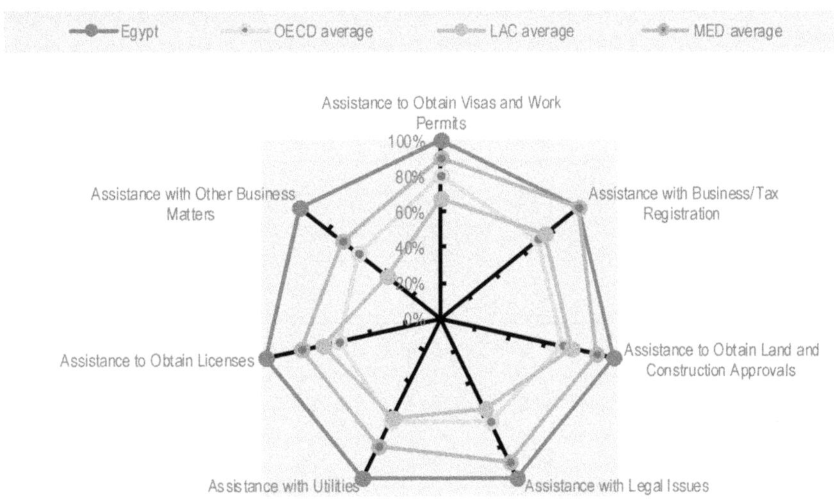

Source: Based on OECD (2018a), OECD (2019) and Volpe Martincus and Sztajerowska (2019).

The pros and cons of one-stop shops have been widely debated in the literature and amongst investment promotion and facilitation practitioners. On the one hand, they can significantly reduce transaction costs for businesses if they are fully-functional but, on the other hand, they can become "one-more stop" if officials from external ministries do not have sufficient decision power and full approval authority. They can also prove costly for governments, as they force ministries to duplicate or multiply the number of officials to allow a presence in both their own administration and in the existing one-stop shop offices.

The Egyptian ISCs follow a number of good international practices. Firstly, unlike in some other countries, they are not mandatory entry points for investors, as businesses can opt for alternative routes to open a business if they so wish, which is an incentive for ISCs to remain efficient. It is the quality of its services that should determine the decision of investors to interact with ISCs or to seek for alternative options. Secondly, ISCs are equipped with a Customer Relationship Management system, which includes key performance indicators for monitoring performance. Customers are also invited to fill in satisfaction surveys and forms. Thirdly, the costs of the ISCs seem to be efficiently and equitably shared between GAFI and external ministries, since, according to the authorities, the basic salaries are paid by the relevant ministries while GAFI covers these extra costs thanks to the revenues made out of lending land in the free zones.

ISCs have been generally welcomed by the international business community established in Egypt but more time is needed to evaluate their long-term influence on the business environment. One of the main points is to ensure the licensing decisions can be taken within the ISCs, particularly when a case is not fully straightforward and the approval process is more complex. The decision power of representatives sitting in the ISCs is the key question as it means bearing the responsibility. It is also important that the decisions to grant or refuse a business licence are transparent and made publicly available, with a right of appeal for those investors who have seen their licence rejected.

Starting and running a business: wider measures

The government's efforts to improve the business environment, especially to facilitate business creation, have allowed the country improve its ranking in the World Bank's overall Ease of Doing Business. Egypt ranked 114 out of 190 in 2020, improving by six notches from 2019 and by 14 notches since 2018. Similarly, the country improved significantly its ranking in the 'Starting a Business' sub-category, from 109 in 2019 to 90 in 2020, which could be largely attributed to the operationalisation of the ISCs. Egypt is gradually reaching the level of some of its peers, especially to start a business, but further efforts are still needed (Table 4.2).

Table 4.2. Doing Business' score in Egypt and selected other countries, 2018-2020

		Egypt	Morocco	Tunisia	Jordan	Turkey	Mexico	Indonesia
Ease of doing business (overall)	2018	**55.8**	69.2	65.3	59.9	70.9	72.5	66.9
	2019	**58.5**	71.7	67.2	61.3	75.3	72.3	68.2
	2020	**60.1**	73.4	68.7	69.0	76.8	72.4	69.6
Starting a business	2018	**80.7**	92.5	81.6	84.4	81.9	85.8	76.1
	2019	**83.8**	93.0	88.5	84.4	88.2	85.9	79.4
	2020	**87.8**	93.0	94.6	84.5	88.8	86.1	81.2

Note: An economy's ease of doing business score is reflected on a scale from 0 to 100, where 0 represents the lowest and 100 represents the best performance
Source: World Bank.

While the establishment of the ISCs under GAFI is a valuable initiative to support new investment, it should not substitute for continuous regulatory reform to quicken and simplify the process of starting a new business. Cutting unnecessary procedures and requirements should remain a top priority of the authorities to provide a healthy business environment to both incoming and already-established investors. Private sector representatives also report that administrative procedures and requirements tend to be burdensome at different stages of their business operations, not only at establishment, and that fulfilling these requirements is a major impediment to their expansion and, at times, an incentive to divest. In this light, the Egyptian government recognises the constant need to improve the business environment so that the private sector can effectively contribute to growth and development. The establishment of ISCs are a good step forward, which were followed by a number of procedural improvements in administrative streamlining and business facilitation. The government should ensure that the focus given to ISCs is not overshadowing other necessary efforts to strengthen the capacities of officials dealing with businesses (including in remote governorates), to enhance the transparency in administrative decision-making.

The authorities should continue their efforts to systematically map all required licences, approvals and procedures to do business in Egypt and identify those that should be streamlined. This would help make ICSs even more efficient and useful for investors. International good practices show that countries that have successfully enhanced their business environment have driven reform from the highest-level of government with strong political support; have involved all relevant stakeholders, both public and private, from the beginning of the process; and have established a dedicated taskforce to suggest and monitor reforms.

Post-establishment: consulting and assisting the private sector

The key role of a high-level public-private dialogue

In their continuous efforts to provide a friendlier investment climate, governments should maintain regular dialogue with the private sector in order to involve them in policy design and to collect feedback on recurrent issues affecting their operations.

The private sector is often consulted on an ad hoc basis in Egypt, notably through the Egypt business association, when new laws and regulations are in preparation. This was the case during the preparation of the 2017 Investment Law, where businesses had the opportunity to comment on early drafts. For a long time, however there has not been a strategic or systemic approach to consult the private sector on investment climate challenges or to collect their views on necessary reforms and priority government actions. In 2019, the MIIC and GAFI established monthly meetings with investors attended in person by the minister. Requests or complaints had to be sent in advance and the authorities addressed them in the meetings. Although this initiative reflects the willingness of the authorities to take investors' concerns seriously and address them, it is too recent to evaluate its impact or effectiveness.

Taking advantage of the new institutional framework for investment, the authorities would be well advised to build on this initiative to reinforce public-private dialogue mechanisms. Meetings should be well-prepared, well-structured and focused on specific topics to make them relevant and constructive. It is also important to invite systematically representatives of relevant ministries and agencies, as investment climate challenges can rarely be solved within a single agency. Such whole-of-government mechanisms have proven extremely useful in other countries to facilitate a constructive and mutually beneficial dialogue. The example of the Vietnam Business Forum demonstrates that holding these public-private dialogue platforms both on a regular basis and with high-level government representation are key ingredients for their success and efficiency (Box 4.4).

Box 4.4. The Viet Nam Business Forum

The Vietnam Business Forum (VBF) was established in 1997 with the support of the World Bank as a not-for-profit, non-political channel for nurturing public-private dialogue to develop a favourable business environment that attracts domestic and foreign private sector investment and stimulates sustainable economic development in Viet Nam. This is done primarily through high profile bi-annual Forums between the business community and Vietnamese leadership and through specialised Working

Groups cutting across sectors (agribusiness, automotive, banking, capital market, customs, education & training, governance & integrity, infrastructure, investment & trade, mining, and tourism).

Key VBF objectives include working with the government to create pathways to long-term and sustainable business performance as well as to promote the interests of national and international business community in Viet Nam and enhance investment and trade in local and overseas markets. The VBF works to provide research, legal analysis, identification of problems and practical solutions.

In early 2012, the co-ordination function of the Forum's secretariat was transferred from the World Bank Group to a Consortium of international and local business associations and chambers of commerce to allow the private sector to play a bigger role in the Forum's sustainable development. The bi-annual Forums are co-chaired by Viet Nam's Minister of Planning and Investment, the World Bank's Viet Nam Country Director, IFC's Regional Manager for Viet Nam and Co-chairmen of the Consortium. The Consortium is led by five Consortium Members and supported by 11 Associate Members which are foreign and local business associations and chambers of commerce in Vietnam.

Public-private dialogue reached a new level beginning in 2014 when former Prime Minister Nguyen Tan Dung started participating personally in the bi-annual Forums. The prime minister's participation since then has been very well received by the private sector, as it sent a strong signal of the government's commitment to a constructive partnership with the business community. Since then, the private sector reports that it fully recognises the VBF as a useful mechanism to interact with the government and suggest reforms that can provide concrete results towards delivering a better business environment.

Source: Vietnam Business Forum (vbf.org.vn) and OECD (2018b).

Aftercare: promoting investment retention and expansions

Beyond a formal public-private dialogue platform, countries are putting in place other measures to consult investors, retain them and encourage their expansion. GAFI is usually recognised by businesses as a trusted government interlocutor, which shows responsiveness and effectiveness when concerns are reported by investors. Proactive aftercare has often been a secondary task of GAFI but recent measures show encouraging signs of systematic post-establishment consultation. For example, GAFI has established a mechanism through the ICSs allowing its staff to follow-up with investors after their establishment. Another way to collect investors' feedback is through surveys. A first survey of companies established in Egypt was conducted over 2018-19, with the results used for internal discussions and policymaking. A second survey started during the second half of 2019. Surveys are very good tools to identify strengths and weaknesses in the business climate, but it is important that the sample be representative of all companies regardless of their size, nationality or sector of activity. Many IPAs in different regions of the world also conduct surveys of foreign investors (see below). These are often considered as an efficient tool for IPAs to gather a comprehensive and systematic understanding of investors' concerns and thus to better tailor their recommendations to policymakers accordingly. The authorities could consider using these surveys to prepare synthesis reports that summarise the findings and are made publicly available.

Aftercare activities have a potentially high impact on retaining investors by keeping them satisfied and encouraging them to expand their activities or reinvest in new ones. It is often also less costly from an IPA perspective than other functions. Aftercare can encourage new investors through word of mouth endorsements by satisfied investors already on the ground. Most well-developed IPAs devote a substantial amount of time to working with their existing company portfolio to try to identify potentially new business opportunities for them to consider.

In this light, targeted aftercare activities by GAFI – but also by the SCEZ in the case of investments in the Suez Canal economic zone – should focus on those investors that have the greatest propensity to expand their activities and on those with the highest developmental impact, not only in terms of job creation but also linkages with the local economy (see below the role of aftercare on promoting business linkages). As a matter of consistency and to develop sector-specific knowledge, GAFI should focus its proactive aftercare activities on companies that operate in the same industries and sectors as those chosen for investment attraction and generation.

Through aftercare, IPAs can also play an important role in preventing potential disputes involving investors, notably through structured trouble-shooting with individual investors, mitigation of conflicts and ombudsman intervention. Structured trouble-shooting with individual investors is the most frequently available service in all three regions covered by the survey of IPAs, with at least 80% of IPAs in OECD, MED and LAC countries providing this service (Figure 4.6).

Figure 4.6. IPAs' aftercare services related to dispute prevention in selected regions

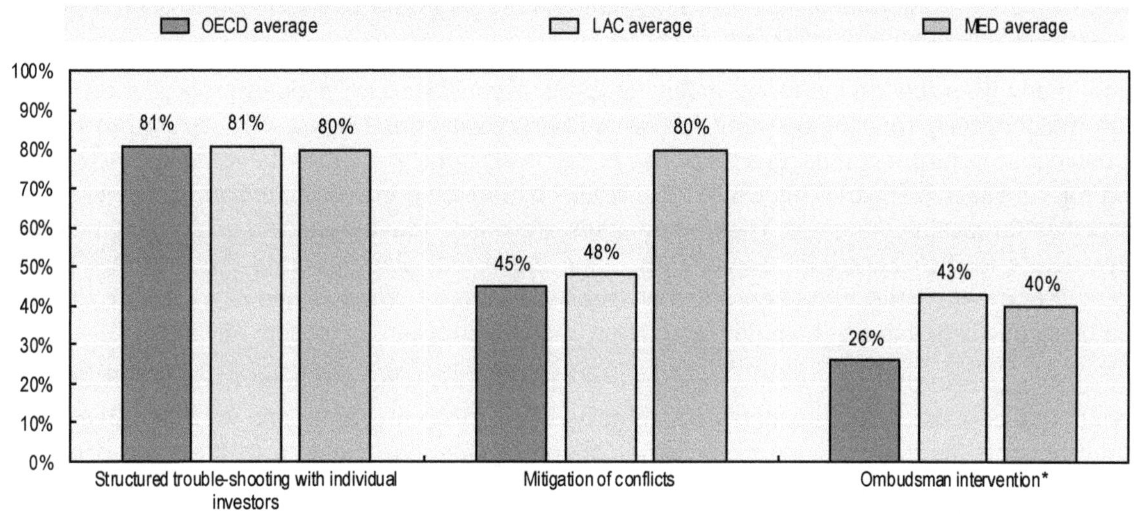

Note: (*) Activities marked with an asterisk are not conducted by GAFI, while the others are.
Source: Author based on OECD (2018a), OECD (2019) and Volpe Martincus and Sztajerowska (2019).

Conversely, ombudsman interventions are the least frequently available activity of the three across IPAs and is not performed by GAFI either. An investment ombudsman can provide a useful avenue for preventing potential disputes. Korea was a forerunner in setting up a foreign investment ombudsman in its IPA in 1999. Its role is to solve complaints reported by foreign investors both by sending relevant experts to business sites and by taking pre-emptive measures to prevent future grievances by encouraging systemic improvements and legal amendments (see below the role of policy advocacy). Drawing on the Korean model, several countries have successfully integrated an investment ombudsman in their IPA, including Brazil, the Czech Republic and Turkey.

GAFI is not the only actor involved in aftercare in Egypt. For example, the Administrative Control Authority (ACA), an independent body under the responsibility of the President, is in charge of fighting corruption within government and monitoring the efficiency of the state. It has a specific investment support centre, established in 2015, to help create a sound investment climate in Egypt. The centre functions as a grievance mechanism where individual companies can file a complaint when they face specific problems. ACA reported receiving 280 complaints the first year, 161 the following year and 39 the one after. ACA has sometimes helped solve investors' complaints by addressing recommendations to line ministries, including sometimes involving the amendment of laws or regulations. ACA has offices in GAFI and in the three main industrial zones.

Through their aftercare activities, GAFI, SCEZ and ACA may also consider working with existing investors to promote responsible business conduct and encourage them to more systematically comply with laws, such as those on the respect for human rights, environmental protection, labour relations and financial accountability, as well as to embrace responsible and sustainable practices in their business operations (see Chapter 7 on Promoting and Enabling Responsible Business Conduct).

Aftercare as a channel for business linkage promotion

MNEs do not necessarily engage in linkages with domestic suppliers automatically – even when local firms are competitive enough and technology-ready. Many MNEs are bound by international contracting arrangements that tie them to international suppliers, offsetting the effectiveness of public policies to promote linkages. In some other cases, MNEs rely on their usual overseas business partners for convenience or because of lack of information, and do not make the effort to look for local firms that can act as suppliers. In this case, the government can bridge information gaps with targeted measures to facilitate exchange of information. By interacting with MNEs on a daily basis, IPAs are often well placed to do so, especially through their aftercare activities.

As such, many IPAs around the world, including GAFI, are involved in linkages programmes, most often through matchmaking services between foreign and domestic firms (Figure 4.7). GAFI, like many other IPAs, could also consider compiling a database of domestic firms and make it available to MNEs that are looking for suppliers in Egypt. This would help MNEs by reducing their transaction costs while providing opportunities for local businesses. These databases are often industry-specific and sometimes focus on priority sectors for FDI attraction. Some IPAs, often those that also integrate the mandate to promote domestic investment, have more sophisticated business support programmes (e.g. cluster programmes and capacity building) that can help domestic firms become suppliers of foreign affiliates.

Evidence shows also that long-lasting foreign investors, by knowing the local context better, are more inclined to use domestic suppliers instead of sourcing internationally (Farole and Winkler, 2014). Aftercare can thus support the double purpose of better anchoring foreign investors in the local economy and enhancing their positive spill-overs.

Figure 4.7. IPA linkage and business support programmes in OECD and MED regions

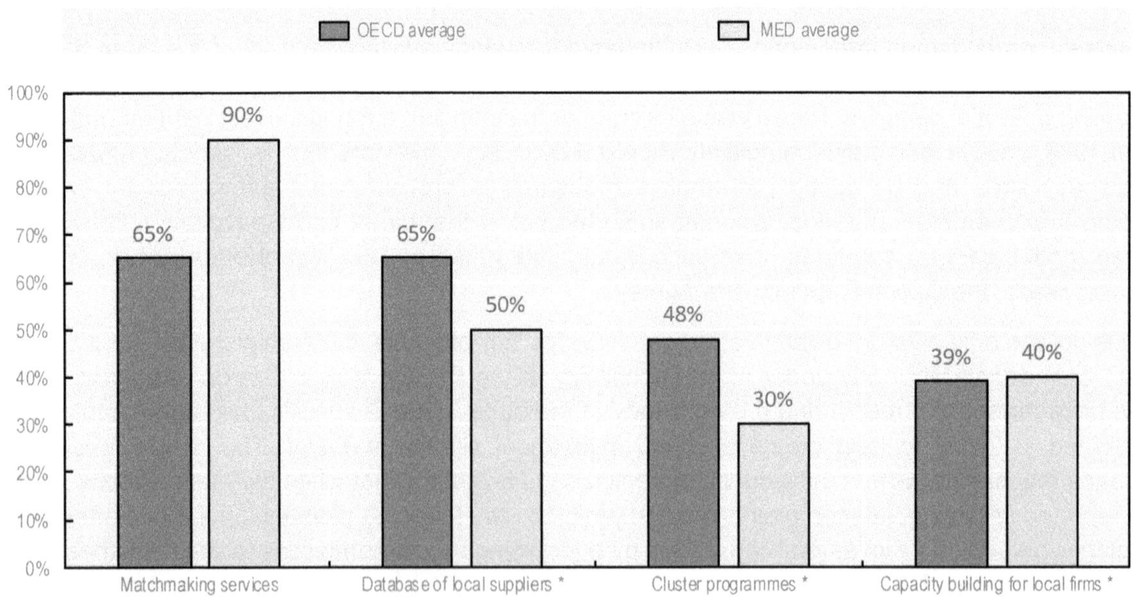

Note: (*) Activities marked with an asterisk are not conducted by GAFI.
Source: Author based on OECD (2018a) and OECD (2019).

Policy advocacy: responding to investors' needs by influencing policymaking

Identifying recurrent problems faced by investors through public-private dialogue and aftercare also effectively contributes to the IPA's policy advocacy role. As a policymaking and regulatory department – previously under the responsibility of the MIIC – GAFI is naturally involved in policy advocacy. It is contributing to the national investment policy agenda and is thus directly influencing changes in regulations, laws, government policies and their administration. The majority of IPAs in the world are involved in policy advocacy, especially through activities that involve meetings with the private sector and with government officials as well as by tracking international rankings and preparing recommendations for policymakers (Figure 8).

A more autonomous IPA is often better placed to find a balanced approach between the government's public policy objectives and the private sector's corporate interests. The question is to what extent it uses the private sector's feedback to feed into its policymaking and advocacy function. It often depends on the efficiency of public-private dialogue and on the quality of aftercare measures, as described above.

Figure 4.8. Frequency of IPA policy advocacy activities in selected regions

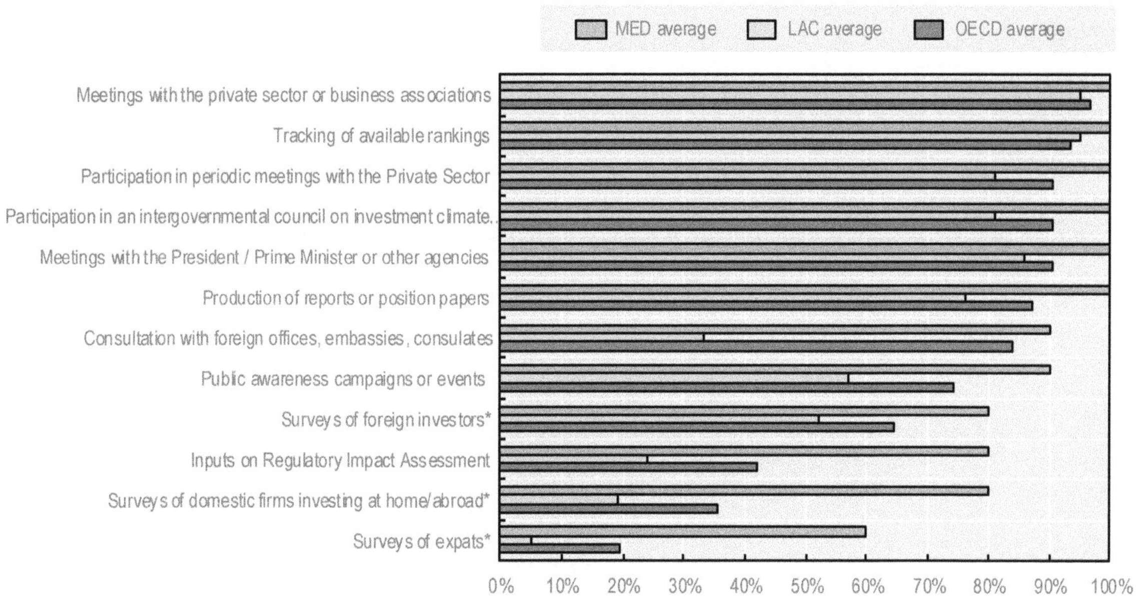

Note: (*) Activities marked with an asterisk are not conducted by GAFI, while all the others are.
Source: Author based on OECD (2018a), OECD (2019) and Volpe Martincus and Sztajerowska (2019).

References

Farole, T. and D. Winkler (2014), Making Foreign Direct Investment Work for Sub-Saharan Africa: Local Spillovers and Competitiveness in Global Value Chains, World Bank, Washington.

IDA Ireland (2014), Winning: Foreign Direct Investment 2015-2019, Dublin.

MIIC (2018a), Investing in Development for the SDGs, Cairo.

MIIC (2018b), Annual Report 2017: Investing in Development, Cairo.

Novik A. and A. de Crombrugghe (2018), Towards an International Framework for Investment Facilitation, OECD Investment Insights, April 2018, https://www.oecd.org/investment/ Towards-an-international-framework-for-investment-facilitation.pdf.

OECD (2019), Mapping of Investment Promotion Agencies in Mediterranean countries, https://www.oecd.org/investment/Mapping-of-Investment-Promotion-Agencies-MED.pdf

OECD (2018a), Mapping of Investment Promotion Agencies in OECD countries, http://www.oecd.org/investment/investment-policy/mapping-of-investment-promotion-agencies-in-OECD-countries.pdf

OECD (2018b), OECD Investment Policy Reviews: Viet Nam 2018, OECD Publishing, Paris, https://doi.org/10.1787/9789264282957-en.

OECD (2015), Policy Framework for Investment, 2015 Edition, OECD Publishing, Paris. http://dx.doi.org/10.1787/9789264208667-en

OECD (2011), Attractiveness for Innovation: Location Factors for International Investment, OECD Publishing, Paris, http://dx.doi.org/10.1787/9789264104815-en

Volpe Martincus, C. and Sztajerowska, M. (2019), How to Resolve the Investment Promotion Puzzle – A Mapping of Investment Promotion Agencies in Latin America and the Caribbean and OECD Countries, IDB, Washington DC.

World Bank (2011), Investment Regulation and Promotion: Can They Coexist in One Body?, Washington.

Annex 4.A. Options to consider when designing or revising Egypt's national investment strategy

An investment strategy, whatever form it takes, consists of a document prepared by the government and highlighting its main orientations in terms of how to use investment to foster economic growth and sustainable development. Preparing a national investment strategy is commonly an inclusive, multi-ministerial process, as the multiple policy objectives pursued by governments all call for a whole-of-government perspective so as to increase policy coherence.

Some strategies are high-level documents with broad orientations and showcasing the country's political will to increase investment, while others are much more detailed and ambitious government action plans setting concrete targets and indicators. Some strategies focus exclusively on FDI while others address foreign and domestic investment equally. Most strategies also address private investment while some include elements on public investment. Some countries also choose not to prepare an overarching investment strategy, but focus instead on sectoral strategies or on investment promotion strategies.

Different types of strategies can be considered by Egypt, depending on the government's objectives, on the target audience and timeframe, and on whether the document includes how the strategy will be implemented. Three main types of national strategies have been used by other countries to guide their governments in promoting investment in a structured, methodical and well-planned manner (Table 4.A.1). They could all three apply in the case of Egypt and guide its investment strategy making. These three options are:

1. **A national policy statement on investment**, which presents and describes the investment landscape and the government's strategic orientations, including its overarching economic goals, regulatory framework for investment, priority sectors and the country's key local value propositions.
2. **An investment promotion strategy** that defines the government's main objectives, tools and performance indicators to attract inward foreign investment. It defines priority sectors and markets for FDI attraction and describes the role and responsibilities of local institutions to support these objectives/targets.
3. **A comprehensive investment strategy** that outlines the government's main objectives and orientations to foster investment and what needs to be done to achieve these goals. It focuses on priority investment policies, measures and reforms as well as on the planned institutional and administrative improvements.

Annex Table 4.A.1. Typology of investment strategies

Strategy	Type of document	Objectives	Recipients	Specific features	Common features
NATIONAL POLICY STATEMENT ON INVESTMENT	Political and succinct, promotional statement	Presenting the government's strategic vision on the role and impact of investment in the economy Demonstrating the government's commitment to foster and attract investment Showcasing investment policy objectives: past, current and future reforms	International community, economic partners International investors National institutions, citizens, businesses and civil society	Presenting the government's economic vision and broader investment objectives Presenting recent achievements and showcasing upcoming ones Presenting the investment regulatory framework and responsible institutions; Presenting investment promotion and facilitation objectives and services	Presenting national development objectives Presenting main economic sectors Presenting key FDI trends Presenting investment policy principles and values Presenting investment policy and promotion objectives Presenting measures to achieve objectives Presenting the country's local value propositions Presenting the target sectors, markets and related activities Presenting performance in international rankings Introducing with a foreword by a senior official (e.g. Minister)
INVESTMENT PROMOTION STRATEGY	Technical and operational action plan	Defining the IPA's the territorial marketing strategy, including: targets, tools, timeframes and performance indicators to attract inward investment Defining the role of the IPA and other institutions involved in FDI promotion	Investment promotion practitioners (IPA's staff) Policymakers (competent ministries) Other implementing agencies	Identifying targets for FDI attraction (sectors, markets, etc.) Defining marketing and targeting tools Defining measures to simplify investors' establishment and expansion Establishing timeframes for activities Establishing monitoring mechanisms and performance indicators	
COMPREHENSIVE NATIONAL INVESTMENT STRATEGY	Technical, comprehensive and descriptive roadmap	Defining the government's vision to foster investment in the country and translating it into an action plan Defining how investment can support economic growth and sustainable development Defining what should be the related reforms and concrete measures Defining the role of national investment-related institutions	Policymakers (competent ministries) IPA and other implementing agencies	Defining the country's objectives and orientations on investment Defining measures to ease the entry, establishment and operation of investors Presenting a detailed action plan, including on investment policy reforms Assigning implementation responsibilities Establishing timeframes for activities Establishing monitoring mechanisms and performance indicators	

Chapter 5. Zone-based policies

This chapter examines zone-based policies in Egypt. It provides an analysis of zones' competitiveness and sustainability as well as of their strategic objectives, their distinct regulatory frameworks, and current policies to attract investment, boost export and foster linkages with the local economy. The chapter also presents evidence on zones' contribution to foreign investment, export, and job creation. It offers some policy options to better align the development objectives of zones in Egypt with the government sustainable development priorities.

Summary and policy recommendations

Zones in Egypt have become central growth locomotives and, as in other emerging economies, they are home to substantial manufacturing activities. They have succeeded in attracting foreign investment, boosting participation in global value chains (GVCs) and creating jobs. By one estimate, they are home to at least one-tenth of FDI stock, generate almost half of non-oil exports and employ nearly 2% of the workforce. The characteristics and outcomes of each type of zone are nevertheless distinct, reflecting the specific development objectives of their corresponding legal and institutional frameworks.

Egypt has a longstanding history of relying on zones for development aims. The government established the first zone in 1974 in the area of Port Said, and has since overseen a proliferation of these areas. Currently, seven types of zones co-exist in Egypt: public or private free zones (FZs), investment zones, technological zones, special economic zones (SEZs), qualified economic zones (QIZs), and industrial zones. Most are governed by specific laws, overseen by different ministries, operate under distinct regulatory and institutional frameworks, provide different types of incentives to investors and often have overlapping goals. According to the government, the different zone types are meant to meet the different needs of investors and various types of investment. Nonetheless, the complex and overlapping landscape of zones has contributed to rivalry between government institutions over new zones management and expansion.

Zones' development objectives and legal frameworks shape to a certain extent their key features and economic outcomes, but the patchwork of policies and regulations surrounding these frameworks makes it hard to assess the benefits and costs of each zone type for investment and wider economic development. Further clarity on each zone's development aims, governance structure and legal and regulatory framework would help policymakers in better aligning zones' strategic objectives with Egypt's long-term development goals.

Several facts can be highlighted when comparing four out of the seven types of zones for which there is sufficient information:

- Zones differ in the size of land allocated to them (Table 5.1). Due to their regional development objectives, SEZs in Egypt are radically different from the other types of zones. They are much larger – for instance, the surface area of the Suez Canal Special Economic Zone (SCZone) is ten times larger than all the free zones put together – and include ports as an integral part of the zone.
- Zones differ in their geographical focus. FZs, investment zones and QIZs are located in the most advanced regions (Cairo, Alexandria and the Suez Canal). Industrial zones are in nearly all of the 27 governorates, including the investment-scarce southern and desert areas.
- Each type of zone attract firms with different features (in terms of size, export potential, foreign-ownership, etc.). Around a thousand firms operate in FZs and a similar number in QIZs. FZs contribute more than QIZs to national exports but they generate a large trade deficit. Investment zones, which have cluster-specific development goals, are substantial job creators due to the relatively larger firms they host.

Zones in Egypt have comparable investment and export outcomes with those in other emerging countries but have a mixed record in generating value-added, fostering innovation, and supporting diversification and sustainable development countrywide. More problematic, they may be impeding fair competition between firms inside and outside of zones, at the risk of creating economic enclaves. They also impose a certain cost on government revenues, as the incentives granted to firms reduce the fiscal base (IMF, 2017). In addition, while foreign-owned businesses take advantage of such tax incentives, they often limit their reliance on local providers of goods and services in order to maintain some degree of locational mobility (Azmeh and Nadvi, 2014). Ties between zones and the local economy may be even narrower in the lower value-added segments of sectors such as textiles and clothing. Linkages between multinationals in Egyptian zones and local suppliers do sometimes exist, but policymakers could support their extension to further rely on higher-skilled labour or on R&D agreements.

Table 5.1. Key features of zones in Egypt in 2018

Zone type	Public and private Free zone	Investment Zone	Special Economic Zone	Qualified Industrial Zone
Year of creation	1971	2008	2002	2004
Size (km2)	48.6	12.7	9'761	n.a
# Active zones	9 public/208 private	18	2	17
# of Firms	1'091	300	n.a	1'030
# governorates (out of 27)	9	7	5	n.a
# of employees	190'035	59'000	n.a	150'000
Avg. exports 2013-18 (% of national non-oil export)*	34.2	n.a	n.a	5.4
Avg. imports 2013-18 (% zone trade)	48	n.a	n.a	9.5

* Excluding sales on the domestic market; Data is for 2018 or last available year. Industrial zones and technology zones are not included.
Source: OECD based on Central Bank of Egypt, QIZ Unit Bulletin, GAFI, and WTO (2018).

Zones in Egypt have comparable investment and export outcomes with those in other emerging countries but have a mixed record in generating value-added, fostering innovation, and supporting diversification and sustainable development countrywide. More problematic, they may be impeding fair competition between firms inside and outside of zones, at the risk of creating economic enclaves. They also impose a certain cost on government revenues, as the incentives granted to firms reduce the fiscal base (IMF, 2017). In addition, while foreign-owned businesses take advantage of such tax incentives, they often limit their reliance on local providers of goods and services in order to maintain some degree of locational mobility (Azmeh and Nadvi, 2014). Ties between zones and the local economy may be even narrower in the lower value-added segments of sectors such as textiles and clothing. Linkages between multinationals in Egyptian zones and local suppliers do sometimes exist, but policymakers could support their extension to further rely on higher-skilled labour or on R&D agreements.

Policy recommendations

- Better align the development objectives of existing zones in Egypt with national and local strategies as well as investment and trade goals. Egypt Vision 2030 calls for "achieving coherence and integration among industrial and free zones, and domestic, regional, and global value chains". To succeed, Egypt needs to develop realistic and coherent objectives for zones that are aligned with national, governorate and sectoral development priorities, including Egypt Vision 2030, the national investment plan, the Trade and Industry Development Strategy 2016-2020, the national SME and Export Development Strategies, and forthcoming decentralisation reforms. The policy dialogue around such objectives (and the actions needed to reach them) should involve a multitude of stakeholders, including GAFI, the QIZ Unit, the Industrial Development Agency, the Export Promotion Agency, the recently created SME agency, governorates, and civil society.
- Assess the longer-term benefits and costs of creating new zones, or expanding existing ones, for sustainable development and economic welfare. The proliferation of zones, created under distinct special regimes and managed by different public entities, without an ex ante assessment, may result in weak development outcomes (e.g. low shares of exports) or, more problematically, to undesired consequences (e.g. distorting competition with the inland regime). Estimating the expected impact of new zones in Egypt should take into consideration the

specificities of the domestic economic environment, including the level of import protection or the complexity of customs procedures.

- Balance the objective of expanding zone activities with a transparent and sequenced plan to level the playing field between the special and the inland investment regimes. The government should gradually eliminate some of the most distortive tax incentives granted in the zones, particularly the exemption from corporate income tax in FZs, in line with the recommendations of chapter 6 and the IMF Article IV. The government should consider setting up zones with a less distortive impact on the economy, i.e. with special regimes that give investors less differentiated treatment with respect to tax incentives. In parallel, Egypt should continue to improve the broader business climate by lowering import and export barriers so as to reduce the incentives gap between the inland and the special regimes.
- Promote private investment in higher value-added segments of the manufacturing sector to unlock zones' export competitiveness potential. This includes promoting investment in capital-intensive, upstream stages of the textile and clothing, food, and chemicals supply chains to modernise their production capabilities. To move towards a cluster-based strategy, the government could support investments aimed at replacing ageing technology in state-owned enterprises, from which downstream clothing firms in zones source their inputs. This would prevent an increase in production costs throughout the supply chain that affects smaller establishments the most. Furthermore, Egypt could align zone-specific and sector-specific objectives to attract investment in higher value-added segments of the logistics, food, chemicals and automotive sectors. It could leverage the advantage of QIZs related to US duty-free market access beyond textile products to also attract investors into the food and chemicals sectors.
- Better use zones as a tool to bridge investment and regional development policies. It is crucial to incorporate the investment aims of the different zones into a regional/governorate development strategy that includes not only the provision of various duty exemptions and other incentives to attract investors, but also a comprehensive reform programme to boost business linkages. Cost-based incentives should be favoured over compulsory linkage requirements to strengthen linkages between foreign MNEs in special regimes and suppliers located in the inland regime. Authorities at the national and zone level could better co-ordinate their efforts to promote the different tools incentivising linkages. The government could also support strengthening local firms' absorptive capacity through skills development training, tailored business development services and partnerships with education entities.
- Clarify zones' institutional and regulatory framework to ensure a level playing field between public and private investors. Zone authorities in Egypt often have the mandate to be both regulators and developers. The institutional framework should therefore ensure that private and public developers are eligible for the same benefits provided by zones. These benefits should be fully defined in the legislation and awarded based on clear, objective and transparent criteria. In the case of new zones, the government should examine how to clearly separate these regulatory and development roles to improve the effectiveness and transparency of zone administration.
- More systematically involve the private sector, local governorates and other relevant stakeholders in the decision-making process of zone authorities. This measure is necessary to build trust and ensure that there is no bias in the decisions of the boards of zones, particularly in light of the limited land available in some zones with many investors already present. The board could include representatives from all governorates within the zone (or otherwise have transparent and clear rules on how governors rotate to sit on the board), as well as private investors, private developers and business representatives, such as SME associations.
- Ensure that investors in zones comply with responsible business conduct (RBC) standards. Adopt RBC policies to ensure that health, safety, labour and environmental norms in zones are

in line with national and international standards. Monitor the impact of more flexible labour regulations on the local labour market in zones, particularly in SEZs as they enjoy more flexible labour and social rules. The more flexible regulations in zones should be designed for a temporary period and closely monitored through regulatory impact assessment tools. Zone authorities should put in place strong and independent institutional tools to monitor labour and environmental rights.

- Provide better statistics on zones to support evidence-based policy making. More granular statistics on exports, investment and jobs in zones are needed to disentangle the contribution of each special regime. The availability of firm-level data, perhaps through annual surveys, would allow authorities to track business features and performance, measure zones' fiscal costs and benefits and, for example, monitor smuggling operations. Such data would offer more room for designing more targeted, evidence-based policies to steer zone outcomes towards their development goals. The statistical bulletin provided by the QIZ Unit could be an initial example to build on.

Overview of the objectives and regulatory frameworks of zones

Egypt opted for the establishment of zones to meet various development objectives, from job creation and increasing export and budget earnings, to attracting investment, especially FDI. Zone-based policies are increasingly common in many developing economies. They can help partly to neutralise the effects of an otherwise less favourable business climate by offering differentiated treatment or services to investors, such as through tax or administrative incentives or better infrastructure than in the rest of the country. The creation of zones is often a reflection of the need to offset a negative impact of stringent import protection on trade or challenges in accessing secured land under the inland regime.

Aligning the objectives of each special investment regime in Egypt with national development goals is more than ever a pressing, yet challenging, policy priority. In recent years the government has based the overall development strategy on the multiplication of both the types of special investment regimes and the number of zones (Table 5.2). The Sustainable Development Strategy: Egypt 2030 Vision and other sectoral or ministerial strategies all have an objective of establishing new zones in the next decade or expanding existing ones to support industrialisation, innovation and exports.

Table 5.2. Tracking Zones in Egypt

Zone type	Name/location of the zone
Free Zones	Alexandria; Damietta; Ismailia; Keft (Qena); Media Production City (Giza); Nasr City and Badr city (Cairo); East Port Said Public Free Zones; Port Said; Shebin El Kom (Monufia); and Suez ; Minya and Nuibaa; and South Sinai and Aswan. Private Free zones are spread around the country.
Investment Zones	CBC Egypt for Industrial Development (building materials); Giza; Polaris International Industrial Park (textiles); Giza; the Industrial Development Group (automotive-related industries); Giza; Pyramids Industrial Parks (engineering industries); Sharqiya; Al-Tajamouat Industrial Park (textiles); Sharqiya; Meet Ghamr (SME); Dakahlia; Al-Saf (SME); Giza; City of Scientific Research and Technology Applications (nanotechnology and biotechnology); Alexandria; Cairo University (higher education and scientific research); Giza; Ain Shams University (higher education and scientific research); Qalyubiya; Faiyum University (higher education and scientific research); Faiyum.
Special Economic Zones	The Suez Canal Economic Zone (SCZone); the Golden Triangle Economic Zone (GTZone).
Qualified Industrial Zones	Alexandria governorate; Dakahleya Governorate; Damietta Governorate; Gharbeya Governorat; Monofeya Governorate; Kafr El-Sheikh Governorate; Damanhour City; Kafr El-Dawar City; Ismailia Governorate; Port Said Governorate; Suez Governorate; Beni Suif Governorate; Al Minya Governorate.

Note: Industrial Zones and Technology Zones are not covered due to limited information.
Source: OECD based on Government websites and documents.

Meanwhile, Vision 2030 calls also for "achieving coherence and integration among industrial and free zones, and domestic, regional, and global value chains" (Economic Pillar, pp. 42). This proliferation of zones, created by different institutions, without a thorough *ex ante* assessment, may prevent them from achieving their objectives or, even worse, lead to undesired outcomes. Evidence from other countries is not conclusive on the estimated effect of introducing such regimes. Their expected benefits in terms of economic development are not necessarily positive or automatic but are greatly contingent on the local business environment, particularly on the stringency of import barriers: zones' export potential is higher the lower are importing costs compared to the inland regime (Davies and Mazhikeyev, 2015).

In terms of legal framework, the 2017 Investment Law defines four special investment regimes: public free zones, private free zones, investment zones and technical zones (Table 5.3). SEZs are governed by a stand-alone SEZ Law. QIZs do not on their own constitute an investment regime and can fall under the jurisdiction of the inland or special investment regimes. They are regulated through a Protocol signed in 2004 between Egypt, the United States and Israel. Industrial zones are governed exclusively by the inland investment regime and therefore do not provide firms with specific custom exemptions or treatment, unlike the special investment regimes. Other chapters of the review provide an in-depth assessment of dispute settlement mechanisms and tax incentives in special investment regimes.

Table 5.3. Differences between regulatory regimes of Zones in Egypt

	Public and Private Free zones	Investment and Tech Zones	Special Economic Zones	Qualified Industrial Zones
Law	Law No. 72/2017 on Investment	Law No. 72/2017 on Investment	Law No. 83/2002 "Economic Zones of Special Nature Law" Amended by Law No. 27/2015	Protocol between Egypt, Israel and the U.S
Executive regulation	Prime Minister decree No. 2310/2017	Prime Minister decree No. 2310/2017	Prime Minister decree No. 1625/2002	--
Competent authorities	Board of the Zone Authority, GAFI	Board of the Zone Authority, GAFI Competent Minister pursuant to the speciality of the Zone	Board of the SEZ Authority	QIZ Unit, Ministry of Industry and Trade
Dispute settlement mechanisms	National Courts; GAFI Dispute Settlement Centre 3 Ministerial Committees The Egyptian Arbitration and Mediation Centre Private arbitration (domestic and international)	National Courts; GAFI Dispute Settlement Centre 3 Ministerial Committees The Egyptian Arbitration and Mediation Centre Private arbitration(domestic and international)	Zone Dispute Settlement Centre (yet to be established) National Courts Private arbitration (domestic and international).	National Courts Private arbitration (domestic and international)
Tax incentives*	Corporate income tax: 0% VAT: 0%	Corporate income tax: 22.5% VAT: 14%	Corporate tax: 22.5%** VAT: 0%	Corporate tax: 22.5% VAT: 14%
Export incentives/requirement	No customs duties and procedures. Minimum export for public free zones projects fixed by a technical committee. Minimum of 80% of export for private free zone projects.	Tech zone: No customs duties on intermediate inputs.	No customs duties	No customs duties and procedures; Duty-free access to U.S market & no quota limit; 35% local content requirement, of which a minimum of 10.5% must be Israeli inputs.

* Goods and services *exported* are exempted from VAT; ** 10% if created before the 2015 amendment. Industrial Zones are not represented as they are governed exclusively by the inland investment regime.
Source: OECD based on OECD (2017), the QIZ Unit Bulletin, and WTO (2018).

The institutional landscape governing zones in Egypt consists of a plethora of public entities at both the national and local levels. Ensuring smooth and effective institutional co-ordination is therefore an essential, albeit challenging task. At the national level, FZs are regulated and overseen by GAFI. In contrast, QIZs and industrial zones fall under the authority of the Ministry of Industry and Trade and the Industrial Development Authority (IDA). In light of their wider mandate and higher level of independence, SEZs report directly to the Prime Minister. At the sub-national level, each zone type is administered by an authority, with a board of directors reporting to the national entity in charge of the zone management. Many other national and sub-national bodies are also involved in zone governance, such as specific ministries in the case of investment and technology zones, and authorities at the governorate and city level.

Box 5.1. Allocation of roles and responsibilities in zones in Southeast Asia

Administrating a zone usually requires multiple bodies at different institutional levels. In general, the government assigns regulatory responsibilities to a public authority administrating the zone. The regulator usually adopts and implements regulations within the zone, designates developers, allocates land, promotes the zone, provides business facilitation services and monitors compliance. Although some functions are distinct for different parties, in practice there is often an overlap of functions, especially at the regulatory and development levels. In some zones, the authority is also a developer, i.e. it is in charge of developing and managing the zone. Often, the authority also holds equity shares in private development companies.

According to the Association of Southeast Asian Nations (ASEAN) Guidelines for SEZ Development and Cooperation, which serve as a reference of best practices for ASEAN countries, there are several roles that should be separated in the institutional framework:

- *Government*: Provides strategic guidance through the establishment of zones in specific areas. It adopts a legal framework for zones, creates the zone authority and appoints the zone managers. The government can also conduct initial feasibility studies in order to develop basic infrastructure. The government can participate in workers' training in order to ensure the quality of the workforce.
- *Regulator*: Zones are usually governed by a regulator, appointed by the government, responsible for adopting the regulations applied within the zone. Thus, the regulator also monitors the compliance with these rules and imposes penalties in case of breach of such regulations. The regulator should provide services – such as licensing and registration – to investors. The regulating entity often selects the developers and operators in the zone but in some cases, the regulator may also act as a developer.
- *Developer*: The developer can be a private investor – usually a real estate developer – a public company or a company established through a PPP with responsibility for building and maintaining infrastructure within the zone.
- *Operator*: The operator is the entity responsible for managing the zone's day-to-day operations. It manages rentals but also ensures the provision of basic utilities (gas, electricity, water, etc.), offers diverse services and is in charge of promoting the zone. Private companies often take over operation and promotion of the zone. Financed by zone user fees, operators maintain infrastructure, recruit zone tenants, enforce rules, and, in some cases, carry out administrative services.
- *Users or tenants*: Users, or resident firms, set up operations in the zone. Some zone users are "anchor tenants", or large firms which, in exchange for concessions, agree to operate in the zone and help attract other, smaller tenants.

Source: OECD (2017) and ASEAN (2016), Guidelines for Special Economic Zones Development and Collaboration.

The organisational prerogatives given to zone authorities vary from one zone type to another. For instance, the SEZ authority is mandated with developing internal regulations and monitoring firms' compliance. At the same time, the authority can assign a developer (either public or private) to execute and manage the land in a delimited area of the zone and conduct promotion activities within this area. The authority can fully or partly own the developer, mainly by allocating a land parcel in return for a usufruct fee. It also has the ability to provide incentives to developers such as endowments, grants, loans and credit facilities. The overlapping mandates held by zone authorities may create confusion as well as possible conflicts of interest as the (public) developer is in charge of regulating itself. Such a framework negatively affects private investors' perception of a transparent and competition-friendly business environment (Farole and Kweka, 2011). The multiple roles of zone authorities also cast doubts on their capacity to effectively administer the zone.

Allocating clear and transparent roles and responsibilities among the authorities administrating zones would improve their efficiency and attractiveness to investors. More specifically, organisational frameworks should as much as possible separate the roles of zone regulator from those of zone developer, owner and operator (Box 5.1). For all zones in Egypt, legislation should therefore ensure that privately-owned developers are eligible for the same full benefits as public developers and that the criteria to obtain these benefits are clear and transparent. Such mechanisms are key to guarantee that public and private developers are competing on an equal basis.

Clarifying responsibilities of zone administrators is a pressing challenge given that Egypt intends to set up in new public FZs under a public-private partnership (PPP) model. Outsourcing the development of the zone to private developers may attract higher levels of investment: private developers tend to offer better quality services because of the self-interest they have in engaging in implicit investment promotion (Moran, 2011). Beyond helping to create a competition-friendly climate, the division of roles also allows for increased efficiency, as the regulator can concentrate on strategic matters while the private developer can focus on performance and commercial outcomes. For instance, in the Mactan SEZ in Philippines, the Philippine Economic Zone Authority employed a private company to develop and operate a zone owned by the Mactan-Cebu International Airport Authority. The private company (the developer) earned fees from investors that settled in the Zone; an incentive for the company to attract new investors (Moran, 2011).

Public and private free zones

Public and private FZs are regulated by Investment Law (72/2017) and the Executive Regulations of the Prime Minister decree (2310/2017). The oldest Egyptian special regime, the public FZ regime, is to a certain extent a typical free trade zone (FTZ), whose primary goal is to support imports and exports by removing customs duties, corporate income tax and VAT (Tables 5.3 and 5.4).[1] Public FZs in Egypt, as FTZs elsewhere, are delimited areas offering warehousing, storage and other services. They also host light manufacturing industries (i.e. limited transformation), producing goods mainly for foreign markets. Beyond boosting trade, Egypt also set up public FZs with the objective of increasing foreign currency reserves.

The private FZ status was removed from the Presidential Decree 17 of 2015, issued to introduce amendments to the old Investment Law No. 8 of 1997, before being restored in the 2017 revision. Private FZs grant the same fiscal incentives as public FZs, but their development objectives differ from a typical FTZ as they aim to attract export-oriented mega-projects, mostly in the manufacturing sector. Often, the mega-project is itself one private FZ that can be located in any area considered as appropriate to conduct the business. They are therefore closer in type to a single factory export processing zone (EPZ) (Table 5.4). Other countries, such as Tunisia, have comparable special regimes where incentives are granted to firms based on their export share requirements (ESR) rather than on their location in a specific fenced-in area.[2]

Table 5.4. General typology of zones

Type of zone	Development objectives	Description	Markets
Free trade zone	Supporting trade	Also known as commercial free zones, these are clearly delimited areas (fenced-in, duty-free), offering warehousing, storage and other services aimed at boosting import-export.	Domestic, re-export
Export processing zones (EPZs)	Export and manufacturing	Industrial clusters offering incentives and facilitation of manufacturing and other activities mostly export-oriented.	Mostly export
Hybrid EPZs	Export and manufacturing	Sub-divided zones with one part open to all industries regardless of their export orientation, and another specifically designed for export-oriented firms.	Export and domestic market
Freeport	Integrated (regional) development	Large territories accommodating all types of activities, providing broad incentives and benefits. Can also include residents on the site.	Domestic, internal and export markets
Enterprise zones	Urban revitalisation	Aimed at revitalising distressed urban and rural areas, enterprise zones mostly flourish in developed countries and are characterised by the provision of tax incentives and financial grants.	Domestic
Single factory EPZ	Export manufacturing	Incentives are provided to a specific enterprise, rather than to a geographic location.	Export market

Source: Adapted from OECD (2017) and FIAS (2008), Special Economic Zones: Performance, Lessons Learned, and Implications for Zone Development, World Bank.

The current investment law makes some significant changes to the FZ regime, limiting the scope of industries that can qualify. To put this new approach into practice, the Law lists several activities that cannot be pursued in a FZ, e.g. petroleum refining, steel, natural gas liquefaction and transport, industries that require high energy consumption, and alcoholic beverages industries (article 34). In case of an investment dispute occurring within such zones, investors can refer to national courts, Dispute Resolution Ministerial Committees, GAFI's Dispute Settlement Centre or the Egyptian Arbitration and Mediation Centre. Investors may also choose to use private arbitration centres (Table 5.3). Investors operating in FZs therefore have as many options to access alternative dispute resolution mechanisms as investors located outside of the zones.

The criteria for establishing a project under the public and private FZ regime are defined by the investment law and corresponding executive regulations. The Investment Law indicates that projects in public FZs are mainly oriented towards exporting.[3] The existing regulation does not specify the ESR but rather states that the minister of investment, in agreement with the minister of trade and industry affairs, sets project obligations in terms of export rates.[4] The conditions for establishing a private FZ, as defined in the legislation, are more stringent and more specific.[5] These conditions include:

- No appropriate location for the project inside a public FZ;
- The geographical location is a detrimental factor for the viability of the project;
- Exports should be no less than 80% (this condition is excluded in the strategic projects of special importance);
- Minimum capital of USD 10 million;
- The local content may not be less than 30% ;
- Permanent employment should not be lower than 500 workers.

The decision-making process of boards of zones could benefit from procedures that are more transparent. In the case of the FZ regime, the board is composed of the zone governor, the city mayor (as chairman of the board), three private sector representatives (investors in the zone) and two employees representatives (from the zone). The chairman has the mandate to issue approvals on projects within the zone (or within private FZs located in their geographic area), in addition to being responsible for issuing licences to authorise these projects. The Board determines the size of the land lot to be allocated to investors, a crucial decision in light of the high demand and limited space available within some zones. A technical committee for FZs affairs, located at GAFI's headquarters, studies the applications for setting up the projects and is in charge of approving them. If dismissed, it is not clear if the rejected investor can appeal the decision.[6]

Investment and technology zones

Egypt introduced investment zones in 2008 and technology zones in 2017. Both are regulated by the 2017 Investment Law and Prime Minister decree No. 2310/2017. They are somewhat similar in their design to EPZs as they aim to create, in an area with defined borders, sector-specific clusters (Table 5.4). In contrast with EPZs set up elsewhere, investment zones and technology zones in Egypt are home to services projects and are intended to serve both foreign and domestic markets. For instance, projects operating within investment and technology zones are not required to export (part of) their production, as is the case under the FZ regime.

The investment law defines investment zones as a special regime that grants administrative facilitation (e.g. exemption from contracts for land registration). Technological zones are similar to the investment zones in that firms benefit from administrative facilitation, but they also qualify for additional incentives such as exemption from taxes and customs duties on the imported machinery and tools required for establishing the project. Because of their sector-specific nature, these two types of zones are established by the ministry that is overseeing the sector (e.g. the Minister of Communications, Information and Technology is the authority in charge of establishing ICT zones).

Investment zones can be established in various fields, through a decree from the prime minister. These zones cover services clusters that are not prioritised by FZs, such as education, scientific research and tourism infrastructure. For instance, Cairo University and Cairo Airport are under this regime. Technology zones in particular aim to promote activities in the fields of technology, including manufacturing and developing electronics, programming, and technological education. In contrast with the FZ regime, the establishment, management and promotion of an investment zone or technological zone are undertaken by a developer, whether public or private.

Special economic zones

Egypt introduced special economic zones (SEZ) with the enactment of the Law No. 83/2002 "Economic Zones of Special Nature Law", amended by Law No. 27/2015. The SEZ Law applies to the zones created by the presidency. The country's first SEZ was developed in 2003, in the northwest Gulf of Suez. The two presidential decrees No. 330/2015 and No. 341 of 2017 declared respectively the areas adjacent to the Suez Canal and the lands located in the Golden Triangle area in Upper Egypt as SEZs (hereafter, referred to as the SCZone and GTZone).

The SEZ regime differs very significantly in its features and objectives from the other zone regimes in Egypt and most clearly resembles what the World Bank classifies as freeports: usually designed as liberalised platforms for diversified economic growth that not only could, but should spill-over into the national economy (Table 5.4). Ranging in size from single digits to thousands of square kilometres, freeports are generally large, usually located at seaports, with a broad range of permissible activities, and exemptions from customs duties for all types of merchandise. As in other SEZ regimes around the world, companies in Egyptian SEZs receive full access to the domestic market upon payment of required import duties and taxes, unlike the FZ regime or other regimes that have export-related requirements.

An important feature of freeports is that they often include residents on the site, which is the case of SEZs in Egypt, making them regional development areas. Similar to the Chinese freeports (e.g. Shenzhen), commonly cited as examples for these types of zones, Egyptian SEZs intend to serve as pilot regions or laboratories for experimentation with different policies. While freeports and similar types of SEZs generally occupy an area around a single port city or province, Egypt's two SEZs, the SCZone and GTZone, span very wide territories covering several different governorates and major port cities. The SCZone is also home to a large population. Despite unique locational features, the sheer size and scope of the two Egyptian SEZs may constitute a challenge in itself (OECD, 2017).

Compared to the FZ regime as defined in the 2017 Investment Law, the SEZ regime is characterised by a higher degree of institutional and regulatory insularity. The Law contains provisions related to business facilitation, through the establishment of a zone authority exclusively responsible for zone regulation and management. It also addresses issues regarding privileges, exemptions and guarantees granted to investors, and provides for the internal organisation as well as, in contrast with the other special regimes, a dispute settlement centre for the SEZ, which has not yet been established (Table 5.3). In light of the multiple mechanisms for dispute settlements that already exist in the country, creating a dedicated dispute settlement centre in SEZs may be counterproductive.[7]

SEZs are overseen by an authority that reports directly to the prime minister. In the context of the Suez Canal area, the SEZ Authority acts as a near-autonomous entity, with the capacity to create a special regime applicable to a delimited territory and hence to introduce its own regulations, including in areas such as labour and social protection. The rationale behind the empowerment of the authority is to enable it to create a framework within the zone that provides stronger protections to investors against political and legislative instability, as well as to experiment with policies that could be extended to the national level.

A variety of other actors contribute to the wider management of the Suez Canal area, beginning with the Suez Canal Authority (SCA), the entity that manages, operates, uses, and maintains the Suez Canal. The SCA issues and enforces the rules of navigation in the Canal and other rules and regulations that provide for a well and orderly run canal. Line ministries, port authorities, state-owned companies, regulatory agencies, and governorates authorities are involved in the management and operations of the territory declared by the government as a SEZ.

The decision-making process of boards of SEZs could be reinforced by involving a wider variety of stakeholders. Strengthening the decision-making process is important in the case of the newly created SEZs. The institutional framework governing SEZs has been substantially revamped with the enactment of the 2015 SEZ Law and amending regulations, aimed at streamlining the allocation of powers and mandates for the governance of the Zone. According to the amended 2015 SEZ Law, the board shall be composed of the chairman, deputy chairmen, two ministers and one governor as well as five financial and legal experts. According to the SCZone authority, there are systematic hearings and open discussions with investors and developers but they are not mandatory (OECD, 2017). Likewise, Law No. 27/2015 and Prime Ministerial Decree No. 3300 of 2015 stipulate the presence of three representatives from development companies and investors on the boards, but it is not clear at this point which role private sector representatives play during the meetings of the boards.

The amended SEZ text also reduces the number of permanent seats allocated to representatives from governorates compared to the 2002 SEZ Law. This governance change may affect the credibility and transparency of board decisions, which has the mandate to grant specific incentives (e.g. allowed ratio of foreign workers within a company) on a discretionary basis. Greater involvement of the private sector and local partners (e.g. sub-national ministerial offices, governorates, municipalities, local business associations) in the oversight of SEZ activities is necessary to ensure that there is no bias in the decisions of the authority. For instance, in the Philippines, the Subic Bay Metropolitan Authority is composed of 15 members, including representatives of all local governments that are part of the Subic Bay Freeport and five representatives from the private sector.

Qualified Industrial Zones

Qualified industrial zones (QIZs) can be considered as a type of zone that is rather unique in both design and objectives. QIZs are regulated through a protocol signed in 2004 between Egypt, the United States and Israel. The protocol allows products jointly manufactured by Egypt and Israel duty-free access to the US market.[8] Jordan signed the same protocol as Egypt in 1997. Investment in a QIZ can fall under the jurisdiction either of the inland investment regime or of a special regime, depending on where the QIZ is located. In the latter case, it combines the privileges associated with QIZ status and those offered by the special investment regime. In terms of development objectives, QIZs fit best with the definition of EPZs (Table 5.4). They are fenced-in areas, confined to boosting exports of processed manufacturing goods, essentially textiles and clothing, to the United States. Ultimately, the QIZ protocol also aims to increase trade between Egypt and Israel, thus contributing to further bilateral cooperation and stability in the region.

To be eligible for QIZ status, the protocol requires firms to source 35% of their content locally, of which a minimum of 10.5% must be Israeli inputs. Recently, Egypt negotiated with the US the possibility to lower the Israeli component to 8%, as applied in the case of Jordanian QIZs, and to expand the scope of the protocol to cover other sectors (e.g. technology companies). Firms operating within the boundaries of a QIZ are free to export within or outside the QIZ framework (i.e. to the US or elsewhere). The QIZ Unit operates under the auspices of the Ministry of Trade and Industry and serves as an executive and technical support unit, as well as an information centre for local and foreign businesses interested in investing under the terms of the QIZ protocol.

Industrial zones

Industrial zones aim to boost industrial development throughout the country by facilitating investors' access to industrial land, including in less developed areas. Contrary to the other types of zone in Egypt, they are not governed by a special legal framework or a protocol and do not offer any tax incentives or duty-free market access. Industrial zones that are confined to the boundaries of one of the special regimes grant the investor the privileges offered by the regime. The Industrial Development Authority (IDA), created in 2005, is in charge of managing the industrial zones. It has the exclusive authority over industrial land, including the development of utilities and infrastructure and is in charge of putting the land up for bids (WTO, 2018). IDA also is responsible for delivering licences for any industrial project in the country, including in FZs or in investment zones, with the exception of SEZs.[9]

The central role of zones in advancing sustainable development

Zones-based policies have succeeded, to some extent, in boosting exports and attracting foreign investment and jobs to Egypt. Combined, FZs and investment zones are home to one-tenth of national FDI stock; FZs and QIZs generate around half of the country's non-oil exports; and FZs, investment zones, and QIZs employ nearly 2% of the workforce. In Viet Nam, for instance, zones also contribute to exports and jobs in a similar proportion; although they are also home to half of the country's FDI stock (Box 5.2).

The lack of data makes it a daunting task to gauge zones' benefits and costs on the Egyptian economy. As in other zone-intensive emerging countries, zones tend to have a mixed record in generating value-added, fostering innovation, and supporting sustainable development more broadly. More problematic, they may be impeding fair competition between firms inside and outside of zones, and risk creating economic enclaves. They also bear a certain cost on government revenues as the incentives, particularly corporate income tax holidays, granted to firms reduce the fiscal base (IMF, 2017).

Even if foreign-owned businesses move to exploit zone-based tax incentives in Egypt, they often are poorly rooted in the local economy (with limited production sites) in order to relocate more easily their activities to another country with more lucrative conditions (Azmeh and Nadvi, 2014). Ties between zones and the local economy may be even narrower in the lower value-added segments of industries such as textiles and clothing, where profit margins are small. For instance, linkages between MNE affiliates in zones and local firms exist but they are confined to the sourcing of low-skilled intermediate inputs (with only a few contractual arrangements involving R&D or other upstream activities).

Box 5.2. Key Features of zones in Asia

In **Viet Nam**, SEZs play a key role in the government's FDI attraction strategy. There are currently 295 industrial parks, 3 technology parks and 15 economic zones, which concentrate over 50% of total FDI and 80% of manufacturing FDI. A master plan approved in 2015 provides for the creation of a total of 400 industrial parks and 18 economic zones by 2020. SEZs currently contribute to 40% of GDP and 45% of export value, and employ approximately 2.5% of the workforce. SEZs are under the responsibility of provinces, with the central government only having a coordinating role. All 58 provinces have at least one zone.

In **Lao PDR**, SEZs have been developed since the early 2000s but remain a relatively new concept. Ten zones have been created, although only two seem to be fully operational. Due to its location on the economic corridor that links Viet Nam, Lao PDR and Thailand, Savan-Seno, the first SEZ established in 2002, attracts investors from a broad range of economic sectors, thereby contributing to the diversification of the economy, currently driven by natural resource extraction. The government is preparing a new SEZ law to ensure that zones have their own regulatory framework, reflecting good international practice.

The **Philippines** hosts well over 300 zones administered by the 18 different investment promotion agencies which have contributed significantly both to FDI inflows and to exports. The Philippines Economic Zone Authority (PEZA) alone owns three eco-zones and administers the incentives for over 300 privately-managed zones. These include 21 agro-industrial economic zones, 216 IT parks and centres, 64 manufacturing economic zones, 19 tourism economic zones, and two medical tourism zones (as of May 2015). PEZA has a good reputation among investors for its one-stop, non-stop service.

In **Cambodia**, the legal framework for SEZs was established in 2005, and there are currently 34 approved SEZs, of which 14 were operational as of September 2015. Most are located along the borders with Thailand and Viet Nam and at Sihanoukville and Phnom Penh. As in the Philippines, these SEZs are often privately owned. These zones have helped to start diversifying the industrial base away from garments towards electronics and electrical products, as well as household furnishings and car parts. The zones are nevertheless relatively small and account for a low share of total investment and employment: 68 000 as of 2014 or less than 1% of total employment and 3.7% of total secondary industry employment.

Myanmar opted early on in its reform process to develop SEZs to attract foreign investment. The first SEZ in Myanmar, the Thilawa Special Economic Zone began operation in late 2015. The majority of the roughly 60 businesses to set up at Thilawa have been Japanese, although investors from China, the United States, Thailand and other countries are also present. Sectors include manufacturing of garments and toys, steel products, radiators, aluminium cans, packaging and waste management. As in other AMS, the SEZs in Myanmar could be used as effective pilot schemes for testing new approaches to boost the investment climate, such as in the area of building capacity for monitoring the environmental, social and economic impact of investments in the zones, streamlining registration and licensing procedures, effectively managing incentives, and promoting linkages.

Source: OECD Investment Policy Reviews of Cambodia (2018), Indonesia (2010), Lao PDR (2017), Malaysia (2013), Myanmar (2014), the Philippines (2016), and Viet Nam (2018)

Further efforts to improve data quality and availability would help Egypt better monitor zone outcomes. In particular, the dearth of robust, more granular, statistics makes it difficult to disentangle the contribution of each regime. For instance, according to the list of firms entitled to QIZ duty-free treatment, published by the QIZ Unit, more than a hundred have an address in GAFI's FZs[10] but GAFI reports that 56 companies located in the FZs are entitled to the QIZ treatment, of which 20 companies are in private FZs and 36 are in public FZs. Finally, anecdotal evidence suggests that some private FZs are located within the boundaries of industrial zones. Potential statistical double counting creates opaqueness with regard to the activities of zones and limits the possibility to assess their benefits and costs on the national economy.

Monitor zones' investment trends to formulate more targeted policies

Examining zones' investment features and performance helps to assess whether objectives are on track and if readjustments in zone policies are desirable. First, it is useful to measure the contribution of all the zones to nationwide FDI. Evidence at hand indicates that around 10.5% of Egypt's national FDI stock is concentrated in public and private FZs and investment zones. Most of this stock is located in public FZs, which have accumulated 5 billion in FDI stock since their introduction in the 1970s (Figure 5.1). Foreign participation makes up 18% of the total issued capital of businesses operating in FZs.[11] Private FZs and investment zones, both introduced later, are each home to a stock of FDI of USD 1.9 billion. Foreign investors' stake in the capital of companies operating in Egypt's FZs has nevertheless diminished over time, partly driven by fiercer global competition for investment and the multiplication of zones worldwide (Mori, 2017; UNCTAD, 2019).

Figure 5.1. Foreign direct investment in Egyptian zones: manufacturing vs. services

USD billion (2017)

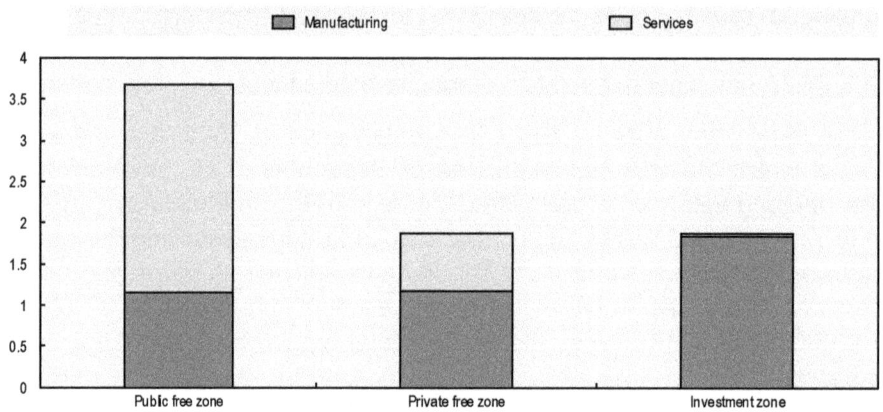

Note: The figures compiled by GAFI use the IMF' Balance of Payments Manual. They are based on actual paid in capital using the company financial statements of unlisted companies, taking into considerations the inter-company debts, equity, and reinvested earnings. Meanwhile, market valuation was used for listed companies. The stocks are compiled based on 2013 End-year exchange rate (USD 1.0 = EGP 6.9).
Source: OECD based on GAFI statistics.

Statistics on investment trends and performance in other zones types are limited. The introduction of QIZs in 2004 coincided with a period of increased FDI flows to Egypt, including in manufacturing, which ended in 2008 with the global financial crisis. Evidence also indicates that QIZs in Egypt performed less well than those in Jordan in attracting FDI (Nugent, 2010; Azmeh, 2014). With the introduction of the new SEZ law in 2015, the government expects to revive cross-border investments in a wide range of sectors. The SCZone multiplied investment deals in steel, petrochemicals and logistics while the GTZone should attract USD 18 billion in investments over 30 years, mostly in the mining sector, according to government estimates.

FDI composition by sector reflects the strategic objectives set by the central government for each zone type. Evidence suggests that there is ample room for policymakers to steer special regime outcomes in the most desired direction in term of FDI flows. In public FZs, the FDI stock is concentrated in services, mostly in shipping, logistics activities (such as storage and warehousing) and media production (Figure 5.1). This is not surprising as in general FTZs are characterised by intense import-export activities with little or no product transformation. The design of private FZs fits with their objective of attracting export-oriented industrial projects. Along with private FZs, investment zones and QIZs also attract foreign investment in manufacturing sectors such as textiles, food products, chemicals and electronics. Investment zones were created to develop both manufacturing and services clusters, such as in education, but available statistics indicate that these zones have been less successful in attracting foreign investors in services projects (Figure 5.1).

The size of investment projects, both in terms of capital and labour, vary substantially depending on the specificities and regulations of the zone type. The average project in a private FZ employs more than 400 workers, twice that of an investment zone (Figure 5.2). Often, one firm (private FZ) or a small cluster of fewer than 20 firms (investment zones) represents the entire zone.[12] Public FZs, QIZs, and industrial zones attract medium-sized firms of 100-150 employees. Available statistics suggest that there is little presence of smaller establishments such as start-ups in Egyptian zones. For instance, in QIZs, only 20% of establishments had fewer than 50 employees in 2016 (QIZ Unit Bulletin). While firm-level data for the SEZ regime areas is limited, it is plausible to assume that this zone type should display greater variety in firm size due to the regime's development objectives and wide geographical coverage.

Figure 5.2. Firm size in zones in Egypt

Average number of employees

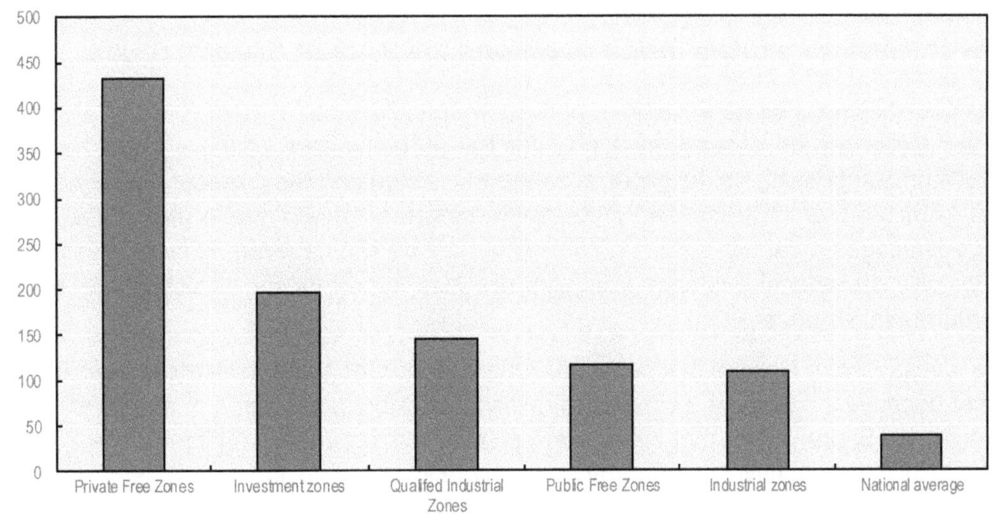

Note: The national average and the average firm size for industrial zones are calculated using firm-level sample weightings. Only firms that are formally registered are included.
Source: OECD based on GAFI Statistics, QIZ Unit Bulletin, and the World Bank Enterprise Survey of Egypt.

Beyond capital and labour size, governments expect the features of firms in zones to be different from those not benefitting from differentiated treatment. International evidence suggests that firms in zones are export-oriented, more integrated into regional and global value chains and more productive (Moran, 2011). These firm-level features are intrinsically linked to the *raison d'être* of zones and should reflect their entry requirements. In Egypt, firm-level data for each zone type are limited, making it difficult to compare the features and performance of firms in zones with those located outside.

The 2016 World Bank Enterprise Survey of Egypt provided insights on establishments located in an industrial zone.[13] These establishments tend to outperform those not located in zones in a number of criteria. They tend to be more productive and are more likely to export, hold an internationally-recognised certificate and offer more training to their staff (Table 5.5). Relatedly, their sales are more than double that of firms located outside industrial zones. Despite stronger performance, the percentage of foreign-owned businesses or of skilled workers is similar within and outside of industrial zones. It may be that foreign investors favour other zone types because of their wider incentives and higher level of protection. With respect to skills, the difference could be driven by low-skilled, labour-intensive activities in industrial zones, potentially explaining at the same time the higher share of female employees (El-Haddad, 2016).

Table 5.5. Firm characteristics in industrial zones versus the rest of the economy

Is the firm located in an industrial zone	Yes	No
Firm size (average number of employees)	101	39
Firm productivity (median)	141 666	71 666
% of foreign-owned firms	4.3%	4.9%
% of exporting firms	30%	15%
% sales that are exported (average)	48.3%	22.7%
% of foreign inputs (average)	22.6%	20.9%
% of women employees (average)	11%	7%
% of high-skilled employees (average)	56%	64%
% of firms that offer training	13.1%	5.9%
% of firms with an international certification	25%	7%

Note: Variables are calculated using sample weightings provided by the World Bank Enterprise Survey.
Source: OECD based on the World Bank Enterprise Survey of Egypt (2016).

Several factors explain MNEs decisions to locate in Egypt's zones

A combination of business-climate, region- and zone-specific factors drive foreign MNEs to invest in Egypt's zones. Country-wide determinants hold for the attractiveness of the various zone types. They include Egypt's unique position as the gateway to the EU, Africa and the Greater Arab Free Trade Area or GAFTA with both preferential trade and investment agreements with these regions, a large domestic market, and advantages in labour costs.[14] The top factors do not necessarily include the granting of tax incentives, which international evidence suggests are less important for attracting FDI but can heavily affect the government's budget.

By providing investors with a range of incentives, zones encourage them to locate in specific geographical regions, either because the areas are close to infrastructure hubs (ports, airports and railways) or markets, or because they are poorer areas that necessitate private investment. For instance, the 2017 Investment Law introduced a new incentives taxonomy to promote investment in certain geographical locations, including greater incentives for firms that locate in SEZs.

Because of the government's location-based investment incentives (and with the exception of Cairo), governorates with zones have become home to relatively higher shares of foreign investment compared to the rest of the country. In the governorates forming the SCZone, the average proportion of foreign investment in a firm reached 19% of the total capital in 2013, well above the 5.5% national average. With the exception of Cairo, FDI is also more concentrated in governorates with larger industrial zone lands (Suez, Alexandria, Giza, and Port Said). For instance, the governorate of Giza, a top FDI recipient, hosts five out of the 13 investment zones, one public FZ and 9% of the governorate land is allocated to industrial zones (Table 5.6). Governorates with FZs also report higher levels of investment, with two-thirds of the total investment in FZs concentrated in the governorates of Alexandria and Cairo.

Table 5.6. FDI is more concentrated in governorates with larger industrial zones

Top 10 FDI recipients	FDI (% total)	Greenfield FDI (% total)	Industrial Zone (% governorate size)
Cairo	32.42	63.80	0.90%
Suez	**6.08**	**11.72**	**4.97%**
Alexandria	**7.16**	**5.41**	**3.99%**
Giza	**27.46**	**3.73**	**8.74%**
Port Said	**2.25**	**3.53**	**10.08%**
Damietta	2.37	1.72	0.33%
Behera	0.92	1.49	0.04%
Aswan	0.81	1.46	0.00%
South Sinai	1.45	1.21	0.00%
Fayoum	0.66	1.08	0.73%

Source: OECD based on GAFI statistics and Dealogic Analytics.

Governorates with FZs are particularly attractive to foreign, non-Arab, investors because they provide, among other services, better access to information (Hanafy, 2015). When prospecting potential investment locations, foreign firms often face information asymmetries and business uncertainties that result in high information costs (Mariotti et al. 2010). In Egypt, as in other developing countries, publicly available information about the business environment at the sub-national level is often scarce. Foreign investors end up relying on signalling effects, i.e. they mimic the location decisions of already established investors, or may choose to set up in a zone because of the quality of the information provided. Governorate, city and zone authorities could co-ordinate their investment promotion and economic development actions to further guide investors in their location decision process. Private sector development of the inland regime areas bordering FZs may encourage stronger business connections between the two regimes and contribute to the wider development of the governorate.

Figure 5.3. The key determinants to open a business in an industrial zone

% of total firms

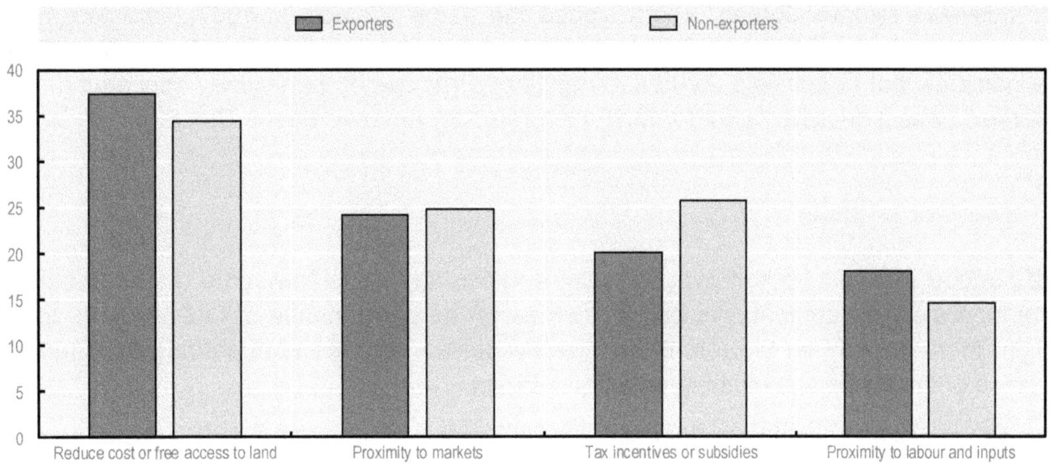

Note: Variables are calculated using sample weightings provided by the World Bank Enterprise Survey.
Source: OECD based on the World Bank Enterprise Survey of Egypt (2016).

Investors in Egypt, as elsewhere, often opt for zones to benefit from a friendlier business environment than in the rest of the country. The first zone-specific determinant that pushes investors to locate in zones is land availability and access, which continue to be a severe barrier to doing business in Egypt (see Chapter 3). Evidence reveals that "access to land at a reduced or no cost" is the most important reason behind manufacturing firms' choice to locate in an industrial zone (Figure 5.3). It is plausible to assume that the *land determinant* holds also for investors that decided to locate in other zone types of Egypt. Proximity to markets, particularly for exporters, followed by tax incentives (or subsidies) are the second and third most important decision factors for firms locating in an industrial zone. This evidence confirms that, while important, specific tax incentives may not be as crucial a factor to investors as Egypt's geographical position and large market size. Agglomeration effects (proximity to inputs and labour) are driving less investors' choice to locate in an industrial zone, suggesting that sourcing from local suppliers close to zones areas is limited.

Figure 5.4. Textile and clothing exports after signing the QIZ protocol (in USD)

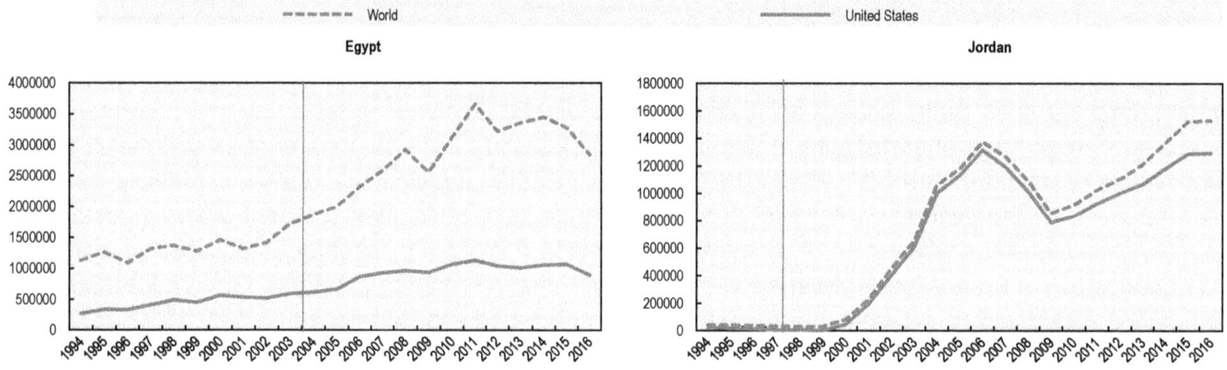

Source: OECD based on the World Integrated Trade Solution (WITS).

Other hurdles investors face in doing business in Egypt (or in certain regions of Egypt) are not necessarily addressed by zones' friendlier environment. These may consist of regulatory challenges such as poor intellectual property rights or of scarcity of resources such as the lack of adequate skills. QIZs are an edifying example of how zones are a second-best policy tool to attract FDI, the first-best being to reform the wider business climate. Jordan, which signed the same Protocol in 1997, attracted more foreign multinationals than Egypt in QIZs, despite higher labour and production costs (Figure 5.4). Comparative evidence indicates that the flexible Jordanian regulatory framework, particularly concerning the hiring of foreign workers, was a decisive factor for MNEs to prefer Jordan over Egypt (Box 5.3).

Box 5.3. The role of Egyptian QIZs in boosting exports: A comparative analysis with Jordan

The QIZ protocol signed by both Egypt (in 2004) and Jordan (in 1997) with the United States provides a natural laboratory for comparative policy analysis of the performance of QIZs in both countries. It sheds light more broadly on the role of special investment regimes in upgrading the manufacturing performance of the textile and clothing industry in Egypt.

The Egyptian textile and clothing sector accounts for 3% of GDP and around 30% of the manufacturing workforce. Exports of textiles and clothing represent 15-25% of non-oil exports depending on the year. QIZ exports made up 33% of exports of textiles and clothing. There are around 7 000 firms in the textile and clothing sector, 196 of which are in free zones. It is likely that these 196 firms are also entitled to QIZ provisions, benefiting from free zones incentives and US duty-free access.

No statistics are available on the amount of foreign investment in Egyptian QIZs but evidence from Azmeh (2014) suggests that MNEs played only a limited role in QIZs expansion. The positive impact of the protocol on exports was driven by an expansion of large firms exporting to the US prior to the introduction of QIZs. Larger firms expanded after the protocol, as they could save on their variable costs when purchasing Israeli products in bulk. Limited shifts in the distribution of textile exports towards SMEs occurred after the establishment of the QIZ protocol. Linkages exist between SMEs and large firms operating in QIZs but remain weak, with little evidence of sub-contracting agreements between large firms and SMEs to improve their capabilities.

In contrast, the QIZ protocol contributed to the emergence of a textile sector in Jordan, mostly through large foreign capital and labour from Asia. Foreign firms indicated that the main reason of choosing Jordan instead of Egypt as a QIZ-investment location (as most firms view them as substitutable locations) was the ability for them to build the production and labour regimes required to meet the needs of their US buyers. The Jordanian framework enabled foreign companies to rapidly bring in qualified, competitive, foreign labour from South Asia, thereby maintaining a high locational mobility.

Regulatory flexibility in zones' framework may nevertheless come with a cost. The fast "entry-exit" GVC governance strategy of MNEs in Jordan's QIZ led to low levels of embeddedness in the local economy. In such a context, it is less likely that there will be spillovers to the local economy as this requires MNEs making organisational and financial investments, which are not part of their governance strategy. Recent reforms in Egypt eased the restrictions on hiring foreign workers, including in the SEZ regime. Under the inland regime the foreign workers rate could be increased from a maximum 10% to 20% of the total number of workers in a company, if it is not possible to hire national manpower with the required qualifications. The impact of this reform may be limited if QIZs' attractiveness depends only on duty-free access to the US market and low-cost labour, however.

Source: OECD based on Azmeh (2014) and Nugent and Abdel-Latif (2010)

Improve zones' attractiveness as export hubs and modernise their industrial capabilities

Zones have helped boost Egyptian manufacturing exports and integrate the economy into GVCs, despite the aforementioned competitiveness challenges. They have become increasingly central in the country's export landscape. A decade ago, a study estimated that 23% of Egypt's exports originated from export processing zones, similar to Morocco (25%) and several other emerging countries. During the same period, they represented half of China's or Mexico's exports (Degain, 2011). Ten years later, export data from public and private FZs and QIZs suggest zones represented 40% of Egypt's non-oil exports in 2018 (Figure 5.5). Public FZs drove the increase in exports, while private FZs and QIZs witnessed a stagnation in exports, at least in the last few years.

Although zones in Egypt certainly stimulated exports, the extent to which their performance has met the objectives set by the government is an open question. Public and private FZ projects, for instance, are not necessarily creating substantial value-added, as they import more than they export (Figure 5.6). FZ projects' trade balance was positive in the last two years, but only when sales on the domestic market are categorised as exports. With such trade outcomes, FZs are falling short of reaching their strategic objectives of contributing to national trade deficit reduction. QIZ firms report higher export-to-import ratios. Only 10% of QIZ exports to the US include intermediate inputs, imported from Israel. There is no publicly available data on exports by SCZone projects.

The trade outcome of public FZs is arguably to be expected, given their design. Firms located there mostly offer transport and warehousing platform services for import-export transit and, therefore, do not necessarily create significant value-added. The causes behind private FZs' trade deficit during this period are less straightforward since they mostly consist of large industrial establishments with, in principle, strong export potential. It is likely that the regional and national contexts in the aftermath of the 2011 events, combined with lukewarm global demand, have affected FZs exports during the last years.

Figure 5.5. Egyptian zones' contribution to non-oil exports

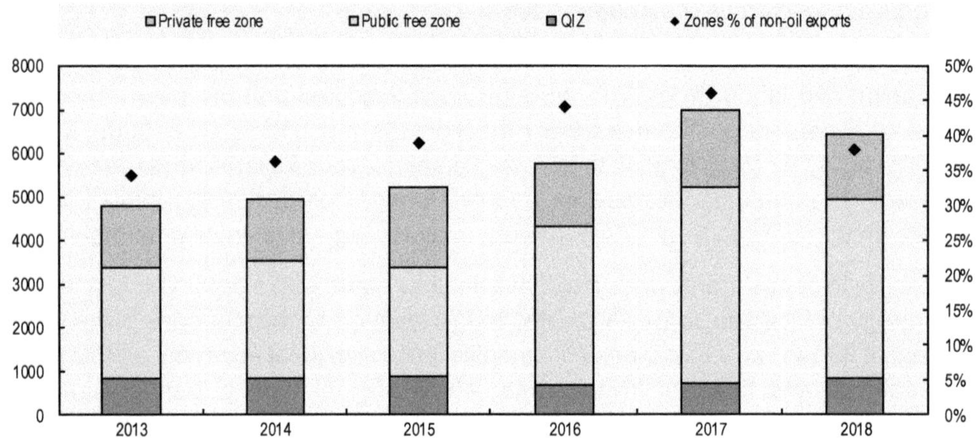

Note: A possibility of double counting exists due to presence of QIZ-listed firms in public Free zones. There is no publicly available data on exports by projects in the SCZone, GTZone and investment zones.
Source: OECD based on GAFI statistics, QIZ Unit Bulletin and the Central Bank of Egypt.

Figure 5.6. Free zones' exports, imports and sales on the domestic market

In USD million

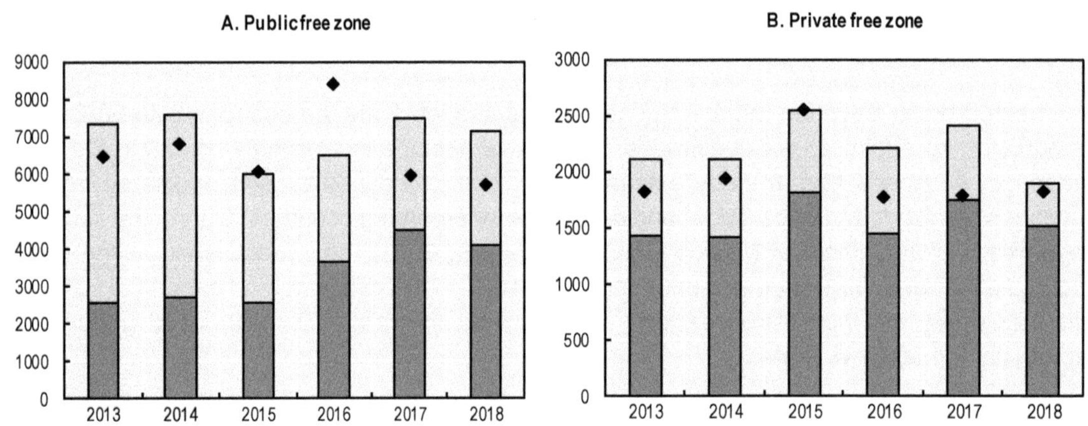

Source: OECD based on GAFI statistics.

Improving zones' attractiveness as export hubs and modernising their industrial capabilities should be among the top priorities of the Egyptian government. The main barriers to export in Egypt in 2016 were the value of the Egyptian pound and foreign exchange controls and restrictions, which affected all firms regardless of their investment regime (Figure 5.7). Despite the provision by the Egyptian authorities of generous fiscal incentives to zone investors, this could not compensate for an overvalued exchange rate, reducing the competitiveness of labour-intensive products and deterring FDI (Moran, 2011). The decision by the Central Bank of Egypt to float the exchange rate in 2016 and the new provisions of the 2017 Investment Law to facilitate the repatriation of benefits are important steps in the right direction to lower these two important barriers.

Figure 5.7. Export constraints in industrial zones versus rest of the economy

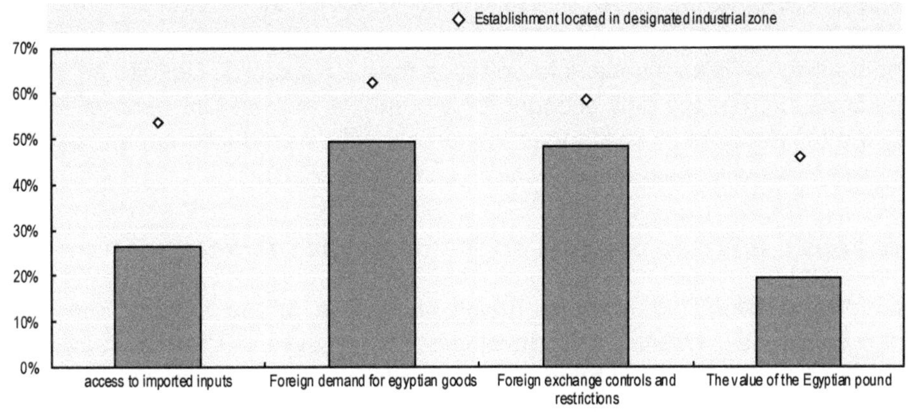

Note: Variables are calculated using sample weightings provided by the World Bank Enterprise Survey.
Source: OECD based on the World Bank Enterprise Survey of Egypt (2016).

Other constraints, such as the lack of access to imported inputs, also negatively affect Egyptian exporters, especially businesses located in industrial zones, which do not receive as much duty-free customs or facilitated import procedures as firms in special regimes. It is plausible to assume that firms under the FZ and SEZ regimes face lower constraints to accessing imports. Industrial zones' competitiveness could be further enhanced if they had easier access to foreign inputs as it would allow them to lower production costs or fabricate better quality goods (or both).

Besides wider investment climate considerations, export capabilities of businesses in zones are also intrinsically linked to the sector in which they operate. In the textile and clothing sectors, firms in FZs and, to a greater extent, in QIZs are essential to the sector's overall production. Firms entitled to QIZ duty-free treatment made up 4.8% of national non-oil exports and half of Egypt's non-oil exports to the US. They also accounted for around a third of exports of textile and clothing products, although QIZ export performance has slightly deteriorated over the last decade. The government should also promote and facilitate investment in higher-value added segments of the flourishing chemicals and food sectors by aligning sectoral strategies with zones' priorities and objectives.

Entities involved in setting the strategic objectives of zones should co-ordinate their efforts to promote private investment in the higher value-added segments of sectors' supply chains. The limited private domestic and foreign investment in the textile and clothing upstream activities, which are capital-intensive as they require modern technologies, hinders potential productivity gains in the whole sector (Nugent and Abdel-Latif, 2010). Egyptian state-owned enterprises (SOEs) dominate the upstream stages of the textile supply chain but produce at a higher cost than competitors abroad due to, *inter alia*, ageing technology. As a result, firms in downstream activities in zones mostly source their inputs from more competitive markets such as China.

Investment that upgrades industrial capabilities within zones is necessary to restore the deteriorating competitiveness of the upstream textile and clothing sector. The need for such investment is even more pressing given the recent increase in electricity and gas prices, which will put pressure on production costs throughout the supply chain. SMEs located in zones will likely be more adversely affected by such cost increases than larger firms and SOEs. More private investment in upstream activities, possibly resulting in technological upgrading, would also foster longer-term business linkages as inputs sourced by downstream establishments would become less costly and of better quality than those fabricated currently. The rise in gas prices also affects the competitiveness of some of the segments of the booming chemicals sector.

Government policies should aim to diversify production away from ready-made garments, which predominates manufacturing production in FZs and QIZs, particularly since the preferential treatment of

Egyptian exports through the QIZ will erode over time due to the widening network effect of US FTAs. To preserve the competitive edge of the QIZ, it is crucial to widen the scope of manufacturing products exported by zones. For instance, food and other non-textile exporters such as chemicals producers have a limited interest in using QIZs as a vehicle to enhance their US exports. Despite an increase, exports of food products by firms in QIZs still only account for around 1% of total QIZ exports. Some firms are not able to export to the US because of challenges in marketing their products, expensive Israeli inputs, lack of skilled labour, and financial constraints (Ghoneim and Awad, 2010).

Mitigate zones' adverse impacts on the domestic market

The large amount of production sold by zones, mainly public FZs, on the domestic market is another facet that reveals zones' challenge in meeting their development objectives.[15] There are several reasons behind these large domestic sales. On the one hand, the access to a large domestic market pushes firms to sell imported goods (instead of using imported inputs in the production process) or to discharge an excess of production that they cannot export. On the other hand, the lack of competitiveness and adequate knowledge of foreign markets reduces the capacity of businesses in FZs to export (Mori, 2017).

Regulatory restrictions and cumbersome import procedures in the inland regime amplify the domestic demand for imported goods transiting via FZs and the SCZone. In both zones, sales by firms in zones to the domestic market are treated as imports and are therefore subject to the general rules applicable to imports from abroad, i.e. they are subject to taxes and customs (Table 5.7). According to consultations with government representatives, public authorities authorise using temporarily zones with duty-free access as import entry doors in periods where the country faces severe shortages in some products.

Table 5.7. Zones' import and export relationship with the inland regime

Zone	Access to the local market	Sourcing from the local market
Free Zone	- Products are subject to the general rules applicable to importation from abroad. - If the products contain both local and foreign components, the customs tax basis applies only to the foreign components. - A fee of 1% of the total revenues realised is charged on local sales by public Free zones industrial projects (same fee than if exported). - A fee of 2% of the total revenues realised is charged on local sales by private Free zones projects (1% if exported abroad).	- Exportation of the production supplies from the local market to the Free zones shall be subject to the rules defined by a decision issued by the minister concerned with foreign trade affairs, in agreement with the Competent Minister and the Minister of Finance. - With the exception of the passenger vehicles, shall be exempted from the customs duties, the VAT, and other taxes and duties all types of tools, supplies, machinery and all kinds of means of transportation, necessary for exercising Free zone projects' activity. - Private Free zones projects shall source no less than 20% locally. - Local suppliers do not need to register in the exporters register. - Local suppliers do not need to obtain approval to source goods subject to quality control.
Investment and Tech Zones	- No restrictions/requirements	- No restrictions/requirements
Special Economic Zone	- Products are subject to the general rules applicable to importation from abroad. - If the products contain both local and foreign components, the customs tax basis applies only to the foreign components.	- Products exported from inside the country shall be treated as if they are exported abroad, and shall fulfil all export and monetary requirements.
Qualified Industrial Zone	- No restrictions/requirements	- 35% of the exported good should be produced locally.
Industrial Zone	- No restrictions/requirements	- No restrictions/requirements

Source: OECD based on the Investment Law, SEZ law, Import and Export law and the QIZ Protocol.

Sales from firms in FZs to the domestic market are even more problematic in light of the ESRs they need to comply with to enjoy the wide array of incentives in zones. Consultations with government representatives in 2019 revealed that public FZ apply a de facto ESR of 80%.[16] In private FZs, exports of the project are required to be no less than 80% of production, as defined in the law.[17] Over the last five years, FZ projects sold half of their production on the domestic market and the other half abroad according to GAFI's statistics. Public FZs drove this pattern, as domestic sales were even slightly higher than exports (Figure 5.6). The years 2016 and 2017 presented encouraging signs with a reverse in the pattern, coinciding with the government decision to float the exchange rate. Projects with a private FZ status have exported 70% of their production over the last five years, below the 80% requirement. Public and private FZs would have had to export 96% and 87% of their production respectively to generate a trade surplus in that period.

The government could better spell out its policy regarding the access of zones-based firms to the domestic market. There are no statutory ceilings on the share of production that can be sold on the domestic market by firms in FZs and SEZs (Table 5.7). At the same time, the government's internal regulations allegedly require zone-based firms to export a share of their production.[18] It is also not straightforward how zone authorities are able to enforce ESRs and how these requirements are linked to tax incentives granted to firms. Beyond the general rules applicable to imports from abroad,[19] public authorities charge firms in FZs a fee on their sales to the domestic market. Recently, an amendment to the investment law increased this fee from 1% to 2% of the total revenues realised, but only for private FZs projects.

Recent policy reforms, while laudable, may prove insufficient to support fairer competition and level the playing field between zones with special regimes and the inland regime. Sales to the domestic market by firms in FZs adversely affect firms in the inland regime by exposing them to unfair competition (IMF, 2017; Mori, 2017). Preferential treatment given to firms in FZs, such as zero corporate taxes or import facilitation measures, probably offset the fees they pay to access the domestic market. Such preferential treatment gives "market-seeking" businesses in FZs a comparative advantage over those under the inland regime, and may incentivise the latter to move to the zones.[20] Lowering import tariffs and easing import procedures under the inland regime while phasing out the use of profit-based corporate tax incentives in the zones would cut this detrimental (and costly) comparative advantage gap. Levelling the playing field between the special regimes and the inland regime is an even more pressing priority in light of the government's strategy to expand the number of zones.[21]

Governments have opted for various policies regarding zones' access to the domestic market. Thailand or Uruguay apply a somewhat similar statutory rule to Egypt, i.e. there are no ceilings on domestic market sales, but neither country fixes any ESRs such as in Egyptian public and private FZs. Conversely, firms in FZs in Bangladesh are allowed to sell up to 20% of production on the domestic market. Other countries permit a fixed percentage of production to be sold on the domestic market without facing customs duties, using duty-free domestic access as an incentive to attract FDI to the zones (Yücer and Siroën, 2017).[22] In Mauritius, for instance, firms are allowed to sell up to 20% of their production duty free on the domestic market, thus offering them preferential, albeit limited, access. In Brazil, the FTZ of Manaus offers tariff incentives conditional on the local value-added created in total production rather than based on ESRs.

Policymakers in Egypt could benefit from the respective experiences of Poland and the Dominican Republic, as both successfully managed to address challenges inherited from their zone-based policies. Poland established zones in the mid-1980s for a temporary period of 20 years (setting a temporary lifespan for zones is in itself a good practice). Zones in Poland contributed to productivity growth in the country but they were not without some adverse consequences. The criteria discriminated against SMEs based outside zones. In addition, neighbouring countries started offering tax incentives regardless of investors' location. As a remedy, Poland introduced in 2018 a new law to expand zones incentives to the entire territory and shifted from geographical and investment scale criteria towards sustainability and innovation criteria (UNCTAD, 2019).

The Dominican Republic established export-processing zones that offered CIT incentives conditional on an ESR, as FZs in Egypt. With the country joining the Central American Free Trade Agreement (2004), the end of the Multi-Fibre Agreement (2005) and the WTO deadline to comply with the Agreement on Subsidies and Countervailing Measures (2015), it became necessary for the Dominican Republic to phase-out such incentives (UNCTAD, 2019). The phase-out strategy consisted of a staggered removal of the ESR: in 2007, the country eliminated the ESR for firms producing leather, textiles and apparel and footwear products (national priority sectors); and in 2011, it lifted the ESR for all firms. Zones in the country remained attractive locations for exporters, with no impact on exports levels (Defever et al., 2018).

Use zones to bridge investment and local development policies

Zones in Egypt have been an instrument at the crossroads of investment and local development policies. If zone-based policies in Egypt have managed to attract foreign MNEs to specific locations, their record in advancing local development objectives is more mixed. To maximise the benefits from investment in zones, Egypt needs to be equipped with a strategy that is aligned with national SME and export goals and coherent with the development priorities of governorates. With no such strategy in place, zones in Egypt may miss their broader development objectives, creating enclaves with limited connections to the local economy, where foreign investors mainly contribute to export hubs without fostering dynamic industry clusters. International experience has shown that the socio-economic benefits governments expect from FDI in zones are not automatic. Successful zones generate robust linkages with the local economy when they are firmly embedded in a wider development agenda that covers, *inter alia*, SMEs upgrading and human resources development (Moran, 2011).

Any strategy to promote the contribution of zones to sustainable development in Egypt should serve to create linkages between MNEs and local suppliers, specifically SMEs. It is critical therefore to examine what sort of linkages exist in the country. Business linkages are contingent on the GVC governance framework of MNEs, which sectors MNEs operate in, and their position in the supply chain. For instance, FDI tends to be less stable in the low capital-intensive clothing sector because of increasingly squeezed margins. Thus, global firms make sure to limit their links with the local economy to be able to "exit" as quickly as possible once another location becomes more attractive (Azmeh, 2014). This is the case in Jordan, where Asian garment MNEs moved to exploit QIZs duty-free access to the US market but have limited embeddedness in the local economy. More problematic, in Lesotho the removal of textile quotas in 2005 led to rapid factory closures and huge job losses (Staritz and Morris, 2013). Connecting MNEs located in Egyptian zones with local suppliers outside of zones would help technology spillovers. It would also help firms manufacture more technologically advanced goods in the textile supply chain and advance sectors with larger margins such as in chemicals or automotive.

Egypt has introduced several tools to forge stronger linkages between MNEs and the local economy and to improve zones' value-added. These policies are framed in some cases as a requirement, which may deter foreign investors, and in others as a soft, proactive tool incentivising relationships with local suppliers. For instance, in private FZs at least 30% of production must come from local inputs. In QIZs, 35% of the exported product should be produced locally to obtain duty-free access to the United States. In contrast, businesses in public FZs get a 7% tax refund on intermediates purchased locally (and 3% if purchased from abroad).[23] Such cost-based incentives could be further increased and financed by raising FZs fees on domestic market sales. The tax refund tool is similar to what is applied in the Manaus FTZ in Brazil, where incentives are conditional on the local value-added, rather than exports, to support the development of areas bordering the zone.

To encourage business linkages, Egypt also eased the regulatory and administrative procedures on local firms that supply businesses in FZs and SEZs, which have duty-free regimes. Although products and services sold to these zones are treated as exports and therefore subject to the same trade rules, including tariffs, some administrative incentives are given to local suppliers. For instance, local suppliers selling inputs to FZ businesses do not need to register in the exporters register or obtain approval from the General Organisation for Import and Export Control to source some agricultural goods subject to quality control (Table 5.7).[24] Such exemptions are not granted to establishments in QIZs, SEZs and Investment Zones.

It is crucial to ensure that incentives and tools to promote business linkages are well promoted by the different responsible entities, i.e. GAFI, the QIZ Unit, the Export Development Authority and zone authorities, and effectively implemented in practice. Both MNE affiliates and domestic SMEs may shy away from using such tools because they lack knowledge about them, face cumbersome administrative steps to request the tool or a lengthy refunding/approval period. In Tunisia, suppliers to firms under the export-only offshore regime face arduous administrative procedures to receive VAT tax refunds, discouraging them from forging business linkages and thereby limiting valuable spillovers from productive exporting firms to the local economy (OECD, 2018a).

Examining whether extending linkages incentives to special regimes other than the FZs is an avenue that Egyptian authorities could consider. In the SCZone area, for instance, the quasi-totality of inputs used in exported products were of domestic origin in 2013. Exemption from customs duties and sales tax since the new SEZ law in 2015 may reduce SCZone businesses' purchases of domestic inputs as these may become more costly than imported goods. In such a scenario, authorities could envisage extending the proactive incentives to promote business linkages in SEZs.

Achieving stronger business co-operation between MNEs established in zones and local suppliers also requires policy actions to upgrade local suppliers' capabilities. Local firms may not be sufficiently well equipped and the labour force may lack the relevant skills to make such co-operation possible. SMEs also sometimes have a poor record in terms of compliance, which may deter foreign investors from engaging in business partnerships. SMEs in Egypt tend to have lower absorptive capacity than in other MENA countries, although this varies greatly across governorates. Firms located in the governorates forming the SCZone (Port Said, Ismailia and Suez) are more likely to hold internationally-recognised quality certifications and are more inclined to train their staff (Figure 5.8).

Figure 5.8. Firms' absorptive capacity across Egyptian governorates in 2013

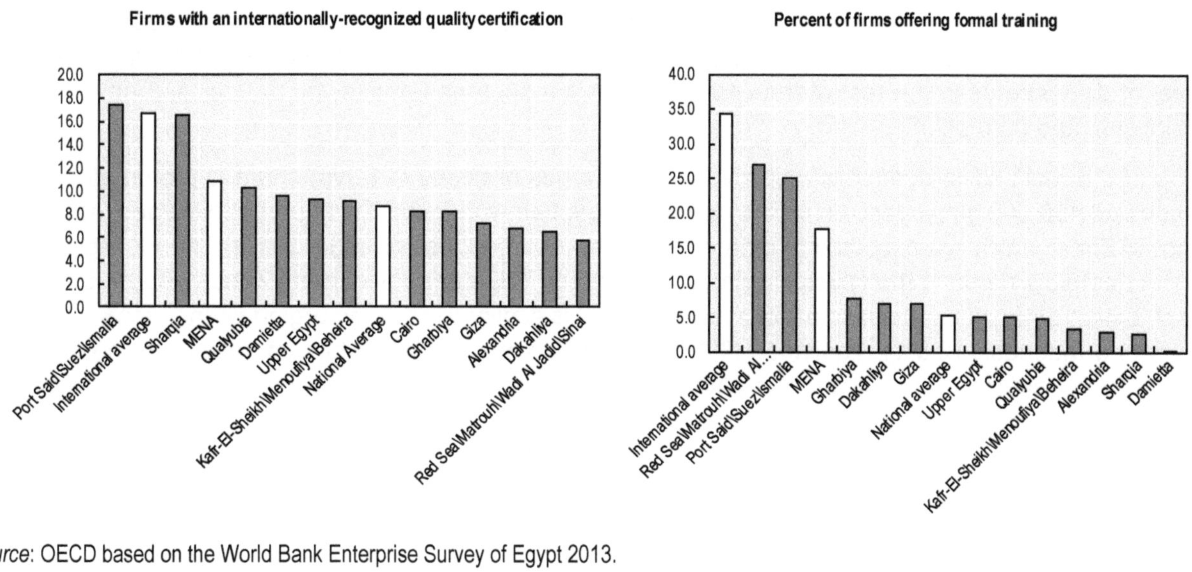

Source: OECD based on the World Bank Enterprise Survey of Egypt 2013.

It is therefore crucial to strengthen the absorptive capacity of Egyptian SMEs located near zones through skills development training, partnerships with education institutions, and better business development services (BDS). More effective coordination between the different public and private entities is required to achieve these objectives. Large zones with a regional development objective, such as the SCZone, could continue intensifying their already existing efforts to forge partnerships with research and education institutes and associations with a view to support innovation, provide adequate training facilities and thereby address skills shortages in local businesses.[25]

Fostering institutional co-ordination is one of the goals of the forthcoming national SME strategy, which the new agency in charge of SME policy, the MSMEs Development Authority (MSMEDA), will implement at a yet-to-be-determined date (OECD/EU/ETF, 2018). One of the pillars of the strategy is the development of value chains and export promotion through upgrading SME capabilities. A national initiative between IDA and the Central Bank of Egypt plans to establish BDS centres in all governorates. MSMEDA, CBE, GAFI, and zone authorities could further co-ordinate their capacity-building activities to ensure that SMEs near zones are equipped with the adequate absorptive capacity to connect with MNEs in the zones.

The extent of geographical proximity between Egyptian SMEs and foreign-owned firms in zones matters for the materialisation of local development benefits from business linkages. Proximity facilitates knowledge spillovers, especially tacit knowledge. One example of a successful linkages strategy is the Penang SEZ, which is hosting one of Malaysia's most developed technology clusters, of semiconductor-based electronic components manufacturing. In combination with vigorous investment promotion policies, the government created an SME Centre within the zone, providing SMEs rental subsidies to help them take advantage of the facility (OECD, 2013). Penang state also established a skills development centre, which was recognised by other countries as a world-class model for partnerships between government, academia and industry (OECD, 2018b).

Ensure zones' social and environmental sustainability

The Egyptian government recently put achieving greater economic, social and environmental sustainability at the forefront of its priorities. Both Egypt Vision 2030 and the 2017 investment law often mention sustainability as an objective. It is therefore crucial to embed sustainability as a priority in the policy framework of special regimes, as they constitute an integral part of the Egyptian economy. International experience shows that countries using special investment regimes as a sustainable development tool should pay close attention to safeguarding treatment of workers and the environment, aligning the zone-based policies with national legislation and its implementation (Moran, 2011). To avoid creating economic enclaves with lower standards and norms, the policy framework of zones in Egypt should apply the same level of diligence as in the rest of the country on issues such as tax evasion, labour and environmental violations, and corruption.

One of the main socio-economic objectives that all types of zones in Egypt share is job creation: with a combined 400 000 employees or 1.7% of the total Egyptian workforce. This number excludes the SCZone and GTZone, which are expected to create more than 600 000 jobs (OECD, 2017). The FZ regime is the largest employer among the special regimes, followed by QIZs and Investment Zones (Figure 5.9).[26] The contribution of Egyptian zones to national employment is similar to other emerging economies such as Viet Nam and Indonesia (2.5%), Thailand (1%) or the Philippines (1.4%). While impressive, zones in Egypt have not yet attained their full job generation potential. For instance, public and private FZs have so far achieved 62% of their job creation objective (Mori, 2017).

Anecdotal evidence from businesses in zones suggests that there are both labour and skills shortages in zones, which are sometimes provoked by restricted access to foreign labour (Ghoneim and Awad, 2010). The impact of the recent reforms aimed at reducing restrictions on hiring foreign workers in zones could be monitored to assess whether such a framework should be extended to the inland regime in the future. In 2011, the Ministry of Manpower and Migration enacted regulations to restrict foreigners' access to Egyptian work visas. According to the regulations, the jobs that are open to foreign workers are only those that Egyptians workers do not have the requisite skills for and nor can they acquire them.

Figure 5.9. Employment by zones in Egypt in 2018 (or latest available year)

In thousands of employees

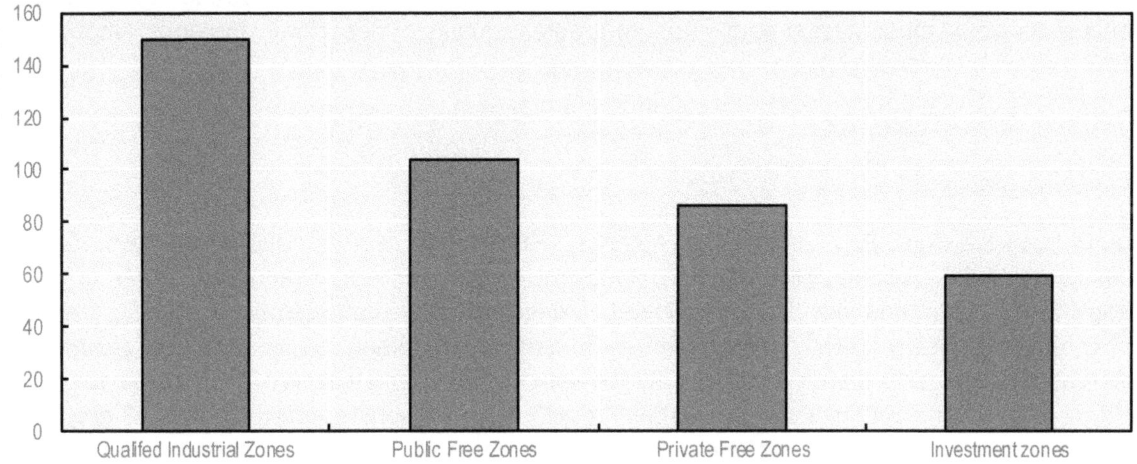

Note: A possibility of double counting exists due to presence of QIZ-listed firms in public free zones.
Source: OECD based on GAFI statistics and QIZ Unit Bulletin.

Addressing the sustainability of zones goes beyond monitoring adherence to job creation goals; it requires ensuring that foreign and domestic businesses create *quality* jobs, notably in terms of working conditions and environmental impacts. FZ and SEZ regimes enjoy more flexible labour regulations than in the inland investment regime. In SEZs, for instance, if parties wish to continue to execute a limited employment contract after its expiration, it will be renewed only for period similar to the period of the expired contract. In the general rule under the Egyptian Labour Law (12/2003), the contract would be converted into an unlimited one.[27] In light of the large population in SEZ territories, such standards might create a dual labour market within the country, if the impact of such policies is not monitored over a defined period of time. Countries with successful special regime strategies allow, for instance, union organising within defined areas or have written in their different laws that environmental and labour standards in the zones should not be below those stipulated in the national legislation.

The framework surrounding zones' governance plays a determinant role in guaranteeing that social and environmental standards are promoted within the zones. If well implemented, the recent decision of GAFI to partner with private developers to set up new FZs may be an opportunity to further enhance Egyptian zones' sustainability standards. Evidence shows that foreign private developers bring in not only innovation and know-how but also contribute to raise labour and environmental standards and conditions (Moran, 2011). In Thailand and Viet Nam, for instance, most FDI and export activities take place in privately-run zones, which also tend to have a better record of social and environmental impact than government-owned zones.

Authorities managing zones play an important role in implementing and monitoring labour regulations. For instance, the SCZone authority has the power to determine internal labour regulations of firms operating within the SEZ. The SEZ authorities can also issue work permits for foreigners (after obtaining the security approvals) and determine the work permit requirements. They also have the right to exempt some projects, entities and companies from the maximum percentage of foreigners determined by the law. Nevertheless, it is not clear what the criteria are for obtaining such exemptions. SEZ authorities are also qualified to establish a special system for social insurance that is more beneficial for employees in the SEZ. The Subic Bay SEZ in the Philippines created ecology and labour centres to monitor and coach firms (Box 5.4).

Zones could be also used as laboratories to experiment with new policies aimed at supporting sustainable development, such as tools and programmes aimed at closing the gender wage gap in the country. Zones also hire relatively more women because they accept lower wages than men but also because they are involved in less skill-intensive activities, such as in textile and clothing (El-Haddad, 2016). Enhancing women's skills would thus, at least partly, ensure greater equality of opportunity in zones' labour market.

Box 5.4. Safeguarding social and environmental norms in the Philippines Economic Zone

In the Philippines, Subic Bay Metropolitan Authority (SBMA) fully applies national laws with regards to labour rights and environmental protection, according to its rules and regulations. It has created an Ecology Centre entrusted with functions linked to environmental management, including monitoring, training and permitting. SBMA also reserves a certain proportion of its land for environmental conservation. As regards labour rights, the SBMA established a labour centre "responsible for studying and amicably settling professional and labour relations and disputes, interpretation of employment contracts, and monitoring work hygiene and safety standards" (OECD, 2016). In addition, every zone also has a staffed monitoring office on behalf of the Philippines Economic Zone Authority which monitors if the zone developers and locators comply with national social and environmental legislation.

Source: OECD (2016).

References

Álvarez-Galván, J. (2015), A Skills beyond School Review of Egypt, OECD Reviews of Vocational Education and Training, OECD Publishing. http://dx.doi.org/10.1787/9789264209626-en

Azmeh, S. (2014), Labour in global production networks: workers in the qualifying industrial zones (QIZs) of Egypt and Jordan, *Global Networks*, 14(4), 495-513.

Azmeh, S., & Nadvi, K. (2014), Asian firms and the restructuring of global value chains, *International Business Review*, 23(4), 708-717.

Davies, R. B., & Mazhikeyev, A. (2015), the impact of special economic zones on exporting behaviour, No. 15/28, Working Paper Series, UCD Centre for Economic Research.

Defever, F. & Reyes, J-D. & Riaño, A. & Sanchez-Martin, M. E. (2018), Special Economic Zones and WTO Compliance: Evidence from the Dominican Republic, *Economica*, Volume 86, Issue 343, July 2019, Pages 532-568.

Degain, C. (2011). Trade patterns and global value chains in East Asia: From trade in goods to trade in tasks, World Trade Organization.

El-Haddad, A. (2016), Female Wages in the Egyptian Textiles and Clothing Industry: Low Pay and Discrimination, *Review of Economics and Political Science*, *415*(3757), 1-36.

Farole, T., & Akinci, G. (2011), Special economic zones: progress, emerging challenges, and future directions, The World Bank.

Farole, T. and Kweka, J. (2011), Institutional best practices for special economic zones: an application to Tanzania, World Bank Africa Trade Policy Notes No. 25, 2011.

Ghoneim, F., and Awad (2011), Impact of Qualifying Industrial Zones on Egypt and Jordan: A Critical Analysis, unpublished manuscript.

Hanafy, S. (2015), Determinants of FDI location in Egypt: Empirical analysis using governorate panel data, *Joint Discussion Paper Series in Economics, No. 13-2015.*

IMF (2017), Arab Republic of Egypt: Selected Issues, December 11, 2017, International Monetary Fund, Washington D.C.

Moran, Theodore H. (2011), International experience with Special Economic Zones: Using SEZs to drive development in countries around the world, Report commissioned by the Centre for Development and Enterprise (CDE)

Mori, I. (2017), Free zones in Egypt: A critical reading, Al-Ahram Centre for Political and Strategic Studies, December 2017.

Nugent, J. B., & Abdel-Latif, A. (2010), "A quiz on the net benefits of trade creation and trade diversion in the QIZs of Jordan and Egypt", In *Economic Research Forum Working Papers* (Vol. 514).

OECD (2013), *OECD Investment Policy Review of Malaysia*, OECD Investment Policy Reviews, OECD Publishing, Paris, https://doi.org/10.1787/9789264194588-en.

OECD (2015), *OECD Policy Framework for Investment, 2015 Edition,* OECD Publishing, Paris, https://doi.org/10.1787/9789264208667-en.

OECD (2016), *OECD Investment Policy Review of the Philippines*, OECD Investment Policy Reviews, OECD Publishing, Paris. https://doi.org/10.1787/9789264254510-en

OECD (2017), Supporting the Development of the Suez Canal Economic Zone: Identifying Priority Actions for a Dynamic and Sustainable Economic Zone, OECD, Paris (unpublished).

OECD (2018a), *OECD Economic Surveys: Tunisia 2018: Economic Assessment*, OECD Publishing, Paris, https://doi.org/10.1787/eco_surveys-tun-2018-en.

OECD/EU/ETF (2018), *The Mediterranean Middle East and North Africa 2018: Interim Assessment of Key SME Reforms*, SME Policy Index, OECD Publishing, Paris, https://doi.org/10.1787/9789264304161-en.

OECD-UNIDO (2019), Integrating Southeast Asian SMEs in Global Value Chains: Enabling

Linkages with Foreign Investors, Paris, www.oecd.org/investment/Integrating-Southeast-Asian-SMEs-in-global-value-chains.pdf.

WTO (2018), Trade Policy Review: Egypt 2018, World Trade Organization, Geneva.

UNCTAD (2019), World Investment Report 2019, UNCTAD Publishing, Geneva.

Yücer, A., & Siroën, J. M. (2017), Trade Performance of Export Processing Zones, *The World Economy*, 40(5), 1012-1038.

Notes

[1] See Chapter 6 for a discussion on the fiscal incentives granted in the different zones in Egypt.

[2] In Tunisia this type of zone is referred to as the offshore regime.

[3] See Article 33 of Law No. 72/2017 on Investment.

[4] See Article 35 of Law No. 72/2017 on Investment.

[5] See Article 75 of the Prime Minister Decree No. 2310/2017.

[6] Licences must describe the purpose and term of the project as well as the amount of financial guarantee to be paid by the licensee. This licence must also state the real estate properties needed to carry out the relevant project.

[7] Chapter 3 provides an assessment of the different dispute settlement mechanisms in Egypt.

[8] The US market is the only main market where Egyptian exporters do not enjoy duty free access as they do in other markets such as the European Union, Arab countries and African countries, where Egypt has concluded free trade agreements.

[9] Procedures to get a licence for an industrial project are governed by law No. 15 of 2017 on the Facilitation of Granting Licences to Industrial Facilities, which applies to all projects in or outside of the Industrial Zones and within FZs and investment zones. Law No. 15 of 2017 applies without prejudice to law No. 83 of 2002 on Economic Zones of a special nature.

[10] The list of companies entitled to QIZ Duty-Free treatment is available here: http://www.qizegypt.gov.eg/images/attachment.ashx.pdf

[11] Foreign participation represents 20% of the total issued capital in public FZs and 17% in private FZs (GAFI Statistics).

[12] According to data provided by GAFI, each Investment Zone is on average home to 16 companies.

[13] Industrial zones in Egypt can be located either within the boundaries of the inland regime or within one of the special investment regimes.

[14] Some large foreign investors in Egypt's zones, such as the Chinese state-owned industrial developer TEDA, the Tianjin Economic-Technological Development Area, established their businesses with the multiple objectives of exporting to Africa and Europe using Egypt's network of preferential agreements, serving the large Egyptian market and exporting intermediate inputs back to China (Farole and Akinci, 2011).

[15] Sales on the domestic market by FZ regime represented USD 3.6 billion in 2016 compared to USD 1.5 billion in 2003 (WTO, 2018).

[16] Article No. 35 of Law No. 72/2017 dictates an obligation of sharing decision between GAFI and Ministry of industry and trade regarding exporting percentage of public FZs projects. There are representative from the Ministry of industry and trade in GAFI' FZ Technical Committee to make decisions regarding exporting percentages.

[17] With the exception of ready-made clothing and furnishing; 95% of these goods must be exported. In the strategic and mining industries the relevant minister decides export rates. Export rates are not applied to strategic projects of national importance.

[18] According to government sources, GAFI is working on issuing a necessary decree to regulate the procedures to determine a fixed export percentage for projects in public free zones. Currently the free zones technical committee determine a percentage for each industry.

[19] Law No. 72/2017 - Article 40.

[20] Chapter 6 addresses the subject of tax incentives in Egypt. The chapter describes how sales by FZ companies on the domestic market may reduce productivity growth.

[21] More effectively combating smugglings operations to penetrate the local market across the custom borders of these zones would also reduce the costs associated with this regime (IMF, 2017).

[22] Higher tariff rates may encourage firms to set up in zones where sales on the domestic market free of import tariffs are possible, leading to higher investment and export rates. It is not clear however that this will outweigh tariffs' wider negative effects (Yücer and Siroën, 2017).

[23] This information needs verification.

[24] The duty drawback scheme allows a full refund of customs duties paid on imports of inputs used in the manufacture of finished products provided that they are shipped to a FZ within two years, but this does not necessarily contribute to forge business linkages.

[25] The OECD reviewed vocational education and training policy in Egypt and provided recommendations on how to improve skills supply in the country (see Álvarez-Galván, 2015).

[26] Information on job creation in the SCZone and GTZone is not available.

[27] In addition, an employer in an SEZ is not restricted by the limited causes of termination stipulated in the Labour Law but compensation will not be less than that provided for in the Labour Law.

Chapter 6. Tax policy and incentives in Egypt

This chapter provides an overview of Egypt's tax system, including recent reforms, and an assessment of the country's investment incentives regime. It provides an overview of existing incentives, their implications for the tax administration and proposes options to ensure that tax incentives achieve the government's policy goals in a cost-effective manner. The chapter also looks at tax governance and transparency issues.

Summary and policy recommendations

Tax policy and administration are important components of an investment climate. Governments worldwide use tax incentives to achieve certain outcomes, whether more investment overall or greater flows to certain sectors, activities or regions. At the same time, corporate income taxes are often an important source of fiscal revenue for governments, particularly in emerging economies which can in turn contribute to improving other aspects of the investment environment such as through public spending on infrastructure or health and education. Sound tax policy requires effective coordination across ministries and agencies and at different levels of government, transparency and consistency in its application and regular monitoring and review of its effectiveness. Tax expenditure reporting should be publicly available and subject to parliamentary oversight. Tax policies that create an uneven playing field for business or that are uneven in their application create uncertainty for investors which might negate any positive outcomes which the policy was intended to achieve in the first place.

The Egyptian government has made substantial improvements in its tax policy in recent years. The 2017 Investment Law includes many positive changes, including limiting corporate income tax holidays to free zone (FZ) companies. Similarly, the 2015 amendment of the Law on Economic Zones of Special Nature no longer includes reduced corporate and income taxes for projects inside special economic zones. The government also has an extensive array of measures to protect the domestic tax base from cross-border tax minimisation techniques used by multinational enterprises (MNEs). The Egyptian Ministry of Finance and the OECD have recently launched an EU-funded project to strengthen domestic resource mobilisation in Egypt. Project elements include guidance on enhancing tax transparency, implementing international standards on exchange of information, capacity building to assist authorities in addressing aggressive tax planning by MNEs, and compiling internationally comparable revenue statistics.

Incentives offered to companies in FZs contribute to revenue leakage when commodities (imported and domestic supplies) enter zones tax-free. They also introduce distortions and hamper productivity growth when FZ companies enjoy competitive advantages focus on the domestic market, as shown by recent figures presented in Chapter 5. To limit revenue leakage, the authorities are encouraged to prescribe and publish lists of commodity inputs currently eligible for customs duty and value added tax (VAT) exemptions. They could also consider mechanisms to monitor firms' export performance until CIT holidays are phased-out in zones.[1].

To ensure consistency with overall tax policy and to strengthen accountability, the government is encouraged to consolidate tax incentive legislation and tax legislation and assign to the Ministry of Finance (MOF) primary responsibility to introduce tax incentive legislation. The report recommends that the tasks of monitoring compliance with tax incentives be assigned to the Egyptian Tax Authority (ETA), and that strict penalty regimes be exercised. The current project to switch to a fully electronic data management platform in the tax system is strongly supported.

Policy recommendations

Guidance on tax policy and tax incentive design

Recommendations on tax policy

- Target the tax deduction for undocumented expenses to small businesses
- Increase the withholding tax rate on dividends paid by resident companies to resident shareholders and eliminate the EGP 10 000 dividend exemption

- Eliminate the personal tax exemption for dividends paid by FZ companies.
- Eliminate the corporate tax exemption for interest on bonds issued by listed companies
- Limit the exemption for pension income
- Supplement or replace the (4:1) thin-capitalisation rule with an interest deduction limitation rule that follows the recommendations of BEPS Action 4
- Discontinue the statutory non-resident withholding tax exemption for interest

Recommendations on tax incentive design

- Target the 30% expensing of capital costs to new investment expenditure
- Prescribe conditions and list commodity inputs eligible for customs duty exemption
- Redesign targeting criteria and clarify terms to minimise discretion in determining eligibility
- Revise the base of the investment tax allowance to investment expenditure on tangible capital (with a 'first-in-use' rule)

Recommendations on tax incentives for Free Zone projects

- No longer provide FZ projects with a CIT holiday (grandfather existing projects)
- Extend the investment tax allowance to include investments by FZ companies
- Ensure electronic tracking of goods entering and exiting FZs
- Monitor very closely export performance of public FZ projects as long as CIT holidays exist
- Align fees on sales by public FZ projects to the domestic market with those of private FZs (i.e. increase them from 1% of sales to 2%).

Guidance on governance of tax incentives

Recommendations on introducing tax incentive legislation

- Consolidate tax incentive legislation and tax legislation
- Reduce discretion of officials in providing tax incentive relief
- Assign to the MOF sole authority to introduce tax and tax incentive legislation
- Strengthen capacity of MOF staff for tax analysis
- Regularise data collection and ensure MOF access to anonymised tax data

Recommendations on monitoring tax incentives

- Assign to the ETA responsibility to monitor compliance with tax incentives
- Ensure electronic tracking of goods entering and exiting FZs
- Apply strict penalty regimes for non-compliance with tax incentive laws and regulations

Recommendations on reporting of tax incentives

- Prepare tax expenditure reports to accompany budget documents[2]
- Prepare reports on purchases, sales and tax relief for FZ companies
- Prepare reports on cost-benefit analysis of main tax incentives

Tax system review and scope for revenue mobilisation

Tax revenues in Egypt have been relatively stable over the past decade but remain below many peers in the region and elsewhere as a percentage of GDP. The government will need to raise revenues over time for public spending on health, education, infrastructure and other areas which, among other benefits, will contribute to improvements in the business climate. Revenue mobilisation will require efforts on several fronts, not least concerning income, property and consumption taxes, as well as on improving tax administration.[3] This section focuses mainly on corporate taxation which has the most direct impact on investor behaviour and on the broader social returns from economic activity. The discussion which follows looks at how taxes on capital are applied and at how Egypt protects its tax base against profit shifting by investors.

Domestic taxation

Table 6.1 reports the tax mix in Egypt in fiscal year 2016/17, including the recent introduction of VAT showing tax revenues in millions of Egyptian pounds and as a percentage of GDP. One notable feature is the relatively low contribution of personal income tax (PIT), due in part to the importance of the informal market and in part to narrow rules governing the taxation of investment returns at the individual level (as noted below).

Table 6.1. Tax mix, fiscal year 2016/17

	Million EGP	Per cent GDP
Total tax revenue	426 007	13.3
Income and property taxes	203 437	5.9
Personal income tax	51 014	1.5
Corporate income tax	115 883	3.3
Property tax	36 539	1.1
Consumption taxes	208 624	6.0
VAT- goods	94 384	2.7
VAT – services	18 139	0.5
Excises	70 949	2.0
Oil excises	33 072	1.0
Non-oil excises	37 877	1.1
Other fees, duties*	25 153	0.7
International trade	34 255	1.0
Other taxes	15 691	0.5

* Development fees, stamp duties and taxes on specific services.
Source: Ministry of Finance.

The corporate tax-to-GDP ratio is not low by international comparison but has declined sharply from 6% over the past decade and may decline further over time, depending on the path of corporate tax policies, administration and governance going forward. The statutory corporate income tax (CIT) rate is moderate at 22.5%, the second lowest rate in the Mediterranean region after Lebanon (Figure 6.1).[4] The CIT base is nevertheless at risk, depending on how broadly the FZ regime is applied (number and size of firms covered), how successful authorities are in protecting the CIT base from profit stripping, and other factors.

Table 6.2 provides a summary of corporate income tax provisions in Egypt. Ordinary business losses may be carried forward for up to five years for both listed and non-listed companies, with few exceptions.[5]

Figure 6.1. The CIT rate in Egypt is in line with many other emerging economies

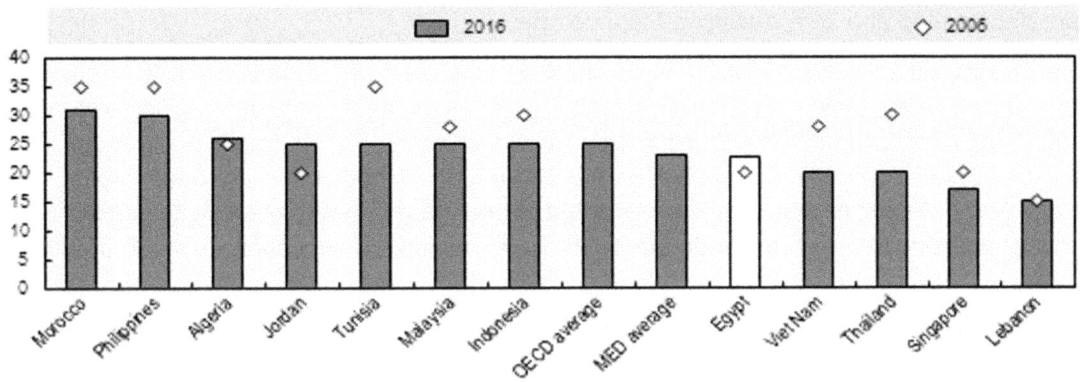

Source: Based on KPMG (2017), Tax Tools & Resources (database).

Table 6.2. Summary of corporate income tax provisions

Basic corporate income tax rate	22.5%
Loss carry-forward	5 years (loss carry-back for long-term contracts)
Inter-corporate dividend tax rate	5% (for direct investments)
Capital gains on shares	Capital gains on listed shares suspended until May 2020
Capital gains on immovable property	No exemption
Branch profit tax rate	Branch taxable profits are subject to the standard CIT rate 22.5% and dividends tax is 5% for branches
	Statutory non-resident withholding tax rates:
- dividends	10% (general) 5% if shareholding > 25% and holding period > 2 years
- interest	20% (general) 0% for foreign loans with maturity of 3 years or longer
- royalties	20%
- technical service fees	20%
- management fees	20%
Inbound anti-avoidance provisions	Thin capitalisation legislation (4:1) Transfer pricing legislation (OECD) General anti-avoidance rule (GAAR)
Outbound anti-avoidance provisions	Controlled foreign company (CFC) legislation
Foreign dividends	Participation exemption
Foreign interest	22.5% (taxable as business income)
Other:	
Capital taxes	No
Property taxes	10% on rental value of the real estate
Transfer tax	2.5% on transfer of immovable property
Stamp duty	10% on premiums for insurance 20% for advertisements 2% for bank loans, overdrafts, and credit facilities (calculated and paid quarterly) 0.3% or 0.6% for transfer of shares (based on percentage of acquisition) 1% for life and health insurance (1%) 10% for other types of insurance *In addition to other type of items subject to nominal stamp tax with different values*

Source: Income Tax Law No. 91 for 2005. Stamp Duty Law No. 111 for 1980.

The tax depreciation system is attractive in its simplicity, based on four asset classes. Buildings and intangible assets are depreciated on a straight-line basis at 5% and 10%, respectively. Computer devices and information-technology assets are depreciated on a declining-balance basis at 50%. Other depreciable assets are depreciated at a 25% declining-balance rate.

Under the Investment Law No. 17 of 2017, businesses may claim an immediate 30% deduction on the machinery and equipment used in production (with 70% of investment costs depreciated according to the above-noted tax deprecation rules). Presumably, this acceleration of depreciation, through immediate expensing of 30% of capital costs, applies to the acquisition of both new and used capital goods. To improve efficiency, the expensing should be targeted at new (rather than pre-existing) capital.[6] This could be accomplished using a 'first-in-use' rule that limits the expensing to new capital used in production.

Egypt is currently planning to implement e-invoicing. One provision that should be reviewed, to assess the implications for income tax revenues, is a general deduction for undocumented business expenses equal to 7% of documented general and administrative expenses (including wages). This provision, which applies to (closely-held) private corporations and unincorporated businesses, may have been understandable in years past, when provided to micro-businesses challenged by tasks of record-keeping. But given current low costs of keeping digital records on expenses (e.g., as required for VAT purposes), this provision appears to be dated and offering poorly targeted tax relief. At a minimum, it would seem appropriate to target the provision (if retained) to small firms that are below the VAT registration threshold.

The personal income tax exemption for dividends on shares in FZ companies is inefficient,[7] providing investors with windfall gains on their returns, as opposed to lower costs of finance for FZ firms. Moreover, to the extent the PIT exemption lowers the rate of return shareholders expect on their investments in FZ companies, this relief tends to favour FZ companies relative to companies outside FZs. As noted earlier, the multiple forms of tax relief targeted at FZ companies may be limiting productivity growth and wages in the economy and should be scaled back.

Tax incentives for investment

Many governments offer incentives in one form or another to achieve certain outcomes related to the overall level of investment or investment in targeted sectors or regions, or to encourage certain activities on the part of businesses such as training or the development of local suppliers. Incentives can take many forms but are usually either a tax holiday or an investment tax allowance or tax credit. Incentives in Egypt have undergone a major reform with the introduction of Investment Law No. 72 in 2017.[8] The current system of tax incentives is reviewed below, with a particular focus on FZ incentives in the final section.

General, special and additional incentives

Tax incentives are included in Income Tax Law No. 91 of 2005 and Investment Law No. 72 (INVL). Tax incentives under the INVL include general incentives, special incentives and additional incentives, and varied incentives across a number of categories of zones. Law No. 83/2002 on "Economic Zones of Special Nature Law", amended by Law No. 27/2015, does not provide for corporate income tax incentives.

a) CIT incentives (Income Tax Law)

The Income Tax Law provides accelerated depreciation, whereby companies can immediately expense 30% of capital costs and depreciate the remaining 70% by applying standard tax depreciation rules. As noted earlier, the 30% expensing provision should be targeted at new (rather than pre-existing) capital, to improve efficiency.

b) General incentives (Article 10 of INVL)

General incentives include a uniform customs duty at 2% on imports of machinery and equipment, and exemption from stamp duty for five years. Furthermore, a customs duty exemption is provided to manufacturing projects for imported items brought into the country for temporary use, although 'temporary' is not defined in the law or Executive Regulations. The CEO of the General Authority for Investment and Free Zones (GAFI) holds the power to grant certificates for general incentives.[9] Presumably, GAFI determines lists of duty-free goods and how the term 'temporary' is to be applied, on a case-by-case basis.

c) Special incentives (Article 11 of INVL)

Special incentives include an investment tax allowance (ITA) deductible against taxable profits, for qualifying investments. The ITA rate differs between Sector A-type and Sector B-type investments. The ITA rate is 50% for Sector A investments, which target geographic areas designated in an 'investment map' determined by Executive Regulations.[10] The INVL regulations specify that Sector A includes investments in the Economic Zone of the Suez Canal, the Economic Zone of the Golden Triangle, and "areas in most need for development as determined by the Council of Ministers".[11]

A reduced ITA rate of 30% applies to Sector B investments which targets certain types of investments in all other locations within Egypt. The list of investment types that qualify (Box 6.1) includes targeting by i) business size (small and medium-sized enterprises (SMEs)), ii) inputs used in production (labour-intensive projects, and projects using new and renewable energy), iii) percentage of production that is exported, iv) strategic importance of production, and v) type of output (projects producing new and renewable energy, and projects in a listed set of industrial sectors).

Box 6.1. Sector B targeting of the ITA – investment types

Sector B-type of investments that qualify for the 30% ITA are investments in:

- SMEs
- Labour-intensive projects, as set out in Executive Regulations
- Projects depending on or producing new and renewable energy
- Projects exporting no less than 10% of products
- National and strategic projects listed under resolution of the Supreme Council of Investment
- Electricity generation and distribution projects listed by a decree of the Prime Minister
- Tourism projects listed under resolution of the SCI
- Automotive manufacturing and the supplying industries thereof
- Wood, furniture, printing, packaging and chemical industries
- Antibiotics, tumour drugs and cosmetic industries
- Food, agricultural crops and agricultural waste recycling industries
- Engineering, metallurgical, textile and leather industries

Sector-B investments include investments in labour-intensive projects. Executive Regulations explain that a project is considered labour-intensive if at least 500 Egyptian workers are employed, and wage costs exceed 30% of total operating costs. The CEO of GAFI (or a representative) has the power to grant certificates for special incentives.[12] Presumably, GAFI rules on whether targeting criteria are satisfied. The prime minister and Supreme Council of Investment (SCI) also have discretionary authority to determine eligibility.[13]

For both sector A and sector B-type investments, the ITA is a one-time deduction, based on investment cost measured on the date when economic activity begins and capped so as not to exceed 80% of paid-up capital. The ITA is available within the first seven years following the commencement of economic activity and is deducted against a company's total taxable profit (and not ring-fenced to be deducted against the revenues of a single investment project).[14]

d) Additional incentives (Article 13 of INVL)

The Council of Ministers may grant additional (non-tax) incentives to projects entitled to special incentives (namely ITAs).[15] In order to assess the rationale for and possible effects of the ITA on investment, a review of the additional incentives is required. Additional incentives include:[16]

- Permission to establish special customs ports of entry, for imports or exports
- A grant covering all or part of the expenses incurred in providing utilities to a project
- A grant covering part of expenses of providing technical training to personnel
- A grant of 50% of the value of land (100% for strategic projects) used for industrial projects, if production commences within two years of the date of transfer of land to the project.

The Executive Regulations (Article 12) explain that projects eligible for additional incentives must satisfy *any* (one or more) of the following conditions:

1. Egypt should be a main country for producing its products. Also, the main country of the company's products should be Egypt.
2. The company shall rely on foreign funds (funds transferred from abroad) for financing.
3. A minimum of 50% of products are exported.[17]
4. Project activities include the transfer of technologies to Egypt and 'exert efforts to support their feeding industries' (to confirm that this means purchasing domestic inputs to production).
5. The project uses local content (domestic inputs) in production, with a minimum local content of 50% of raw materials and (other) production requirements.
6. The company's activity should be based on the output of research projects in Egypt.

The conditions required for eligibility, as specified, are generally not demanding and investors need only satisfy one of them. For example, it would appear (without further guidance) that the financing requirement (condition 2) can be met in cases where domestic funds are invested through offshore conduits.

Tax incentives for investment in zones

There are multiple zone designations applied in Egypt, as described extensively in Chapter five. This chapter focuses on public and private FZs. Two other zones (not described in detail here) which were created by the new investment law (INVL) are investment and technological zones. Incentives offered for investment in these latter two zones are as follows.

- *Incentives for investment zone projects*: Projects located in investment zones, established by the prime minister, are eligible for general incentives, special incentives and additional incentives (as described above).[18] Each investment zone is governed by a board of directors which approves projects, subject to the approval GAFI,[19] and sets rules and requirements.
- *Incentives for technological zone projects*: Projects specialised in communications and information technology located in technological zones, established by the prime minister, are eligible for special incentives (as described above)[20] and are exempt from customs duties on machinery and equipment.[21] Each technological zone is governed by a board of directors, which approves investment projects, and sets rules and requirements.

The most extensive tax incentives are available to investment projects in FZs. A FZ established for a single large-scale project is designated as a private FZ. Other FZs are designated as public FZs. Private and public FZs (and their shareholders) enjoy the same tax incentives. Fees and taxes on domestic sales differ between the two. Certain business activities are denied registration in FZs:[22] oil processing; natural gas processing, liquidation, transport; energy-intensive industries; fertiliser industries; iron/steel industries; liquor and alcohol industries; guns, ammunitions and explosive industries; and other industries of national security interest. The INVL and Executive Regulations do not set minimum export percentages for public FZ projects (the percentage of output that must be exported). Instead, the power to set requirements on export percentages is assigned to relevant ministers.[23]

Tax incentives provided to FZ companies are as follows:

- Exemption from corporate income tax on business profits (indefinite CIT holiday)[24]
- Exemption from personal income tax on dividends and gains on FZ company shares
- Exemption from customs duties and VAT on imports of goods and services[25]
- Zero-rating of VAT on purchases of domestic goods and services (with VAT charged on goods and services sold to the domestic market).[26]

The exemption from customs duties and VAT (third bullet) continues to apply for machinery and equipment (other than passenger cars) that "temporarily exit" FZs into the domestic market. The conditions (and presumably the maximum amount time for "temporary exit") are established by the Council of Ministers. While providing these exemptions, the INVL imposes certain charges on imports, and charges akin to turnover taxes on domestic sales and exports of FZ products, as summarised in Table 6.3.

Table 6.3. Free zone charges on imports, domestic sales and exports

Type of business activity	Charges on projects in public free zones	Charges on projects in private free zones
Storage projects	2% of value of imports	2% of value of imports.
Manufacturing/assembly projects	1% charge on export revenues 1% charge on revenues on sales to domestic market	1% charge on export revenues 2% charge on revenues on sales to domestic market
Business service providers (neither importing nor exporting)/1	1% charge on revenues	2% charge on revenues
Transit goods	No charges	No charges

1. MOF authorities confirm that the text used in the INVL, "projects whose main activity does not require entry or exit of commodities" refers to companies providing business services (e.g., accounting or legal services).
Source: INVL.

For storage projects,[27] the 2% charge on imports matches the 2% customs duty provided by the INVL as a general incentive (noted above). For manufacturing and assembly projects, the charge (1 or 2%) on gross revenues on sales (export or domestic) is akin to a turnover tax. Presumably, the turnover taxes are applied given the exemption from CIT on profit. A well-known problem with a turnover tax is that, when used as a substitute for taxation of profit, the effective tax rate on profit increases inversely with the profit rate – less profitable firms bear a higher tax rate on their profit. Given the distortions to competition amongst firms that this creates, turnover taxes are typically targeted in other countries at small firms as a simplification measure, substituting for tax on profit and/or VAT. Turnover taxes are targeted to small firms by applying only to firms with turnover below a 'small business' threshold.

Concerns with customs duty exemptions and design of the ITA

The customs duty exemption for imported items brought into Egypt for temporary use should be circumscribed to a fixed list of products, and the term 'temporary' should be defined with objective criteria and prescribed in the associated Law.[28] Presumably the exemption is provided to reduce the cost of business inputs, and therefore the list should be specified to exclude final consumption goods. To mitigate against tax avoidance, conditions should be specified in regulations that indicate when a duty exemption can be provided, and the considerations determining the maximum duration of 'temporary.'

According to the authorities, the new Investment Law (art. 39) and its executive regulation regulate the movement of local and foreign goods, materials, parts, and raw materials between the Free Zone and the domestic market, as well as the allowed time periods. The technical committee recommendations of Free Zones (no. 2/206/2011) specifies three months with a possible renewal for another three months for local and foreign goods and materials.

The basic design of the investment tax allowance is also problematic for the following reasons:

- The ITA is based on the 'investment cost of a project' determined as the amount (value) of equity rights plus long-term liabilities of a company invested in fixed assets, intangible capital and working capital.[29] By focusing on balance sheet amounts, rather than actual expenditures on physical capital assets, the base of the ITA could include amounts invested abroad (foreign assets generating income outside of Egypt), and tangible and/or intangible assets licensed to foreign companies. The base is too broad where the purpose is to incentivise investment in production in Egypt.
- The 'one-time' feature means that where the amount of capital injected into a company is increased following the commencement of activity, the additional investment is not included in the base of the ITA (an additional deduction is not available).
- The Article 12 restriction to curtail churning is limited to tangible assets.[30] Given that the investment deduction can be claimed in respect of intangible ('non-material') assets, as indicated in the Executive Regulations, this means that the base of the ITA could include pre-existing intangible assets. MOF authorities explain that the reason for this is to avoid instances where investors are denied an ITA where 'investment cost' includes amounts paid for an existing trade name.
- The targeting of the 30% ITA for Sector B investments is imprecise. For example targeting to SMEs is imprecise as the term 'SMEs' is not defined (e.g., with reference to turnover or asset size). Similarly, there are no thresholds given that specify 'projects depending on or producing new and renewable energy'. This lack of precision makes it unclear whether a project that uses a minimal amount of new or renewable energy (e.g., a single solar panel) qualifies.
- Determining how to treat firms that operate in targeted and non-targeted regions (and sectors) is difficult, requiring separate accounting of the base that is used to determine the incentive amount – which enables creative accounting by tax advisers.[31] Tax incentives to stimulate economically depressed areas should be subject to proper cost-benefit analysis, given the poor track record worldwide of location-based targeting.
- Rather than listing qualifying sectors, consideration should be given to listing non-qualifying sectors – for example where national security concerns arise and foreign investment is less desirable. This would recognise the difficulty for policy makers to identify sectors where markets fail in allocating capital or where net benefits to society from investment are the greatest.

Concerning additional incentives, the scope of subsidies provided is uncertain. Neither the law (Article 13) nor the Executive Regulations specify the types of technical training that qualify, or the training institutions (including in-house) that qualify, or the fraction of expenses that are covered. Similarly, under Article 13, all or part of expenses incurred in providing utilities to an investment project are subsidised. This provision raises questions over the types of utility expenses that qualify (electricity, gas, water?) and the fraction of expenses that are covered. Decisions to be taken are based on decisions of the Council of Ministers and GAFI, presumably on a case-by-case basis.

The Executive Regulations that specify conditions for obtaining additional incentives also raise questions, requiring administrative discretion in deciding whether conditions are met in practice.[32] The requirements and measures of technology transfer are not specified in the law or regulations. Similarly, requirements and measures of research findings used in production are not specified. Presumably, GAFI holds the power to determine how the conditions are to be interpreted on a case-by-case basis.

The imprecise nature of the targeting (scope) of these incentives and conditions on eligibility create uncertainty and require further guidance from authorities. In general, this approach is problematic as it involves significant discretion on the part of authorities in awarding subsidies. As observed elsewhere, administrative discretion should be kept to a minimum through greater guidance and specificity in the laws and regulations themselves (and not on their interpretation by officials) to avoid opportunities for corruption. Moreover, where rules are applied on a case-by-case basis in a non-uniform manner across taxpayers, unfair competition results. Uncertainty over eligibility, the cost of bribes, and scope for an uneven playing field all pose a deterrent to investors.

Investment zone and technological zone projects are eligible for general incentives, special incentives and additional incentives and the concerns identified above in relation to these (see sub-section 2) apply. In particular, the conditions for duty exemptions should be clarified in regulations (including lists of eligible products and conditions around temporary use). Also, the investment tax allowance should be based on expenditures on depreciable capital used in Egypt and targeting criteria should be clarified and sharpened to avoid efficiency losses and specified in regulations to reduce discretionary power in deciding how subsidies are allocated.

Tax incentives for free zone companies come with challenges

Egypt provides generous tax incentives to projects in FZs, which raises three concerns. The first is with the efficiency of corporate tax holidays.[33] A second concern is the tendency for FZ companies to sell into the domestic market where they enjoy a competitive advantage over companies outside of FZs (non-zone companies) owing to indirect (and direct) tax relief targeted at FZs. Total factor productivity growth in the economy may be impeded where FZ companies are able to largely avoid export markets and attendant pressures for business efficiencies needed to be profitable at internationally determined output prices.

Third, indirect tax relief for FZ companies – which waives VAT and customs duties on imports and zero-rates for VAT purposes purchases of domestic supplies – offers opportunities to evade taxes. These opportunities arise under provisions that allow tax-free transfers of commodities of FZ companies into the domestic market on a temporary basis, and tax-free transit through FZs of commodities moved from one border point to another. As tax-free entry of goods into FZs effectively multiplies opportunities to evade tax on goods brought into the country, total revenues lost to avoidance and evasion may be significant.

Efficiency concerns with corporate tax holidays for free zones

As highlighted in a recent report to the G20 by international organisations,[34] profit-based tax incentives, such as corporate tax holidays, are generally less efficient than cost-based tax incentives, such as accelerated tax depreciation and investment tax allowances and tax credits. This observation, based on many years of disappointing experience with CIT holidays, is an important consideration for Egyptian authorities as they seek to revitalise their investment promotion strategy.

As noted in the previous section, the current tax system in Egypt provides two main corporate income tax incentives[35] – a CIT holiday that exempts profit from corporate income tax, available to FZ companies, and an ITA that provides a deduction against the CIT base, available to non-FZ companies. The authorities are encouraged to reconsider the relative advantages of granting an ITA rather than CIT holiday to new investments.

Under the new Investment Law No. 72, the rate of ITA differs depending on targeting criteria including the location of investment – sector A (50%) and sector B (30%). As noted in the previous section, the ITA is a one-time deduction earned as a percentage of investment (equity plus long-term debt) in a project assessed at the start of production. While the more limited targeting of newly granted CIT holidays in the new Investment Law is a positive development,[36] the continued reliance on this form of tax incentive is of concern given the relatively large scale of FZ companies, the corresponding amounts of profit that escape CIT and the profit-shifting possibilities that continue to exist.[37]

Key factors in a cost-benefit assessment of corporate tax incentives for investment include returns on estimated additional capital and employment, and the social opportunity cost of forgone CIT revenues that inevitably result when tax relief is provided to redundant investment – that is, investment that would have occurred without the tax incentive. The review draws on the G20 report on effective and efficient use of tax incentives. In anticipation of next steps of incentive reform, the review is intended to offer general guidance in identifying the types of data that would be needed, to factor into a formal cost/benefit assessment of past and current incentives in Egypt.[38]

Productivity concerns from direct and indirect tax relief to free zones

Direct tax relief (profit exemption) and indirect tax relief provided to FZ companies raise concerns about reduced productivity growth in the Egyptian economy. Productivity growth may be hindered where these tax reliefs encourage firms to supply the domestic market where they enjoy a competitive advantage, rather than export markets where greater efficiency of business operations may be required to be competitive and profitable. These mechanisms are at play in Egypt's FZs, as described in chapter 5 and according to the IMF (2017) and Mori (2017).

FZ companies enjoy considerable indirect tax advantages, including indirect tax deferral. FZ companies are encouraged to purchase inputs from domestic suppliers producing outside of FZs (non-FZ companies). Such purchases (backward linkages) are intended to bring wider benefits to the Egyptian economy of the FZ system. As non-FZ companies must compete with foreign suppliers, sales by non-FZ companies to FZ companies are zero-rated for VAT purposes. With zero-rating of sales by domestic suppliers, FZ companies are not charged VAT on domestic purchases and domestic suppliers are provided with tax credits to offset VAT paid on their inputs. Thus, VAT is removed from the entire chain of production underlying domestic supplies to FZ firms. This treatment matches that of foreign supplies, which are zero-rated exports in the host (source) country and are exempt from Egyptian VAT when imported by FZ companies.[39]

A non-negligible portion of FZ output is supplied to the domestic market (see Chapter 5 for further evidence). When output is sold to domestic purchasers, VAT should apply in full, without input tax credits, and customs duties should be collected on the foreign content of products sold. As noted below, the practice of waiving duties and not collecting any VAT on supplies to FZs creates opportunities for tax evasion. However, even in instances where taxes due are collected on sales to the domestic market,[40] the ability to defer payment of tax provides cash-flow advantages and a lower effective tax rate on business supplies to FZ firms (with tax payments measured on a present value basis). In addition, profits of FZ companies are exempt from corporate income tax, and dividends, capital gains and interest on investments in FZ companies are exempt from personal income tax. These tax policies tend to lower the cost to FZ companies of domestic sources of finance.[41] FZ firms are also exempt from paying property taxes, as well as enjoying other cost advantages.

These indirect tax and direct tax reliefs provide FZ companies with a competitive advantage when supplying goods and services to the domestic market relative to non-FZ firms. Given this advantage, FZ companies may be oriented to domestic markets.[42] Chapter 5 provides evidence that this is the case, as a sizeable fraction of output of FZ companies (particularly those in public FZs) is sold to the domestic market, rather than exported. If tax policy does indeed encourage FZ firms to supply the domestic market, then this outcome raises a concern to the extent that it lessens pressures for FZ firms to innovate and transition to productivity-enhancing business strategies generally required to compete successfully in export markets. Moreover, tax policies that place non-FZ companies at a competitive disadvantage, tending to limit their domestic sales, may seriously curb their ability to achieve economies of scale required in order to position themselves to compete successfully in export markets.

Tax revenue losses from tax avoidance and evasion possibilities

While normally VAT and customs duties should be levied when products are sold by FZ companies into the domestic market, opportunities may arise whereby these taxes can be avoided, as the Investment Law allows commodities to be brought into the domestic market in some cases on a temporary basis free of VAT and customs duties.[43] Neither the Investment Law nor the Executive Regulations define ‘temporary’, implying an uncertain deferral advantage. Additionally, as some tax/customs officials may succumb to accepting returns to facilitate a side-stepping of the law/administrative practices, the unfortunate reality is that VAT and customs duties are illegally avoided in some cases. While this outcome can occur under any system, the possibilities of deferral and the creation of multiple border crossing and transit check-points under a zone system multiply these opportunities.

Tax revenues are also lost where FZ companies use their CIT holiday status to shelter profits of other companies from corporate tax. Because profits of FZ companies are exempt from tax, while profits of non-FZ companies are not, tax-planning opportunities are created to artificially shift taxable profit to FZ companies. One way is through commodity transactions between FZ companies and related non-FZ companies, with non-arm’s length pricing used to shift taxable profit. Taxing projects rather than entities through a modified form of group taxation can provide partial tax base protection, but such measures are limited in scope and reach. Financing arrangements (including back-to-back loans) and other arrangements may be used to shift otherwise taxable profit into a CIT-free enclave.

Proper management of tax holidays requires continuous monitoring of operational activities and financial arrangements of tax holiday firms, to verify compliance with qualifying conditions and to detect tax evasion. Where key conditions for tax holiday status are not observed, then it would be appropriate that actions be taken to withdraw tax relief that has been provided.

The treatment of transit goods, free of all taxes and charges, would be expected to encourage businesses to consider ways in which non-transit goods could be mischaracterised as transit goods. Given this, it would be prudent to ensure that goods passing through the country as transit goods be subject to inspection, while the Executive Regulations appear to allow for random verification. The Executive Regulations (Article 37, paragraph 3) state that “The Zone Management shall inspect the goods once they reach the Zone through random sample or detailed inspection.”

Given opportunities created for avoiding customs duty and VAT on goods brought into the country through FZs, and opportunities for avoiding VAT on zero-rated domestic supplies purchased by public and private FZ companies, it is prudent to monitor export percentages, as per the requirements defined in the Investment Law. Export share percentages should however be a temporary measure. Such requirement should be removed in cases where CIT holidays are phased-out and/or the gap in customs duty and VAT rates between the FZ and inland regime are reduced. The terms of the export share percentage should not raise potential risk of non-compliance with WTO rules, notably the Agreement on Subsidies and Countervailing Measures (ASCM).

Governance of tax incentives

This section addresses the governance of tax incentives – including current and best practice in introducing and amending tax incentive legislation, the monitoring of tax incentives, and reporting on them. Authorities are encouraged to consider reform of the mandates of the public institutions engaged in tax incentive policy and implementation, and how reform has the potential to go a long way in improving overall governance in Egypt. As in other countries where corruption is a serious problem, the tax system can be a major fault line. By sharpening legislation and regulations on tax incentives (covering implementation, monitoring and reporting), accountability of the institutions involved is increased, and the rule of law and role of parliament are strengthened. Through this process, fundamental tax incentive reform has the potential to profoundly shape and strengthen governance.[44]

Introducing and amending tax incentive legislation

Accountability of government over tax incentives is weakened by diffuse legislative powers, the involvement of multiple ministries and agencies in setting tax incentive policies, and broad discretion in interpreting tax incentive eligibility. Each of these contributes to the opaqueness of tax incentive policy and administration, which translates into reduced government accountability. A review of the new Investment Law finds a complex and non-transparent tax incentive policy decision-making structure, with diffuse responsibilities and powers amongst the Ministry of Finance, GAFI, and relevant ministers. The current patchwork complicates decision-making and creates a lack of accountability, which limits analysis, evaluation and fundamental reform. The Prime Ministerial Decree No.7/2020 identifies Zones A and B and provides for tax incentives specific to each zone. Zones A, which include South of Giza Governorate, Governorates affiliated to the Suez Canal Region (Suez - Ismailia - Port Said) and Border Provinces (Governorates of the Red Sea from the South of Safaga), are identified as priority development areas. Prime Ministerial Decree (6/2020) clarifies the conditions of project expansion benefitting from investment incentives.

While certain improvements have been made, including less pervasive use of corporate tax holidays, relief from income taxes, VAT and customs duties is still embedded outside of the main legislation.[45] In particular, tax incentives are provided mainly in the new Investment Law or in the SEZ Law, and not in the Income Tax Law, VAT Law and Customs Law that the tax incentives provide relief from. This makes it difficult to determine the net implications of various provisions that together determine effective tax rates and the amount of tax due. This practice also clouds responsibility over tax policy.

To address this, legislation that authorises the provision of tax incentives should be embedded in main statutes that the tax incentives provide relief from (e.g., law providing an investment tax allowance should be contained in the Income Tax Law; law providing for a VAT exemption should be contained in the VAT Law). With this change, the recently enacted Investment Law would be amended, so that articles that currently provide for tax incentives are revised to reference new articles in the Income Tax Law, VAT Law and Customs Law. Similarly, regulations for tax incentives should be included in the regulations of the relevant tax legislation.

Box 6.2. The need to limit discretion in providing incentives

Good practice in providing tax incentives involves prescribing qualifying conditions in laws, regulations and bulletins (official interpretations of laws) and minimising the discretion of tax administration and other officials in determining eligibility. The Minister of Finance should have final authority over the determination of the design and targeting of tax incentives. Limiting discretion helps serve various objectives. First, it curbs opportunities for corruption involving tax officials accepting compensation for the granting of tax relief. Second, limiting discretion in determining eligibility helps provide certainty of tax treatment, which reduces uncertainty for taxpayers in determining after-tax returns on projects – including their own projects, and those of competing firms. By reducing uncertainty, investment is encouraged. Third, where tax incentives are granted on a case-by-case basis, involving private negotiations with taxpayers, the fiscal and broader implications of agreements are not known by the general public – and possibly not known by tax official, which inhibits assessments of impacts and determinations of whether policies or practices should be revised.

Furthermore, following best practice, the Minister of Finance should have sole authority to introduce, amend or withdraw tax incentive legislation, after approval of the Council of Ministers.[46] This could be anchored in the Constitution or in public finance management legislation.[47] Responsibility for deciding tax incentive policy and design should be centralised within the Ministry of Finance and the Egyptian Tax Authority, drawing on tax experts from multiple fields (e.g., economists, lawyers, accountants). The General Authority for Investment and Free Zones (GAFI), as well as other ministries should be involved in the design process.[48] In deciding upon tax incentive design, a main objective should be to minimise the discretion of government officials in determining eligibility for tax relief (Box 6.2).

The government is encouraged to provide the Ministry of Finance with the necessary resources to finance the hiring of highly-qualified staff to undertake economic analysis of current tax policies and possible reforms.[49] Staff need to be trained in modern public finance theory, frameworks and toolkits to assess tax proposals submitted to government for consideration, and to propose and analyse reform agendas.

Analysis of tax policy, including the costing of tax incentives, is data intensive. Given this, and the importance of the Ministry of Finance being equipped to provide high-quality, independent policy analysis, it is imperative that tax authorities regularly collect taxpayer-level data (gathered from tax returns) to feed into revenue estimation (microsimulation) models. Comprehensive taxpayer data collection requires that all businesses, including FZ companies, complete and file tax returns. These changes will involve institutional arrangements that may require legislative action. The ETA is currently undertaking a wide-ranging business process reengineering project, whereby all tax administration processes will be automated. This provides a timely opportunity to address key governance issues.

Monitoring tax incentives

As a check on the operation and outcomes of any tax incentive regime, careful monitoring is essential. As reviewed earlier, the tax incentive regime has many concessions intended to limit unintended distortions. Examples include the duty exemptions provided to domestic firms supplying zone companies, the temporary exit of goods to the domestic market and the allowance of transit commodities without VAT and duties that would otherwise apply. Given these concessions, data collection and monitoring are needed as a check on the integrity of the system and to make adjustments to policies and practices where fraud is detected. It is not clear from a review of the investment promotion legislation and regulations which government body is responsible for monitoring tax incentives, including data collection on take-up, the measurement of forgone tax revenues, and the determinations of whether investors (FZ companies) are complying with commitments in relation to export percentages and employment of local workers. It is also not clear which entities are tasked with determining corrective interventions when tax incentive design is found to be problematic.

Legislation authorising tax incentives should specify which government agency has responsibility for monitoring compliance and enforcing penalties in cases of non-compliance. In practice, experience shows that electronic tracking is required of transactions in goods and services (quantities and values) – including the tracking of commodity codes and values for commodities receiving duty waiver, duty drawback, transit goods, exported goods, goods sold to domestic market, and goods temporarily brought into the domestic market.

Strict and proportionate penalties are required as a deterrent to fraud, including a claw-back of tax relief in cases of non-compliance (e.g., export requirements as percentage of production, local hiring commitments). Where FZ companies are permitted to continue (under grandfathering rules) to benefit from FZ incentives provided to them, these firms should be held to account for the commitments made to the government in benefiting the host country (e.g., in terms of local hires, and exports).

Reporting of tax incentives

Annual tax expenditure reporting to parliament of revenues forgone by tax incentives (part of tax expenditure reporting), as part of the annual budget and budget documentation cycle, is recognised as a cornerstone of good practice in providing tax incentives. Tax expenditure reporting is required to ensure transparency and oversight, in the same way that tabling direct expenditure programmes is of central interest to parliament.

In its pursuit of best practice, the government is encouraged to introduce legislation requiring tax expenditure reports to be included with budget documents (annually or bi-annually). The reporting of tax incentives should identify the policy purpose (as specified when introduced or amended) and the estimated amount of forgone tax revenue. Consistent with this, legislation should be introduced that requires the ETA each year to provide the Ministry of Finance with anonymised micro-level data (e.g., gathered from tax returns) to enable robust estimates of forgone tax revenues. Furthermore, given the extensive tax incentives provided to FZ companies, reports should be prepared (annually or bi-annually) giving aggregate data by sector, on total production, inventories (storage), export and domestic sales, customs duty waivers and customs duty drawbacks (for FZ companies and separately for domestic suppliers).

Lastly, it is recommended that the government instruct the MOF to undertake cost-benefit analysis of FZ incentives and other major tax incentives (identified by a ranking of tax revenue forgone estimates). While resource demanding, it is important given the scarcity of public funds that societal benefits and costs be compared, and corrective action taken when necessary. Of major fiscal policy concern are instances of incentives having limited impact in boosting investment expenditure, and yet involving significant forgone revenue, due to tax relief provided to redundant investment, and limited success in countering tax avoidance and evasion by MNEs, facilitated by tax incentives (most notably CIT holidays).

References

Aitken, B. and A. Harrison (1999). "Do Domestic Firms Benefit from Foreign Direct Investment? Evidence from Venezuela." *American Economic Review*, 89, 605-618.

Boadway, R., N. Bruce and J. Mintz (1984). "Taxation, Inflation and the Marginal Tax Rate on capital in Canada." *Canadian Journal of Economics*, 15, 278-93.

Clark, W. (2000). "Tax Incentives for Foreign Direct Investment: Empirical Evidence on Effects and Alternative Policy Options." *Canadian Tax Journal*, 48, 1139-1180.

_______ (2010). "Assessing the Foreign Direct Investment Response to Tax Reform and Tax Planning." in Cockfield, Arthur J. (ed.), *Globalization and its Tax Discontents—Tax Policy and International Investments*, University of Toronto Press, 84-114.

Clark, W. and A. Klemm (2015). "Effective Tax Rates and Multinationals: The Role of Tax Incentives and Tax Planning." *Canadian Tax Journal* 63(1), 133-148.

De Mooij, R. and S. Ederveen (2008). "Corporate Tax Elasticities: A Reader's Guide to Empirical Findings." *Oxford Review of Economic Policy*, 24 (4), 680-697.

Defever, F. and A. Riaño (2017), "Subsidies and export share requirements in China", *Journal of Development Economics*, 126, pp. 33-51.

Department of Revenue, India (2014). Report by the Comptroller and Auditor General for India – Performance of Special Economic Zones, No. 21.

Devereux, M.P. and R. Griffith (1998). "The Taxation of Discrete Investment Choices", Institute for Fiscal Studies Working Paper 98/16.

IMF (2017). "Arab Republic of Egypt – Selected Issues." (December)

IMF, OECD, World Bank, and United Nations (2015). "Options for Low Income Countries' Effective and

Efficient Use of Tax Incentives for Investment." Study and Background Paper Prepared for the G20 Development Working Group. Washington.

Jorgenson, D. (1963). "Capital Theory and Investment Behavior." *American Economic Review* 53, 2, 247-259.

King. M. (1974). "Taxation, Investment and the Cost of Capital." *Review of Economic Studies*, 41, 21-35.

King, M. and D. Fullerton (1984). *The Taxation of Income from Capital: A Comparative Study of the United States, The United Kingdom, Sweden and West Germany*, Chicago: University of Chicago Press.

Mori, I. (2017), Free zones in Egypt: A critical reading, Al-Ahram Centre for Political and Strategic Studies, December 2017.

OECD (2002). *Foreign Direct Investment for Development – Maximising Benefits, Minimising Costs*. Paris, https://www.oecd.org/investment/investmentfordevelopment/1959815.pdf.

_______ (2007). *Tax Effects on Foreign Direct Investment – Recent Evidence and Policy Analysis*. OECD Tax Policy Studies, No. 17. Paris, http://www.oecd.org/tax/tax-policy/39866155.pdf.

_______ (2013). *OECD Principles to Enhance the Transparency and Governance of Tax Incentives for Investment in Developing Countries*. Paris.

OECD (2015), *Designing Effective Controlled Foreign Company Rules, Action 3 - 2015 Final Report*, OECD/G20 Base Erosion and Profit Shifting Project, OECD Publishing, Paris, https://doi.org/10.1787/9789264241152-en.

OECD (2016), *Limiting Base Erosion Involving Interest Deductions and Other Financial Payments, Action 4 - 2016 Update: Inclusive Framework on BEPS*, OECD/G20 Base Erosion and Profit Shifting Project, OECD Publishing, Paris, https://doi.org/10.1787/9789264268333-en.

UNCTAD (2000). *Tax Incentives and Foreign Direct Investment: A Global Survey*.

UNIDO (2011). *Africa Investor Report: Towards evidence-based investment promotion strategies*.

U.S. Council of Economic Advisors (2015). *Economic Report of the President*. Washington.

Van Parys, S. and S. James (2010). "The Effectiveness of Tax Incentives in Attracting Investment: Panel Data Evidence from the CFA Franc Zone," *International Tax and Public Finance*, 17, 400-429.

Notes

[1] An export share requirement of 80% of production exists for private FZ companies. It was set by the Investment law Executive Regulations Article No. 76. Export share requirements could have unintended consequences by lowering export prices and increasing those of goods sold on the domestic market (Defever and Riaño, 2017). They also must be designed to ensure compliance with WTO rules, notably the Agreement on Subsidies and Countervailing Measures. Chapter 5 provides further analysis on ESR effects on Egyptian zone-based exports.

[2] For example, IMF, OECD, UN, World Bank (2015[69]) describe different methods to calculate revenue forgone from tax expenditures, while IMF (2019[70]) sets out guidelines for tax expenditure reporting.

[3] The Egyptian government is currently drafting a Medium-Term Revenue Strategy that also considers current and new reforms of tax policy and tax administration.

[4] A 40% CIT rate applies to the Central Bank, the Suez Canal, and the General Authority for Petroleum. A slightly higher rate (44.5%) applies to oil exploration and production companies.

[5] The exemption involves the prohibition of loss carryover if 50% or more of the ownership of share capital changes, or if a company's main business activity has changed. This provision is limited to listed companies.

[6] Current rules encourage 'double-dipping', whereby machinery and equipment is sold from one taxpayer to another, to obtain multiple tax savings from the same unit of capital.

[7] Exempting capital gains on shares in zone companies tends to reward and thereby incentivise patient capital invested in growth-oriented firms. In contrast, exempting dividends tends to reward investment in mature firms that distribute (rather than reinvest) their profits.

[8] The Investment Law No. 72 of 2017 repealed application of the (previous) Law on Investment Guarantees and Incentives No. 8 of 1997 (incentives granted in the past under Law No. 8 are grandfathered under the new Law No. 72). Under previous law (No.8), a 20-year CIT holiday was provided to companies located outside the old valley, in areas designated by the Council of Ministers. A 10-year CIT holiday was provided to companies in new industrial zones and located in remote areas determined by decree by the Prime Minister. In other cases, firms engaged in (any) commercial or industrial activity were provided a 5-year CIT holiday.

[9] Article 14 of INVL.

[10] Article 10 of the Executive Regulations of INVL.

[11] The regulations explain that such areas are characterised by i) poor levels of economic development, low gross domestic product and the surge of the informal sector; ii) poor operation level, low employment opportunities and rising unemployment rates; iii) remarkable population surge, poor education quality and rising illiteracy, poor health services and high poverty rates."

[12] Articles 11 and 14 of INVL.

[13] Article 11 of INVL states that the Prime Minister may determine by decree sub-sectors that the ITA applies to, for sector A and B-type of investments. The Supreme Council of Investment may add qualifying activities.

[14] Presumably an ITA claimed by an unincorporated business may be used to offset wage and non-business income.

[15] Article 13 of INVL.

[16] Under Article 13, the Council of Ministers may also grant other non-tax incentives.

[17] The English translation of the Executive Regulations show a 20% export requirement, but MOF authorities advise that the text should read 50%.

[18] Under Article 28 of the INVL, investment projects located in Investment Zones are eligible for incentives provided under Part I and Part II of the INVL. Chapter II of Part II (Investment Guarantees and Incentives) provides General Incentives described in Article 10, Special Incentives in Article 11, and Additional Incentives in Article 13.

[19] Approval is required from the Board of Directors of GAFI.

[20] The customs duty exemption is more generous than the 2% customs duty rate under General Incentives.

[21] Under Article 32 of INVL, investment projects located in Technological Zones are eligible for Special incentives described in Article 11.

[22] Article 34 of INVL.

[23] Article 35 of INVL assigns this power to 'appropriate' ministers including the minister of industrial affairs.

[24] Article 41 of INVL provides an exemption for corporate and personal income tax.

[25] Article 39 INVL.

[26] Article 6 of VAT Law No. 67 of 2016. Zero-rating of VAT on domestic supplies does not apply to passenger cars.

[27] A storage project is a project where the sole business activity is storing (housing) commodities.

[28] While the (temporary) customs duty exemption is targeted at the manufacturing projects, the exemption is prone to abuse if the targeting is not also limited to specific commodities (e.g., machinery and equipment).

[29] Executive Regulations, Article 11.

[30] The INVL aims to curtail 'churning', whereby pre-existing capital is misrepresented as new capital, to qualify for the ITA. Article 12 stipulates that to qualify, "neither shareholders nor partners nor owners of establishments have offered, contributed or used any of the tangible assets of a company or an establishment, existing since the date on which the provisions of this Law come into force, in setting up, incorporating or launching an Investment Project enjoying the incentives awarded by this Law."

[31] Targeting concerns are generally the greatest when profit-based tax incentives are used. Profit-based tax incentives (like corporate tax holidays) provide tax relief to firms that are investing and to firms that are not – in which case the incentive merely waives tax on profit from prior-year investment. Given the scope for pure windfall gains (tax savings) to investors, it is understandable that governments would wish to target tax relief to growth-oriented sectors. But this is difficult to determine and accomplish. An advantage of cost-based tax incentives is that they provide tax relief only to firms that are investing (making targeting less of a concern).

[32] MOF authorities explain that the condition under Article 12 of the Executive Regulations, requiring that "Egypt should be a main country for producing its products. Also, the main country of the company's products should be Egypt" concerns where production occurs (not where products are sold) and that thresholds are determined by GAFI.

[33] An analysis which compares CIT revenues forgone by a CIT holiday with CIT revenues forgone by an investment tax allowance (which when granted at a 33% rate is predicted to provide the same boost to the level of investment) will be available separately in a link (to be established). The analysis, based on standard investment theory, is carried out at the investment-project level using illustrative tax and non-tax parameters for Egypt.

[34] See IMF, World Bank, OECD and United Nations (2015).

[35] The term 'corporate income tax incentive' refers to measures that provide an offset to (relief from) corporate income tax, intended to encourage investment. The CIT holiday for zone companies and the ITA are prescribed in INVL, which repealed the provision of incentives under the Law on Investment Guarantees and Incentive No. 8 of 1997. Under this previous law, a 20-year CIT holiday was provided to companies located outside the old valley, in areas designated by the Council of Ministers. A 10-year CIT holiday was provided to companies in new industrial zones and located in remote areas determined by decree by the Prime Minister. In other cases, firms engaged in (any) commercial or industrial activity were provided a 5-year CIT holiday. CIT incentives previously granted under Law No. 8 are grandfathered under the new Law No. 72.

[36] The new Investment Law includes 'grandfathering' provisions that continue to provide an exemption for current and future profit on projects that were granted CIT holiday status under the old investment law.

[37] The profit-shifting opportunities concern the use of non-arm's length transfer pricing and financing arrangements to shift otherwise taxable profits from companies outside FZs to related companies inside FZs.

[38] A recent reform requires FZ companies to report income tax statements. This positive development should be strengthened to require reporting of tax returns.

[39] As customs duties are waived on imports by FZ companies, neutrality would require that a duty drawback is provided to domestic suppliers to FZ companies. A duty drawback aims to provide domestic suppliers with an offset to customs duty paid on imported foreign products used as inputs in the production of output sold to FZ companies.

[40] While required by law to charge customs duties on foreign content, when selling products into the domestic market, opportunities are created to avoid customs duties on imports as the amount and true value of foreign content is often difficult to establish.

[41] Where investors require a fixed after-tax rate of return (e.g., available on other investments), policies that lower personal tax on dividends, capital gains and interest may operate to lower the pre-tax rate of return that investors are willing to accept. Where this is the case, the cost of financing of firms may be significantly reduced.

[42] As a result of tax advantages implying lower costs, FZ companies may be (inadvertently) provided scope to charge below-market prices on products sold in domestic markets. This advantage may limit pressure to innovate production and distribution strategies, in order to achieve cost savings and competitive pricing in export markets.

[43] This recognises that the present value of deferred tax payments declines as the period of deferral is extended. In the limiting case, the present value approaches zero.

[44] See OECD (2013).

[45] Income Tax Law No. 91 of 2005, and VAT Law No. 67 of 2016.

[46] Meetings of the Council of Ministers and other committees arranged to decide on applications for tax incentives (those decided on a discretionary basis) should be recorded to provide an auditable account of the application assessment process and the criteria used in determinations.

[47] Public finance management (PFM) legislation should authorise only the Minister of Finance to introduce legislation that imposes (or provides relief from) national taxes and duties. Under this structure, the Minister of Finance would have sole authority to introduce, amend or revise tax relief including targeted tax incentives.

[48] Other relevant ministries to contribute to discussions would presumably include the Ministry of Commerce and Industry, the Ministry of Investment and International Cooperation, the Ministry of Petroleum and Mineral Wealth, and the Ministry of Local Development.

[49] In March 2016, the organisation of the Ministry of Finance was changed to include three Vice Ministers, including a Vice Minister of Finance for Tax Policy. Since then the tax policy analysis has been centralised in the MOF.

Chapter 7. Toward sustainable economic development through promoting and enabling responsible business conduct

This chapter provides an overview of the responsible business conduct (RBC) landscape in Egypt, outlining steps taken by the government to promote and enable responsible business practices. It provides concrete examples of actions the government could take to facilitate implementation of RBC standards and foster trade and investment in key economic sectors. It proposes policy recommendations to further enhance the climate for RBC, with a view to improving economic and sustainability outcomes and supporting Egypt's development objectives.

Summary and policy recommendations

Promoting and enabling responsible business conduct (RBC) is of central interest to policymakers wishing to attract quality investment and ensure that business activity in their countries contributes to broader value creation and sustainable development. RBC principles and standards set out an expectation that all businesses avoid and address negative impacts of their operations, while contributing to sustainable development where they operate.

RBC expectations are affirmed in international principles and standards and increasingly in legislation. Recent years have seen a proliferation of high-level statements, including by the G7 and G20, national legislation, economic instruments and industry initiatives on RBC. Policy action has focused on promoting the integration of RBC in core business operations, including also in how companies manage and deal with their supply chain. Any company that wishes to integrate in the global economy and participate in trade and investment must be aware of the fact that their buyers, clients, and partners may have various obligations when it comes to RBC. Broadly speaking, RBC is also an entry point for any company that wishes to contribute to the Sustainable Development Goals (SDGs) or to achieve specific economic and sustainability outcomes.

The notion that businesses should contribute to society is part of Egyptian business culture and is rooted in local traditions. A number of programmes and initiatives that aim to address societal challenges from a business perspective exist in Egypt. They have predominantly been based on philanthropy or social investments, but, in line with global trends, awareness of RBC in Egypt is evolving to align with the understanding that impacts on society and the environment are also a matter of core business operations.

The government has taken steps to support various initiatives and promote RBC. Egypt is an adherent to the OECD RBC instruments since 2007 and the establishment of a National Contact Point (NCP) on RBC is an important milestone in this endeavour. NCPs are agencies established by governments to promote the OECD Guidelines for Multinational Enterprises, and to handle cases as a non-judicial grievance mechanism. NCPs have a mandate to consider RBC issues and impacts in global supply chains and can receive cases from any individual or organisation with a legitimate interest in the matter. They are in that sense distinct from mechanisms existing in Egypt for the settlement and resolution of disputes that may arise between investors and the state, or among investors (See Chapter 3). Although the functioning of Egypt's NCP has not been consistent over the years, the continued co-operation with the OECD in the context of a country programme aimed at enhancing the investment climate and participation in the OECD Working Party on RBC offers an opportunity to renew various commitments on RBC, engage in dialogue with peers, and benefit from international good practices on RBC.

The government has every interest in using the recent momentum on RBC in the country to promote a wide dissemination and implementation of internationally recognised RBC standards. This is especially true as a way to ensure that businesses conduct due diligence to identify, prevent, avoid and mitigate environmental and social risks which can have a significant impact on key economic sectors. For example, in the garment industry, which is a strategic industry in Egypt, RBC can be instrumental in building a reputation for quality and sustainability that is increasingly essential. In infrastructure projects, risk-based due diligence can contribute to minimising potential environmental and social impacts.

Implementing RBC standards requires broad engagement with businesses but also with all stakeholders, including relevant government ministries and agencies, NGOs and trade unions. The government can take strategic actions to create an enabling environment for all relevant stakeholders to contribute to the design and implementation of RBC standards. A particular opportunity exists to promote collaborative initiatives. The policy recommendations listed below address both opportunities on RBC in depth and in breadth.

Policy recommendations

- *Engage with other NCPs in order to build the capacities of the Egyptian NCP.* The NCP is an instrumental tool in the government policy toolbox that has so far been under-utilised. A well-functioning NCP can be instrumental for engagement with business and other stakeholders due to its unique non-judicial mandate and it can support the sound design and implementation of RBC-related policies.
- *Undertake a voluntary NCP peer review by 2023.* In line with calls from the international community and commitments made in June 2017 at the OECD Ministerial Council Meeting, Egypt is encouraged to undergo a voluntary peer review of its NCP. Peer reviews provide an important means to assess the practical aspects of NCP functioning and have been used by various government to assess opportunities for further improvements.
- *Develop a National Action Plan on RBC, in line with international best practice and in wide consultation with stakeholders.* A NAP process would be an opportunity to build multi-stakeholder support in key areas for Egypt's development trajectory and in complex areas where action by one stakeholder would not be enough. A consultative and inclusive NAP process is an opportunity to strengthen knowledge about the linkages of various policy areas that address business practices in the country and help build the capacity of local industry to participate in global supply chains.
- *Facilitate meaningful stakeholder engagement in the design and implementation of RBC policies and processes.* Particular attention should be paid to ensuring meaningful engagement in the early stages of policy development. In the planning and implementation of state-led projects, such as infrastructure projects, it is particularly important to engage meaningfully with affected stakeholders.
- *Support, enable and promote RBC due diligence among businesses.* Egypt should explicitly support multi-stakeholder initiatives and promote broad dissemination and implementation of the OECD due diligence instruments. In particular, facilitating dialogue between various stakeholders in the garment sector and supporting application of the *OECD Due Diligence Guidance for Responsible Supply Chains in the Garment and Footwear Sector* in Egyptian factories would help improve industrial relations and enhance competitiveness of the garment sector.
- *Require the integration of RBC due diligence standards at all stages of infrastructure project life cycle, including in tendering and contracting processes.* Potential contractors and suppliers should be explicitly asked to follow international standards on RBC such as the OECD Guidelines and UN Guiding Principles and to demonstrate that they do so.

Scope and importance of responsible business conduct

Responsible business conduct (RBC) principles and standards set out an expectation that businesses should avoid and address negative impacts of business activities, while contributing to sustainable development in countries where they operate. RBC is an integral part of a quality investment climate and, as such, is at the heart of the OECD *Policy Framework for Investment* underpinning this review. In recent years, RBC has been a priority policy area in the international economic agenda (Box 7.1).

Box 7.1. Rising expectations and demands on RBC

The financing needs for achieving the SDGs, as well as the essential role of the private sector as a driver of economic growth and job creation, have placed businesses at the centre of the global development agenda. UN member states have also committed to foster a well-functioning business sector and protect labour rights and environmental and health standards in accordance with relevant international standard (United Nations, 2015).

High-level commitments at G20 and G7 have also made it clear that RBC has become a priority in the international agenda. In September 2018, G20 Ministers of Labour and Employment committed to promote due diligence and transparency in global supply chains, and encouraged businesses to consider the 2018 OECD Due Diligence Guidance for Responsible Business Conduct (G20, 2018). In July 2017, G20 Leaders committed to foster the implementation of labour, social and environmental standards and human rights in line with internationally recognised frameworks, including the OECD Guidelines. The G20 Leaders' Declaration also expressed support for access to remedy and, where applicable, non-judicial grievance mechanisms, such as the NCPs, and underlined the responsibility of businesses to exercise due diligence (G20, 2017). In June 2015, G7 leaders pledged to lead by example to promote international labour, social and environmental standards in global supply chains; to encourage enterprises active or headquartered in the G7 to implement due diligence; and to strengthen access to remedy (G7, 2015).

RBC expectations are also reflected in domestic legislation. Several countries have passed laws to strengthen due diligence requirements to address supply chain and sustainability risks. The UK Modern Slavery Act, adopted in 2016, requires that commercial organisations prepare an annual statement and report on their due diligence processes to manage the risks of slavery and human trafficking within their operations and supply chains (UK, 2015). Australia passed a similar act on 29 November 2018, which includes expectations for the government itself to report on its own activities. In France, since 2017, the French Due Diligence law requires certain companies to develop and implement due diligence plans to identify and address risks related to human rights, fundamental freedoms, health and safety, and the environment (French Government, 2017). In the United States, the US Trade Facilitation and Trade Enforcement Act of 2015 repealed the exceptions to the prohibition on imports of goods mined, produced or manufactured in any foreign country by forced or indentured child labour, including child labour (US CBP, 2016 and 2018).

RBC is also increasingly referenced in various economic instruments, such as trade or co-operation agreements. For example, the EU commonly includes RBC in its Trade and Sustainable Development chapters. The EU Trade for All policy aims to respond to consumers' concerns by reinforcing CSR initiatives and due diligence across supply chains (EC, 2015). The OECD Recommendation of the Council on Common Approaches for Officially Supported Export Credits and Environmental and Social Due Diligence encourages members, via their export credit agencies (ECAs), to promote the Guidelines, consider the outcomes of NCP cases when undertaking project reviews, as well as to give consideration to policy coherence with the Guidelines. The majority of ECAs of OECD member countries have incorporated reference to the Guidelines within their policies and actively promote the Guidelines as a tool for RBC. Some of them, such as Austria, Canada, the Netherlands and Slovenia, have reported that they have formal processes in place for considering any statement made public by their NCPs when undertaking project due diligence. In addition, some ECAs exchange information with their NCPs on specific instances. For example, the US ECA is a member of the US NCP Interagency Working Group and participates in regular Group meetings to discuss specific instances (OECD, 2017).

RBC means integrating and considering environmental and social issues within core business activities, including throughout the supply chain and business relationships. Although RBC is sometimes used interchangeably with corporate social responsibility (CSR), it is understood to be more comprehensive and integral to core business than what is traditionally considered CSR (mainly philanthropy). A key element of RBC is risk-based due diligence – a process through which businesses identify, prevent and mitigate their actual and potential negative impacts and account for how those impacts are addressed.

The main OECD instrument for promoting and enabling RBC is the OECD *Guidelines for Multinational Enterprises* (the *Guidelines*). The *Guidelines* are a part of the OECD *Declaration on International Investment and Multinational Enterprises* (the *Declaration*), a policy commitment to provide an open and transparent investment environment and to encourage the positive contribution businesses can make to economic and social progress. Egypt adhered to *Declaration* in 2007 and as such has committed to promote and implement the *Guidelines*.

The *Guidelines* are practical recommendations from governments to businesses on how to act responsibly. They cover all areas of business responsibility, including information disclosure, human rights, employment and labour, environment, anti-corruption, science and technology, competition, taxation and consumer interests. To support implementation of the *Guidelines*, the OECD has developed due diligence guidance which provide practical recommendations to businesses on how to identify and respond to risks of adverse impacts associated with particular products, regions, sectors or industries[1].

Because of their breadth and scope, the *Guidelines* are relevant to a number of policy areas on RBC and are referenced in various OECD instruments including the *Policy Framework for Investment*, the G20/OECD *Principles on Corporate Governance*, the OECD *Guidelines for State-owned Enterprises*, the OECD *Anti-bribery Convention*, or the *Recommendation of the Council on Principles for Private Sector Participation in Infrastructure*. The *Guidelines* are also linked with other key international standards, notably the *UN Guiding Principles on Business and Human Rights* (UN Guiding Principles) and the fundamental International Labour Organisation (ILO) Conventions.

To date, 36 OECD members, as well as 12 additional economies – including Egypt, Jordan, Morocco and Tunisia – have adhered to the *Guidelines*. Governments that adhere make a binding commitment to implement them and encourage their use. The *Guidelines* have a unique implementation mechanism – the National Contact Points (NCPs) – which are agencies established by governments. Their mandate is twofold: to promote the *Guidelines*, and related due diligence guidance, and to handle cases (referred to as “specific instances”) as a non-judicial grievance mechanism. Adhering governments have an obligation to establish an NCP to further the effectiveness of the *Guidelines*.

Awareness and understanding of RBC is deepening in Egypt

The notion that businesses should behave ethically and contribute to the society is intrinsic in Egyptian business culture. One of the five pillars of Islam is *Zakat*, or an obligation of charity which is a common practice of organisations and individuals in Egypt where 90% of the population identify with the religion and many companies donate funds to charities. A corporate philanthropy concept, *Awqaf*, dates back to the 11th century and is a charitable endowment under Islamic law which typically involves donating assets for religious or charitable purposes (Jamali, 2017).

Rooted in this culture and traditions, awareness of various aspects of RBC is not new in Egypt. While philanthropy and social investments tend to be the main form of engagement by businesses, understanding of RBC is gradually evolving towards a more comprehensive approach that looks at how core business operations affect society (El Shobargi, n.d; Kindornay et al., 2018). A 2016 analysis of the terminology used in various CSR events between 2007 and 2015 reveals an increased focus on issues that go beyond charity such as labour rights and environmental issues (UNDP, ECRC, 2016).

The evolution of various business initiatives align with that trend. For example, the Egyptian chapter of the UN Global Compact Network was launched in 2004, following the global launch of the network in 2000. An early initiative by the Egyptian Mansour Group and UNDP Egypt, the network counts 84 active members as of July 2019, which represents one of the highest participation levels in the region (UNGC, 2019). In 2008, UNDP, the government-initiated Industrial Modernization Centre (IMC) and the Egyptian Institute of Directors (EIoD) jointly launched the Egyptian Corporate Responsibility Center (ECRC), which was given a mandate to empower businesses to develop sustainable business models and to improve the national capacity to design, apply and monitor sustainable corporate social responsibility-related policies (ECRC, 2017). The Federation of Egyptian Industries (FEI), in cooperation with the ILO, also established a unit dedicated to CSR in 2015 to provide FEI members with expertise and technical assistance. The unit organised the first CSR matchmaking in April 2017, where the Cairo CSR Declaration was announced to showcase commitment to CSR and put forth principles for promoting CSR in Egypt (OECD, 2017c).

Egypt's businesses have also been early adopters of initiatives in the financial sector, where attention has grown exponentially in recent years. In March 2010, the Egyptian Stock Exchange (EGX), in partnership with Standards and Poor's, launched the S&P EGX ESG to track the performance of Egyptian companies listed on the Egyptian stock exchange that demonstrate leadership in environmental, social and corporate governance (ESG) issues (Hebatallah, 2017). In 2016, the EGX published a *Model Guidance for Reporting on ESG performance and the SDGs*, to help listed companies on EGX in integrating ESG information into effective capital market communication. The guidance recognises that many investment funds now seek investment in more sustained, socially and environmentally responsible listed companies (EGX, 2016). In January 2019, Egypt's Financial Regulatory Authority joined the UN Global Compact, explicitly expressing support to the ten principles of the Compact with respect to human rights, labour, environment and anti-corruption (UNGC, 2019).

Despite these various initiatives, several studies have pointed out that there is significant opportunity to further link and integrate RBC within core business operations widely in the corporate culture. In addition, while the size and scale of initiatives related to RBC have increased, they are more widely prevalent within large businesses and multinational enterprises. As a result, understanding of RBC may vary among businesses, especially of different sizes, and between different stakeholders. In particular, meaningful engagement with local communities is an important aspect of RBC that has not been at the forefront of discussions (UNDP, ECRC, 2016; ILO, 2015).

The government has committed to promote and enable RBC

Egypt's 2015 *Sustainable Development Strategy - Vision 2030* recognises the important role of the private sector in achieving the SDGs. The strategy notably aims to activate public private partnerships to support and stimulate innovation; encourage the private sector's contribution to technical education development; and encourage civil society and private sector participation in preserving and protecting biodiversity (Government of Egypt, 2017a). This expectation is also reflected in legislation with the Investment Law of 2017 which underlines that all investments shall make a "[…] contribution to the comprehensive and sustainable development of the State". Social objectives and protection of the environment are included in the principles expected to guide all investments, with tax incentives envisioned as a tool to promote these objectives. Art. 15 of the law states that a maximum of 10% of net profit can be dedicated in this regard. Such projects may comprise environmental protection, health care, technical education, social services, and other developmental initiatives (Government of Egypt, 2017b).

Egypt's formal adherence to the *Guidelines* in 2007 and establishment of an NCP constitute important milestones in the promotion of RBC principles and standards in the country. Since then, the government supported several projects to promote RBC, such as annual CSR forums. Seven CSR forums were held between 2015 and 2018 to integrate efforts by the government, business community and civil society organisations to promote CSR in Egypt (Egypt CSR Forum, 2019). The last edition of the CSR Forum, held in April 2019, focused on the integration of sustainability considerations into core business strategies (Egypt CSR forum, 2019). In 2018, the Ministry of Investment and International Cooperation (MIIC) launched a contest to select the leading companies in the field of CSR. Companies are assessed based on environmental, social and governance criteria and compliance with international CSR standards. The winning companies receive incentives including visibility in the media and on governmental web portals, promotion in conferences, and the allocation of a liaison officer in an Investor Service Centre to provide dedicated support and facilitate administrative procedures (MIIC, 2018a).

Although the Egyptian NCP's activity has been sporadic since 2008 (Section 7.4.3), the appointment, in 2019, of a contact person within MIIC, demonstrated renewed efforts to promote RBC in Egypt. Ensuring that an effectively functioning NCP is in place is essential to support wide dissemination of the *Guidelines*, engage with stakeholders on RBC, and strengthen accountability. The government has an opportunity to build on the progress made and develop a robust NCP in support of its commitment to foster a wide understanding and adoption of international RBC standards in the country.

Actively promoting and implementing RBC principles and standards can improve economic and sustainability outcomes and support Egypt's development objectives

Building on the efforts already undertaken by the government to promote RBC, this section provides concrete examples where the government could foster implementation of RBC standards to support further trade and investment in key economic sectors and to ensure that the risk perceptions of foreign investors looking to invest in Egypt are well-founded.

Attracting investment, facilitating trade, and participating in the global economy

The impetus to promote RBC among Egyptian businesses is not only a social matter but also an economic one. Companies that want to participate in global supply chains must be aware of the global expectations on RBC. For example, in the UK, which was Egypt's largest foreign direct investor in 2017 (See Chapter 1), it is a legal requirement for companies of a certain size as of 2015 to prepare an annual report on modern slavery and human trafficking, indicating the steps taken to ensure that modern slavery is not occurring in the companies' supply chain or business operations (Box 7.1).

The EU, which is both Egypt's largest import and export partner, has integrated RBC principles and standards in a number of policies, legislations and economic instruments. The EU Trade for All policy includes objectives to reinforce CSR initiatives and due diligence across the production chain (EC, 2015). EU Directive 2014/95/EU on non-financial disclosure requires that certain companies disclose non-financial and diversity information, and encourages businesses to rely on relevant frameworks such as the *Guidelines* to provide this information (European Parliament, 2014). Binding sustainability provisions have been included in all EU Free Trade Agreement negotiations since 2011 (Business Europe, 2017). In 2013, the EU and Egypt started discussions to widen the existing trade agreement through the completion of the Deep and Comprehensive Free Trade Agreement (Council of the Association between the EU and Egypt, 2017), which could increase GDP by 1.8% in Egypt, and an estimated increase of 25% for both imports and exports in the long run (European Commission, 2016). Any supplier to EU businesses that integrates internationally recognised RBC instruments like the OECD *Guidelines* will have a comparative advantage over those that do not as they can more easily address concerns about environmental, social, human rights or labour issues that may come up in the due diligence processes of MNEs when assessing country and supplier risks.

Furthermore, various studies have demonstrated that RBC enhances the financial performance of businesses that implement RBC principles and standards. Empirical evidence from a study led by the OECD on 6 500 companies showed that the "social score" – a measure of a company's capacity to generate trust and loyalty with its workforce, customers and society – had a highly-significant positive effect on companies' return on equity and return on assets (OECD, 2017d). This business case is obvious when looking at Egyptian companies. Figure 7.1 shows a comparison between S&P EGX ESG with the EGX100, which shows that more responsible companies perform better. The EGX100 tracks the performance of 100 large companies in a variety of sectors, while the S&P EGX ESG index includes 30 companies leading on environmental and social criteria, from the pool of the EGX100 Egyptian companies screened annually (Hebatallah, 2017; EIOD, 2010)[2].

Figure 7.1. Performance of the S&P EGX ESG vs EGX100

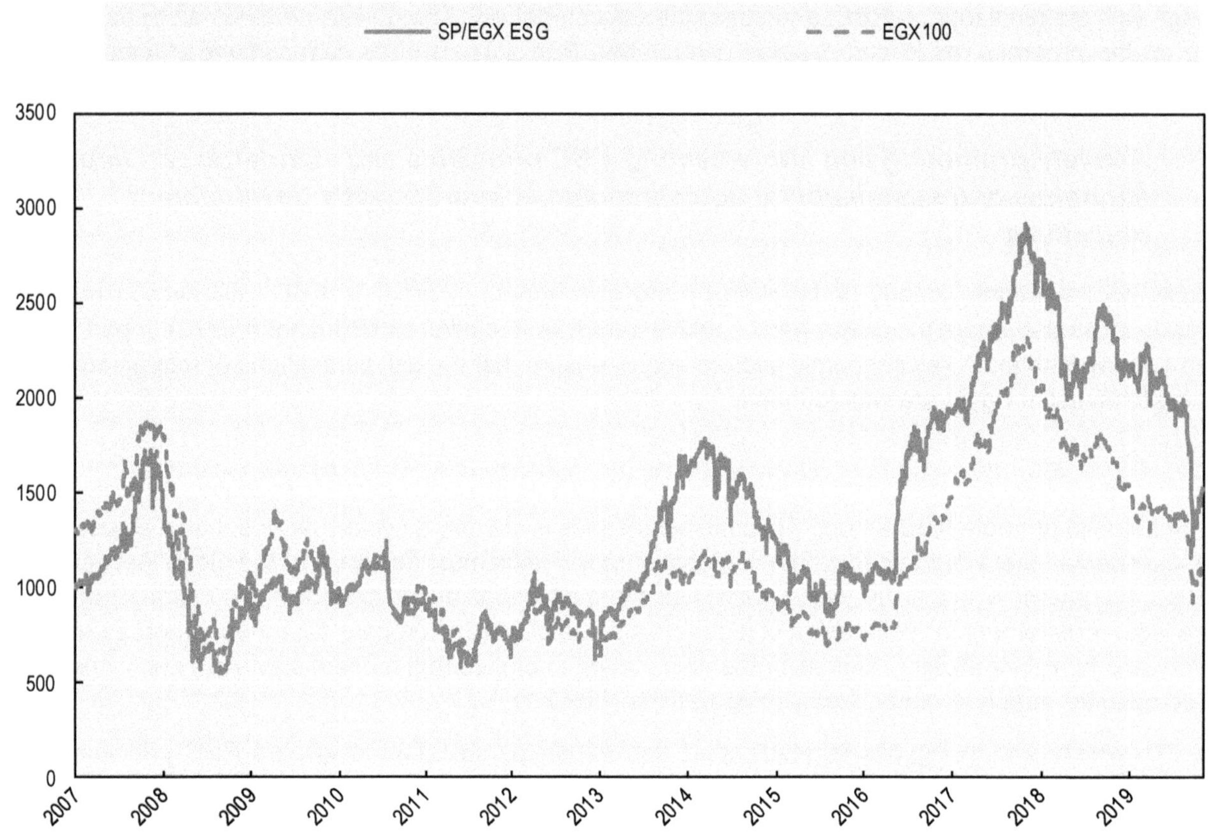

Source: OECD Secretariat based on data retrieved from the Egyptian Stock Exchange. http://www.egx.com.eg

Therefore, embedding RBC into Egypt's business culture and facilitating businesses in meeting RBC expectations is important to ensure participation in global supply chains in the long term and to achieve sustainable economic growth. To support implementation of international RBC standards, the OECD has developed guidances for businesses on how to implement the recommendations of the *Guidelines* which provide practical recommendations to help businesses identify and respond to risks of adverse impacts associated with particular products, regions, sectors or industries. As an adherent to the *Declaration*, Egypt has committed to promote the use of these instruments. Translating these guidances, starting with the OECD *Due Diligence Guidance for Responsible Business Conduct,* and ensuring their wide dissemination can facilitate the integration of Egyptian firms in global supply chains and give them a competitive advantage.

Supporting collaborative initiatives for a sustainable textile supply chain

One sector where particular attention to promoting RBC would be useful is the garment industry, due to its importance in Egypt's trade and investment portfolio. In 2017, the textile industry alone contributed 3% to the country's GDP, and employed approximately one-third of the industrial workforce (with about one-half being women, higher than national average of 23% (Oxford Business Group, 2018a; ILO, 2017b; World Bank, 2018a). Textiles were the largest export commodity after mineral products, accounting for 12% of Egypt's total exports (UN Comtrade, 2017). Egypt's textile industry is vertically integrated, with the entire production process – from the cultivation of cotton to the production of yarns, fabrics and ready-made garments – carried out domestically (GAFI, 2019). RBC risks occur throughout this supply chain and the implementation of the OECD *Due Diligence Guidance for Responsible Supply Chains in the Garment and Footwear Sector* can help to address them.

The guidance highlights that cotton harvesting often employs high rates of informal seasonal migrant workers and is exposed to risks of child labour (OECD, 2017e). In Egypt, cotton production has traditionally been a key industry, with its reputation of quality making it an international luxury standard (Oxford Business Group, 2016). Reports highlighting the presence of child labour in agriculture and in cotton production in particular have surfaced since the early 2000s. The National Child Labour Survey conducted in 2010 by the Egyptian Central Agency for Public Mobilisation and Statistics (CAPMAS) estimated that 9.3% of Egyptian children were engaged in child labour, nearly one third working in agriculture. According to the same survey, 89.3% of child labourers worked in hazardous conditions (CAPMAS, 2010). In 2001, the international NGO Human Rights Watch estimated that over 1 million children between the ages of 7 and 12 were working in cotton pest management, often forcibly and in hazardous conditions (HRW, 2001). In 2015, according to the UNESCO Institute of Statistics, 6.7% of children in the age group 5-14 were working overall, with 52% working in agriculture, including cotton production (Khatab et. al., 2019).

Ensuring that Egypt's cotton production is free of child labour and any form of modern slavery is paramount in all regards – including respecting Egyptian law, meeting international human rights standards and commitments, developing an educated workforce, and participating in global supply chains. The Egyptian government has already taken important steps to fight child labour. The *National Action Plan for Combating the Worst Forms of Child Labour in Egypt and Supporting Family for 2018-2025* includes activities targeting businesses on how to detect, mitigate and end child labour in business and in supply chains (Box 7.2). The government should consider clustering participants by industry and tailoring activities to the specific risks associated with each sector. Basing such activities on internationally recognised RBC due diligence standards can help Egyptian businesses and suppliers communicate with their buyers according to the same language and expectations on how they are addressing these phenomena. Additionally, the guidance can be useful in terms of building capacity and common expectations on all relevant stakeholders

Setting and communicating clear expectations more broadly about what constitutes RBC is key to ensure the sustainability of Egypt's cotton industry and maintain its reputation. In 2016, an announcement by the Cotton Egypt Association (CEA) that 90% of global supplies branded as Egyptian cotton were fake led to increased scrutiny on Egyptian sourced cotton by international retailers. That same year, Egypt's cotton production hit a 100-year low as a result of loosened quality controls which eroded quality and trust in cotton producers. In response, the CEA started a programme aimed at licensing manufacturers through a comprehensive DNA analysis programme to certify authenticity and merit the use of the official Egyptian cotton logo. The government also made efforts to tighten quality assurance and crop testing, leading to a rebound in cotton production in 2017-18 (Oxford Business Group, 2018). In 2019, the CEA, in partnership with UNIDO and the Better Cotton Initiative, launched a pilot aimed at creating a sustainable supply chain supporting the welfare of cotton workers and the environment. This initiative aims to modernise the industry to meet modern customers' expectations and cement the reputation of quality, integrity and sustainability of Egyptian cotton (Knitting Industry, 2019). The government could use this important momentum to encourage the industry to come together on RBC due diligence in quality assurance, training and licensing initiative. This could include supporting pilots and collaborative initiatives in sustainable cotton to build an 'Egyptian cotton' brand synonymous with responsible business practices as well as quality.

Box 7.2. Egypt's actions for the elimination of child labour

Eliminating child labour and all forms of modern slavery has become a priority in many countries. In 2017, G20 leaders committed to eliminate child labour, forced labour, human trafficking and all forms of modern slavery by 2025, and endorsed the G20 Strategy to eradicate child labour, forced labour, human trafficking and modern slavery in the world of work (G20, 2018). In June 2018, Thailand ratified the Protocol of 2014 to the 1930 Forced Labour Convention, a legally-binding treaty that complements the Forced Labour Convention of 1930 by adding new elements such as a requirement that employers exercise due diligence to avoid forced labour in their business practices or supply chains (ILO, 2018-2019a). On 29 November 2018, Australia passed a Modern Slavery Act, which requires businesses based or operating in Australia to report annually on the risks of modern slavery in their operations and supply chains, as well as the actions they have taken to address those risks. The government itself is expected to report on its own activities. This law echoes earlier legislative developments in the UK, France, US and the EU related to modern slavery, transparency in global supply chains, and disclosure (Box 7.1).

Egypt has ratified 8 of 9 core international human rights instruments, including the Convention on the Rights of the Child, and all 8 ILO fundamental conventions, including the Worst Forms of Child Labour Convention (UN OHCHR, 2019). The government has participated in several programmes to tackle child labour, including a project implemented with the ILO between 2016 and 2018, focused on school feeding, expanded access to education (including for refugee Syrian children), and awareness raising events (ILO, 2017a). Egypt is currently participating in a regional four-year programme (2018-2022), in partnership with the ILO and the Netherlands to accelerate the elimination of child labour in supply chains in Africa. The Egypt chapter of the project focuses on eliminating child labour in the cotton, textile and ready-made garment supply chain (ILO, 2019b). In 2018, the Egyptian government adopted a National Action Plan for Combating the Worst Forms of Child Labour in Egypt and Supporting Family (2018-2025). The plan includes the organisation of child labour sessions for members of the federation and chambers of industry and employers on how to detect, mitigate and end child labour in business and in supply chains. The plan also includes activities to build the capacity of concerned entities (e.g, child labour department, labour inspectors, occupational health and safety inspectors, child labour focal points) and staff to ensure better identification, intervention and reporting of those issues (Government of Egypt, 2018).

Environmental and social risks also exist in midstream and downstream processes of the garment and footwear supply chain. For example, in garment manufacturing, strikes to protest working conditions have occurred in Egypt. Between 2006 and 2017, eight strikes were reported in the news that took place on issues related to market reforms and working conditions (Ah-Wahaidy, F., 2017), with the most recent one in 2017 gathering 6 000 workers demanding bonuses and payments of wages of a state-owned enterprise (Adham, 2017). Such issues are detrimental to workers, but also to businesses. Costs of production delays can be substantial for certain product categories and any delays due to, for example, labour unrests or environmental damage, contributes to those costs (OECD, 2014b).

Businesses in Egypt are well aware of this reality and some companies have taken action to improve working conditions in Egyptian garment factories. An Egyptian factory participating in a programme initiated by Levi Strauss to build a network of better-run factories reported that the programme had a 4 to 1 return on investment, largely because of interventions focused on women (Fry, 2017). Nevertheless, this view is not fully mainstream in the industry, although there has been improvement in recent years. For example, in 2017, Walt Disney Company instituted a ban on the production of its merchandise in Egypt, following a decline in Egypt's Worldwide Governance Indicators and Egypt's decision at that time not to join the ILO/IFC Better Work Programme. The ban was lifted shortly thereafter following Egypt's commitment to participate in the programme (Egypt Independent, 2017).

The ILO/IFC Better Work Programme aims to improve working conditions and respect of labour rights for workers, and to boost the competitiveness of apparel businesses. It is currently active in 1 600 factories and employs more than 2.2 million workers in seven countries (Better Work, 2018b). Evidence from the programme shows that at country level, participation in the programme is associated with significant increases in apparel exports (World Bank, 2015). A pilot programme was implemented in Egypt between July 2017 and December 2018, at the request of the government following consultations with all industry stakeholders. The pilot engaged the government, manufacturers and their associations, all trade unions, international apparel brands and their suppliers. However, at the conclusion of the pilot, Better Work decided not to pursue a full Better Work programme, in part due to considerations relating to Egypt's conformity in law and practice with international labour standards, as determined by the ILO's supervisory bodies (Better Work, 2019). Better Work stated that conformity with international labour standards helps create an enabling environment for constructive engagement with social partners, which facilitates continual improvements in workplace compliance that are critical to the programme's success. Better Work website stated that the ILO remains committed to constructive dialogue and engagement with Egypt towards the realisation of shared objectives and that Better Work will consider the implementation of a programme in Egypt in the future, should the enabling conditions permit (Better Work, 2019).

The government's continued support of collaborative initiatives is critical, as well as efforts to create an enabling environment for such initiatives. Collaborative initiatives are particularly relevant when it comes to identifying and addressing complex and systemic risks that cannot be addressed by one actor alone. Collaboration can be beneficial in many aspects. For example, businesses and stakeholders can pool knowledge on sector risks and solutions in order to make due diligence more efficient for all. This can also facilitate cost sharing and savings. The government should use its convening role in order to assess where the gaps in the industry still exist and where the opportunities would be for its support. Experience from other governments in this regard can be useful. The Dutch government, for example, supported a multi-stakeholder initiative that led to a Covenant Agreement on Sustainable Garments, through which parties agree to conduct RBC due diligence in line with OECD RBC standards (SER, 2016).

Building sustainable infrastructure

Infrastructure is vital to economic development; it connects people to economic activity, lowers production and transaction costs for firms, and facilitates growth in a variety of sectors that serve global markets. The scaling-up of infrastructure investment has been identified as a priority by the G20 (G20, 2019). In Egypt, as mentioned in Chapter 8, estimated infrastructure investment needs by 2040 amount to an average of USD 675 billion, or 5% of GDP. There is now substantial evidence that without adequate consideration to environmental and social risks throughout infrastructure projects life-cycles, such projects are not likely to yield the intended economic or development outcomes, and at worst, could lead to negative impacts. A 2018 joint study by UN OHCHR and the Heinrich Boell Foundation showed that large transport projects in Africa, Asia, Latin America and elsewhere have been associated with serious and sometimes irreparable harm to people and the environment (UN OHCHR, 2018). Ensuring that RBC principles and standards are implemented across all steps of infrastructure life cycle can directly contribute to minimising potential negative impacts and can also foster RBC promotion across a number of key economic sectors in Egypt.

Addressing environmental and social risks associated with infrastructure projects through risk-based due diligence

In a context of broader reforms intended to achieve inclusive and sustainable economic growth, the government has initiated a number of mega-projects in diverse sectors such as agriculture, transport, housing, as well as solar and nuclear energy. This includes the building of over 4 000 km of new road, the expansion of the power capacity, and the building of twenty new cities, among which a New Administrative Capital 45 km east of Cairo in the desert (Box 8.2). In addition to improving access to services such as electricity, or water and sanitation, these projects are envisioned as a way to mobilise the private sector in the pursuit of development objectives, and create opportunities for Egyptian citizens (MIIC, 2018b).

Past experience has highlighted a number of environmental and social risks that may be associated with such projects. For example, the New Towns programme launched in the 1970s, which led to the creation of 23 new towns in underpopulated areas, has come at environmental cost. Water is an area of particular concern, as the irrigation needs for green areas, golf courses, as well as urban use including thousands of swimming pools requires pumping volumes from the Nile river to high elevations, where it cannot be recharged to the underground Nile Valley aquifers (Sims, 2014). Since the 1980s, the development of tourism facilities in coastal areas has also led to the deterioration of the coral reefs ecosystem, which in turn threatens the long-term sustainability of a sector largely reliant on its exceptional coasts, scuba diving and snorkelling activities (Sims, 2014).

Infrastructure projects often entail risks for local communities, notably in relation to land use and indigenous people's rights. It is important that the government considers carefully the benefits of meaningful engagement. Many international investors that may invest in large projects will have obligations and expectations to meet either by their own governments or in the context of the implementation of international RBC expectations. In Egypt, for example, the construction of the Aswan High Dam between 1961 and 1964 led to displacements of Nubian communities that have been claiming a right to return for decades. The sale of land considered Nubian territory in 2016 in the context of the development of the Toshka project – a project to build a system of canals to carry water from Lake Nasser to reclaim half a million acres in the Sahara desert – revived these concerns (Mahmoud, 2018; Michaelson, 2017).

Avoiding and addressing risks of adverse impacts in infrastructure projects requires embedding RBC principles into all phases of infrastructure project planning and across the entire supply chain of infrastructure provision. OECD RBC standards provide practical guidance to carry out such a process. For example, the OECD *Due Diligence Guidance for Responsible Business Conduct* offers operational guidance on how to integrate stakeholder engagement into project planning; how to prioritise engagement with the most severely affected stakeholders; how and why to share decision-making with interested and affected parties; what does ongoing consultation and follow-through look like in practice, and other issues. These standards are relevant to all actors involved in infrastructure provision, including businesses – whether private or state-owned, local or foreign, as well as the government itself in its capacity of economic actor, for example in public procurement and tendering processes.

Safeguarding Egypt's water security

Water demands associated with mega-projects are an important issue in a context where projections indicate that Egypt could fall below the threshold of absolute water scarcity as early as 2030[3] (FAO, 2016). While the government is aware of the necessity to manage water resources efficiently, as demonstrated by several national plans and strategies to ensure water balance, limited data are currently available on the impact of the new mega-projects on Egypt's water system. It is important to consider the impact of multiple projects on water and how that relates to continued economic and sustainable development. For example, academic analyses conducted on two of Egypt's land reclamation mega-projects, namely the El-Salam canal west of the Suez Canal and El-Sheikh Jaber east of the Suez Canal (Sinai project) and the El-Sheikh Zayed canal (Toshka project), showed that these projects would increase pressure on Egypt's water system (Dawoud, Sallam, 2014) (Box 7.3). This question is relevant in the context of new development plans as well. For example, plans for building the New Administrative Capital anticipate the use of treated wastewater for the irrigation of the "Green River", which is projected to be the largest park in the world, however, the resources to provide water for the new city and its expected 7 million residents are still to be defined (Farouk, 2019).

Box 7.3. Egypt water balance equation

Approximately 95% of Egypt's annual renewable water resources comes from the Nile River, with the rest coming mostly from precipitation (3%) and ground water aquifers (1.5%) (Elsaeed, 2011; Sims, 2014). Out of the Nile average annual flow of 84 billion cubic metres (BCM) per year that reaches Lake Nasser, a share of 55.5 BCM per year is allocated to Egypt according to the 1959 Nile Water Agreement (Sims, 2014).

Egypt's annual water demand is of approximately 77 BCM per year. Consumption is mainly for agriculture (62 BCM), while an additional 8 BCM (10%) is used as drinking water. The remaining demand (7.5 BCM) comes from industry (Elsaeed, 2011). The gap between water supply and demand creates a deficit estimated between 7 to 30 billion cubic meters annually, which is compensated by the recycling of drainage water (Rehab, 2018; Srour, 2018; Mohie El Din, Ahmed, 2016).

Efficient water resources management has long been a focus of the Egyptian government. Egypt prepared its first water policy in 1975, following the construction of the Aswan High Dam. Several national water strategies and plans have been developed since then, to safeguard Egypt's water balance through various means (Dawoud, Sallam, 2014). The Water Resources Supply Management Vision for 2050 focuses notably on increasing sea water desalinisation for drinking water purposes in coastal areas, water reuse programmes, and increasing the efficiency of water conveyance and water use systems (Dawoud, Sallam, 2014). The National Water Resource Plan for 2017-2037 aims to improve the enabling environment for integrated water resource management; increase the availability of freshwater sources; improve water quality; and enhance the management of water use (Nicklin,Cornwell, 2018).

Ensuring water security in Egypt remains an important issue in a context where Egypt faces increased pressure on its water system. The construction of the Grand Ethiopia Renaissance Dam, started in 2011 and expected to be completed by 2022, has raised concerns amongst Egyptians that the dam could block the flow of the Blue Nile (Wirtschafter, 2019). Additional threats may come from the water requirements of some of the mega-projects initiated to propel Egypt's development, such as the Toshka Project project, designed to pump approximately 5.5 BCM per year from Lake Nasser, i.e 10% of Egypt's total allotment. Estimated water requirements for the Sinai or Al Salam Canal project are nearly 4.5 BCM of fresh Nile water yearly – 8% of the total available (Sims, 2014; Dawoud, Sallam, 2014). The development of a large number of mega-projects, including the reclamation of one and a half million acres of desert land, the establishing of 20 new cities, or the creation of a new industrial hub in Upper Egypt, will increase pressure on water resources. Finally, climate change could have a dramatic impact on Egypt's water resources, with a diminution of Nile flows from 5% to 50% by 2025 according to some projections (Elsaeed, 2011).

It is important in this context to consider the cumulative impact of multiple projects on the environment, including in particular on water security. Some cities around the world are already dealing with water scarcity impacts (see for example FT (2019) and Middle East Water Forum (2019). The private sector can play a significant role in supporting government efforts to preserve water.

Although the Law for the Environment provides that environmental impact assessments (EIA) must be conducted for projects with potential environmental impacts (EEAA, 2017), such assessments are made at project level and do not provide an analysis of the relevance and sustainability of allocating water resources to one project in relation to another. In addition, the focus of the assessment in relation to water tends to be on the potential impacts on water quality (e.g. pollution) while limited analysis is required with respect to quantity. No law currently defines or mandates strategic environmental assessment (SEA), which could provide a mechanism for integrating environmental considerations at policy, national plans and programme levels (Ezzat et al., 2017). While these aspects are relevant for the environment as a whole, considering the importance of water in Egypt's national context, the government would benefit from developing a robust water data collection and management system, as well as centralising the project review approval process for projects with potentially significant water requirements, and requiring a systematic analysis of estimated water requirements in EIAs. SOEs and private sector participants should be asked to pay particular attention to water risks.

Using government leverage to foster wide implementation of RBC standards

The above section showcases that the impact on Egypt if environmental and social issues are not integrated in the infrastructure calculus could be quite significant. The government both as a policy-maker – for example, through land use and infrastructure planning – as well as an economic actor – notably through SOEs, tendering and public procurement processes – can lead by example in ensuring that environment and society are included in the risk assessments.

Governments are expected to lead by example on RBC, including in their own practices, i.e. as employers, business partners, through procurement and contracting practices, and in commercial activities, including activities of SOEs. The *Guidelines* apply to all businesses, regardless of their legal status, size, ownership structure or sector.

In Egypt, SOEs dominate infrastructure provision. In the energy sector, generation, transmission and distribution remains predominantly with the publicly-owned companies under the umbrella holding company, Egyptian Electricity Holding Company. Sectors such as water and transport are also largely publicly owned, with a few private concessions for example in ports and airports (GIF, 2018). A recent World Bank report identified weak SOE governance as one of the main constraints to the development of sustainable infrastructure that maximises private sector involvement (World Bank, 2018b). RBC expectations should be made clear in the context of SOE expectations. The importance of RBC in SOE activity is recognised in the 2015 OECD *Guidelines on Corporate Governance of State-Owned Enterprises*, which recommend making clear any expectations the state has in respect of RBC by SOEs, and further recommend extensive measures to report on foreseeable risks, including in the areas human rights, labour, the environment, and risks related to corruption and taxation (OECD, 2015b).

The government should establish and publicly disclose clear expectations on RBC in the context of infrastructure projects. RBC could also be an explicit requirement in tendering and contracting processes. Complexity and lack of transparency around financing and operations of infrastructure projects amplifies the risks that environmental and social issues will not only not be dealt with but perhaps even exacerbated due to the fact that efficient and meaningful risk-based due diligence may not be possible. For example, a 2016 analysis by SOMO, the coordinator of OECD Watch, of the involvement of foreign companies in the context of dredging of the new Suez Canal showed the risks of not adequately conducting risk-based due diligence and engaging meaningfully with affected stakeholders prior to the start of the project. The study highlighted the lack of engagement with villagers, the destruction of homes, and harmful impacts on biodiversity (SOMO, 2016).

The government can also play an important role in promoting RBC among Egyptian companies operating abroad. Encouraging RBC due diligence is an important element of promoting and enabling RBC and ensuring that environmental and social risks are adequately assessed and addressed. For example, several Egyptian businesses are involved in the building of a dam in Tanzania in the context of the

Stiegler's Gorge hydropower project (also known as Rufiji hydropower project). Located on the Rufiji River, the site for the proposed project is within the Selous Game Reserve, which was made a UNESCO World Heritage site in 1982. A study published by OECD Watch in 2019 highlighted a number of environmental and social risks associated with the project, including impacts on biodiversity, social disruption and potential displacements. The research also highlighted gaps in the assessment of the environmental and social impact of the dam (Hartmann, 2019). As Egyptian enterprises increase their investments abroad, it will be important for both their reputation but also the quality of their investment that RBC considerations are integrated as a matter of practice.

Deepening policy reform to enable RBC

Beyond RBC promotion and facilitation, it is important to also remove legal or regulatory obstacles for RBC. This not only requires creating an environment that encourages responsible behaviour and enables dialogues between relevant stakeholders, but also a policy environment that is clear and predictable and allows for mechanisms to ensure accountability when RBC expectations are not met. This section highlights areas where the government could focus its policy efforts to support the development of an enabling environment for RBC.

Meaningful stakeholder engagement is key for implementing RBC standards

A key component of what constitutes an enabling environment for RBC is one where meaningful stakeholder engagement and dialogue is a way of doing business. The *Guidelines* explicitly recommend that enterprises participate in private or multi-stakeholder initiatives and social dialogue on responsible supply chain management. Enterprises are also encouraged to co-operate with governments in developing and implementing policies and laws, and to consider the views of other stakeholders in society. Additionally, the OECD *Policy Framework for Investment* emphasises that greater participation of stakeholders in policy design and implementation leads to better targeted and more effective policies. Creating an environment where stakeholders are empowered to express their views and actively participate in policy design as well as consultations organised by businesses, the government or a group of stakeholders, is therefore essential for RBC.

Foreign investors, especially those for which implementing RBC standards is a legal obligation, may also have concerns about their ability to conduct risk-based due diligence when stakeholders cannot actively engage in the due diligence process. The *OECD Due Diligence Guidance for Responsible Business Conduct* lays out clear expectations that due diligence should be informed by meaningful engagement with stakeholders such as workers, workers' representatives, trade unions (including global unions), community members, civil society organisations, investors and professional industry and trade associations. Meaningful stakeholder engagement is characterised by two-way communication, through which enterprise and stakeholders freely express opinions, share perspectives and listen to alternative viewpoints to reach a mutual understanding. The government can play an important role in supporting this process by ensuring that the legal and judicial framework empowers stakeholders to express their views and engage with businesses.

Egypt has ratified 64 ILO Conventions, including the eight fundamental ones (ILO, 2017c). The right to establish unions and federations is also protected by Article 76 of the 2014 Egyptian Constitution. However, the ILO has pointed out that in effect, the current legislative framework does not ensure full recognition of independent trade unions, which in the past had negative effects on industrial relations (OECD, 2017c; ILO, 2017d-e). In November 2017, a draft law (213/2017) was submitted to and approved by the parliament. Critics have argued that it effectively institutionalises the Egyptian Trade Union Federation as the sole union body for Egypt by setting membership thresholds that are too high for independent trade unions to meet (ITUC, 2017; Kindornay et al, 2018). Recently, Law No. 142 of 2019, which amended some provisions of the earlier Law, reduces the number of workers required to form independent trade unions from 150 to 50, and abolishes imprisonment penalties.

Concerns have also been raised about laws governing NGOs. The May 2017 Law on NGO, in particular, drew criticism for restricting NGO activities. The law notably introduced an administrative body including members of security services that could regulate all NGOs receiving foreign funding (U.S State Department, 2017). In 2017, the UN Office of the High Commissioner for Human Rights issued a statement citing that the law was "damaging for the enjoyment of human rights and leave rights defenders even more vulnerable to sanctions and reprisals than they already are" (UN OHCHR, 2017). In July 2019, Egypt's Parliament approved a new NGO law that aims to address some of these concerns, and notably eliminates criminal penalties for non-compliance, and which executive regulations are yet to be released. It also allows NGOs to receive foreign funding, under the condition that the NGOs obtain approval from administrative authorities. Some NGOs have noted that while the new law is widely considered to be an improvement from the 2017 NGO law, concerns still remain over restriction of activities and cooperating with foreign organisations or experts (see for example Amnesty, Access Now, HRW, 2019).

Tackling corruption

Tackling corruption is another important component of building this enabling environment. The *Guidelines* emphasise that bribery and corruption discourage investment and distort international competitive conditions. In particular, the diversion of funds through corrupt practices undermines attempts by citizens to achieve higher levels of economic, social and environmental welfare, and it impedes efforts to reduce poverty. Both businesses and governments have a role to play in addressing corruption. For example, the *Guidelines* specify that enterprises should not, directly or indirectly, offer, promise, give, or demand a bribe or other undue advantage to obtain or retain business or other improper advantage, and should also resist solicitation of bribes and extortion. Governments also have a responsibility to ensure that a legal and regulatory framework is in place and enforced to deter corruption. They can also lead by example by observing the highest integrity standards in their own actions as economic actors.

Tackling corruption has been high on the political agenda in Egypt. Vision 2030 also has a strong focus on strengthening reform and good governance in the civil service to combat corruption and promote transparency and integrity. According to Transparency International, a number of institutional reforms, as well as deepened co-operation with international organisations, have strengthened the country's anti-corruption framework (Transparency International, 2015a). Several government agencies share responsibility for addressing corruption in Egypt, including the Administrative Control Authority (ACA), which has jurisdiction over state administrative bodies, SOEs, public associations and institutions, private companies undertaking public work, and organisations to which the state contributes in any form (IBP, 2018). In 2017, the Egyptian parliament adopted amendments to the law governing the work of ACA. The amendments included transferring the subordination of the ACA to the President, appointing the head of the ACA by the president following the parliament's approval and recognising the authority as a state body with technical, financial and administrative independence. The amendments also introduced the creation of several bodies to fight and prevent corruption including creating a specialised national academy to build the capacity of ACA staff (Al Wahaidy, 2018).

The Egyptian criminal code criminalises active and passive abuse of power including facilitating payments and bribes. In 2013, Egypt adopted a Conflict of Interest Law targeting senior public officials. In 2014, the government adopted an anti-corruption strategy for 2014-18, developed by the National Coordinating Committee for Combating Corruption (NCCCC) and implemented by a technical committee headed by the Administrative Control Authority (Al Wahaidy, 2018). The strategy was updated in December 2018 for the period 2019-22 (MENA, 2018). Egypt ratified the UN convention against Corruption in 2005 (UNTC, 2019) but is not party to the OECD *Convention on Bribery of Foreign Public Officials in International Business Transactions*. Egypt has also joined a number of international initiatives and projects to combat corruption including the MENA-OECD Task Force on Anti-Bribery, the OECD Good Governance for Development in Arab Countries Initiative, the Arab Anti-Corruption and Integrity Network and the UNDP-POGAR project to support the Ministry of Investment in the fight against corruption (FEMISE, 2017). In 2017, Egypt signed a memorandum of understanding with UNODC to combat corruption in Egypt (UNODC, 2017).

In practice, however, several studies point to a gap between a relatively strong legislative framework and the implementation of the law (FEMISE, 2017). In 2018, Egypt ranked 105th out of 180 countries in perceived corruption (Transparency International, 2018). According to the 2016 World Bank Enterprise Survey for Egypt, 68% of firms surveyed identified corruption as a major constraint to doing business (World Bank, 2016). The 2017-18 World Economic Forum Global Competitiveness Index reports that corruption is the third most problematic factor for doing business, after political instability and inflation (WEF, 2018).

One area where future reforms could focus is on strengthening the involvement of the private sector and civil society in the implementation and monitoring of efforts to promote integrity. This could involve raising awareness on the risk of corruption, encouraging the reporting of misconduct, and ensuring access to remedy when corruption occurs. A 2015 report by Transparency International identified a gap in the protection of whistle-blowers in Egypt. Although a draft Witnesses and Whistle-blowers Protection law was proposed in 2013, no dedicated law exists yet to regulate whistle-blowing. In addition, potential whistle-blowers face challenges and fear retaliation, which hinders reporting instances of corruption (Transparency International, 2015b). The government could consider introducing legislation to provide protection to whistle-blowers. Encouraging the public to monitor, detect and report misconduct, and creating a safe space for civil society organisations to play the role of watchdogs, could increase accountability and enhance integrity and transparency in both the public and private sector.

The government would also benefit from strengthening its anti-corruption efforts in the public sector. Areas such as public procurement, customs administration and land administration are especially vulnerable to risks of corruption in Egypt (GAN Integrity, 2019). Cases relating to land administration have involved high-ranking officials accused of accepting bribes against land licences (GAN Integrity, 2019; Egypt Today, 2018a-b). The issue has also been raised by businesses in recent surveys. For example, the 2016 World Bank Enterprise surveys indicated that 28% of firms surveyed expected to give gifts to get a construction permit, 26% expected to give gifts to get a water connection, and 19% expected to give gifts to public officials to "get things done" (World Bank, 2016). A 2017 survey by Transparency International indicated that 40-50% of respondents reported paying a bribe when they came into contact with a public service in the last 12 months prior to when the survey took place (Transparency International, 2017).

The government has indicated to the OECD that several of its recent initiatives in the context of implementation of Egypt Vision 2030 have been envisioned in response to the above challenges, notably the adoption of the Civil Service Law 81 in 2016; the Investment Law in 2017; Prevention of Conflict of Interest Law and the law broadening the mandate of the Administrative Control Authority to include corruption prevention in the public sector; establishment of the National Anti-corruption Academy to conduct training and raise awareness on for civil servants on anti-corruption and transparency and integrity in the delivery of public services; as well as programme for the automation of public service delivery; establishment of Investment Service Centres and others to enhance the efficiency and transparency of service provision to investors.

Strengthening Egypt's NCP

NCPs have a mandate to further the effectiveness of the *Guidelines* by undertaking promotional activities, handling inquiries, and contributing to the resolution of issues that arise relating to the implementation of the *Guidelines* by businesses in specific instances. Several mechanisms for settlement and resolution of disputes exist in Egypt, as discussed in Chapter 3. These mechanisms provide an alternative to judicial courts and private arbitration centres when disputes arise between investors and the state, or among investors. NCPs are complementary to these mechanisms and represent at present the only state-based non-judicial grievance mechanism with a mandate to consider RBC issues and impacts in global supply chains. Any individual or organisation with a legitimate interest in the matter can submit a case to an NCP regarding a company, operating in or from the country of the NCP, which has not observed the *Guidelines*.

Operating with this global mandate, NCPs offer and, with the agreement of the parties involved, facilitate access to consensual and non-adversarial means, such as conciliation or mediation, to resolve issues that arise if the *Guidelines* are not observed – called specific instances. NCPs also have an important promotion and stakeholder engagement function. They are expected to develop and maintain relations with representatives of the business community, worker organisations and other interested parties that are able to contribute to the effective functioning of the *Guidelines*. NCPs are expected to make the *Guidelines* known and available by appropriate means, to raise awareness about them and their implementation procedures, including also with prospective investors (outward and inward).

Adherents to the *Declaration*, have a legal obligation to establish an NCP and to make available human and financial resources so that the NCP can effectively fulfil its responsibilities. Adhering governments have flexibility in how they structure their NCP, but all NCPs must be given adequate resources to fulfil their functions. The NCP structure must enable the NCP to deal with the broad range of issues covered by the *Guidelines*, develop and maintain relations with stakeholders and operate in an impartial manner. When establishing their NCPs, governments are also expected to ensure that they can operate in accordance with the core criteria of visibility, accessibility, transparency and accountability.[4] When handling specific instances, NCPs should observe the principles of impartiality, predictability, equitability and compatibility with the *Guidelines*.[5]

Egypt adhered to the *Declaration* in 2007 and established an NCP located in the Ministry of Investment, assisted by a multi-stakeholder Advisory Committee (OECD, 2008). Between 2008 and 2011, the Egyptian NCP established a website that featured the *Guidelines* in both English and Arabic, adopted rules of procedures for handling specific instances, and undertook promotional activities such as reaching out to major MNEs and asking all enterprises to adhere to the *Guidelines* (OECD, 2009-10). After a period of interruption, Egypt reported having reactivated its NCP in 2013 (OECD, 2013). In that same year, the Egyptian NCP supported the US NCP in handling a specific instance requested by the International Union of Food, Agricultural, Hotel, Restaurant, Catering, Tobacco and Allied Workers' Association, which alleged that Mondelez International had breached the human rights and employment and industrial relations provisions of the *Guidelines* in Tunisia and Egypt. However, Mondelez stated that it would not participate in the mediation offered by the NCP, and the specific instance was closed (OECD, 2014a). No NCP activity was reported Egypt in 2014-16. During those years, Egypt did not attend the annual meetings of the NCPs in Paris or report to the OECD Investment Committee and did not appear to have an NCP contact or website in place (OECD, 2014a-16). The Egyptian NCP was not represented at the NCP meetings of the OECD in Paris in June and November 2017.

Between 2016 and 2018, the OECD Secretary General issued three letters to the Minister of Investment and International Cooperation to remind Egypt of the commitments associated with adherence to the *Guidelines* and request that the Egyptian government report to the OECD Secretariat on concrete actions taken regarding the NCP. In response, the Minister of Investment and International Cooperation reiterated Egypt's commitment to set up an NCP and implement the *Guidelines*, and reported on steps taken toward the establishment of an NCP in two letters addressed to the OECD Secretary General in December 2017 and January 2018. These steps included a national consultation meeting and capacity-building exercise held in November 2017, during which representatives of the Egyptian government and the OECD discussed the next steps for moving forward with the NCP. The NCPs of France and Morocco participated in this event. In addition, the MIIC designated three members to take part in the NCP in 2017. This structure was revised and a new contact person appointed in January 2018, in the context of a broader institutional restructuring of the MIIC.

A new NCP head was appointed in 2019. In September 2019, the proposed composition of the NCP was a Coordinator/Focal Point from the Ministry of Investment and International Cooperation, senior representatives from GAFI, Ministry of Trade and Industry, and the Ministry of Justice. In 2019, Egypt reported to the OECD on the Egyptian NCP's activities for 2018. The NCP did not undertake or participate in any promotional activities in 2018 but it did adopt a plan for promotional activities in 2019. A webpage providing general information about the NCP as well as contact information to reach the NCP was created in 2019. However, the webpage does not provide detailed information on, for example, promotional activities and rules of procedures for specific instances. Making this information public would be important to ensure that the NCP operates in accordance with the core criteria. At present, the NCP does not have any rules of procedures in place, making it challenging for stakeholders to understand what the specific instance procedure entails in practice. The NCP participated in the June 2019 meeting of the Network of NCPs in Paris and shared recent updates, such as the ongoing review process of the ministerial decree setting up the NCP. The team leader of the NCP was also Egypt's delegate to the March 2019 WPRBC meeting.

In 2018, the government requested the OECD's assistance to facilitate the pairing of the Egyptian NCP with a suitable NCP, under a project implemented in partnership with the World Bank and aimed at enhancing the investment climate. These developments are positive and could greatly contribute to reinforcing the Egyptian NCP. Egypt should continue its efforts to strengthen its NCP. The government could, for example, consider a peer review evaluation of the NCP, which is an important means to highlight both strengths and improvements, and could facilitate the development of an action plan for strengthening the Egyptian NCP. To ensure that the NCP can fulfil its mandate effectively, the government is encouraged ensure that it has adequate human and financial resources, meets its reporting obligations and participates at relevant meetings at the OECD.

Developing a National Action Plan on RBC

Policy coherence is crucial to ensure sound policy design and implementation. This is recognised in the *Policy Framework for Investment*, which encourages governments to co-operate internally as well as externally with foreign governments and stakeholders to ensure coherence and support of policies relevant to RBC. Such co-operation should involve all relevant stakeholders, including among government agencies, companies, worker associations, professional associations, employer associations, civil society, and local communities.

Despite important commitments made toward RBC, Egypt has not yet developed an overarching framework defining clear actions, timelines and responsibilities for the promotion and implementation of RBC standards. In line with international good practice, Egypt could consider working with stakeholders to develop a National Action Plan (NAP) on RBC, based on the *Guidelines*. The UN Human Rights Council and the UN Working Group on Business and Human Rights have called on governments to develop, enact and update NAPs to disseminate and implement the *UN Guiding Principles on Business Human Rights*. A number of OECD governments, notably the United States, have decided to broaden these efforts and include all RBC issues, based on the *Guidelines*, in their NAPs. To date, 20 countries, all adherents to the *Declaration* have already produced a NAP, and 21 more are in the process of developing or have committed to developing one. Developing a NAP is an effective way to prioritise actions for the implementation of RBC standards, support policy coherence and reinforce coordination of efforts related to RBC within the government.

The process of developing a NAP would also be a good way for the government to engage with stakeholders and the wider public on a range of issues related to RBC, to promote the *Guidelines*, as well as policy coherence and alignment on RBC. As indicated in the Guidance on National Action Plans for Business and Human Rights developed by the UN Working Group on Business and Human Rights, NAPs need to be developed in inclusive and transparent processes, taking into account the views of relevant stakeholders in the development and update of the NAP.

In Egypt, overcoming potential barriers related to the complexity of the institutional framework will be of particular importance to ensure successful development and implementation of the NAP. This notably requires having a clear structure in place, with designated leadership and a format for cross-departmental collaboration and stakeholder engagement (UNWG, 2016). The NCP for the OECD *Guidelines*, in coordination with relevant government and other stakeholders, could lead the process. The process of developing the NAP would also be an opportunity for the government to understand and eventually remove barriers that influence RBC uptake by businesses, as well as to facilitate collective initiatives, in the government's role as a convener, to promote RBC among industry and other stakeholders.

References

Access Now (2019), *Access Now issues a red card to Egypt for new repressive NGO law,* https://www.accessnow.org/access-now-issues-a-red-card-to-egypt-for-new-repressive-ngo-law/

Adham, Y. (2017). *Thousands of workers strike at Mahalla textile factory.* https://www.dailynewsegypt.com/2017/08/08/thousands-workers-strike-mahalla-textile-factory/

Al Tamimi & Company (2018). *Egypt's Economic Renaissance: Mega Projects and their Framework.* Retrieved from Lexology. https://www.lexology.com/library/detail.aspx?g=034e7e38-5827-4975-959a-68f25f19e8ce

Al-Wahaidy, F. (2017). *Ghazl El-Mahalla textile workers' strike is not the first.* . Egypt Today. http://www.egypttoday.com/Article/2/18861/Ghazl-El-Mahalla-textile-workers%E2%80%99-strike-is-not-the-first

Al Wahaidy, F. (2018). *Sisi meets ACA Chairman to discuss anti-corruption strategy.* http://www.egypttoday.com/Article/1/60842/Sisi-meets-ACA-Chairman-to-discuss-anti-corruption-strategy

AmCham (2018). *Egypt and the United States. A shared Future.* http://www.amcham-egypt.org/Missions/csrprograms2018.pdf

Amnesty International (2019), *Egypt: Amendments to repressive NGO law little more than token 'cosmetic' changes,* https://www.amnesty.org/en/latest/news/2019/07/egypt-amendments-to-repressive-ngo-law-little-more-than-token-cosmetic-changes/

Amnesty International (2011). *We are not Dirt. Forced evictions in Egypt's Informal Settlements.* https://www.amnesty.org/download/Documents/32000/mde120012011en.pdf

Bales, K. (2007). *What Predicts Human Trafficking.* International Journal of Comparative and Applied Criminal Justice 31(2), 269-279.

Banco Santander (2018). *Egypt: Foreign Investment.* https://en.portal.santandertrade.com/establish-overseas/egypt/foreign-investment

Barma, M. (2012). *Private Sector boasts strong record in CSR.* American Chamber of Commerce in Egypt. https://www.amcham.org.eg/publications/business-monthly/issues/195/March-2012/2813/

Bedawy, R. (2014). *Water Resources Management: Alarming Crisis for Egypt.* Journal of Management and Sustainability. Vol.4, No.3, 2014.

DOI: 10.5539/jms.v4n3p108. Retrieved from Research Gate.

Better Work (2019). *Better Work pilot in Egypt.* https://betterwork.org/where-we-work/better-work-pilot-in-egypt/

Business Europe (2017). *Trade and Sustainable Development chapters in EU FTAs.* https://www.businesseurope.eu/sites/buseur/files/media/position_papers/rex/2017-11-

06_sustainability_and_ftas.pdf

CAPMAS (2010). EU-Egypt Partnership Priorities 2017-2020. https://ec.europa.eu/neighbourhood-enlargement/sites/near/files/eu-egypt-partnership-priorities.pdf

Council of the Association between the EU and Egypt (2017). EU-Egypt Partnership Priorities 2017-2020. https://ec.europa.eu/neighbourhood-enlargement/sites/near/files/eu-egypt-partnership-priorities.pdf

Dawoud, M.A., Sallam, O.M (2014). *New Reclamation Mega Projects and Increasing the Pressure on Water System in the Nile Valley and Delta in Egypt.* DOI: 10.13140/RG.2.1.1845.4564.

Egypt Independent (2017). *Walt Disney lifts ban on merchandise produced in Egypt: Trade minister.* https://ww.egyptindependent.com/disney-lifts-ban-egypt/

Egypt Today (2018). *Game-changing Insights into the Real Estate Market.* http://www.egypttoday.com/Article/3/48476/Game-changing-Insights-into-the-Real-Estate-Market

Egyptian Exchange – EGX (2016). *Model Guidance for Reporting on ESG Performance & SDGs.* http://www.egx.com.eg/getdoc/98b4f610-5544-4f93-a36e-636d3baf8f45/EGX-Model-Guidance-on-ESG_en-11-10-2016.aspx

EIoD (2010). *The Third Annual Conference on Corporate Social Responsibility. "Transparency & Reporting on CSR practices, Towards Sustainable Competitive Environment"* . The Executive. http://www.eiod.org/uploads/publications/pdf/issue10-eng.pdf

Elsaeed, G. (2011). *Effects of Climate Change on Egypt's Water Supply.* Conference Paper. DOI: 10.1007/978-94-007-2430-3_30. Retrieved from Research Gate.

European Commission (2019). *U-Viet Nam free trade agreement - Joint press statement by Commissioner Malmström and Minister Tran Tuan Anh.* http://trade.ec.europa.eu/doclib/press/index.cfm?id=2041

European Commission (2015). *Trade for All. Towards a more responsible trade and investment policy.* http://trade.ec.europa.eu/doclib/docs/2015/october/tradoc_153846.pdf

European Union External Action – EEAS (2018). *Preparation of the National Water Resources Plan for Egypt 2017-2037 (NWRP 2017-2037) (€2 million grant).* https://eeas.europa.eu/headquarters/headquarters-homepage/43747/preparation-national-water-resources-plan-egypt-2017-2037-nwrp-2017-2037-%E2%82%AC2-million-grant_en

European Parliament (2014). Directive 2014/95/EU of the European Parliament and of the Council of 22 October 2014 amending Directive 2013/34/EU as regards disclosure of non-financial and diversity information by certain large undertakings and groups Text with EEA relevance. https://eur-lex.europa.eu/legal-content/EN/TXT/?uri=CELEX%3A32014L0095

ECRC (2017), Egyptian Corporate Responsibility Center Website, http://www.ecrc.org.eg/WhoWeAre.aspx.

Egypt CSR Forum (2018). *Third CSR Forum in Governorates.* http://www.egyptcsrforum.com/#Intro

Egypt Today (2018a). *ACA arrests head of FIHC, major officials in bribery case.* http://www.egypttoday.com/Article/1/51163/ACA-arrests-head-of-FIHC-major-officials-in-bribery-case

Egypt Today (2018b). *Cairo Court holds 4 officials in detention for 15 days over bribery charges.* http://www.egypttoday.com/Article/1/51302/Cairo-Court-holds-4-officials-in-detention-for-15-days

El Shorbagi (n.d). *Supporting Egypt's Corporate Responsibility Framework.* Presentation. Egyptian Corporate Responsibility Center. http://ecrc.org.eg/uploads/documents/Egyptian%20Corporate%20Responsibility%20&%20the%20Way%20Forward.pdf

European Commission (2018). *Countries and Regions. Egypt.* http://ec.europa.eu/trade/policy/countries-and-regions/countries/egypt/

European Commission (2016). *European Commission Services' position paper on the trade sustainability impact assessment in support of negotiations of a deep and comprehensive free trade area between the European Union and Egypt.* http://trade.ec.europa.eu/doclib/docs/2016/december/tradoc_155189.pdf

Ezzat, E.E., Gallal, R., Hesham, P. (2017). *Strategic Environmental Assessment (SEA) Criteria formulation; The Egyptian Case Study.* International Journal of Applied Engineering Research ISSN 0973-4562 Volume 12, Number 21 (2017) pp. 11130-11138. Research India Publications. https://www.ripublication.com/ijaer17/ijaerv12n21_86.pdf

Fair Labor Association (2016). *Independent Trade Unions in Egypt.* http://www.fairlabor.org/tr/node/2278

FAO (2016). *Egypt.* Aquastat. http://www.fao.org/nr/water/aquastat/countries_regions/EGY/

Farouk, M. (2019). *Egypt's new administrative capital getting its own 'Nile'.* https://www.al-monitor.com/pulse/originals/2019/01/egypt-administrative-capital-nile-river-green-park.html

FEMISE (2017). *Potential Accession to the Revised WTO Government Procurement Agreement: The Cases of Egypt and Turkey.* FEM42-02. FEMISE Research Papers. https://www.euneighbours.eu/sites/default/files/publications/2017-11/The%20case%20of%20Egypt.pdf

French Government (2017). LOI n° 2017-399 du 27 mars 2017 relative au devoir de vigilance des sociétés mères et des entreprises donneuses d'ordre (1). https://www.legifrance.gouv.fr/eli/loi/2017/3/27/2017-399/jo/texte

Fry, E. (2017). *Can Levi's Make Life Better for Garment Workers?* Fortune. http://fortune.com/2017/09/08/levis-change-the-world/

FT (2019), *India's precarious water security takes toll on farmers*. Financial Times. https://www.ft.com/content/ff8dfc64-be7b-11e9-9381-78bab8a70848

G7 (2015), Leaders' Declaration G7 Summit, 7–8 June 2015, available at https://www.g7germany.de/Content/EN/_Anlagen/G7/2015-06-08-g7-abschluss-eng_en.pdf?__blob=publicationFile&v=3

G20 (2019) G20 Principles for Quality Infrastructure Investment, https://g20.org/pdf/documents/en/annex_01.pdf

G20 (2018) Fostering Opportunities for an Inclusive, Fair and Sustainable Future of Work, http://www.g20.utoronto.ca/2018/2018-09-07-employment.html#annex2

G20 (2017), G20 Leaders´ Declaration: Shaping an interconnected world, Hamburg Summit, 7-8 July 2017, https://www.g20.org/gipfeldokumente/G20-leaders-declaration.pdf.

GAFI (2019). *The only fully vertically integrated textile industry in the Middle East*. GAFI Website. Accessed 07.01.2019. https://www.gafi.gov.eg/English/Sectors/TargetedSectors/Pages/Textiles.aspx

GAN Integrity (2016). *Egypt Corruption Report.* https://www.business-anti-corruption.com/country-profiles/egypt/

Global Infrastructure Facility – GIF (2018). *Egypt : Scaling up Private Investments in Infrastructure*. https://www.globalinfrafacility.org/sites/gif/files/GIFBriefs_PDA_April2018_Egypt%20Scaling%20Up.pdf

Government of Egypt (2018). *National Action Plan for Combating the Worst Forms of Child Labour in Egypt and Supporting Family (2018-2025).* https://www.ilo.org/wcmsp5/groups/public/---africa/---ro-addis_ababa/documents/publication/wcms_633743.pdf

Government of Egypt (2017a), *Sustainable Development Strategy: Egypt Vision 2030,* http://sdsegypt2030.com/economic-dimension/economic-development-pillar/?lang=en&lang=en

Government of Egypt (2017b) Law No. 72 of 2017 Promulgating the Investment Law, http://www.investment.gov.eg/Front/Investment/LawsList.aspx?CatId=14

Hartmann, J. (2019) Economic Feasibility of the Stiegler's Gorge Hydropower Project, Tanzania, https://www.oecdwatch.org/wp-content/uploads/sites/8/2019/02/Economic-Feasibility-of-the-Stiegler's-Gorge-Hydropower-Project-Tanzania.pdf

Hebatallah, E.S. (2017). *The Egyptian Exchange (EGX) Experience with Corporate Governance & Sustainability*. International Finance Corporation. https://www.ifc.org/wps/wcm/connect/ce9465db-6487-4699-948c-72ef4b1bf640/Hebatallah_El_Serafi.pdf?MOD=AJPERES

HRW (2019), Egypt: New NGO Law Renews Draconian Restrictions, https://www.hrw.org/news/2019/07/24/egypt-new-ngo-law-renews-draconian-restrictions

HRW (2017), Egypt: New Law Will Crush Civil Society, 2 June 2017, https://www.hrw.org/news/2017/06/02/egypt-new-law-will-crush-civil-society.

HRW (2001), Underage and unprotected : child labour in Egypt's cotton fields, https://www.hrw.org/legacy/reports/2001/egypt/index.htm

ILO (2019a). The Protocol. 50 for Freedom Campaign website. Accessed 12.07.2019. http://50forfreedom.org/the-protocol/

ILO (2019b). *Accelerating action for the elimination of child labour in supply chains in Africa*. https://www.ilo.org/wcmsp5/groups/public/---ed_norm/---ipec/documents/publication/wcms_698538.pdf

ILO (2018), Thailand joins the global movement to combat forced labour, https://www.ilo.org/global/standards/information-resources-and-publications/news/WCMS_631435/lang--en/index.htm

ILO (2017a), Project description - Capacity of Egyptian Government, Workers' and Employers' Organizations Strengthened to Combat Child Labour, http://www.ilo.org/addisababa/technical-cooperation/WCMS_548918/lang--en/index.htm.

ILO (2017b), *ILO improves working conditions in 30 factories in Egypt*, Better Work. https://www.ilo.org/addisababa/media-centre/pr/WCMS_565938/lang--en/index.htm

ILO (2017c), Ratifications country websites, www.ilo.org/dyn/normlex/en/f?p=1000:11200:0::NO:11200:P11200_COUNTRY_ID:103542 (accessed 18 December 2018).

ILO (2017d). Definitive Report - Report No 375, June 2015, *Case No 3025 (Egypt)*, http://www.ilo.org/dyn/normlex/en/f?p=1000:50002:0::NO:50002:P50002_COMPLAINT_TEXT_ID:3241132

ILO (2017e). Individual Case (CAS) - Discussion: 2017, Publication: 106th ILC session (2017). https://www.ilo.org/dyn/normlex/en/f?p=1000:13100:0::NO:13100:P13100_COMMENT_ID:3330989

ILO (2016). *Progress and potental: How Better Work is improving garment workers' lives and boosting factory competitiveness: A summary of an independent assessment of the Better Work programme*. International Labour Office. Geneva. https://betterwork.org/blog/portfolio/impact-assessment/

ILO (2015). *CSR. Industrial Leaders of Egypt. Towards Creating Shared Value. Volume I.* http://schools.aucegypt.edu/Business/gerhart/Documents/Publications/CSR-V1.pdf

IOM (2016), *Egyptian Unaccompanied Migrant Children. A case study on irregular migration.* https://publications.iom.int/system/files/egyptian_children.pdf

International Business Publications – IBP (2018). *Egypt Clothing and Textile Industry Handbook. Strategic Information, developments, contacts.* Washington DC, USA.

ITUC (2017). *Egypt: New Draft Trade Union Law Suppresses Freedom of Association*. https://www.ituc-csi.org/egypt-new-draft-trade-union-law

Jamali, D. (2017). *Comparative Perspectives on Global Corporate Social Responsibility*. IGI Global. Hershey PA, USA. Print Version.

Khaled, F. (2018). *A Good Year for Real Estate*. Egypt Today. http://www.egypttoday.com/Article/3/39037/A-Good-Year-for-Real-Estate

Khatab, Khaled & Raheem, Maruf & Sartorius, Benn & Ismail, Mubarak. (2019). *Prevalence and risk factors for child labour and violence against children in Egypt using Bayesian geospatial modelling with multiple imputation*. PLOS ONE. 14. e0212715. 10.1371/journal.pone.0212715.

Kindornay, S., Kocaata, K., Boehler, T. (2018). *Private sector engagement through development co-operation in Egypt*. Country Case Study. Global Partnership for Effective Cooperation. OECD. http://www.oecd.org/dac/effectiveness/PSE-case-study-Egypt.pdf

Knitting Industry (2019). *Egyptian Cotton launches BCI pilot project*. https://www.knittingindustry.com/egyptian-cotton-launches-bci-pilot-project/

Mahmoud, K. (2018). *Dashing Nubians' Hopes of Returning Home*. https://carnegieendowment.org/sada/77026

MENA (2018). *ACA: Sisi launches 2nd phase of anti-graft strategy*. http://www.egypttoday.com/Article/1/61742/ACA-Sisi-launches-2nd-phase-of-anti-graft-strategy

Michaelson, R. (2017). *Egypt's Nubians fight for ancestral land earmarked for mega-project*. https://www.theguardian.com/global-development/2017/feb/13/egypt-nubians-fight-for-ancestral-land-earmarked-for-mega-project

Middle East Water Forum (2019). Website. https://www.mewf.de/

Ministry of Environment, Egyptian Environmental Affairs Agency – EEAA (2017). *Environmental Impact Assessment (EIA)*. http://www.eeaa.gov.eg/en-us/services/eia.aspx

Ministry of Investment and International Cooperation – MIIC (2018a). *Corporate Social Responsibility*. http://www.miic.gov.eg/English/Investment/Pages/Corporate-Social-Responsibility.aspx

Ministry of Investment and International Cooperation – MIIC (2018b). *Investing in Development for the SDGs. Maximising Impact through partnerships and stronger private sector engagement.* http://www.miic.gov.eg/English/Resources/Publications/Periodical/DOCUMENTS/IID4SDGS2.PDF

Ministry of Investment and International Cooperation – MIIC (2017). *Investing in Development. Annual Report 2017.* http://www.miic.gov.eg/English/Resources/Publications/Periodical/DOCUMENTS/AR2017_EN.PDF

Mohie El Din, M.O, Ahmed, O (2016). *Water management in Egypt for facing the future challenges*. Journal of Advanced Research, 7, 403-412. Cairo University. https://dx.doi.org/10.1016/j.jare.2016.02.005

Nicklin, S., Cornwell, B. (2018). *Volume 3: Ensure Access to Water and Sanitation for All*. Better World. Tudor Rose Publication. http://digital.tudor-rose.co.uk/a-better-world-vol-3/index.html#IFC/z

OECD, (2018b). *Promoting and Enabling Responsible Business Conduct through Development Co-operation Efforts. Stocktaking of initiatives by donor agencies and national development finance institutions*. OECD. http://mneguidelines.oecd.org/Promoting-and-enabling-RBC-through-development-cooperation.pdf

OECD (2017a). *Contributing to the Sustainable Development Goals through responsible business conduct.* https://mneguidelines.oecd.org/global-forum/2017-GFRBC-Session-Note-Contributing-to-SDGs.pdf

OECD (2017b). *2017 Annual Report*. Annual report on the OECD Guidelines for Multinational Enterprises. http://www.oecd.org/investment/mne/annualreportsontheguidelines.htm

OECD (2017c). *Sustainable investment and responsible business conduct*. Report. http://www.oecd.org/mena/competitiveness/Sustainable-investment-and-responsible-business-conduct-report-Cairo-Nov-2017.pdf

OECD (2017d). *OECD Business and Finance Outlook 2017*. OECD Publishing, Paris. https://doi.org/10.1787/26172577

OECD (2017e). *OECD Due Diligence Guidance for Responsible Supply Chains in the Garment and Footwear Sector*. OECD Publishing, Paris. http://www.oecd.org/industry/inv/mne/responsible-supply-chains-textile-garment-sector.htm.

OECD (2017f). *Responsible business conduct and infrastructure. Session Note. 2017 Global Forum for Responsible Business Conduct.* OECD Publishing, Paris. https://mneguidelines.oecd.org/global-forum/2017-GFRBC-Session-Note-RBC-Infrastructure.pdf

OECD (2016a). *Trafficking in Persons and Corruption: Breaking the Chain,* OECD Public Governance Reviews, OECD Publishing, Paris. http://dx.doi.org/10.1787/9789264253728-en

OECD (2016b). *Annual Report on the OECD Guidelines for Multinational Enterprises 2016.* http://www.oecd.org/daf/inv/mne/2016-Annual-Report-MNE-Guidelines-EN.pdf

OECD (2015a). *Annual Report on the OECD Guidelines for Multinational Enterprises 2015.* http://mneguidelines.oecd.org/2015-Annual-Report-MNE-Guidelines-EN.pdf

OECD (2015), *OECD Guidelines on Corporate Governance of State-Owned Enterprises, 2015 Edition*, OECD Publishing, Paris, https://doi.org/10.1787/9789264244160-en.

OECD (2014a). *Annual Report on the OECD Guidelines for Multinational Enterprises 2014. Responsible Business Conduct by Sector.* https://www.oecd-ilibrary.org/docserver/mne-2014-en.pdf?expires=1549310829&id=id&accname=ocid84004878&checksum=F2021008B04DAC460266157CED2337F4

OECD (2014b). *Responsible Business Conduct Matters. OECD Guidelines for Multinational Enterprises.* http://mneguidelines.oecd.org/MNEguidelines_RBCmatters.pdf

OECD (2013). *Annual Report on the OECD Guidelines for Multinational Enterprises 2013. Responsible Business Conduct in Action*. http://www.oecd.org/daf/inv/mne/MNE-Annual-Report-2013-NCP-Activities.pdf

OECD (2010). *2010 Annual Meeting of the National Contact Points. Report by the Chair.* http://www.oecd.org/daf/inv/mne/46385752.pdf

OECD (2009). *2009 Annual Meeting of the National Contact Points. Report by the Chair.* http://www.oecd.org/daf/inv/mne/43753441.pdf

OECD (2008). *2008 Annual Meeting of the National Contact Points. Report by the Chair.* http://www.oecd.org/daf/inv/mne/41721195.pdf

Oxford Business Group (2018). Egypt. The Report 2018. https://oxfordbusinessgroup.com/egypt-2018

Oxford Dictionary (2018). *Hawala.* https://en.oxforddictionaries.com/definition/hawala

Reeve, C. (2011). *What ever happened to Cairo 2050?*. https://ww.egyptindependent.com/what-ever-happened-cairo-2050/

Rehab, I. (2018). *Facts about water resources and rationing in Egypt.* http://www.egypttoday.com/Article/2/44255/Facts-about-water-resources-and-rationing-in-Egypt

Reuters (2019). *Egypt revamps law curbing NGOs, critics unimpressed.* https://www.reuters.com/article/egypt-rights/egypt-revamps-law-curbing-ngos-critics-unimpressed-idUSL8N24F0K8

SER (2016). *Agreement on Sustainable Garment and Textile.* https://www.oecdguidelines.nl/binaries/oecd-guidelines/documents/publication/2016/3/09/agreement-on-sustainable-garment-and-textile/160309-agreement-sustainable-garment-textile.pdf

Sims, D. (2014). *Egypt Desert Dreams: Development or Disaster?* Oxford University Press. Print Version.

SOMO (2016). Dredging in the dark. An analysis of the Dutch dredging industry's failure to identify, prevent, and mitigate adverse impacts in dredging the Suez Canal. https://www.somo.nl/nl/wp-content/uploads/sites/2/2016/03/Dredging-in-the-Dark.pdf

Srour, M. (2018). *Water Scarcity and Poor Water Management Makes Life Difficult for Egyptians.* http://www.ipsnews.net/2018/09/water-scarcity-poor-water-management-makes-life-difficult-egyptians/

Transparency International (2018). *Corruption Perceptions Index 2017.* https://www.transparency.org/news/feature/corruption_perceptions_index_2017

Transparency International (2017). *Global Corruption Barometer: Citizen's Voices from Around the World.* https://www.transparency.org/news/feature/global_corruption_barometer_citizens_voices_from_around_the_world

Transparency International (2015a). *Overview of Corruption and Anti-Corruption in Egypt.* Anti-Corruption Helpdesk. https://www.transparency.org/files/content/corruptionqas/Country_profile_Egypt_2015.pdf

Transparency International (2015b). *Egypt Whistleblowing Overview.* https://www.transparency.org/whatwedo/publication/egypt_whistleblowing_overview

UNDP, ECRC (2016). *Expanding Horizons in Development: The Rising Role of the Private Sector.* http://www.eg.undp.org/content/egypt/en/home/library/poverty/publication_1.html

U.S Customs and Border Protection – CBP (2018). *Forced Labor.* U.S Department of Homeland Security. *https://www.cbp.gov/trade/programs-administration/forced-labor*

U.S Customs and Border Protection – CBP (2016). *Trade Facilitation and Trade Enforcement Act of 2015. Repeal of the Consumptive Demand Clause.* U.S Department of Homeland Security. *https://www.cbp.gov/sites/default/files/assets/documents/2016-Oct/Fact%20Sheet%20-%20Repeal%20of%20the%20Consumptive%20Demand%20Clause.pdf*

UK (2015), Modern Slavery Act, www.legislation.gov.uk/ukpga/2015/30/contents/enacted

UNICEF (2017). *Water, Sanitation, and Hygiene.* https://www.unicef.org/egypt/water-sanitation-and-hygiene

United Nations (2015). *Transforming our world: the 2030 Agenda for Sustainable Development.* https://sustainabledevelopment.un.org/post2015/transformingourworld/publication

UNDP (2016). *Supporting Businesses and its Corporate Social responsibility efforts.* http://www.eg.undp.org/content/egypt/en/home/presscenter/pressreleases/2016/10/04/supporting-businesses-and-its-corporate-social-responsibility-efforts-.html

UN GC (2019), Participant list, www.unglobalcompact.org/what-is-gc/participants (accessed 26 June 2019)

UN OHCHR (2019). *UN Treaty Body database.* Accessed 02.07.2019 https://tbinternet.ohchr.org/_layouts/15/TreatyBodyExternal/Treaty.aspx?CountryID=54&Lang=EN

UN OHCHR (2018). *The Other Infrastructure Gap: Sustainability. Human Rights and Environmental Perspectives.* https://www.ohchr.org/Documents/Publications/InfrastructureGapSummary.pdf

UN OHCHR (2017), *Repressive new NGO law deeply damaging for human rights in Egypt – Zeid, 1 June 2017*, http://www.ohchr.org/en/NewsEvents/Pages/DisplayNews.aspx?NewsID=21678&LangID=E

UNODC (2018a). *Developing a community of practice: How training prosecutors in Egypt will help in the fight against human trafficking and migrant smuggling.* https://www.unodc.org/unodc/en/human-trafficking/glo-act/developing-a-community-of-practice-how-training-prosecutors-in-egypt-will-help-in-the-fight-against-human-trafficking-and-migrant-smuggling.html

UNODC (2018b). *Global Study on Smuggling of Migrants.* https://www.unodc.org/documents/data-and-analysis/glosom/GLOSOM_2018_web_small.pdf

UNODC (2017). *UNODC and Egypt sign Memorandum of Understanding to combat corruption.* https://www.unodc.org/unodc/en/frontpage/2017/November/unodc-and-egypt-sign-memorandum-of-understanding-to-combat-corruption.html

UNODC (2013). *Corruption and the Smuggling of Migrants*. Issue Paper. https://www.unodc.org/documents/human-trafficking/2013/The_Role_Of_Corruption_in_the_Smuggling_of_Migrants_Issue_Paper_UNODC_2013.pdf

UNTC (2019). Chapter XVIII. Penal Matters. https://treaties.un.org/pages/ViewDetails.aspx?src=IND&mtdsg_no=XVIII-14&chapter=18&lang=en

UNWG (2016). *Guidance on National Action Plans on Business and Human Rights*. https://www.ohchr.org/Documents/Issues/Business/UNWG_NAPGuidance.pdf

U.S State Department (2017). *Country Reports on Human Rights Practices for 2017*. Bureau of Democracy, Human Rights and Labor. https://www.state.gov/j/drl/rls/hrrpt/humanrightsreport/index.htm#wrapper

Wirtschafter, J. (2019). *Egypt confronts water 'poverty' in shadow of Ethiopia's dam*. https://www.washingtontimes.com/news/2019/jan/2/egypt-water-anxiety-grows-over-ethiopia-dam-nile/

World Bank (2018a). *World Development Indicators*. https://data.worldbank.org/indicator/SL.TLF.TOTL.FE.ZS

World Bank (2018b). *Egypt: Enabling Private Investment and Commercial Financing in Infrastructure*. https://www.worldbank.org/en/country/egypt/publication/egypt-enabling-private-investment-and-commercial-financing-in-infrastructure

World Bank (2016). *Enterprise Surveys. What businesses experience*. http://www.enterprisesurveys.org/data/exploreeconomies/2016/egypt

World Bank (2015). *Interwoven - How the Better Work Program Improves Job and Life Quality in the Apparel Sector*, https://openknowledge.worldbank.org/bitstream/handle/10986/22699/99729.pdf?sequence=1&isAllowed=y.

World Economic Forum (2018). *The Global Competitiveness Index 2017-2018 edition. Egypt.* http://www3.weforum.org/docs/GCR2017-2018/03CountryProfiles/Standalone2-pagerprofiles/WEF_GCI_2017_2018_Profile_Egypt.pdf

Notes

[1] OECD RBC Due Diligence instruments are: the *Due Diligence Guidance for Responsible Supply Chains of Minerals from Conflict-Affected and High-Risk Areas minerals*, the *OECD-FAO Guidance on Responsible Agricultural Supply Chains extractive industries*, the *Due Diligence Guidance for Meaningful Stakeholder Engagement in the Extractive Sector,* the OECD *Due Diligence Guidance for Responsible Supply Chains in the Garment and Footwear Sector* and the OECD *Due Diligence Guidance for Responsible Business Conduct*

[2] The Egyptian stock exchange tracks 8 indices, namely the EGX30, EGX50 EWI, EGX20 Capped, EGX70, EGX100, the Banks Sector Index, the Nile Index and the S&P EGX ESG. The rationale for comparing the S&P EGX ESG with the EGX100 is that it is includes a broader range of companies, both in terms of sector and size. The EGX100 combines constituents of the EGX30 and EGX70. In addition, the list of current constituents indicated that as of today, all the 30 constituents of the S&P EGX ESG are also constituents of the EGX100. Therefore, the S&P EGX ESG as it stands today could be understood as a selection of the 30 best performing companies in terms of ESG among the 100 companies listed in the EGX100. By

comparison, the ESG30 can be understood as the top 30 companies by liquidity and activity among the 100 listed in the EGX100.

[3] The threshold of absolute water scarcity corresponds to 500 m3 of renewable water sources per capita and per year (FAO, 2016).

[4] OECD Guidelines 2011, II. Implementation Procedures to the OECD Guidelines for Multinational Enterprises. Procedural Guidance: I. National Contact Points.

[5] OECD Guidelines 2011, Commentary on the Implementation Procedures to the OECD Guidelines for Multinational Enterprises. Paragraph 9.

Chapter 8. Infrastructure connectivity

This chapter examines the current context of infrastructure development in Egypt. It reviews connectivity challenges and recent reforms to boost infrastructure investment, including private participation in infrastructure through public-private partnerships. It also proposes recommendations to overcome the remaining obstacles to improving the enabling environment for private investment in infrastructure.

Summary and policy recommendations

Infrastructure is critical for Egypt's productivity and sustained long-term economic growth. Its essential function is to enhance connectivity, which can allow firms to integrate into regional and global value chains (RGVCs). Under the right conditions, it can reduce trade and logistics costs, foster export product diversification and increase competitiveness by fostering the development of large and efficient markets. Such benefits cannot materialise without adequate infrastructure networks linking markets efficiently, predictably and sustainably. When transport costs are high, and procedures are unclear and uncertain, only large firms can avail themselves of the opportunities brought about by RGVCs. Bringing new actors into RGVCs, including Egyptian small- and medium-sized enterprises (SMEs), requires connectivity that is more readily accessible to all. Connectivity is not just important for firms in Egypt, but for households as well. It plays a critical role in enabling access to new jobs, skills development, and higher wages, as well as greater access to a diversity of goods and services. As Egypt continues to experience rapid population growth and economic and industrial transformation, the need for effective and high-value infrastructure connectivity remains crucial.

The low levels of investment in infrastructure have raised concerns that Egypt may not be able to sustain the current stock of infrastructure given its natural depreciation and aging, let alone expand it to meet growing demand. According to the Ministry of Investment and International Cooperation, in the past five years, Egypt has invested around USD 61.4 billion in infrastructure to connect governorates, enhance accessibility and mobility of goods. The Global Infrastructure Hub estimates that Egypt needs an average of USD 675 billion of investment, or 5% of GDP, between now and 2040. At current levels of spending, this translates to an investment gap of USD 230 billion per annum, or 1.7% of GDP. The infrastructure gap is especially high for critical infrastructure such as energy, telecommunications and transport. Bridging this financing gap requires a more cross-cutting approach to mobilise quality investment for connectivity infrastructure. Such endeavours are a challenge, but the payoffs from successfully improving infrastructure connectivity can be large.

While in recent years Egypt has significantly improved the quality of its trade and transport infrastructure, it still faces important infrastructure shortcomings. These include the lack of multi-modal transport, an over-reliance on roads, a rail sector in need of reform, and a fragmented port system. This leads to high transport costs and poor logistics performance compared to other countries in the region. Logistics costs in Egypt account for around 20% of GDP compared with a global average of 10-12%, and the operating costs for trucks are approximately 30-50% higher than in Lebanon and Jordan (IFC, 2013; World Bank, 2015a). Overall, such bottlenecks in infrastructure constrain economic growth by around two percentage points per year, hindering the distribution of resources and contributing to a disproportionate concentration of economic activity in metropolitan areas (EBRD, 2017).

The need to improve connectivity is acknowledged in Egypt's "Vision 2030" and its transport and infrastructure plans, which aim to increase the capacity of the transport sector and boost its share in international and regional transport volumes. To achieve these objectives, the government has embarked on a number of ambitious mega-infrastructure plans, including the new Suez Canal Zone (SCZone). Currently, the Canal handles close to 10% of global seaborne trade connecting Africa, Asia and Europe, representing an effective logistics and strategic base for ships and trade transiting the Suez Canal; it can also have significant development benefits for Egypt. Close co-ordination of logistics sector development with business operations and activity in the industrial and free zones will be crucial to meet these objectives.

Egypt's connectivity depends on how well it is positioned in global logistics networks, infrastructure and services. While the economy moved up four places (from 56th to 52nd) in the infrastructure pillar of the Global Competitiveness Index 2019 (WEF, 2019), and made considerable strides in areas such as maritime connectivity, it has much to do to improve connectivity with the rest of the world in other areas that are relevant to today's globalised world. The DHL Global Connectedness Index, which measures cross-border flows of trade, investments, information and people, reveals a low connectivity for Egypt, placing it below similar peers such as Morocco, the United Arab Emirates and Panama. While most other countries have experienced a rising trajectory since 2008, Egypt experienced the opposite in part due to the very low intra-regional integration across all four pillars (Figure 8.1) (Steven et. al, 2019). According to the Index, improving the operating environment and developing infrastructure links could have a significant positive impact on the depth of Egypt's connectivity and would further connect the economy to world markets.

Figure 8.1. Global Connectedness Index (0-100) (2005-17)

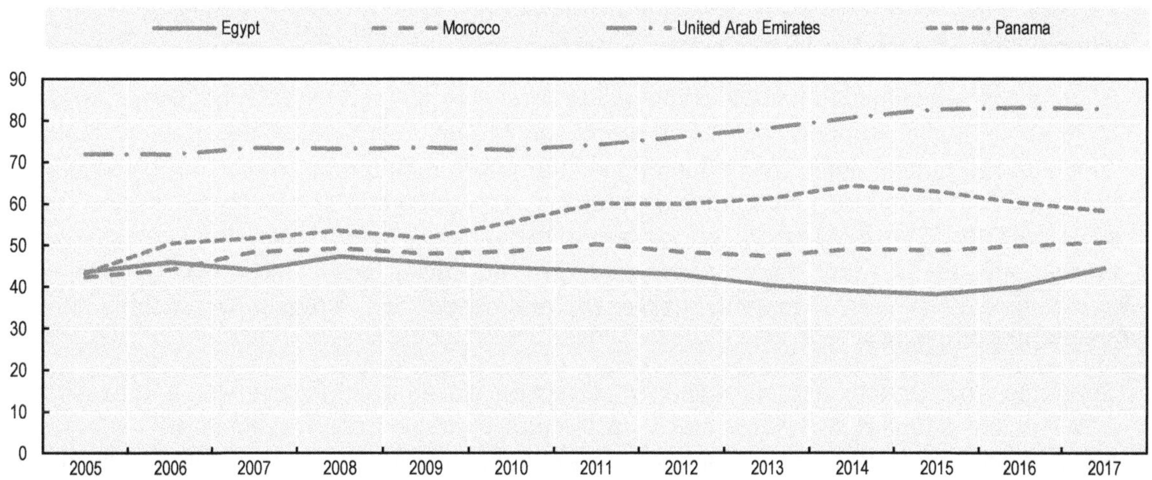

Note: Global Connectedness is measured in this report based on the depth and breadth of countries' integration with the rest of the world as manifested by their participation in international flows of products and services (trade), capital, information, and people (the four pillars of the DHL Global Connectedness Index).
Source: Steven A. Altman, Pankaj Ghemawat, and Phillip Bastian, "DHL Global Connectedness Index 2018," Deutsche Post DHL, February 2019

Egypt has adopted major economic liberalisation policies since the 1970s leading to sector-specific laws to allow private sector provision of public services, and opened the door for more private investments in infrastructure, although it only introduced a regulatory framework for public-private partnerships (PPPs) in 2010. PPPs bring some important regulatory and institutional mechanisms to improve Egypt's infrastructure delivery capacity. Yet, there is a lack of a track record, capacity and experience to develop PPPs by the PPP Central Unit, and public support for PPPs is low. While the framework is considered to be in line with international best practices, it does not replace the old sector-specific laws that regulate the procurement of infrastructure projects. This old system may still be used by the government in the future, especially in the power sector (EBRD, 2011).

Notwithstanding the recent efforts to provide a framework for public procurement, the government also needs to strengthen its planning capacity and coordination for infrastructure projects. Currently, numerous infrastructure priorities in Egypt are laid out in different strategies. Often, the allocation of budget for the national plans is an annual exercise, despite the fact that various ministries have to prepare their investment planning estimates over various time horizons such as the 5-year plans. The government plans to strengthen its fiscal planning by introducing the medium-term expenditure framework, which will set multi-year expenditure ceilings by major spending categories, including infrastructure (IMF, 2018). Such planning of current and capital expenditure within a medium-term budget framework could also ensure that infrastructure investments are sustainable and that maintenance spending is fully taken into account (IMF, 2014).

Policy recommendations

- Clarify the regulatory frameworks for infrastructure investments to provide potential investors with clear, predictable and consistent policies. Currently, the PPP Law coexists with other channels of procuring infrastructure projects such as the public utilities legislation and a number of sector-specific or project-specific laws. The government should build a clearer and more transparent regulatory framework governing infrastructure activities.
- Provide more opportunities for private participation in infrastructure, including through PPPs. Despite Egypt's robust PPP regulatory framework, private sector participation in the infrastructure and energy sectors has been limited.
- Engage with stakeholders in local communities to ensure support for PPP projects. Currently, there is low public support for PPP projects, partly due to a lack of adequate community consultation to guide project selection and secure public support for projects. In order to gain more public support for infrastructure projects, the government needs to involve more systematically all the relevant stakeholders from the earliest stages of infrastructure planning to ensure support and that their needs – as well as social, economic, environmental and governance risks – are correctly assessed, addressed and adequately reflected in the contractual structures.
- Strengthen the capacity and co-ordination across the government for planning and assessing infrastructure priorities to ensure that infrastructure strategies are well integrated with other types of planning such as industrial development strategies and land use plans. For example, infrastructure plans in special economic zones such as the SCZone should be well connected with the hinterland. Achieving this also requires better co-ordination between different branches of government.
- Prioritise the completion and upgrade of the rail lines as well as other projects that will facilitate multi-modal freight and passenger traffic. Despite ambitious modernisation projects currently undertaken, the rail network is still not competitive enough. Further strengthening the legal framework and actively promoting private investments in railway projects could make the railway system a reliable alternative to congested roads.
- Improve coordination of port and multimodal transport planning to facilitate more river-based transport. Currently, ports contribute less than 1% of inland transport, which is mainly due to the poor integration of river transport to the country's transport networks.
- Further strengthen the legal framework for public procurement to increase tender participation, supplier diversity and a more competitive procurement environment. While the 2016 Law on Public Procurement introduces procedures to enhance transparency and reduce discretion in public procurement, the consistent application and enforcement of the law by the involved procurement entities is weak.
- Ensure that infrastructure projects are grounded in efficiency rather than fiscal motivations. Building capacity among government entities to assess value for money over the lifecycle of an infrastructure asset is crucial to make sure that investments benefits users and society at large.

Connectivity matters for Egypt's economy

In recent years, the setting up of highly connected locations such as Dubai, Singapore and Panama highlights how countries with regional transhipment ports have leveraged global connectivity to deepen their role in the global economy by using hubs, gateways or ports as drivers of regional economic growth (OECD, 2013). A common trend is the development of logistics zones to capture opportunities from global outsourcing and offshoring (Rodrigue, 2017). Egypt's recent expansion of the Suez Canal, coupled with reforms to attract foreign investment to establish export-oriented industries, aim to transform the country into a global logistics hub and increase its participation in regional and global value chains (RGVCS).

More broadly, connectivity can be understood as infrastructure supporting cross-border trade and investment flows. The connectivity of individual economies, or how they are positioned in global trade networks, matters for the cost of trade, competitiveness, and integration in RGVCs. The performance of these networks sustaining trade such as shipping, logistics and data, is influenced by private investments in physical infrastructure, such as roads, railroads, and airports.

Key infrastructure challenges

Egypt's economic infrastructure, including transport, energy, ICT and water resources and the associated services is vital for industrial development. It is not only used as an input in production sectors, but also contributes to making Egyptian industrial output competitive in domestic, regional and international markets. Yet, numerous deficiencies across all sectors of infrastructure currently limit the contribution made by infrastructure to the country's industrial development.

Egypt has made progress in terms of infrastructure networks but transport costs are very high

In recent years, Egypt has significantly improved its performance under the indicator of "quality of trade and infrastructure" (e.g. ports, roads, airports, information technology) of the World Bank's *Logistic Performance Index* between 2010 and 2018 (Figure 8.2). According to this Index, Egypt advanced its score from 2.22 in 2010 to 2.82 in 2018 on a scale from 1 (worst) to 5 (best), ranking from 106th (out of 155) in 2010 to 58th (out of 160) in 2018. Yet, despite significant progress achieved since 2010, Egypt still faces some important infrastructure shortcomings as reflected in a number of infrastructure stock indicators and perception assessments (Table 8.1). Currently, there is no large logistics provider with a consistent distribution of services around road-based transport in Egypt. More than one third of the road fleet is owned by small fragmented firms, with cooperatives or public firms owning the rest. This poses challenges for big consignments and leads to a high cost of domestic transport.

These high transport costs make Egypt a relative outlier in terms of its logistics performance compared to its regional peers (Figure 8.3). Because of Egypt's high logistics costs, which account for around 20% of GDP compared with a global average of 10-12%, and inadequate infrastructure, operating costs for trucks are approximately 30-50% higher in Egypt compared to countries such as Lebanon and Jordan (IFC, 2013; World Bank, 2015). Furthermore, transport costs can vary by a factor of 2.5 across Egypt, with more distant regions experiencing worse delays. Inefficient logistics also adds significant cost and time to trade operations, especially for agribusiness exporters. This hinders the distribution of resources and contributes to a disproportionate concentration of economic activity in metropolitan areas (EBRD, 2017).

In order to improve the logistics system and address the high logistical costs, the Ministry of Transportation is currently planning to establish a network of logistical areas and villages. A law was drafted to organise the establishment and management of logistical areas and villages to establish seven logistical cities in Damietta, Sohag, 10th of Ramadan, Borg El Arab, Sadat and Beni Suef, and 6th of October. The establishment of the logistical areas and villages is expected to contribute to industrial and trade promotion, but also to increase investments and further reduce logistical costs.

Figure 8.2. The World Bank's Logistic Performance Index, Infrastructure Indicator

(score from 1 to 5 (best))

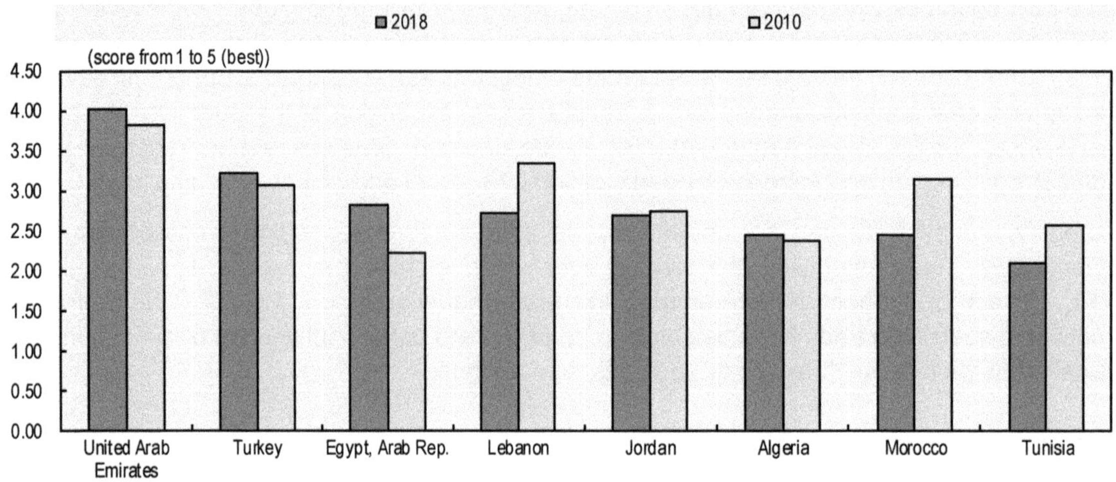

Source: World Bank Logistics Performance Index database

Table 8.1. Selected infrastructure indicators across selected peer countries

	Egypt	Morocco	Panama	Saudi Arabia	Singapore	South Africa	Tunisia	Turkey	United Arab Emirates	Middle East and North Africa
Electricity										
Access to electricity (% of population) 2016	100.0	100.0	93.4	100.0	100.0	84.2	100.0	100.0	100.0	98.0
Electric power transmission and distribution losses (% of output) 2014	11	15	14	7	2	8	15	15	7	14
Quality of electricity supply (1-7 (best), WEF 2017-2018	5.0	5.6	5.2	6.2	6.9	3.9	5.1	4.4	6.5	5.1
ICT										
Mobile telephone subscriptions (per 100 people) 2017-2018	114	121	172	158	147	142	126	97	204	140
Individuals using the internet (% of population) 2016	41	58	54	74	81	54	50	58	91	43
Fixed broadband internet subscriptions (per 100 people) 2017-2018	5.2	3.7	9.5	10.8	25.4	2.8	5.6	13.6	13.3	10.3
Transport										
Quality of roads, 1-7 (best), WEF[1] 2017-2018	3.9	4.5	4.4	4.8	6.3	4.4	3.7	5.0	6.4	4.4
Quality of railroad infrastructure, 1-7 (best), WEF[1] 2017-2018	3.3	3.9	4.5	3.3	5.9	3.5	2.8	n/a	3.3	4.4

	Egypt	Morocco	Panama	Saudi Arabia	Singapore	South Africa	Tunisia	Turkey	United Arab Emirates	Middle East and North Africa
Liner shipping connectivity index (maximum value in 2004 = 100)³ 2016	62.5	64.7	53.4	61.8	122.7	37.1	6.3	49.6	70.6	-
Quality of port infrastructure, 1-7 (best), WEF¹ 2017-2018	4.7	5.0	6.2	4.7	6.7	4.8	3.3	4.5	6.2	4.4
Growth of Container port traffic (TEU: 20 foot equival. unit, CAGR, %) 2007-16	24	76[1]	36	45	9	14	14	47	35	38
Quality of air transport infrastructure, 1-7 (best), WEF¹ 2017-2018	5.1	4.8	6.0	4.9	6.9	5.6	3.9	5.4	6.6	4.6

1. data for Morocco is 2008 instead of 2007

Source: World Bank World Development Indicators database, World Economic Forum Competitiveness Index (2018).

Figure 8.3. Egypt is an outlier relative to its peers in terms of logistics costs and trade openness

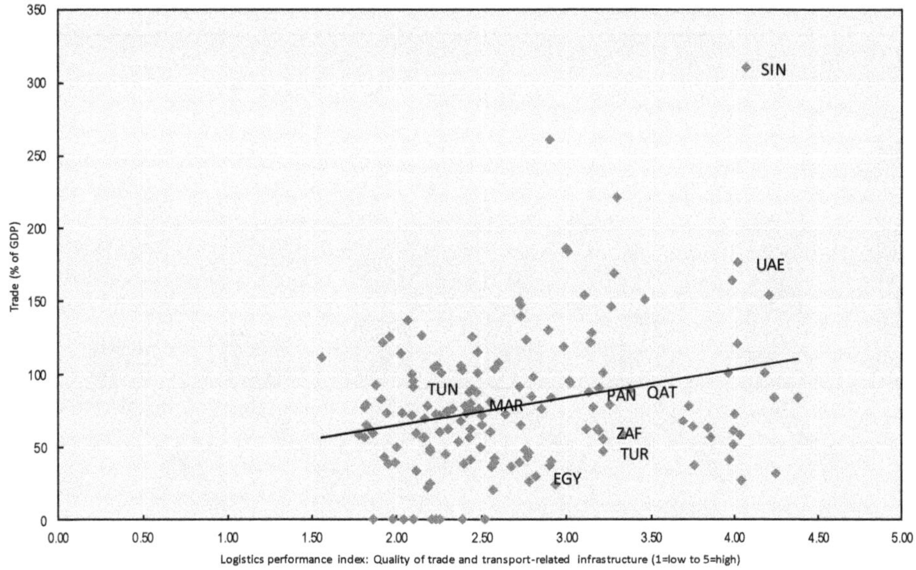

Source: World Bank Development Indicators

Transport connectivity

Transport infrastructure has improved recently, but multimodal connectivity is still lacking

Current transport infrastructure bottlenecks and lack of multimodality act as key constraints to trade, mobility, job creation and service delivery across Egypt (World Bank, 2015). The transport sector in Egypt serves an area of around 1 million km^2 and a population of close to 100 million. While road infrastructure is relatively dense and of good quality, with 95% of its roads paved, all alternative transport systems remain inadequate. For freight, there is not yet an integrated scheme that would encourage intermodal rail-road-river transport. More than 99% of Egypt's international freight relies on maritime transport, both in terms of volume and external logistics costs (EIB, 2013), while roads, followed by railways (4%) and the Nile River (1%), move more than 95% of domestic freight. Trucks move 90% of the country's domestic freight, but given that the biggest trucking companies have at most a 10-truck fleet, this leads to an inefficient system where quality is not considered and creates a missing link in Egyptian export chains. While most OECD and MENA countries also rely heavily on road transport for domestic logistics, they tend to use rail services in a higher percentage than Egypt does. Because of road congestion in Egypt, railways could be an alternative for freight transport, but the rail network does not offer a viable alternative to the road network at present.

According to the World Bank Enterprise Survey of Egypt (2016), over 17.4% of domestic firms reveal that transport is a major constraint to their current operations (Figure 8.4). While this is lower than Morocco's 27% and slightly below the MENA average of 20%, it is significantly higher than in peer economies in the region (Tunisia 7%, Turkey 6.5%). Compared to their domestic peers, foreign manufacturing firms face higher constraints to their operations in Egypt. Around 25% identified infrastructure in Egypt as a major constraint, as compared to 11% in Tunisia, 4.1% in South Africa, 3.6% in Turkey, or only 0.6% in Panama. While these obstacles apply to firms across the whole of Egypt, they are less important for those in special economic zones such as the Suez Canal region (9.4% compared to 32.4% in Southern Upper Egypt).

Figure 8.4. In general, foreign firms have higher transport constraints than domestic firms

(percentage of firms listing transport as a major constraint)

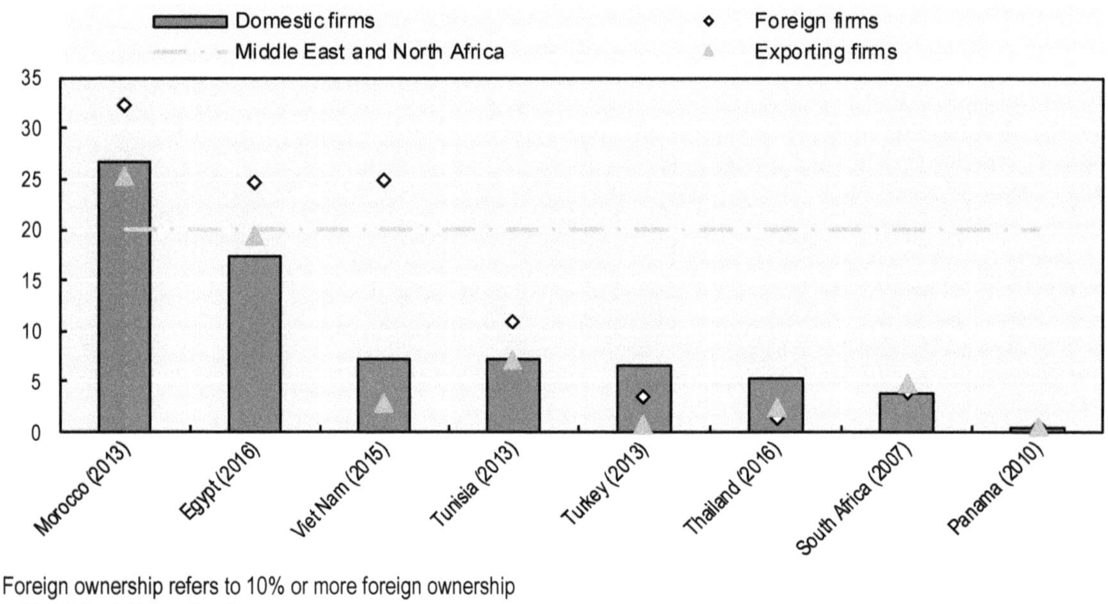

Note: Foreign ownership refers to 10% or more foreign ownership
Source: World Bank Enterprise Survey

Despite government efforts to address traffic congestion, this remains a serious problem especially in urban areas, in part due to gasoline price subsidies and low road maintenance. In Greater Cairo, where the density of the most heavily inhabited areas is 1500 inhabitants/km², which is almost triple the global average (World Bank, 2015), commuting times amount to 90 minutes. Past attempts to address congestion and road safety at the city level have resulted in modest increases in road construction, but the results have been mixed.

The dependence of the Egyptian logistics chain on road services makes it even more vital for these problems to be corrected to decrease export time and increase product quality, thereby opening up new markets for Egyptian exports. Recognising the importance of facilitating cross-border movement of goods, in 2016 Egypt started preparations to join the International Road Transports Convention system, which is the only universal customs transit system in existence for road transport (IRU, 2016). Such a system would further increase the transit volumes in Egypt and would strengthen its strategic position as a logistics and transport hub between Europe, Asia and Africa.

Infrastructure accessibility varies greatly across regions

The road network is mostly concentrated in and around Cairo and the Nile Delta area. A substantial part of the road network outside those areas remains substandard and needs upgrading, despite major improvements in connecting the major cities of Upper Egypt to the Greater Cairo Area. For Egyptian firms, the lack of road connection to rural areas leads to up to 40% of losses in the value of products transported from Upper Egypt to wholesaler. This may also explain why only a small share of Egyptian firms export to global markets (EBRD, 2017). Significant improvements in transport and logistics infrastructure will help to spread economic activity outside metropolitan Egypt and help increase market access and agricultural income for farmers especially in rural Upper Egypt, where they experience long shipping times. The government has focused on further improving infrastructure accessibility across the country. For instance, the Ministry of Transportation developed horizontal roads[1] connecting locked governorates in Upper Egypt and Oasis to other governorates near the Red Sea and helping to spread economic activity outside of metropolitan areas while increasing market access and exports from Red Sea ports.

Limited upgrading has left the rail network sector of poor quality and uncompetitive

A public monopoly on the existing railway network in Egypt has led to under-investments and the need to update services and improve safety. The railway system is the oldest in the world, after the United Kingdom. The network composed of around 9 800 kilometres of railways is currently being used for freight and passenger services, providing relevant supply chain links between the key seaports and the main cities. Due to under-investment and reliance on low fare passenger traffic, the system is operated inefficiently with low environmental performances. The lack of ICT also makes rail transport risky. An estimated 85% of the signals in the system are mechanical and in need of maintenance or replacement, while only 15% are electrical signals (Egyptian National Railways, 2018). Discussions on the need to reform the state-owned Egyptian National Railway have led to the recently approved Law No. 20 of 2018, which ended state monopoly over the national rail system projects and gave the private sector the legal framework to be able to participate in such projects (Amereller, 2018).

Egypt suffers from a fragmented port system with considerable excess capacity

In contrast to roads and railways, port infrastructure has been the main recipient of investments by the Egyptian government over the past decade. Yet, the lack of a co-ordinated port and multimodal transport planning and development strategy has resulted in a fragmented port and maritime terminal system with considerable excess capacity even in some key economic regions, such as the Southern region. Egypt's ports are geographically fragmented (World Bank, 2015a). Main challenges facing the Egyptian ports include: (i) limited multimodal connectivity regarding rail access and high speed road connection to ports; (ii) lack of logistical platforms; (iii) IT infrastructure not fully compliant with international standards on safety and security (EIB, 2013).

Egypt has 1 850 km of navigable waterways with more than 40 ports, of which 12 are commercial ports, but they currently account for less than 1% of inland transport in the country. This low level is mainly due to the poor integration of river transport in the country's transport networks (EBRD, 2013). Instead, Egypt's ports handle the majority of its international trade. Among the most important ports in terms of capacity are Alexandria, the biggest port in Egypt, and the Port of Dekheila, which is a natural extension to the Port of Alexandria, followed by Damietta and Port Said (Table 8.2) jointly handling 85% of Egypt's cargo tonnage and 92% of its containerised trade. Alexandria Port is by far the most important, handling about 60% of Egypt's foreign trade. There is also a relatively elevated concentration of container traffic in ports with a high trans-shipment activity, of which Damietta and Port Said handle the majority.

Table 8.2. Commercial Port Capacity in Egypt

	Maximum capacity		Area	
	Cargo (million TEUs)	Containers (Million TEUs)	Land (km²)	Total (km²)
Alexandria	37.9	1.0	1.60	8.40
El Dekheila	27.1	1.0	3.50	6.20
Damietta	19.75	1.2	7.9	11.80
Port Said	12.78	0.8	1.30	3.00
El Arish	1.2	0	0.05	0.23
East Port Said	12.0	2.7	70.60	72.10
Suez	6.6	0	2.30	
Petroleum Dock	4.14	0	1.16	162.40
Adabiya	7.93	0	0.85	
Sokhna Port	8.5	0.4	22.30	87.80
Hurghada	0	0	0.04	9.94
Safaga	6..37	0	0.62	57.11
El Tour	0.38	0	0.43	1.65
Nuweiba	1.9	0	0.4	9.9
Sharm El Sheikh	0	0	0.2	88.31
Total	**146.55**	**7.1**	**113.25**	**518.84**

Source: Ministry of Transport. Maritime Transport Sector (MTS). The Egyptian Port's Capacity http://www.mts.gov.eg/en/content/275/1-83-The-Egyptian-Ports-Capacity

Despite improved maritime transport in Egypt, the ports transhipment function is still limited

The Suez Canal, which plays such a strategic role in international trade, mainly benefits Egypt through the tariffs collected from ships and vessels that cross it (UNECA, 2015). But the potential opportunities offered by the Canal to attract foreign manufacturers that are looking for locations close to markets in Europe, the Middle East and Africa are still to be seized. In contrast to other canals and straits, the port transhipment function related to the Suez Canal traffic is partly captured by other ports in the region such as Djibouti in the South of the Canal, and Piraeus in the North, as well as a range of other transhipment ports in the Mediterranean. In comparison, the three main ports along the Malacca/Singapore Straits (Singapore, Port Klang and Tanjung Pelepas) capture almost all of the transhipment cargo in the region, whereas the main ports at both sides of the Panama Canal also capture a dominant share of the regional transhipment cargo, even if there are various large transhipment hubs in the Caribbean. Maersk is now using East Port Said as one of its main hub locations, moving activities from some Mediterranean hubs to Suez, but almost all shipping companies use several options, so there is a need for transhipment ports to continuously improve the attractiveness and competitiveness of the Egyptian ports. In order to achieve more transhipment, ports along the Suez Canal need to attract more calls from shipping lines.

A preliminary assessment of Suez Canal ports seems to indicate that main bottlenecks could consist of relatively high ship-turnaround times and the low level of value-added services for shipping firms compared to its regional competitors such as Turkey and Morocco (OECD, 2017a) (Figure 8.5). The great majority of world ports manage to achieve average ship turn around in under two days, most ports in Asia even less than one day. Another bottleneck for Suez Canal ports is the fairly low level of value added services for shipping firms. Other transshipment ports are developing services such as ship repair, value added logistics and well-developed feedering and short-sea services. Average ship turn-around time is a very relevant performance indicator, since longer than expected port times present additional costs to shipping lines, which might offset any cost advantage that the Suez Canal ports might be able to offer due to lower port labour costs.

Figure 8.5. Med container ship turnaround times per country in 2014

In days, 2014

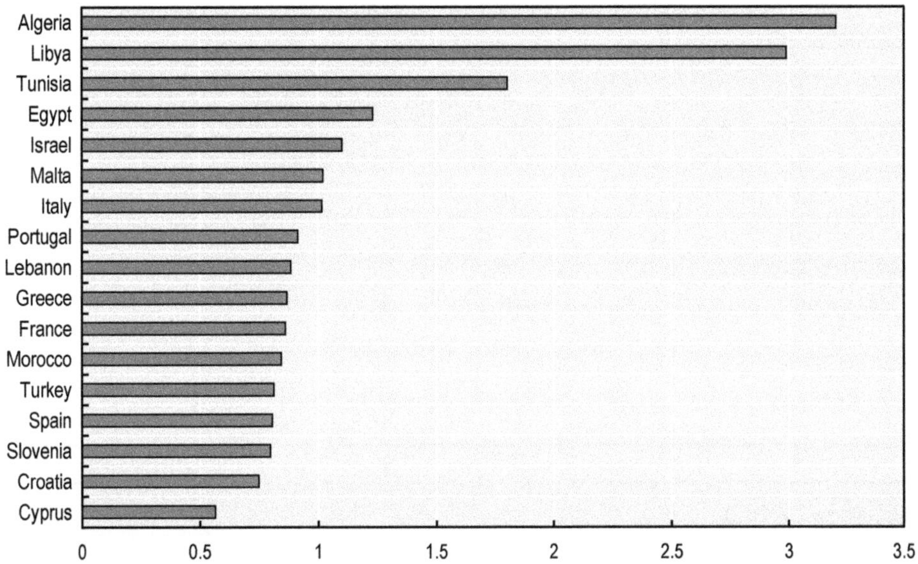

Note: The calculations of ship turn-around times are based on vessel movement data over May 2014 and from Lloyds Intelligence Unit. The estimated coverage of this database is > 95% of all vessel movements. For the purpose of this analysis only fully cellular container ships with GT >100 were taken into account. The database has per vessel call an arrival time at berth and a departure time from berth, allowing for calculation of duration of port stays. For our analysis all port stays were excluded that were smaller than 0.20 days and longer than 7 days. In this way, bunkering calls and extreme values were excluded. The database that resulted included 38,843 port calls in May.
Source: ITF/OECD elaborations based on data from Lloyds Intelligence Uni

Energy and ICT connectivity

Access to electricity has greatly improved, but its reliability remains a concern for investors

Access to reliable and affordable electricity is a key decision factor for investors in higher-value added industries where electricity is a major component of their cost structures. According to the World Bank Doing Business Report 2020, Egypt has improved the reliability of electricity supply by implementing automated systems to monitor and report power outages (World Bank, 2020). This performance is relatively better than the average of the MENA region, but it is still lower than some of its regional peers (Table 8.3). Egypt also performs well compared with its peers in terms of obtaining a permanent electricity connection for a newly constructed warehouse. Until recently, the economy was facing significant electricity supply problems, causing repeated power outages around the country, which led to a low quality of electricity supply (U.S. Energy Information Administration, 2014).

For years, energy subsidies have created significant distortions in the economy. They are partly responsible for bottlenecks in supply chains and declining investments across the supply chain, including oil and gas exploration and production. Although Egypt is currently a relatively low carbon economy, its carbon emissions per GDP and energy consumption per GDP, are among the highest in the region and almost double the global average (World Bank, 2015b). As a consequence, there are limited commercial incentives for efficiency in the provision of energy supply.

Table 8.3. Getting electricity in selected MENA countries

	Getting Electricity Rank	Procedures (number)	Time (days)	Cost (% of income per capita)	Reliability of supply and transparency of tariff index (0-8)	Price of electricity (US cents per kWh)
Algeria	102	5	84	967	5	2.1
Egypt	77	5	53	180.2	5	9.7
Jordan	69	5	55	285.3	6	24.6
Morocco	34	4	31	1308.8	6	12.4
Oman	35	5	30	50.0	7	6.0
Saudi Arabia	18	2	35	27.9	6	7.4
Tunisia	63	4	65	719.1	6	7.7
Turkey	41	4	34	62.3	5	8.9
United Arab Emirates	1	2	7	0.0	8	10.9
Middle East and North Africa	86	4.4	63.5	419.6	4.4	
OECD	43	4.4	74.8	61.0	7.4	

Source: World Bank Doing Business 2020.

The government has recently implemented a reform programme targeting gradual removal of energy subsidies, which is critical to enhance its power generation capacity and the industry's ability to support industrial development. According to the authorities, energy subsidies were reduced by over three percentage points of GDP in the FY20 budget compared to FY17. In the electricity sector, prices were already raised by an average of 30% in July 2016, and by another 40% in July 2017.

Reforming other subsidies such as fuel will also help reduce traffic on the roads (World Bank, 2015b). This will facilitate the elimination of existing distortions to the costs of production factors that have disproportionately benefited energy-intensive industries (IMF, 2018).

Egypt has not yet managed to diversify its power supply for sustainable industrial development

Wind and solar energy represent two good alternatives for producing new and renewable energy in Egypt. The country is endowed with among the best solar resources in the world, as the number of sun rising hours in the remote areas can vary between 2300 to 4000 hours per year (Ministry of Petroleum, 2018). But despite this, it has not yet managed to diversify its power supply and is still relying on fuel consuming power plants for over 60% of its power supply. While all citizens have access to electricity, which has resulted in improved education and health outcomes, companies requiring significant energy supply still face numerous challenges.

The government has shown commitment to deepen the use of renewables both at the policy and strategic level. In 2014, it adopted the Sustainable Energy Strategy 2035 to deepen the use of renewables with a target of meeting 20% of its electricity needs from renewable sources by 2022 from just 3% today with wind providing 12%, hydro power 5.8%, and solar 2.2% (UNECA, 2015). This was followed by the Feed-in-Tariff Act to encourage private investments in the renewable energy sector (EIU, 2018). Importantly, the Act allocates state-owned lands to renewable power projects, for purchasing electricity from solar and wind renewable sources, makes it mandatory for electricity companies to source and trade the energy produced via these projects, and provides attractive tax incentives for private investments in renewable projects (UNECA, 2015). Another major power sector policy reform is the new Electricity Law (Law No. 87 of 2015), which was approved in 2015 to gradually liberalise the electricity transmission market towards a competitive model where private sector producers can sell electricity directly to consumers at market prices. Such policies have already led to a number of projects, particularly in the Zaafarana area of the Gulf of Suez, where the wind speed reaches 10m/second and the capacity for renewables is higher.

ICT infrastructure has been expanding fast in recent years. Further investments can catalyse industrial growth and promote high-tech industries

ICT infrastructure in Egypt has expanded significantly in recent years, driven by government initiatives as well as by the private sector. This expansion was facilitated by a partial deregulation and liberalisation of the ICT sector, especially in wireless and data services areas (UNCTAD, 2011). ICT also contributed to improving the way in which services are delivered to industry and indirectly to the industrial development of the country, which in turn provides skilled and productive human resources for the manufacturing sector (MCIT, 2016). The sector currently represents 3.9% of GDP, and the government aims to achieve 8.4% of GDP by 2020, creating 250 000 direct job opportunities. The government recently introduced 4G data connectivity and issued four 4G LTE licences in 2016, accelerating further the growth of the sector. Currently, there are four mobile telecom providers namely Vodafone Egypt, Etisalat Misr, Orange Egypt and WE, some of which are investing heavily in network expansion, quality of service improvements and new technologies ((Egypt Independent, 2017). According to the Mobile Connectivity Index[2] 2018, which measures the performance of countries against the key enablers of mobile internet adoption – infrastructure, affordability, consumer readiness, and content and services – Egypt is a "transitioner" in the MENA region (54.2), similar to Jordan (54.2) and above Algeria (51.6), but below its regional peers such as Morocco (57.7), Tunisia (60.3) (GSMA, 2019).

To keep up with increases in demand, the fixed and mobile broadband transmission capacity overall will need to grow at double-digit rates for the near future. Significant investments are still necessary to expand broadband access and to alleviate overloaded networks that affect the quality of services. While the coverage of mobile phones surpasses the population (114 subscriptions per 100 inhabitants), this is lower than the MENA regional average of 140 or other comparator countries such as Morocco (121) or Tunisia (126). Egypt also faces medium to high barriers in internet accessibility (McKinsey, 2016). By 2017, the internet penetration rate reached 47% (although Egypt has the largest population of internet users in the MENA region), compared to Tunisia (64), Morocco (65) and Turkey (71) (World Bank, 2020). The government's strategy includes structural measures to accelerate private sector participation in ICT to expand basic infrastructure including the broadband optic fibre networks, cloud computing infrastructure, in addition to submarine cables. Better ICT infrastructure is also expected to increase the volume of e-commerce given that Egypt has the largest population of prospective online shoppers in the Arab world (MCIT, 2016).

Taking stock of public and private investments in infrastructure

Estimated investment gap in infrastructure amounts to USD 675 billion or 5% of GDP until 2040

Infrastructure investments rebounded in 2013 when the idea that infrastructure would revive growth was the main driving principle of an economic revival programme that was introduced in August 2013. The government then allocated USD 3.2 billion in additional infrastructure spending (1.2% of 2012 GDP) to help raise GDP growth from 2.3% to 3.5%, reduce unemployment from 13% to 9% and reduce the government's budget deficit from 14% to 9% of GDP (ibid). Data by the Central Bank of Egypt suggests that the government is still the main provider of infrastructure, investing over 56% of total public investments in economic infrastructure in FY 2016-17, up from 47% in FY 2007-08 (Figure 8.6). Private sector investments in infrastructure have been only 17-20% of total investments.

Figure 8.6. Public and private investments in economic infrastructure assets

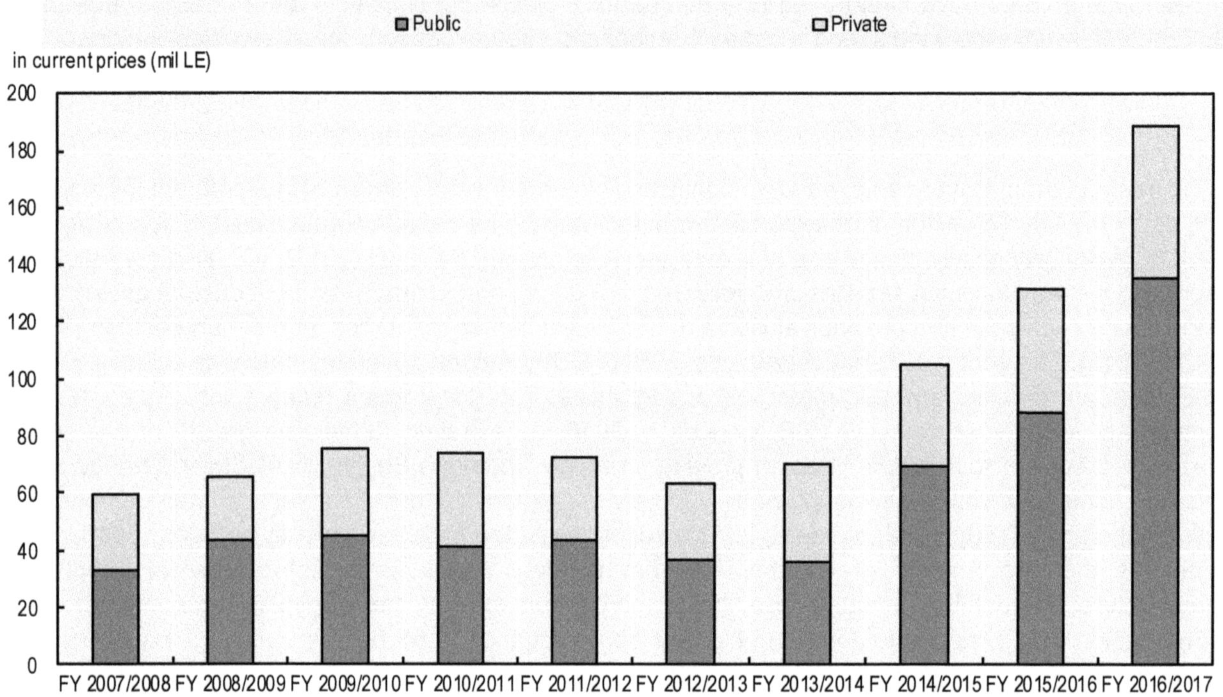

Note: Economic infrastructure covers investments in "Electricity", "Water", "Drainage", "Construction and Building", "Transportation and Storage", "Communications", "Information", and "Suez Canal".
Source: Central Bank of Egypt

According to recent estimates by the Global Infrastructure Hub, under a 4% GDP growth assumption each year[3], Egypt's investment needs are USD 675 billion or 5% of GDP on average until 2040 (Figure 8.7). At current levels of spending, the investment gap in Egypt amounts to around USD 230 billion (or 1.7% of GDP) across all sectors, but it is more prevalent in cross-border infrastructure and in energy and transport. With such a high gap, there are concerns that the economy has reached a level of infrastructure investment that is unlikely to sustain the current stock of infrastructure given its natural depreciation and aging (UNIDO, 2017). Such concerns are also valid across the African continent, where the infrastructure deficiency alone is estimated to lower companies' productivity by 40%, which leads to increased production and distribution costs, lowers competitiveness and deters the adoption of new innovation technologies (ibid).

Closing such a high infrastructure gap is expected to have a significant impact on jobs in Egypt, especially given that it is only one of the two countries in the region together with Saudi Arabia to employ more workers in the infrastructure sector than in construction. Similarly, across the MENA region, meeting annual investment needs would lead to around 2 million direct jobs and 2.5 million direct, indirect and induced infrastructure related jobs throughout the region.

Figure 8.7. Infrastructure investments in Egypt needs to be scaled up significantly

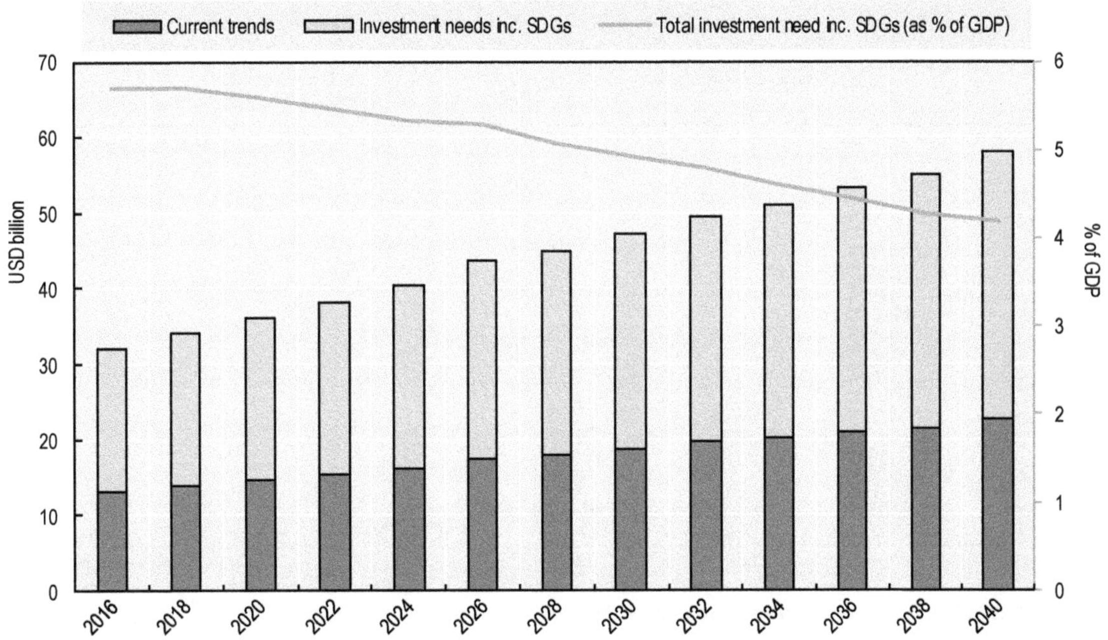

Source: Global Infrastructure Hub, Global Infrastructure Outlook 2016

Private sector participation in infrastructure has been limited, leading to irregular or low quality of service provision.

The magnitude of private investments in transport, municipal and energy infrastructure sectors has been rather limited, leading to irregular or low quality service provision. The prevalence of private ownership is still low, while foreign ownership is even more limited. It is only in recent years that Egypt has been able to attract considerable private investments in infrastructure, owing to a national policy encouraging private investments. For example, the number of infrastructure projects with private participation went from only two in 2016 to 25 in 2017. Most of these investments were in renewable energy, particularly within the Benban Solar Park (World Bank PPI, 2018). Nevertheless, there are still large gaps in terms of private investments at the sectoral level. The sectors requiring more investments by 2040 are electricity, roads, telecoms and water (Figure 8.8). The largest gaps are in the electricity and road sectors, which will require investments of around USD 251 billion and USD 212 billion respectively. Some sectors also present a large gap between the relative investment needs and current investment, particularly for road and water infrastructure, where there is an estimated gap of around USD 177 billion and USD 49 billion respectively. The government as well as private institutions will need to mobilise taxes, savings, capital markets, and private equity to finance this multibillion-dollar infrastructure gap.

Despite requiring less significant amounts of investment compared to other sectors, railways have increasingly been a high priority for investment. Egypt has been working to upgrade its railway system with some capital investments from development banks and foreign contractors. For instance, in 2017, Thalis, the French group was awarded a EUR 109 million contract to renovate a signalling system on a 208-km route between Cairo and Alexandria, and the World Bank financed more than 90% of it (Oxford Business Group, 2017). Siemens was awarded a similar contract for upgrades along the Port Said and Benha route and between Zagazig and Abu Kebir. Other similar deals include a USD 600 million contract with China Railway Construction Corporation to renovate tracks in necessary areas and a USD 125 million loan to Egypt National Railways from the EBRD to hire a private company to procure more rolling stock and for the maintenance of its fleet (ibid). This investment can help bring the much needed expertise and enhance competition and innovation.

Figure 8.8. Egypt infrastructure: current trends and relative investment needs 2016-40

In USD billion

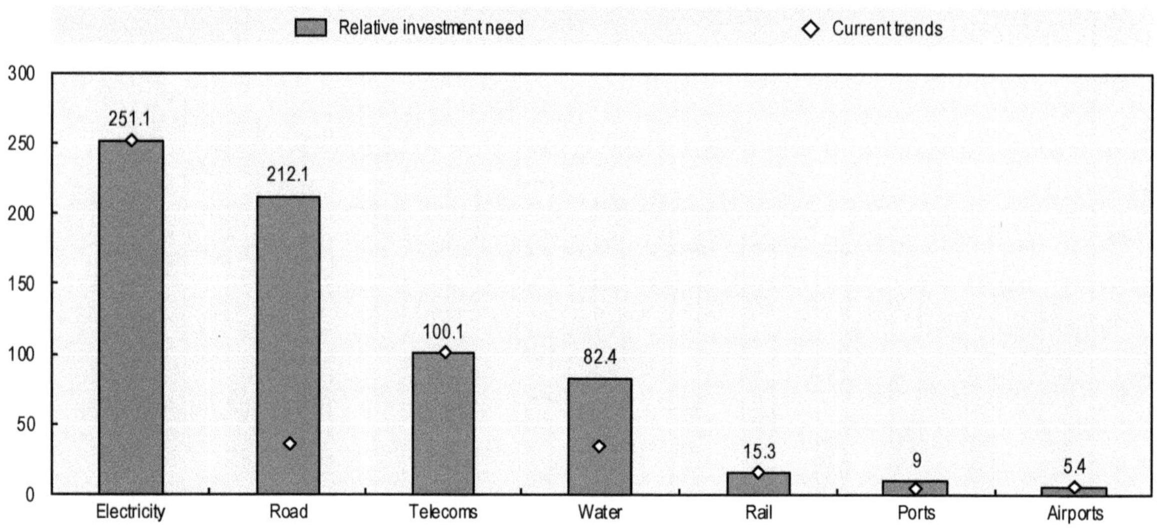

Source: Global Infrastructure Hub, Global Infrastructure Outlook 2014

Establishing an enabling environment for connectivity and infrastructure investments

The government's goal of making infrastructure networks attractive for private participation is made easier when infrastructure policy priorities are fully embedded in the country's economic development strategies and are supported by a clear regulatory and institutional environment. This helps to secure greater policy co-ordination and alignment across levels of government and to assure investors of the long-term political commitment to infrastructure development. This section will focus on Egypt's current strategies for developing connectivity infrastructure and the accompanying regulations to achieve such strategies.

The infrastructure development strategy

Developing a strategy for connectivity infrastructure involves developing integrated strategies between trade, investment and infrastructure, dealing with the governance of infrastructure, and infrastructure financing. Integrated strategies should focus on including facilitation measures and multimodal infrastructure planning that can further facilitate trade and investment. At the same time, these strategies require overcoming a range of co-ordination and government capacity challenges, including: identifying infrastructure needs across sectors and regions; appropriate prioritisation of these projects; ensuring that they are affordable and represent value for money; preparing and procuring projects adequately; monitoring asset performance and properly scrutinising any necessary modification.

The Sustainable Development Strategy, Egypt Vision 2030 and the Transport Sector Master Plan

Infrastructure development is high on Egypt's agenda. The Sustainable Development Strategy, Egypt Vision 2030 recognises infrastructure development as one of the priority areas to improve competitiveness, alongside developing human resources and skills to support the development of a modern industry and innovation, and improving governance to maximise the positive effects of reforms. In particular, the

Economic Pillar of Egypt Vision 2030 incorporates infrastructure mega-projects. The most important mega-project is the expansion of the Suez Canal and the Development of the Suez Canal Economic Zone.

Other mega projects include constructing and rehabilitating 3 000 kilometres of roads; reclaiming one million acres of land; renewable energy projects; and fostering development in the Golden Triangle for touristic, industrial, commercial, and agricultural activities (Box 8.1). For transport projects, aims include achieving multi-modal transport chains and enhancing the role of the private sector in investing or participating in transport sector projects (Egypt Vision 2030, 2015).

The targets established in Egypt's Vision 2030 are achieved through five-year sustainable development plans (2021-25 and 2026-30), where the government sets its work programme objectives, the budget expenditures as well as the economic and social reform programme priorities. The current plan, which exceptionally focuses on the period 2018-20, recognises investments in big national projects such as the national housing programme, the national road network and the expansion of subway systems as a strategic priority (Ministry of Planning, Monitoring and administrative Reform, 2017). For 2018, the government plans to spend around USD 36 billion, 60% of which would be injected into transport infrastructure, housing, public utilities, irrigation and electricity among other priority investments to achieve social and human development across the country. The budget also includes a 6% of investments in local development programmes, particularly targeting governorates of Upper Egypt, marginalised border zones, and squatter settlements (ibid).

Box 8.1. Selected Infrastructure Projects for Economic Development to 2030

The Egyptian government has introduced a list of mega projects that are expected to jumpstart the economic recovery and continue to facilitate internal and cross-border transportation and trade.

The Suez Canal Area Development Project

The Suez Canal Area Development Project stands as a high priority for Egypt. It comprises three main components aimed at reinforcing the position of the Suez Canal as a global maritime trade route, and exploiting its potential for investment attraction and export-oriented growth:

- The "New Suez Canal", involving a major expansion to increase capacity and allow ships to navigate in both directions at the same time, which will decrease waiting hours from 18 to 11 for most ships and double the capacity of the Canal from 49 to 97 ships a day. This project is expected to lead to enlarged transit capacity and increased industrial activity in the area, which will raise the international profile of Egypt as an international logistical and industrial hub.
- The "East Port Said" development project, involving the construction of a 9,5-km side channel bypassing the Suez Canal entrance, port expansion works, a new industrial zone and logistics centre as well as four new East-West tunnels to increase cross-canal connectivity and link the Sinai Peninsula to Egypt's mainland.
- The "Suez Canal Economic Zone" (SCZone) established on 461 km² of land and six maritime ports strategically located along the international waterway with direct access to ports, to serve as an international logistics hub and areas for light, medium and heavy industry as well as commercial and residential developments.

Golden Triangle Project

This project entails the development of an area from the Eastern Desert between Qena, Al-Qusayr, and Safaga to the Red Sea Coast. The total land area of the Golden Triangle is 38 000 m2. The development plan would include initiating extraction activities in addition to manufacturing, trade, mining, infrastructure, ports, tourism and urban developments. The aim of the project is to attract more than USD 12.8 billion in investments and create around 400 000 job opportunities.

Damietta Logistical Centre

The project aims to transform the Damietta governorate into a global logistics centre for handling and storing grain and food commodities. This would be achieved through various works, including through (i) the establishment of two sea piers to receive ships carrying up to 150 000 tons of grain, (ii) the construction of five investment and industrial zones for grains and food commodities.

The New Capital

The project entails the construction of a new administrative city on a total area of 700 km2 between the East of Cairo and the Red Sea. The new city will host the Egyptian Parliament building, all ministries and government authorities, as well as all foreign embassies. As part of the project, 25 residential districts will also be built to house more than 25 million people, as well as an international airport, an electric train and solar farms on an area of 90 million^2. With an estimated cost of USD 45 billion, the New Capital is considered the largest administrative city in the world.

National Roads Project

Launched in 2014, the National Roads Project includes 39 roads with a total length of 4 400 km at an investment of USD 2 billion. The focus is on linking remote areas to the national network, including Upper Egypt, the Sinai Peninsula and western Sahara. Through this work, the government has also placed an especially high priority on growth in associated areas such as export-oriented manufacturing and tourism.

One and a Half Million Feddan Project

This project entails the reclamation and development of one and a half million acres of undeveloped land to be used for agriculture in 11 areas in the Western Desert and Sinai. It is part of a larger scheme to reclaim a total of four million feddans to increase the agricultural land by 20% and create investment opportunities that create jobs and sustainable growth.

Major power generation projects

To increase its power generation capacity, Egypt also aims to build conventional and renewable power plants. A first project was already awarded to Germany's Siemens to build a combined cycle power plant with a total capacity of 11 GW and install a wind-power with a capacity of 2 GW. The second project, awarded to Saudi ACWA Power Corporation and UAE Masdar Corporate, plans to build a 2.2 GW combined cycle power plant in western Damietta. Solar power stations expected to generate about 1.5 GW and 0.5 GW respectively are also in the pipeline.

Sources: Invest in Egypt, https://www.investinegypt.gov.eg/English; Country Report: On the Road to Recovery. Bank of Alexandria (2014); Suez Canal Authority Website, www.suezcanal.gov.eg; N Gage Consulting (2016), The Suez Canal Economic Zone: A Strategic Location and Modern Day Innovation

The Transport Master Plan 2027 (MINTS) is the government's current strategy developed by the Ministry of Transportation for all transport sectors to achieve a multi-modal future with seamless connections. It aims to connect national, regional and gateway centres and create agglomerations of various activities that either generate or attract freight and passenger demands, serve as important distribution centres for hinterland activities, or provide international linkages. The required investments of around USD 15.5 billion between 2011 and 2027 would produce around USD 657 million of economic benefits by year 2027 with an economic internal rate of return of 17.8% (JICA, 2012). The MINTS is coordinated with other development plans introduced by other Ministries and entities such as the General Organization for

Physical Planning, Ministry of Agriculture, Ministry of Industry and Ministry of Tourism. The most important corridors that the MINTS aims to create are:

- The Mediterranean Corridor linking Libya with Palestine via Marsa Matrouh, El Alamein, Greater Cairo (Northern segment of Cairo Outer Ring Road), Ismailia, and the Suez Canal-North Sinai Area.
- The Intermodal Transport Corridor (ITC) linking the 6th of October Value Added Center with both the Alexandria-area seaports and Sokhna port. The corridor is expected to focus on the logistics of efficient freight flow. The ITC is seen as directly linking with the European Union "motorway of the sea" connecting Alexandria, Genoa and Koper ports.
- The Red Sea Corridor parallels the Red Sea/Gulf of Suez between approximately Zafarana and Bernees, with a potential for strengthening the current linkage with Sudan. Key intermediate points are Gharib, Hurghada and Safaga.
- The Upper Egypt Corridor paralleling the Nile River between Greater Cairo and Aswan, with a potential extension to create a new gateway to Sudan (Khartoum).

In the long term, the government is also seeking to transform the transport system through high-speed rail going at 300-350 km/h from Alexandria to Aswan through Cairo, Asyut and Luxor for a 1087-km line (Ministry of Transport, 2012). The line is expected to be built in three Phases (Phase I: Cairo – Alexandria, Phase II: Cairo – Luxor, and Phase III: Luxor – Aswan). However, talks with investors are still ongoing and no specific plans have been finalised (Oxford Business Group, 2017).

The recent industrialisation strategy also stresses the enabling role of infrastructure

Consonant with Egypt Vision 2030 is the government's Industry and Trade Development Strategy 2016-2020, which recognises the critical importance of economic infrastructure to industrial development where the manufacturing sector plays a leading role. The strategy aims to increase the contribution of the industrial sector to the country's GDP by 21% in 2020 and generate 3 million jobs, as well as to integrate SMEs into local and global supply chains and link them to major economic centres (MTI, 2017). The new strategy comes with a more integrated and targeted approach than the previous one. It recognises that achieving these objectives requires, among other things, the development of infrastructure and logistics, and linkages to roads and services (UNECA, 2015). These services serve not only as inputs in production sectors but also contribute to making Egyptian industrial output competitive in domestic, regional and international consumption markets. Under this strategy, a more integrated package of reforms focusing on trade, industry and infrastructure targeting sector-level development, land and industrial clusters supply, land and industrial clusters, and attractive investment incentives attractive to local and foreign investment (MTI, 2017).

The need for improved infrastructure planning and prioritisation

Securing the necessary resources to develop infrastructure will also require careful planning and prioritisation. Currently, numerous infrastructure priorities in Egypt are laid out in different strategies. Often, the allocation of budget for the national plans are an annual exercise, despite the fact that various ministries have to prepare their investment planning estimates over different time horizons such as the 5-year plans. The request for funds could also often exceed the funds available. There needs to be a path towards more clear and more predictable medium-term planning and funding allocations to increase stability for priority infrastructure projects and programmes and facilitate the co-ordination with donors. Currently, the government plans to strengthen its fiscal planning by introducing the medium-term expenditure framework, which will set multi-year expenditure ceilings by major spending categories, including infrastructure (IMF, 2018). Such planning of current and capital expenditure within a medium-term budget framework could also ensure that infrastructure investments are sustainable and that maintenance spending is fully taken into account (IMF, 2014).

The regulatory environment needs to be improved

In order for the private sector to be able to participate more in infrastructure delivery and services, an adequate policy environment is required, which involves removing administrative bottlenecks to investment and improving the regulatory environment. In recent years, the government has boosted efforts to build a credible environment for PPPs and has passed a number of reforms to create a more competitive and transparent legal PPP regime to attract qualified international and domestic investors.

Removing regulatory barriers to investment into sectors that are relevant to connectivity

While Egypt is an open market to foreign investments overall, some restrictions are still relatively high compared to some of its regional peers on infrastructure services and the construction sector, which could partly explain the fragmented infrastructure sector, especially for ports. According to the OECD *FDI Regulatory Restrictiveness Index*, Egypt presents higher restrictions in the construction sector, maritime, air, and transport services than the OECD average and some of its peers such as Tunisia (Figure 8.9). Egypt's Maritime Law 1 of 1998, for instance, only allows foreign investments in the form of joint venture companies in which foreign equity does not exceed 49% (OECD, 2017). The Construction Law 104 of 1992 also restricts foreign investment to joint-ventures in which foreign equity does not exceed 49%. In addition, foreign participation in electrical wiring and other building completion and finishing services is restricted to projects valued over USD 10 million (ibid). Such restrictions on investment could affect the competition in the market as well as the quality of infrastructure services that is needed to improve connectivity.

Removing restrictions on services sectors such as maritime air and transport, could also allow Egypt to enhance investments into high-quality logistics and move into higher-value added industries. In particular, improving the maritime services and related logistics could have a significant impact on enhancing FDI and creating jobs in the Egyptian economy (Ghoneim and Helmy, 2007).

Figure 8.9. OECD FDI Restrictiveness Index, Egypt (2017), (Closed=1; Open= 0)

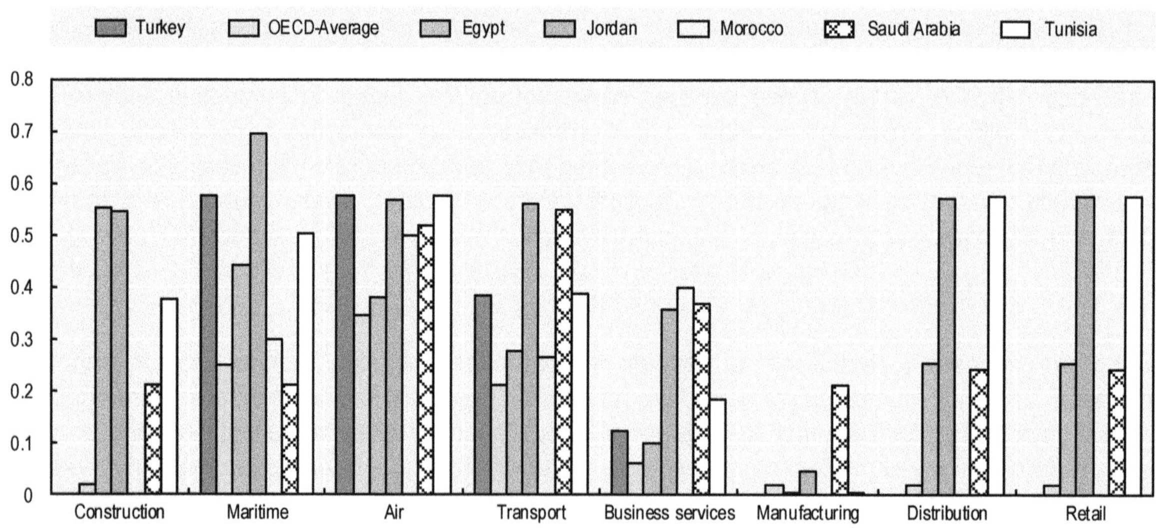

Source: OECD FDI Regulatory Restrictiveness Index database, http://www.oecd.org/investment/fdiindex.htm

Beyond removing restrictions, appropriate market-based mechanisms are also necessary to facilitate private investments

According to a Private Sector Diagnostics carried out by the EBRD, a number of sectors, notably transport and municipal infrastructure, are characterised by the absence of market-based mechanisms for the pricing and delivery of services (EBRD, 2017). The state, often through state-owned enterprises is the main administrator of transport and municipal infrastructure, leading to insufficient client orientation, maintenance and investment and therefore efficiency losses. Often, the regulated tariffs are low and below cost recovery levels. In an attempt to respond to such challenges, the government enacted a new law (law no 182/2018), which regulates public contracts and aims at improving the efficiency of government spending. Further reforms should move beyond tariffs and focus on governance to commercialise public service provision of infrastructure, which are critical to improve the operational and financial sustainability, facilitate greater private sector participation, unlock higher investment and deliver much-needed improvements in service quality.

Reforms in public spending and transport regulation could also crowd in more efficient investments

Efficient public governance in infrastructure can have a significant effect in mobilising further private investments. Yet, poor project selection and implementation have historically led to low returns on public investment in many developing countries, including in Egypt (Dabla-Norris et al, 2012). The country faces surprisingly low returns on connectivity infrastructure investments, which calls for deeper reforms regarding the distribution of budget resources and accountability across ministries as well as the central and local governments (Abdellatif 2012). For example, infrastructure spending in Upper Egypt has historically been much less effective than anticipated since projects have too often been focused in the past on building new roads rather than maintaining existing ones (World Bank, 2009). This would require the project selection process to be guided by technical cost-benefit analysis and public spending be routinely evaluated and monitored.

The IMF Public Investment Management Index also indicates the need for more efficient public investment management in Egypt (IMF, 2011 and 2018). The Index, which assigns scores for the four phases of public investment management – project appraisal, selection and budgeting, implementation, and ex post evaluation – places Egypt in the second quartile, behind peers (Figure 8.10). The Index calls for better public governance across all areas, but more significantly in the selection and management phases. Improving these areas has also been a priority for the World Bank in Egypt, which has incorporated institutional changes in project design, including grievance mechanisms in large transport and energy projects in order to promote institutional forms and leverage further resources, including from the private sector (World Bank, 2015). Further addressing such dimensions in Egypt could be a starting point to identify areas of reforms and more nuanced policy diagnosis.

Egypt has a tradition of public-private partnership (PPP)-type financing structures such as build-operate-transfer (BOT). In 1869, it was the first country in the region to complete the famous concession of the Suez Canal through a BOT project. More recently, the government has been favouring modern PPPs as a potential financing solution for infrastructure projects. In 2006, a dedicated PPP Central Unit (PPPCU) was established within the Ministry of Finance to create a consistent framework for PPPs that applies across all sectors including social sectors such as education and health. The principal role of the PPP unit is to support contracting authorities in preparing, implementing and monitoring PPP projects.

In 2010, the government formalised the institutional and regulatory framework for PPPs by enacting a PPP law (67/2010) entitled "Promulgating the Law Regulating Partnership with the Private Sector in Infrastructure Projects, Services, and Public Utilities" based on the PPP model of the UK. The new PPP law allows the government to enter into PPP contracts with private entities, enabling the private sector to finance, construct, and operate large infrastructure projects and public utilities for contracts of up to 30 years (World Bank, 2011).

Figure 8.10. Public Investment Management Index scores in Egypt and selected countries

0-4 high

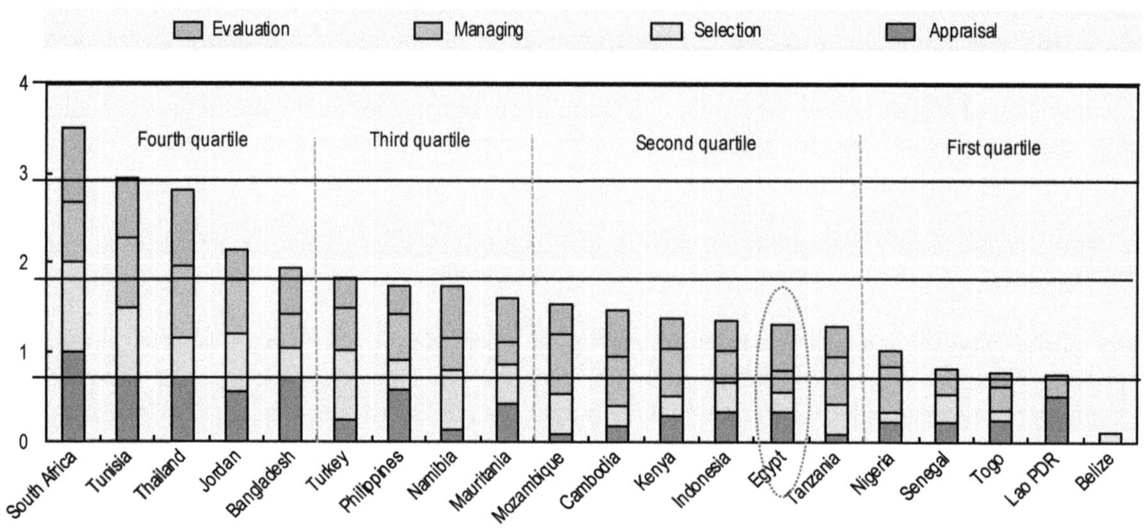

Source: IMF

The new legal framework for mobilising private investments in infrastructure brings an important financing solution for infrastructure projects

The 2010 PPP Law made official the establishment of the PPPCU. It provides that the Minister of Finance stipulates the structure of the unit, while the Executive Regulations of the Law determine the administrative and financial framework for its operation. In addition to the PPPCU, the law provides that a Supreme Committee for Public Private Partnership Affairs (the "PPP Supreme Committee") shall be formed to be chaired by the prime minister and comprising the Ministers of Finance, Investment, Economic Development, Legal Affairs, Housing and Utilities and Transportation, as well as the Head of the PPPCU.

Recognised as the best PPP Law in the world of the year 2010 by the World Bank (Ministry of Finance, 2015), such an institutional and legal element for enhancing private participation in infrastructure represents a solid foundation on which to build a PPP programme. Despite such achievements, a number of challenges with the PPP mechanism remain, including the lack of clarity in allocating land for PPP projects, the absence of a long-term vision for prioritised PPP projects, lengthy procedures for the endorsement and implementation of PPP projects, and financial and technical limitations encountered in conducting necessary feasibility studies for PPP projects (GPEDC, 2018). Nonetheless, the government has started to take steps to tackle some of the abovementioned challenges.

Regarding land allocation for PPP projects, the PPPCU currently requires that any Public Authority shall have the legal documents of the land allocated for the project. The PPPCU is also performing due diligence with the assistance of the project transaction advisors before tendering process for any land proposed from any public authority to implement a PPP project. According to the Ministry of Finance, the PPPCU also engages closely with tendering authorities and governorates in order to choose the right land for PPP projects. A permanent joint committee was also formed, by virtue of a prime minister decree (605/2019), between the Ministers of Finance, Investment, Economic Development, Legal Affairs, Housing and Utilities and Transportation. The main purpose of this committee is to create a PPP pipeline of infrastructure projects for each line ministry and review available pre-feasibility studies to select projects that comply with the PPP criteria. This pipeline is then presented to the PPP Supreme Committee, which approves the initial structure of projects, timeline for feasibility studies, project preparation and tendering.

Despite government efforts, the uptake of public-private partnerships is currently low. While the current PPP framework is considered to be in line with international practices, only limited progress has been made in terms of preparing and implementing actual projects. Currently, there is a lack of track record, capacity and experience to develop PPPs (EBRD, 2017). Areas for improvement include strengthening the capacity of the PPPCU to allow it to prepare complex projects and further developing PPP financing schemes, particularly in the transport sector where they are not yet widely used. The OECD also finds that the PPPCU is understaffed and points to difficulties in securing PPP buy-in from line ministries. To address these issues, according to the Ministry of Finance, the PPPCU is currently working on hiring more staff and developing an organisational structure in line with international best practices.

Elsewhere in the region, Morocco and Jordan lack PPP units while in Tunisia both the Prime Minister's Office and the Ministry of Finance have PPP units (OECD, 2014). In Egypt, the tendering process was disrupted by political instability during 2011-13, and only two hospitals have been built since then, but 14 projects worth over USD 4 billion are at various stages in the project cycle, including ports, roads, rail and ferries.

Moreover, the new PPP law does not replace the old laws that regulate concessions. Egypt finds itself in the position of having a general legal PPP framework coexisting with alternative channels for procuring infrastructure projects, such as the system of public economic entities, public utilities legislation and a number of sector specific or project specific laws (EBRD, 2011). As a result, administrative entities may still grant concessions, BOTs and BOOs (build-own-operate) based on the old scheme. Traditionally, these were granted under the general public utilities legislation (Law 129 of 1947 and Law 61 of 1958) or sector-specific laws (including electricity, specialised ports, airports, trains and roads) issued during 1990s when Egypt pursued economic liberalisation policies (*Infitāḥ*) to allow private sector provision of public services (Montaser et al, 2017). The old utilities legislation includes restrictive requirements, such as limits on the investor's profit and setting a maximum duration for the concession of 30 years (EBRD, 2011). While these old laws may not generally apply on modern PPP projects, an assessment by the EBRD finds that the sector-specific approach may be used in the future, particularly for the power sector.

According to the Ministry of Finance, the government is in the process of addressing these issues by proposing new amendments in the PPP Law and reviewing the old sector-specific laws. Such amendments are currently being discussed in the parliament. Since the issuance of the PPP Law in 2010, the sector-specific laws were only used in tenders that cannot be tendered through the PPP programme. Most international investors have also requested to tender in infrastructure projects through the PPP Law, which is more structured, contains clear procurement procedures, and provides for investor protection.

Public support for PPPs is also low. With a past legacy of non-transparent privatisation processes that led to corruption, there is a traditional negative perception and lack of trust in the private sector, potentially including on cooperation projects between the private and public sectors (EBRD, 2011). This may also be due to the current lack of adequate community consultation to guide project selection and secure public support for PPP projects. According to the Ministry of Finance, this is partly due to the revolutions of 2011 and 2013, which created political and economic uncertainty, and led to a mixed understanding between privatisation and PPPs. It may also be due to the lack of adequate community consultations to guide project selection and secure public support for PPP projects. Yet, since 2014, PPPs are heavily supported at the political level and promoted more actively through media, awareness campaigns and conferences. Given the complex long-term nature of PPP projects, before the decision is made to launch a PPP project, the procuring authority should perform sufficient due diligence and rigorous community consultations. Ensuring responsible business conduct (see chapter on responsible business conduct) is also an important aspect of this process and could help mobilise more public support for infrastructure projects involving the private sector.

The legal framework for public procurement also needs to be updated and strengthened to increase tender participation and supplier diversity.

A more recent challenge for private sector engagement in infrastructure projects has been the fact that some well-developed infrastructure and energy projects involving the private sector have not proceeded as planned, sending a potentially confusing message to investors. This is partly because there is minimal online access to information on procurement opportunities, information on procurement decisions and debriefing procedures for unsuccessful decisions is unavailable, and there is no review and remedies mechanism to protect private sector suppliers competing for public tenders (EBRD, 2017). Overall, the legislative framework is outdated, and the public procurement process overregulated and bureaucratic. The Egyptian public procurement regulation[4] dates back to policy standards from the 1980s.

Local practitioners in Egypt have not in the past considered the national public procurement legal framework to be clear, comprehensive, and conducive to a competitive procurement environment (EBRD, 2011). While open tenders are the default procurement method, which is a positive feature, the extensive use of direct contracting has limited competition in public tenders and works against efficient public spending (ibid). The assessment also reported gaps in transparency, integrity and accountability in public procurement processes. Enhancing the institutional framework for regulating the public procurement sector in Egypt would require making it more attractive to investors and increasing transparency with respect to the review and remedies processes.

The government has shown a preference for direct awards for public sector works, which are perceived to be faster in execution and lack complexities such as public procurement processes. Following the two revolutions, the government increased its role in infrastructure investments in the economy, which led in large part to an increased role of SOEs in building roads and other infrastructure projects.

Many of the projects are awarded to the National Service Projects Organisation, General Authority for Roads & Bridges and Land Transport, and Central agency for Reconstruction, which often serve as a contractor and typically awards subcontracts to private sector entities as part of this process, including to foreign investors. The 2016 Law on Public Procurement introduces procedures to enhance transparency and reduce discretion in public procurement, but the consistent application and enforcement of the law by the involved procurement entities is lacking (EBRD, 2017). The introduction of simplified procedures for small value contracts could also encourage the participation of local SMEs in public tenders (ibid).

Assessing value-for-money is crucial to make sure that investments benefit users and society at large.

Value for money can be defined as what a government considers to be an optimal combination of quantity, quality, features and price (i.e. cost), expected over the whole of the project's lifetime. Even when public funds are not being used to finance infrastructure directly, value for money is important so that society does not overpay for services. Choosing the wrong projects diverts scarce resources from projects with potentially higher social returns. Therefore, value for money must be assessed over the lifecycle of an infrastructure asset, encompassing the construction, operating and maintenance phases. According to the EBRD, as there is no legal requirement in Egypt for the public entities to consider the whole life cycle costing of the goods or services procured, or seeking value for money, no appraisal was undertaken in the past on any other aspect of procured goods or services (EBRD, 2013). Moreover, contracting entities are = cost conscious and the lowest price is more frequently selected in practice than best value for money evaluation.

References

Abdellatif, L. (2012). "Understanding the Role of Public sector in Deepening Spatial Inequality in Egypt." in Reshaping Egypt's Economic Geography, vol. 2. (Washington, DC: World Bank).

Amereller (2018). Client Alert: Liberalization of Egypt's Railway Sector. http://amereller.com/wp-content/uploads/2018/04/180423-Egypt-Rail-Privatization.pdf

Bank of Alexandria (2014). Egypt Country Report: On the Road to Recovery. https://www.alexbank.com/Cms_Data/Contents/AlexBank/Media/Publication/Egypt-Country-Report-2014.pdf

Dabla-Norris, E., J. Brumby ,C. Papageorgiou, A. Kyobe, and Z. Mills (2012). "Investing in Public Investment: An Index of Public Investment Efficiency." Journal of Economic Growth 17(3): 235–66.

EBRD (2017), Strategy for Egypt. As approved by the Board of Directors at its meeting on 8 February 2017. https://www.ebrd.com/what-we-do/strategies-and-policies/egypt-strategy.pdf

EBRD (2013). Public Procurement Sector Assessment - Review of laws and practice in the SEMED region. http://www.marchespublics.gov.tn/onmp/upload/documents/ebrd_report_eng.pdf

EBRD (2011). Egypt Assessment of the Quality of the PPP Legislation and of the Effectiveness of its Implementation. 2011. https://www.ebrd.com/downloads/legal/concessions/egypt.pdf

EIB (2013). Regional Integration through Trade and Transport Corridors (TRANSTRAC) -Egypt activities.

EIU (2018). Economist Intelligence Unit, Country Report for Egypt.

Egypt Independent (2017). Telecom Egypt to go live with country's 4th mobile operator "WE" in a week. https://ww.egyptindependent.com/telecom-egypt-go-live-countrys-4th-mobile-operator-week/

Egypt Vision 2030 (2015). Vision 2030: sustainable development strategy and medium-term investment framework 2014/15 – 2018/19". Paper prepared for the Egypt Economic Development Conference, 13-15 March 2015, Sharm El-Sheikh, Egypt. http://extwprlegs1.fao.org/docs/pdf/egy151569.pdf

Egyptian National Railways (2018). https://enr.gov.eg/ticketing/public/smartSearch.jsf

Ghoneim, Ahmed F. and Helmy, Omneia A. (2007) Maritime Transport and Related Logistics Services in Egypt, ICTSD Trade in Services and Sustainable Development Series. International Centre for Trade and Sustainable Development, Geneva, Switzerland.

GSMA (2019). GSMA Global Mobile Connectivity Index. http://www.mobileconnectivityindex.com/#year=2018&secondaryMenu=about&id=abouttheindex

GPEDC (2018). Private sector engagement through development co-operation in Egypt. Country Case Study. Global Partnership for Effective Development Co-operation. 8 October 2018.

IFC (2013). Egypt Trade Logistics Project.

IMF (2018). Arab Republic of Egypt 2017 Article IV Consultation, Second Review Under the Extended Arrangement under the Extended Fund Facility

IMF (2014). World Economic Outlook (WEO), October 2014; Chapter 3: Is It Time for an Infrastructure Push? The Macroeconomic Effects of Public Investment; October 7, 2014

IMF (2011). Investing in Public Investment: An Index of Public Investment Efficiency. https://www.imf.org/en/Publications/WP/Issues/2016/12/31/Investing-in-Public-Investment-An-Index-of-Public-Investment-Efficiency-24651

Invest in Egypt Portal, https://www.investinegypt.gov.eg/English

IRU (2016). World Road Transport Association: Egypt to join TIR. https://www.iru.org/resources/newsroom/egypt-join-tir

Japan International Cooperation Agency (2012). The Comprehensive Study on the Master Plan for Nationwide Transport System in the Arab Republic of Egypt. http://open_jicareport.jica.go.jp/pdf/12057584.pdf

MCIT (2016). Yearbook 2016. Ministry of Communication and Information Technology. http://www.mcit.gov.eg/Publication/Publication_Summary/1041/

Mckinsey (2016). Digital Middle East: Transforming the region into a leading digital economy October 2016

Ministry of Finance (2015). Public Private Partnership PPP & The Egyptian Experience http://www.mcit.gov.eg/Upcont/Documents/20134151031MoF-%2011%20Apr%202013.pdf

Ministry of Petroleum (2018). Egypt is an International Economic Center for Oil and Natural Gas Trade. http://www.petroleum.gov.eg/en/Investment/InvestmentElements/Pages/default.aspx

Ministry of Planning, Monitoring and Administrative Reform (2017). Strategies and Plans. http://mpmar.gov.eg/en/strategies-and-plans/previous-plans/

Montaser, Ali & Kamel, Muhammad & Abd El-Rashid, Ibrahim. (2017). Public Private Partnerships in Egypt.

MTI (2017). Ministry of Trade and Industry. Industry and Trade Development Strategy 2016-2020. http://www.mti.gov.eg/English/MediaCenter/News/PublishingImages/Pages/2017-Strategy/2017%20Strategy.pdf

N Gage Consulting (2016). The Suez Canal Economic Zone: A Strategic Location and Modern Day Innovation.

OECD (2017a), Supporting the Development of the Suez Canal Economic Zone: Identifying Priority Actions for a Dynamic and Sustainable Economic Zone, OECD, Paris, (unpublished).

OECD (2017b). National Treatment for Foreign Controlled Enterprises, Including Adhering Country Exceptions to National Treatment. https://www.oecd.org/daf/inv/investment-policy/national-treatment-instrument-english.pdf

OECD (2014). Public-Private Partnerships in the Middle East and North Africa A Handbook for Policy Makers. https://www.oecd.org/mena/competitiveness/PPP%20Handbook_EN_with_covers.pdf

OCDE (2014), *The Competitiveness of Global Port-Cities*, OCDE,Paris, https://doi.org/10.1787/9789264205277-en.

Oxford Business Group (2017). Egypt's government and private sector work to expand transport infrastructure capacity and boost capacity. https://oxfordbusinessgroup.com/overview/prime-location-government-and-private-sector-are-working-expand-infrastructure-capacity-and-boost

Rodrigue, J-P (2017), Developing the Logistics Sector: The Role of Public Policy: Dubai, Morocco, Panama and Colombia as Maritime Logistics Platforms, prepared for the OECD.

Steven A. Altman, Pankaj Ghemawat, and Phillip Bastian, "DHL Global Connectedness Index 2018," Deutsche Post DHL, February 2019.

UNCTAD. 2017. Economic Development in Africa Report: Tourism for Transformative and Inclusive Growth. United Nations Conference on Trade and Development. New York and Geneva.

UNCTAD (2011). ICT Policy Review. Egypt. http://unctad.org/en/Docs/dtlstict2011d6_en.pdf

UNECA (2015). Egypt Country Profile 2015. United Nations Economic Commission for Africa

UNIDO (2017). Africa Industrialisation Day. Background Paper. https://www.unido.org/sites/default/files/files/2017-11/AID2017_Background_EN.PDF

US Energy Information Administration. 2014. Country Analysis Brief: Egypt

World Bank (2020). World Bank Development Indicators. https://data.worldbank.org/indicator/IT.NET.USER.ZS?view=map

World Bank (2020), Doing Business 2020. Washington, DC: World Bank.

World Bank (2018a) Public Participation in Infrastructure (PPI). Annual Report 2017.

World Bank Enterprise Surveys (2016). Egypt 2016 Country Profile. https://www.enterprisesurveys.org/data/exploreeconomies/2016/egypt. Washington, D.C.: World Bank Group.

World Bank. (2015a). Egypt - Promoting poverty reduction and shared prosperity : a systematic country diagnostic (English). Washington, D.C.: World Bank Group. http://documents.worldbank.org/curated/en/853671468190130279/Egypt-Promoting-poverty-reduction-and-shared-prosperity-a-systematic-country-diagnostic

World Bank (2015b). Egypt, Arab Republic of - Country partnership framework for the period FY2015-19 (English). Washington, D.C.: World Bank Group. http://documents.worldbank.org/curated/en/773051468197407822/Egypt-Arab-Republic-of-Country-partnership-framework-for-the-period-FY2015-19

World Bank (2011). PPIAF Support to Legal and Institutional PPP Development in Egypt. https://ppiaf.org/impact_story/ppiaf-support-legal-and-institutional-ppp-development-egypt

World Bank. (2009). Upper Egypt: Pathways to Shared Growth. Report 49086-EG (Washington, DC).

World Economic Forum (2019). *The Global Competitiveness Index 2019 edition. Egypt.* http://reports.weforum.org/pdf/gci4-2019/WEF_GCI4_2019_Profile_EGY.pdf

World Economic Forum (2018). *The Global Competitiveness Index 2017-2018 edition.* http://www3.weforum.org/docs/GCR2017-2018/05FullReport/TheGlobalCompetitivenessReport2017%E2%80%932018.pdf

Notes

[1] According to the Ministry of Transportation, the established horizontal roads connect Kuraymat to Zaafarana, Minya to Ras Ghalib, Assuit to Safaga, Qena to Quseer and Aswan to Baranis. These roads facilitate the accessibility of Ports on the Red Sea including Hurghada Maritime Port, Ein El Sokhna Port, Safaga International Maritime Port, and Baranis Port.

[2] The Mobile Connectivity Index is an input index that measures the performance of 163 countries – representing 99% of the global population – of a range of metrics that are essential to create an effective enabling environment for mobile internet adoption. The corresponding output measure is the number of people accessing the internet via mobile.

[3] Egypt's population is estimated to reach 140 million people by 2040, exerting significant pressure on resources and services including energy, water and transport. Given the already high unemployment rate, the economy would require an average annual GDP growth rate of 4% just to absorb the new entrants.

[4] Public procurement refers to the process of identifying what is needed; determining who the best person or organisation is to supply this need; and ensuring what is needed is delivered to the right place, at the right time, for the best price and that all this is done in a fair and open manner. In the MENA region, public procurement is above the OECD average, representing around 17% of GDP.

www.ingramcontent.com/pod-product-compliance
Ingram Content Group UK Ltd.
Pitfield, Milton Keynes, MK11 3LW, UK
UKHW051459290926
15471UKWH00008B/1300

9 789264 122888